A Weaver-Poet and the Plague

Cultural Inquiries in English Literature, 1400–1700

Rebecca Totaro, General Editor

ADVISORY BOARD

Joe Campana
Rice University

Hillary Eklund
Loyola University, New Orleans

Katherine Eggert
University of Colorado, Boulder

Wendy Beth Hyman
Oberlin College & Conservatory

Julia Reinhardt Lupton
University of California, Irvine

Vin Nardizzi
The University of British Columbia

Gail Kern Paster
Folger Shakespeare Library

Garrett A. Sullivan Jr.
Penn State University

Tiffany Werth
University of California, Davis

Jessica Wolfe
University of North Carolina, Chapel Hill

Books in the Cultural Inquiries in English Literature, 1400–1700, series acknowledge the complex relationships that link disciplines in the pre-modern period and account for the lived experience represented in literary and cultural texts of the time. Scholars in this series reconnect fields often now considered distinct, including cuisine, ecology, cartography, the occult, meteorology, physiology, drama, popular print, and poetry.

OTHER BOOKS IN THE SERIES:

Emily Griffiths Jones, *Right Romance: Heroic Subjectivity and Elect Community in Seventeenth-Century England*

Nancy L. Simpson-Younger and Margaret Simon, eds., *Forming Sleep: Representing Consciousness in English Renaissance*

A WEAVER-POET
AND THE PLAGUE

Labor, Poverty, and the Household in Shakespeare's London

Scott Oldenburg

THE PENNSYLVANIA STATE UNIVERSITY PRESS
UNIVERSITY PARK, PENNSYLVANIA

Library of Congress Cataloging-in-Publication Data

Names: Oldenburg, Scott K., 1969– author.
Title: A weaver-poet and the plague : labor, poverty, and the household in Shakespeare's London / Scott Oldenburg.
Other titles: Cultural inquiries in English literature, 1400–1700.
Description: University Park, Pennsylvania : The Pennsylvania State University Press, [2020] | Series: Cultural inquiries in English literature, 1400–1700 | Includes bibliographical references and index.
Summary: "A narrative of Elizabethan London through the eyes of William Muggins, an impoverished silk-weaver who wrote poetry about the plague, motherhood, childrearing, poverty, and the responsibility individuals have to one another"—Provided by publisher.
Identifiers: LCCN 2020027061 | ISBN 9780271087153 (hardback)
Subjects: LCSH: Muggins, William. Londons mourning garment, or funeral teares. | Plague—England—London—History—17th century. | Working class—England—London—History—17th century. | Poor—England—London—History—17th century. | Women—England—London—History—17th century. | English poetry—17th century—History and criticism. | Working class writings, English—History and criticism. | London (England)—History—17th century. | London (England)—Social conditions—17th century.
Classification: LCC DA681.O43 2020 | DDC 942.106/1—dc23
LC record available at https://lccn.loc.gov/2020027061

Copyright © 2020 The Pennsylvania State University
All rights reserved
Printed in the United States
Published by The Pennsylvania State University Press,
University Park, PA 16802-1003

The Pennsylvania State University Press is a member of the Association of University Presses.

It is the policy of The Pennsylvania State University Press to use acid-free paper. Publications on uncoated stock satisfy the minimum requirements of American National Standard for Information Sciences—Permanence of Paper for Printed Library Material, ANSI Z39.48–1992.

CONTENTS

Acknowledgments | vii

Introduction: The Silk-Weavers' Song | 1

1. Company and Complaint: The Limits of Craft Identity | 45

2. Life and Debt in the Poultry: The Communal Bonds of the Parish | 75

3. Grief and Grievance: Communal Elegy in St. Olave's Parish | 109

4. The Jeremiah of Southwark: The Prophetic Poetry of William Muggins | 139

Epilogue: The Horizon of the Past | 169

Appendix: London's Mourning Garment | 173
Notes | 207
Bibliography | 239
Index | 271

ACKNOWLEDGMENTS

From the first chapter on a collective petition to the final chapter about a vision of the perfect commonwealth, *A Weaver-Poet and the Plague* is focused on collaboration and mutual aid. Like its subject, this book would not have been possible without substantial support from a number of generous individuals. First and foremost, Michelle Kohler endured my endless talking about William Muggins. Her support, intellectual insights, and love were invaluable as the book developed. Librarians and archivists were especially helpful. Olwen Myhill of the Centre for Metropolitan History; Penelope Fussell, archivist for the Drapers' Company; Alice Dowhyj at the Society for Antiquaries of London; and numerous others showed care and enthusiasm in helping me locate many of the archival materials that form the basis of this project. William Ingram of the University of Michigan provided some early guidance on Southwark's parish registers. Several of my colleagues at Tulane University either listened to me talk about Muggins or performed invaluable department service that freed me up to pursue this work. Series editor Rebecca Totaro and acquisitions editor Kathryn Bourque Yahner were marvelous throughout the publication process, engaging with the manuscript in meaningful ways and working with dazzling speed and enthusiasm. Finally, I am grateful for the work of Brian Beer, Maddie Caso, Janice North, Laura Reed-Morrisson, Regina Starace, Nicholas Taylor, and others at Penn State University Press who helped bring this book to print.

Introduction

The Silk-Weavers' Song

> Silence mou'd to pitty,
> Sy, wherefore vndon:
>
> Shep[herd]. Wayling for a City,
> Woeful London.
> —HENRY PETOWE (1604)

"CAST OUT YOUR DEAD!"

Sometime in late August 1603, Mary Black of St. Olave's parish in Southwark started showing signs of the plague: a fever and maybe a blister at first or a swelling around the neck, armpit, or groin. Probably within a day she felt joint pain, nausea, and delirium. Sores were soon visible, and the swelling would have grown to the size of a chicken egg until it burst, tearing the skin in a painful wound.[1] By August 29 she was dead.[2] Mary Black may have been the ten-year-old daughter of Nicholas Black, also of St. Olave's.[3] At the time she was an apprentice to the silk-weaver William Muggins, who had lived in the parish since 1598.[4] She had been learning lacemaking, buttonmaking, and silkthrowing.[5] Her training was cut painfully short by the plague. Like several of their neighbors in St. Olave's parish, the Muggins household was quarantined as soon as it was found that one of its members had been infected.

Shortly before Mary Black's death, one of Muggins's other apprentices, Robert Redman, also began showing signs of infection. Four days after Black's burial, Redman, too, was laid out on the street to be found by the parish's searchers, two older women whose job it was "to be viewers of the boddies of such as shall dye in tyme of Infeccon."[6] They were followed by the parish's bearers, two men who made daily rounds traditionally crying "Cast out your dead" as they approached to cart away the corpses.[7] A mix of grief and dread overshadowed the household as one after another showed signs of the plague.[8] A week later William Muggins's eldest daughter, Elizabeth, had also been taken by the plague. Two days after that another apprentice, Henry Beste, also died.

Muggins's wife had just given birth. In an era with a high mortality rate for new mothers and their infants, would she or the newborn be infected? Would the other children in the household catch the plague? How would the family sustain themselves under quarantine? What would happen to the household if Muggins himself fell ill? It was in this setting, in September or early October with the plague deaths mounting outside, that William Muggins, unable to leave his home, first sat down to write *London's Mourning Garment*, a pamphlet dedicated to alderman and sheriff of London Sir John Swinnerton. The dedication was followed by a twenty-page poem, a plague prayer, and a table of the dead organized by parish up through November 17. The cover of the pamphlet featured a printer's device, the image of a scale balanced on an hourglass atop a winged skull with a cross formed out of a bone and a scythe. Judgment, time, death—the woodcut deployed the stock imagery of the *memento mori* tradition. Beneath this was carved "NON PLVS," Latin for "no more." As perfect as the image is for a plague pamphlet, it was not made especially for *London's Mourning Garment*. Rather, it had been used on numerous pamphlets printed for bookseller William Barley: a 1592 reprint of Edward Webbe's travel narrative *The Rare and Most Wonderfvll Things Which Edward Webbe an Englishman Borne, Hath Seene and Passed in His Troublesome Trauailes*; a 1595 sermon (or revision of a sermon) titled *A Salade for the Simple. Gathered out of the Fourth Verse of the First Chapter of the Proverbes of Salomon*; and a translation of the French romance *The Delig[h]tfvl History of Celestina the Faire*, among others.[9] The device at one point included Barley's initials beneath the motto "NON PLVS," but the letters "W B" were apparently effaced when the device was transferred to another printer. Of all the death's head device's uses, however, *London's Mourning Garment* seems to have been its most perfect fit. In part the pamphlet argues that Londoners were terrifyingly indifferent to the tragedies that surrounded them; the woodcut called out to its viewers to remind them of the frailty of all human life and their own mortality in the time of plague.

Described by Rebecca Totaro as "one of the first brief plague epics in English," Muggins's ninety-seven-stanza poem presents a female personification of London as spokesperson for the plight of Londoners.[10] As Paul Gleed has demonstrated, gendered personifications of London typically resulted in sexualized extremes: thus in 1543 Henry Howard declared London to be a "shameless whore," while in 1580 Thomas Churchyard took the opposite view, depicting London as "a maiden town that keeps herself so clean."[11] But Muggins's London defines herself in the first person. The closest the poem gets to a sexualized personification occurs in a description of the excitement around King James's anticipated coronation and royal entry to the city. London compares herself to "a Bryde against her nuptiall day" with James as the metaphorical groom, but the plague intervenes, postponing the monarch's entry to the city. London then describes herself as "poore London" and "helplesse Lady" (sigs. B1r, line 8; B1v, line 29; B2r, line 85).[12] As the title *London's Mourning Garment* suggests, the London of Muggins's poem is a woman in mourning dress, an eyewitness to the loss of lives and livelihoods during the plague.[13]

Muggins's poem is especially concerned with the plight of London's laboring class, those vulnerable not only to the plague but also to the smallest of fluctuations in the city's economy. While writers like Ben Jonson maintained their membership in one of London's livery companies, very few actually labored in a handicraft. This book charts Muggins's unique perspective as a poet of London's laboring class. While the plague prompted Muggins to write *London's Mourning Garment*, the pamphlet is also very much about the experience of London's poor workers confronting the indifference of the city's elite and surviving the frustrations of debt, as well as facing the terrors of the plague. In addition to deploying a female London as spokesperson, Muggins's poem is especially concerned with women. The poem describes the joys and pains of childbirth and childcare, the education of young women, the work women do, the sacrifices they make. Moreover, in the middle of the poem, several impoverished women describe their economic distress.

The plague of 1603 ravaged London. Although the city was rarely completely free of the plague, the growth in population in and around London, the additional throngs of people arriving to view the arrival of the new king, and the heat of the summer conspired to make this wave of plague deaths particularly bad. Although bills of mortality retroactively counted the plague deaths from December 1602, it was not until March that people seemed especially concerned with the epidemic. In that month a spy using the alias Antony Rivers wrote, "The Plaugue begynneth in the cittye and suburbs, especially in Southwark," on the south bank of the Thames where Muggins lived. Before moving onto other matters, the letter explained, "It is feared this next yeare will prove very contagious."[14] A few weeks later, the plague deaths had been noted by the Court of Aldermen, who began to take action to provide for the afflicted.[15]

The city had been busy preparing for the festivities surrounding the coronation of King James I, a welcome change from the public mourning for Queen Elizabeth's passing in late March. Scaffolds and decorations for various pageants had been prepared throughout the city. Preacher James Godskall asserted that the plague had truly struck London in early May, "when all things did flourish in the Countrey, and in the Citie, when we were merrie as the sonnes of the world, marrying, feasting, building, and erecting our armes trivmphants, when we lesse expected it, which hath turned also our joy into sorrow."[16] The incongruence of the plague's intrusion on the preparations for celebrations was noted by several Londoners. Thomas Dekker surmised, "Behold, that miracle-worker, who in one minute turnd our generall mourning [for the passing of Queen Elizabeth] to a general mirth [for the coronation of King James], does now againe in a moment alter that gladnes to shrikes and lamentation."[17] Poet John Hanson, expressing a similar shock at the rapid changes in circumstances for the city, described the city's change in fortune as "Londons late lamentable heroicall comi-tragedie" and succinctly dubbed time "a turne-coate."[18]

The miseries of the plague lasted much longer than did the lamentations for the dead monarch or the planned huzzahs for the new one, however. The plague did not subside until December 1603. James held his coronation at Windsor and did not conduct the traditional royal entry to the city until the following year. By that time the epidemic had resulted in the death of one in every five Londoners. There is no question that the plague threatened everyone in the city, but the ratio of one in five can be deceiving. Those with means fled the city. And wealthier parishes of the city, because they were less densely populated, experienced a far lower rate of plague deaths than did their poorer, more densely populated counterparts.[19] For instance, for the two-week span beginning July 21 and ending August 4, 1603, the wealthy parish of St. Mary le Bow buried four people, three of the plague. In the previous five years for the same span of weeks, the church only buried two people in total, and none in the three years just prior to the plague.[20] Similarly, St. Benet Gracechurch saw no burials during the weeks of July 21 through August 4 in 1598, 1599, and 1601, and just one burial each in 1600 and 1602. For those same weeks the bills of mortality in 1603 recorded three burials at St. Benet's, but only one of the plague.[21] Wealthy parishes saw a considerable spike in deaths during the plague, but not the decimation of the population other parishes experienced.

In the poor and crowded parish of St. Giles, Cripplegate, the numbers are more striking. From 1598 to 1602 the parish averaged fourteen burials during the late July through early August span. In 1603, the same fourteen days involved a staggering 333 burials, 248 of the plague.[22] Whereas the wealthier parishes experienced a three- to four-fold increase in burials, St. Giles witnessed a twenty-three-fold increase in deaths. A similar story can be discerned in the even harder-hit parish where Mary Black and William Muggins lived and worked. Whereas in the previous five years St. Olave's in Southwark buried an average of 11.8 people between July 21 and August 4, during the same two-week stretch in 1603 the parish experienced a thirty-four-fold increase in burials—401 deaths, 377 of the plague.[23] While one in five Londoners died of the plague in 1603, the disease disproportionately affected the poorer sort in the city.

As the numbers suggest, non-plague deaths also increased during the plague of 1603. St. Giles reported an unusual eighty-five non-plague deaths from July 21 to August 4, 1603. This is not an anomaly. The next week St. Giles reported fifty non-plague deaths, and the week after that forty-three. St. Olave's seems to have held a narrower gap between plague and non-plague deaths. From July 21 to August 4 the parish counted twenty-four non-plague deaths, considerably lower than St. Giles's, but still twice the average of the previous five years for the parish. Some of these deaths may have had to do with comorbidities or deficient assessment of the cause of death, but many were probably due to the breakdown in poor relief and informal networks of support for the most vulnerable in the parish.[24]

Parishes like St. Giles and St. Olave's were overwhelmed with burials and care for the poor and quarantined. Each afternoon bearers and searchers would pass through the streets of their respective parishes. In St. Olave's they did not always have the time or energy to track down even the names of all the dead: here and there throughout the pages of the parish's register one finds blanks where the names of the deceased should be; on September 10 the clerk listed, a little below Muggins's apprentice Henry Beste's name, what he could quickly obtain of the nameless: two listings for "_____ of Robt. Parker."[25] These were presumably children or apprentices of Robert Parker, but their names were too difficult to come by in neighborhoods where so many people were shunning contagion or shut up in their homes under quarantine.

Households like Parker's and Muggins's were devastated. The loss of family members, often children, was painful enough, but they would face significant economic hardships as well. Merchants were reluctant to trade in the city for fear of infection. The plague orders demanded that any household infected by the plague self-quarantine for six weeks. The family's economic activity would be brought to a halt, and members of the household would have to rely on the parish's fund of poor relief for sustenance. Week after week saw the piling of corpses on the streets to be collected by the bearers and duly recorded in the parish register. By December 22, 1603, Muggins's parish of St. Olave's had buried 2,383 victims of the plague, more than any other parish in or around London.

The magnitude of the plague and the personal losses at home must have weighed heavily on William Muggins. Neighbors, friends, members of his own household, even his daughter—all endured gruesome, agonizing deaths. The terror of the plague was most keenly felt at the level of the individual household, where the course of the illness was observed up close, where family members required care despite fear of contagion, where none could look away or flee for open air.[26] Foreign merchants brought trade to a standstill as they refused to load their ships with goods from the infected city. Many among the wealthy, who might make significant contributions to poor relief, facilitate charity, or help maintain order, had fled the pestilence. The sick and the poor were left in desperation. What could an individual householder like William Muggins do? *London's Mourning Garment* attests to a profound sense of helpless isolation, a search for fellow mourners and some form of practical action to aid himself and his neighbors. Muggins reread parts of the Bible to compose the prayer included in *London's Mourning Garment*, and he almost certainly rehearsed his prayer at home with his surviving family members. What emotions might have coursed through them as William Muggins began: "o LORD God Almightie, the Father of mercies and God of all consolation, we miserable distressed creatures, wounded with the multitude of our grieuous sins, repayre vnto thee (the Phisition of our soules) for Balme to cure our Sores" (sig. D3r)?

The poem, however, dominates the pamphlet. It begins with a description of London weeping and a command that "London lament." It is here that the poem announces its epic aspirations: London declares that even Homer could not properly recount the city's tragic fall from fame and prosperity to plague and poverty (sig. B1r, lines 5–7).[27] The poem may be usefully broken down into several parts: London describes her former state of plenty until "Vnwelcome death" intrudes (stanzas 1–8). London then seeks fellow mourners but at first finds that Londoners are largely indifferent to the suffering of their neighbors and friends; many even attempt to take advantage of the crisis by swindling orphans and widows (stanzas 9–15). London then seeks parents and singles out mothers in particular, appealing to their shared experience of childbirth (stanzas 16–39). Prompting their tears anew, London invites the mothers to describe their troubles. A mother mourns the death of her children; an elderly widow bemoans the losses that have rendered her homeless; a young widow worries about how she will make ends meet (stanzas 40–59). London then recounts again her former fame in terms of an Icarus-like hubris. For this reason, she argues, the plague hurts all stations of life, the young and the old, the rich and the poor, the sinner and the godly (stanzas 60–76). Of all those afflicted by the plague, London laments the plight of the poor, and listens in on a family worrying about poverty and crushing debt as fears of contagion cause trade to stagnate (stanzas 77–83). Having given voice to mourning mothers and widows and the family in debt, London turns to the city's authorities to demand reforms that she says will bring an end to the plague, a new spiritual and economic covenant to alleviate suffering and appease God (stanzas 84–96). The final stanza presents a vision of King James's long-awaited entry to the city, signaling an end to the plague and the fulfillment of all London has demanded for the city's renewal.

London's concern with mothers and dying children leads Totaro to dub the speaker of Muggins's epic "Mother London" grieving the losses of her "citizen-children."[28] Although London never explicitly describes her inhabitants as her offspring, the concern she shows for them is certainly maternal (even as she describes herself as virgin bride or forlorn lady). This image of London as mother appears to have been influential. By 1612, Thomas Middleton's lord mayor's show, *The Triumph of Truth*, performed in honor of the new mayor, Sir Thomas Middleton of the Grocers' Company, begins with a song for London noting that the new mayor had not yet arrived:

Mother of many honorable sons,
Think not the glass too slowly runs
That in Time's hand is set,
Because thy worthy son appears not yet.[29]

After the song, Middleton explains that "a grave feminine shape presents itself, from behind a silk curtain, representing *London*, attired like a reverend mother, a long white hair naturally flowing on either side of her; on her head a model of steeples and turrets, her habit crimson silk, near to the honourable garment of the city; her left hand holding a key of gold" (lines 117–23). With the city's skyline for a crown, Middleton's London asks that her auditors not "esteem / My words the less, 'cause I a woman speak, / A woman's counsel is not always weak" (lines 128–30). Like Muggins's London, Middleton's recites her bountiful wealth, laments the neglect and indifference of some, and proceeds to advise the new mayor. Muggins's London is more radical and less apologetic, however, insisting that the wealthy give to the poor, that magistrates develop economic policies to ensure the livelihoods of laborers, and that the city's civic leaders fulfill their oaths of office. This, she argues, is the only way to ameliorate God's wrath, the presumed cause of plague.

As Middleton's pageant suggests, there was something audacious about a woman, even an allegorical woman, advising men on how to govern. Patricia Phillippy, who wrote the first extended analysis of *London's Mourning Garment*, notes the disruptive power of maternal mourning, its ability to challenge conventions of masculine control and to rebuke the wrongdoing of male rulers.[30] A lowly silk-weaver's advice to magistrates similarly ran the risk of appearing subversive. As Sir Thomas Smith put it in *De Republica*

Anglorum (1583), "The fourth sort or classe amongst vs, is of those which the olde Romans called *capite censii proletarii* or *operae*, day labourers, poore husbandmen, yea marchantes or retailers which haue no free lande, copiholders, and all artificers, as Taylers, Shoomakers, Carpenters, Brickemakers, Bricklayers, Masons, &c. These haue no voice nor authoritie in our common wealth, and no account is made of them but onelie to be ruled, not to rule other."[31] For Smith, weavers and others of the laboring class should be politically mute. Although out of necessity they might serve as constables or churchwardens, for Smith they had no right to tell the authorities about policies or how to implement them. Smith was describing the governance of the commonwealth as a whole, but the attitude he expresses regarding those who worked with their hands was often true of civic office as well. London's aldermen and mayors were drawn from the elite members of the Twelve Great Companies of London; all were wealthy merchants or retailers, men "of some substance" as Smith would have it, and as a matter of course, each mayor was elevated to the status of knight.[32] Muggins was not among the elite of his company, and in any case, his company, the Worshipful Company of Weavers, was not among the Twelve Great Companies of the city. The preeminence of the powerful men of the Twelve Great Companies is depicted in Anthony Munday's 1615 lord mayor's show, which featured the "Monument of London and her twelue Daughters," with each daughter representing one of the twelve powerful guilds or livery companies.[33] If this "Mother London" had any other daughters, they were clearly not important enough to be part of the symbolic fanfare for the mayor's show. Although the mayor's shows sometimes valorized labor, they also replicated Smith's sense that some of the poorer crafts ought to be passive spectators rather than active participants.[34]

In comparison, *London's Mourning Garment* evinces its own peculiar radicalism, but Muggins does not seem focused on disrupting the whole structure of society. His was not a world to be turned upside down. Rather, amid rapid economic changes, Muggins wanted to stabilize and restore the world as he imagined it was supposed to work. In a 1595 co-authored petition and in his 1603 pamphlet, Muggins argues that early modern society had lost its way, that the balance of justice needed to be recalibrated, not toppled over. He sought not a classless society but instead a delicate reciprocity, a finely tuned Christian commonwealth resistant to acquisitive impulses and oligarchical control. Part of the value of an intensive study of

London's Mourning Garment is the way it sheds light on how London's struggling members of the middling sort saw the economic and social changes around them, and how the experience of the plague made problems already inherent in early modern society more visible and more sharply felt.

Muggins had experienced breakdowns in the system. Discussed in greater detail in chapter 1, the 1595 petition he had a hand in composing complained that his own livery company had failed to enforce its regulations, making it difficult for struggling silk-weavers to compete in the marketplace. Although Muggins's household appears to have been productive, by October 1595 his debts were such that he was forced to appear in court before Chief Justice Edmund Anderson. Chapter 2 deals with this episode and its expression in *London's Mourning Garment* in greater detail, but the court ordered that a team of "witnesses," nearby citizens, compile an inventory of Muggins's household goods. The inventory includes the tools and raw material of Muggins's craft—looms, needles, pins, bolts of silk thread; and the finished products—various types of lace and ribbon, gloves, girdles, and garters, all assessed for their resale value.[35] The inventory also lists "fyve dozen & x paire of playinge cardes" and on the next line "iij dozen & a half of playing cards," in all estimated as worth twenty-seven shillings.[36] It would seem that Muggins's household sold playing cards as a side business, as the number of cards makes no sense for personal use. Further in one finds the household stuff, bedding, chairs, a Bible, and "sev[er]all english printyd Bokes." Much of this, especially the more valuable items, would be sold by the state to pay off Muggins's debt.

Following the language of the period, most historians would categorize Muggins as part of "the middling sort."[37] Primarily an urban category, according to one contemporary account in accord with Smith, this "sort" comprised "the moste part of Retaylors, and all artificers" who were by and large "neither too rich nor too poore but doe live in the mediocritie."[38] The men who assessed the goods in Muggins's household were all of the middling sort. Among them was a grocer, an innkeeper, a skinner, a plasterer, and a mercer. Their wealth varied dramatically. In the tax known as the lay subsidy of 1599, grocer David Floud was assessed at four times the wealth of his fellow witness, innkeeper James Leather; and one of the men who compiled Muggins's inventory does not appear in the subsidy at all, presumably because his household's worth was below the threshold of three pounds. It is not clear if these men would have categorized themselves as of the middling sort, but there is a value in the term "middling" in that the gerund form emphasizes that people like Muggins had a less than static, secure place in London's turbulent economy: a craftsman could make a very good living, just get by, or slip into the ranks of the dispossessed.

The term "middling sort," while current in the period, is an imperfect replacement for class, however. Lumping together extremely wealthy merchants with impoverished craftsmen, the term always risks occluding meaningful differences that class analysis seeks to emphasize. The language of estates and sorts rather than class has been upheld in the name of a pure historicism that seeks to examine the past on its own terms. But, as Keith Wrightson has pointed out, since the tracts about sorts and estates are almost always written by and for elites, this historicism lends itself to an almost exclusively ruling-class understanding of society.[39] Clearly, the wealthiest in early modern England preferred to present their society as an orderly one that naturalized exploitation or rendered it indistinguishable from matters of family and status. It is no coincidence that this period saw an increasing alliance between the gentry and the wealthiest of the middling sort, with these groups clearly recognizing shared interests, the foundation of a class consciousness.[40] Yet Muggins's participation in the 1595 petition and his subsequent 1603 pamphlet suggest that Smith's "*proletarii*," too, had developed a class consciousness, a sense that people in similar economic predicaments might band together to improve their condition.

In the passage by Smith cited above, the author equates "sort," "classe," and "*proletarii*" in rapid succession.[41] Smith, at least, saw Elizabethan sorts as synonymous with classes, and while one might allege that he did not mean class in the Marxist sense, he did see artisans as the contemporary version of the Latin word Marx would seize on, "proletarians." Evident from the number of looms counted in the inventory of his household, Muggins employed not only apprentices but one or two journeymen weavers as well. While Muggins's status as an employer of others complicates a simple view of his class, silk-weavers themselves were beholden to silk-merchants who commissioned their work and controlled the supply and price of the weavers' raw materials. As with the members of the commonalty discussed by David Rollison, silk-weavers like Muggins had every reason to feel a degree of class resentment for the wealthy who exerted so much influence over the markets and laws of the city as well as country as a whole.[42] It should be clear in the chapters that follow that Muggins identified less with wealthy retailers and merchants and more with the laboring class of which he was a definite part. Indeed, in all periods the exploiters and the exploited display a practical knowledge of class consciousness with the potential for oppressive alliances or revolutionary praxis.[43]

Smith's description of "the fourth sort" as having "no voice" suggests a significant problem for the study of the middling sort: If they have no voice, what traces could they have left in the historical record? Indeed, in her study of Star Chamber cases, Hillary Taylor argues that even when the poor were called to testify, fear of reprisal from the elite and wealthy tended to silence or distort their statements.[44] Some recent case studies—like those contained in Tara Hamling and Catherine Richardson's *A Day at Home in Early Modern England* and Robert Tittler's *Townspeople and Nation*—have helped redress this problem, especially in studies of the upper echelon of the middling sort.[45] Meanwhile, Alexandra Shepard and Paul Griffiths have offered exciting research on the poorer sort as they presented themselves before the authorities.[46] One of the goals of this book is to highlight how at least one member of the poorer end of the middling sort, poet and silk-weaver William Muggins, saw early modern society and his place in it in a variety of contexts—not only before authorities but also among his peers and as he presented himself in print. This study thus redresses a significant dearth of knowledge about how the poorer end of the middling sort conceived of themselves and their society.

In a petition from 1595, Muggins counted himself among the "Freemen of the Cittye and the Yeomanry of the Company of distressed Weavers."[47] Freemen of the city had the right to practice their trades independently, sell their own wares on the open market, and employ apprentices and journeymen. There were two paths to gaining the freedom of the city: one earned it through an apprenticeship in the city, or one inherited it from one's father who had been a freeman of the city and enjoyed good standing with his livery company.[48] Because most of the apprenticeship records of the London Weavers' Company were lost in the fire of 1666, it is not known how Muggins obtained the freedom of the city. The petition he signed and helped draft describes the freeman as "he whoe was brought up in the Cittye, served many yeares to have the pryviledge thereof, who is alsoe sworne to all manner of Charges, who payes all dutyes belongeinge to a Subject."[49] Given the petition's definition of a freeman of the city, it seems likely that Muggins had served an apprenticeship somewhere in London.

That Muggins counted himself among "the distressed" highlights the precarious position of craftsmen in the city. Some experienced financial stability or even upward mobility, but most were especially vulnerable to inflation, market fluctuations, and the economic fallout of natural disasters like the plague. Simply adding a child to the household might severely strain the household's resources, as it introduced a new mouth to feed and limited the mother's economic contributions for a time. The inventory of Muggins's home, after all, was occasioned by a suit for unpaid debt. With several children to feed, Muggins was often on the brink of abject poverty.

Like the ruling-class pamphlets on the organization of early modern society, in *London's Mourning Garment* Muggins describes society as organized by "degrees" or "States." At the bottom of Muggins's organization was the "poorest begger" and, toward the top, "the wealthiest Squire" (sig. C3v, line 454). In between Muggins enumerates artisans, tradesmen, and merchants. This is in line with *De Republica Anglorum*'s schema, but the very fact of writing a plague pamphlet, of dedicating it to an alderman, of inserting himself in the public discourse, gives the lie to Smith's notion of a voiceless and politically passive "fourth sort." Indeed, men and women of the poorer end of the middling sort are central to Muggins's portrait of the city.

It is Muggins's status as a poor craftsman, after all, that allows for the insights offered in the poem. The mothers who mourn in *London's Mourning Garment* are destitute—one faces homelessness while another worries about being forced into prostitution. The family in debt must pawn clothing to survive the economic crisis that accompanied the plague. Like her sympathies, Muggins's personified London makes demands that are aimed at helping workers and those too old to work. The radical, polyvocal poem is in many respects a petition in verse form, a plea that those in power attend to the needs of those who make their lives possible. Moreover, the poem presents the voices of precisely those marginalized in London's political discourse: women and the poor. In 1595 Muggins sought to speak narrowly on behalf of his fellow "distressed weavers." By 1603 he had expanded his view, writing his London as a spokesperson "For such as worke and take exceeding care," those preyed on by pawnbrokers or simply impoverished by the economic disaster that came with the plague. From 1595 to 1603, from his immediate economic situation to the broader situation of the working poor in London, then, one can see the development of something very much like class consciousness in Muggins's writing. The paratexts of *London's Mourning*

Garment—a dedication to the sheriff at the outset, and an official-looking table of the dead in each parish at the end—might in part have functioned as ways of mitigating some of the pamphlet's potentially seditious edge. They lend an appearance of authority to the silk-weaver's politically charged plague poem.

This book is about *London's Mourning Garment* and its author, his social network, and the cultural and material forces that informed his minor epic. His social network included members of the Weavers Company, writers, printers, preachers, and neighbors. Some, like Swinnerton and a few wealthy grocers, were well-to-do and elite, but for the most part Muggins associated with men and women of his social and economic station. The chapters that follow look at the conditions of Muggins's life, the problems he faced, and how he translated these into poetry that sought not only to reflect but also to change those conditions. More often than not, literary scholarship on early modern England's laborers—craftsmen and -women, peasants, and day laborers—has relied on representations mediated by members of the ruling class or those patronized by them. But a huge chasm exists between the way farmers thought about their lives and the representation of rustics in Sir Philip Sidney's *Arcadia*, for example. Even stage representations were often necessarily caught up in appealing in part to the conventions expected by high-paying audience members and the powerful patrons who lent their names to the various London theater companies.[50] *London's Mourning Garment*, on the other hand, affords readers a street-level view of early modern London as represented by a member of the poor end of the middling sort. The pamphlet was certainly subject to its own conventions and distortions—no text can offer an unmediated and comprehensive view of the past—but the radically different perspective offered by *London's Mourning Garment* is important in supplementing the statistical work of social historians and complicating our necessarily fragmented understanding of life and literature in the early modern world.[51] This book follows Muggins and those in his social network from 1595 to 1603, providing an early modern laborer's perspective on the economy, religion, authority, and local community amid the plague. At times this book confirms assumptions about members of the poorer end of the middling sort, but Muggins often surprises and complicates long-held views of his class. His reading is wider, his criticism of the authorities more incisive, and his attention to women of the middling sort more sensitive than one might expect.

WEAVER-POETS IN THE SIXTEENTH CENTURY

Among William Muggins's associates, if not close friends, was Thomas Deloney. In 1595 Deloney is known to have visited Muggins's household, and the two were briefly cellmates at Newgate. Like Muggins, Deloney was a silk-weaver, but by 1595 Deloney had also acquired considerable fame as a writer of ballads, and in the later 1590s as a writer of prose fiction. Deloney's notoriety was such that by 1596 Thomas Nashe had dubbed him "the Balletting Silke-weauer" in his *Haue with You to Saffron-Walden*.[52] Although Deloney worked with a number of printers in his career, toward the end of his life he developed a significant professional relationship with the printer Ralph Blower.[53] In 1597 Blower entered his right to print Deloney's *The Gentle Craft*, probably the first edition of part 1 of that book.[54] Blower also had a hand in the earliest extant edition of Deloney's *Thomas of Reading*, and there is no reason to doubt that he was involved in its initial printing.[55] Finally, Blower appears to have printed an edition of Deloney's *Strange Histories* for William Barley, and again, Blower may well have been involved in earlier printings.[56] Blower was also the printer of *London's Mourning Garment*, and it was probably through association with the aforementioned William Barley that Blower acquired the death's head device for the cover of Muggins's pamphlet. It would seem that Deloney and Muggins had a fairly close relationship: the two shared a craft, a cell, and a printer.

Whatever deeper connections existed between William Muggins and Thomas Deloney, it is significant that both were weaver-poets. Although it is not known what Muggins had written in the 1590s, it is unlikely that his 1603 ninety-seven-stanza poem was his first attempt at writing poetry. Unlike Deloney, however, Muggins does not seem to have sought to have his work printed until 1603. He describes his pamphlet as "this my poore labour," but it is clear that for the most part Muggins earned his living in the silk trade (sig. A2r). Laurie Ellinghausen has shown how early modern professional writers born into the middling sort posed "a challenge to aristocratic literary culture" by highlighting the labor that went into writing.[57] Muggins's fleeting description of his own entry into print as the product of his "poore labour" suggests a humble awareness of this trend, although he seems not to have gone beyond this instance to forge a professional persona like those of the writers described by Ellinghausen.[58] Still, Muggins's sympathies might well complement Ellinghausen's work on more prolific non-elite writers of the period. Of the writers discussed by Ellinghausen, Muggins most closely resembles John Taylor, "the Water-Poet"; but while Taylor joined the elite of his company, Deloney and Muggins were among the poorer weavers in the London Weavers' Company. As will be seen in chapter 1, there was a deep divide between the company's elite and the rank and file. The connections between Deloney and Muggins, moreover, suggest that there was a circle of weaver-poets in the 1590s, a group of writers who may not have always seen their work in print but who, like the writers discussed by Ellinghausen, nonetheless had participated in a non-aristocratic aesthetics.

Around the time that Muggins and Deloney shared a cell, William Shakespeare's *A Midsummer Night's Dream* featured Nick Bottom, a weaver who memorizes verses from popular plays. Bottom, whose name refers both to his place in the socioeconomic hierarchy and to the technical term for the core around which a weaver's thread was wound, recites:

> The raging rocks
> And shivering shocks
> Shall break the locks
>   Of prison gates,
> And Phibus' car
> Shall shine from far
> And make and mar
>   The foolish Fates. (1.2.24–31)[59]

Reflecting on the image of breaking the locks of prison gates, the weaver appraises, "This was lofty" (1.2.32). When he finds himself abandoned in the woods, Bottom sings, "The ousel cock so black of hue" and then begins, like a natural literary critic, to evaluate the lyrics (3.1.110–20). And after awaking from his transformation into an ass and his tryst with the queen of the fairies, Bottom aspires to collaborate with the carpenter Peter Quince "to write a ballad of this dream. It shall be called 'Bottom's Dream', because it hath no bottom." Whether he may be called a poet or not, Nick Bottom is clearly a poetry enthusiast, albeit with popular rather than courtly tastes. Audiences are thus left uncertain as to whether Bottom's synesthetic "The eye of man hath not heard, the ear of man hath not seen, man's hand is not able to taste, his tongue to conceive, nor his heart to report" may be taken as garbled scripture or a clever appropriation of Paul's epistle for the purpose of expressing the unfathomable experience the weaver has had (4.1.204–9). The actor who likely played Bottom, William Kempe, would later discuss Deloney's writing in his *Kemps Nine Daies Wonder* (1599).[60] Shakespeare's Bottom was likely intended as a lighthearted jab at the poetic aspirations of weavers like Deloney and other craftsmen in London.

A thread connecting weaving to poetry runs throughout Shakespeare's play. Even in the "Pyramus and Thisbe" play within a play, *A Midsummer Night's Dream* alludes to a close connection between poetry and weaving.[61] The tale of Pyramus and Thisbe had a special significance for silk-weavers like Deloney and Muggins. In Ovid's *Metamorphosis* the tale culminates in the lovers' blood changing the fruit of the mulberry tree from white to black, a sign of mourning.[62] Whereas mulberries were considered a delicacy, the mulberry tree's leaves provided the main sustenance for silkworms and therefore the cultivation of raw silk. It would be ten years before England embarked on its own experiment in sericulture, but the centrality of the mulberry tree for the production of silk was already widely understood.[63] In 1599 Thomas Moffett's *The Silkewormes and Their Flies* presented in verse an argument for planting mulberry trees in England for the propagation of silkworms.[64] By 1607 King James planned to have more than ten thousand mulberry trees planted in England for the express purpose of silk production.[65] Thus, as an ass-headed Bottom reclines with the queen of fairies, she offers him mulberries not only because the fruit tended to be consumed by the privileged, but also because of its relation to Bottom's trade. More to the point, Bottom plays Pyramus, the tortured lover who, believing his beloved Thisbe dead, kills himself, declaring "O fates, come, come, / Cut thread and thrum" (5.1.275–76). Here the classical Fates with the thread of life are imagined to be involved in the technical work of weavers, "thrum" being the weavers' term for the thread that remains on the loom after the web or cloth is cut from it.[66] Is this Quince framing the role to his friend's profession, or is it Bottom's improvisation? Either way the weaver's craft becomes entangled in that of the poet.

Moreover, there appears to have been a longer history of weaver-poets in sixteenth-century England. Forty years before Muggins's and Deloney's stay at Newgate, several prisoners there (perhaps sitting in the same space Deloney and Muggins would later occupy) received letters from another weaver-poet, John Careless of Coventry. Careless wrote to his fellow prisoners in Newgate from the King's Bench, a prison located in the south of London where he languished for roughly two years while awaiting execution for his outspoken Protestantism. Printed several times in the sixteenth century, Careless's letters provide a window into the weaver's experience of Protestantism amid Mary I's re-Catholicization of England. He wrote not only to his wife, Margaret, and bedfellow William Tyms but also to prominent reformers like John Bradford, John Philpot, and Augustine Bernher, as well as imprisoned Protestants like Harry Adlington, the wives of several of the imprisoned, and others.[67] Interspersed among the letters Careless also penned several devotional poems and a record of his interrogation under Dr. Thomas Martin.[68]

Although he describes himself as "a poor man without learning," Careless's letters not only offer comfort to his fellow Protestants but also often evoke a degree of playful wit.[69] In his letter to John Philpot, Careless writes, "O my good master Philpot, which art a principal pot indeed, filled with most precious liquor, as it appeareth by the plenteous pouring forth of the same—O pot most happy, of thy high Potter ordained to honour, which dost contain such heavenly treasure in thy earthen vessel."[70] To Master Bartelet Green, one of the Newgate prisoners, he wrote, "A full dainty dish art thou for the Lord's own tooth. Fresh and *green* shalt thou be in the house of the Lord, and thy fruits shall never wither nor decay."[71] Writing to his bedfellow William Tyms at Newgate, Careless again punned on a surname: "Blessed be God for thee, my dear brother Tyms, and blessed be God again that ever I knew thee, for in a most happy *time* I came first into thy company."[72] John N. King suggests that such passages are to be read as an imitation of St. Paul's admonition that martyrs find joy in their suffering, but Careless also offers more macabre linguistic play, as when he describes Bishop Bonner as "the common slaughter-slave of England," or when he glosses bishops as "bite-sheeps."[73] Careless's particular habit of constructing spiritual meaning in puns and extended metaphors suggests an allegorical turn of mind whereby the world is replete with spiritual meaning to be deciphered through the poetic play of language.

Careless's own name presented the most contentious of spiritual meanings for the Protestant weaver-poet. Careless recalls that at the start of his interrogation, Dr. Martin declared, "Careless! By my faith I think the same; and so I ween it will appear by thy conditions, by that time we have done with thee."[74] Careless retorts, "Though my name be Careless, yet perchance you shall not find me so careless in my conditions as your mastership doth presuppose." Whether Martin actually punned on Careless's name, the debate over the meaning of his name is emblematic of the larger battle over interpretation of scripture that ensues, a contest in which Careless proves to be an astute lay theologian and an extraordinarily deft debater. Similarly, John Philpot's letter to Careless was largely organized around a series of puns on the word "care": "Since God hath willed you at your Baptism in Christ to be Careless, why do you make yourself careful? Cast all your care on him."[75] Careless seizes on Philpot's conceit, at one point signing a letter "John Careless, still careful for you," and later signing a poem "Continue constant in Christ and Careless," where careless comes to mean not ignorant or reckless but focused on the spiritual rather than the worldly.[76]

Deloney and Muggins were likely familiar with at least some of Careless's writing. Foxe's *Acts and Monuments* was widely read, and Deloney reworked material from *Acts and Monuments* in his ballad "The Duchess of Suffolk's Calamity." Careless's poetry, moreover, was well-known independently of Foxe. One of his poems originally appearing in Miles Coverdale's *Certain Most Godly, Fruitful, and Comfortable Letters* (1564) also circulated separately as a broadside ballad.[77] Careless's poem begins:

> Some men for sudden joy do weep,
> And some in sorrow sing,
> When that they lie in danger deep,
> To put away mourning.
>
> Between them both will I begin,
> Being in joy and pain,
> In sighing to lament my sin,
> But yet to rejoice again.[78]

As with his letters, the twenty-eight-stanza poem consoles the suffering Christian. "A ballad of John Careless &c." was licensed for publication in 1586, and presumably again under a slightly different title in 1624 and another time in 1635. But the ballad was already known by 1583: *A Declaration of the Death of John Lewes* (1583) was "to be sung to the tune of John Careless."[79] As late as 1635 printers of ballads could still confidently instruct that a ballad be sung to "To the tune of, *O man in desperation* or, *Some men for sudden joys do weep*."[80]

The enduring popularity of Careless's poem is further attested to by Thomas Nashe, who in *Haue with You to Saffron-Walden* refers to it disparagingly as "the godly ballet of John Careless, or Green Sleeves moralized."[81] In *Medicines for the Plague* (1604) Nicholas Bownd speaks admiringly of the poem, however, arguing that Careless describes for readers the appropriately Christian attitude toward the plague.[82] In a further indication of its popularity, Shakespeare adapted the poem in *King Lear* (1606), when the fool remarks:

> Then they for sudden joy did weep,
> And I for sorrow sung,
> That such a king should play bo-peep,
> And go the fool among.[83]

Similarly, Thomas Heywood alludes to the poem for a song in *The Rape of Lucrece* (1608):

> When Tarquin first in Court began,
> And was approved King:
> Some men for sudden joy gan weep,
> But I for sorrow sing.[84]

The last two lines nod to Careless's poem, but the first two adapt Deloney's ballad, "The Noble Acts of Arthur of the Round Table," printed in his collection of ballads *The Garland of Goodwill* (1596).[85] Deloney's ballad begins, "When Arthur first in Court began, / and was approued king."[86] That Careless and Deloney were thus yoked together in the poem hints at Heywood's awareness of a tradition of popular weaver-poets in early modern England.[87] By the same token, Nashe singles out Careless and Deloney in *Haue with You to Saffron-Walden*, a pamphlet that primarily ridicules the writer Gabriel Harvey for, among other things, his humble birth as "the eldest sonne of the halter-maker." Nashe's allusions to weaver-poets fits a general pattern of the pamphlet to lump Harvey in with the poor craftsmen who lacked university education.[88] Nashe's antipathies aside, the allusions to and adaptations of Careless demonstrate the poem's popularity. Surely, two Protestant weaver-poets like Muggins and Deloney took an interest in the substantial literary notoriety of one of their brethren from the previous generation.

The link between poetry and weaving goes back well into classical antiquity when the likes of Homer, Sappho, and Pindar drew attention to the physical similarity between loom and lyre and therefore used weaving as a metaphor for poetry and storytelling.[89] Anthony Tuck, moreover, theorizes that many songs and stories of antiquity may have developed as mnemonic devices for the production of complex patterns in textiles. This, argues Tuck, explains the images of Circe and Calypso singing while weaving in Homer's *Odyssey* as well as the frequent link of storytelling with weaving in the plays of Euripides.[90]

The connection between text and textile, singing and weaving, persisted into the sixteenth century. In chapter 3 of Thomas Deloney's *Jack of Newbury*, for instance, the eponymous broadcloth weaver, is visited by Henry VIII and his entourage. After dining, Jack invites his guests to view his people at work. They first view weavers attending one hundred looms and singing "The Weauers Song," a ten-stanza poem that charts the "band of amity" among weavers, with allusions to Hercules and the biblical giants whose spears were like "Weavers beames."[91] "The Weauers Song" argues that the unity of weavers is such that the fall of Troy would not have occurred had Paris or Helen been involved in the craft.

After praising and rewarding the weavers, the king advances to view women carding and spinning wool, who "in dulcet manner chanted out this song, two of them singing the Ditty, and all the rest bearing the burden."[92] The song, called "The Maidens Song," is about the earl of Northumberland's daughter, who helps a Scottish knight escape prison.[93] She travels with him to a river, which she must be importuned to cross; once she does so, the knight abandons her for his wife and children in Edinburgh. The song's refrain—"follow my love, come over the strand"—refers to (and only really makes sense at) the dramatic moment of crossing the river's strand, where the lady is in fact stranded. If such refrains also functioned as mnemonic devices, however, "come over the strand" probably referred as well to the repeated act of adding carded strands of wool in the process of spinning.[94] Along the same lines, the emphasis on amity among weavers in "The Weauers Song" relates directly to the cooperation needed between weavers in operating a broadcloth loom. The production of poetry entwines itself in the material process of weaving and serves a mediating function in establishing collaboration and community among laborers. The production of poetry among the weavers here seems to be pragmatic and fundamentally social. It provides mnemonic devices but also inducts weavers into an aesthetic of shared practices that define the community.

These instances from *Jack of Newbury* need to be read in part as entertainment for Jack's royal guests, but the idea that weavers had a special relation to song was prevalent in the period.[95] In Shakespeare's *Twelfth Night*, Duke Orsino remarks of the song "Come away, come away death," "The spinsters and the knitters in the sun / And the free maids that weave their thread with bones / Do use to chant it"(2.4.42–44). And in the folio printing of *Henry IV, Part 1*, Sir John Falstaff laments, "I would I were a weaver; I could sing all manner of songs" (2.4.119–20). Stage directions to John Phillips's *The Play of Patient Grissel* (1560) indicate that Grissel is to "sing some song, and sit spinning," while in Thomas Middleton's *A Trick to Catch the Old One* (1608) it is clear that Audrey is to sing while spinning.[96]

The association of weavers with singing and poetry continued into the nineteenth century when, in 1809, Lord Byron complained of "Moorland weavers" who "boast Pindaric skill," a fairly pointed reference to sometime poet Thomas Bakewell of Staffordshire, who was not really a weaver for much of his life but identified as such; like Nashe two hundred years earlier, Byron's point seems to have been to disparage more generally weavers and other artisans who tried their hands at poetry.[97] Among the weaver-poets hailing from England, Scotland, and Ireland around that time were John Webb (1768–1840), Robert Millhouse (1788–1839), Samuel Bamford (1788–1872), Robert Tannahill (1774–1810), James Maxwell (1719–1801), James Orr (1770–1816), Bernard Short (1803–1842), Thomas Stott (1755–1829), James Campbell (1758–1818), and Francis Boyle (1810–1881), to name only a few.[98] One might attribute the rise of weaver-poets in the late eighteenth and early nineteenth centuries to an increase in literacy and a contemporary taste for seemingly "authentic" portrayals of working-class life à la Stephen Duck, but these poets were preceded by other weaver-poets—Careless, Deloney, Muggins, and any number of others invisible to us because they printed anonymously or not at all.

In *Rhymes and Recollections of a Hand-Loom Weaver* (1845), Scottish weaver-poet William Thom (1799–1848) reflected on the link between weaving and poetry and its relation to his own development as a writer. Thom explains that poems and songs were often recited to keep up the morale of the many impoverished weavers as they worked: "Let me again proclaim the debt we owe those Song Spirits as they walked in the melody from loom to loom, ministering to the low-hearted; and when the breast was filled with everything but hope and happiness, and all but seared, let only break forth the healthy and vigorous chorus 'A man's a man for a' that,' the fagged weaver brightens up. His very shuttle skytes along, and clatters through in faithful time to the tune of his merrier shopmates!"[99] The songs set the rhythm of weavers' labor on the loom. As with the examples from *Jack of Newbury*, the poetry of weavers, as Thom describes it, again appears to be geared to the communal and the pragmatic.

Thom then describes the development of new weaver-poets in the shops. "It was not enough that we merely chaunted or listened," writes Thom, "but some more ambitious or idle if you will, they in time would try a self-conceived song."[100] So began Thom's career as "the factory-distinguished writer."[101] Early nineteenth-century Scotland differed a great deal from sixteenth-century London, but Thom's description of the recitation of poetry or song while weaving bears a striking resemblance to Deloney's in *Jack of Newbury*: they even use the same verb, "chanted," emphasizing the rhythmic, repetitive nature of the work. As weavers were taught their craft, so they came to be attuned to listening to or chanting the poetry of the past, and whether out of boredom, a desire for praise, or genuine inspiration this incited some to write their own verses. One imagines a similar set of material conditions leading Deloney and Muggins to compose poetry, at first for their fellow weavers but eventually for a larger audience. Deloney made his fame as a writer of ballads and then prose fiction, but Muggins seems to have only entered print for the purposes of collective action in petition or poem.

In addition to their own tradition of poetry and song, sixteenth-century weaver-poets were likely influenced by developments in vernacular drama. Bottom, after all, is a theater enthusiast. David Katham has noted that companies had long paid players for entertainment during feast days. By the mid-sixteenth century, however, players began paying companies, among them the London Company of Weavers, for the use of their halls until the professional playhouses eliminated the necessity.[102] Deloney, moreover, occasionally alludes to Shakespeare's plays and especially to his narrative poem *Venus and Adonis* (and some of Deloney's works were adapted to the stage in turn).[103] In 1554, while imprisoned in Coventry and waiting to be transferred to the King's Bench, John Careless was briefly released from prison so that he could participate in the Weavers' play of the Nativity, one of only two parts of the Coventry Corpus Christi cycle to survive.[104]

One wonders if Careless, accused of heresy, might have infused his role with any signs of Protestant zeal. Ultimately, the Bible and Reformation theology had a greater influence than did theater on sixteenth-century weaver-poets. Careless willingly embraced the role of Protestant martyr in the 1550s. By 1560 Bishop of London Edmund Grindal included two weavers, William Betts and Thomas Upcher, among the sixty men he ordained as deacons, and he made Walter Richardson, probably also a weaver, into a priest.[105] In 1579 a utopian dialogue concerning the fictive commonwealth of Crangalor explained that silk-weavers were the most zealous of their citizens, devoting all their time to weaving and praying.[106] In the 1580s and 1590s Deloney promoted his Protestant faith in such ballads as "A Pleasant Dialogue between Plaine Truth, and Blind Ignorance" where Truth is a zealous Protestant who successfully convinces Ignorance to reject Catholicism, and "The Duchess of Suffolk's Calamity" which framed Protestant exile Catherine Brandon as a national hero.[107] And the quarto of *Henry IV* has Falstaff wishing he were a weaver so that he could "sing psalmes," decidedly more pious than the vague "songs" of the folio.[108]

Although many craftsmen sang psalms (and songs), there is a consistent notion in the period that weavers were particularly pious. In the archives of the Worshipful Company of Weavers, amid copies of their early ordinances, are three folio pages on which someone copied out extracts from the Gospels in Latin; and the ordinances of 1379 begin, "In the name of the Fader, of the Sone and the Holy Gost," a decidedly spiritual preamble for secular rules of the craft.[109] By the late sixteenth century weavers came to be associated with zealous Protestantism, so much so that at times weavers were satirized for their outspoken Puritanism. In George Chapman's comedy *Monsieur D'Olive* (1606), the title character recalls an encounter with "Upstart, a weaver," a moralizing artisan who, though "a little fellow," had been "blown up by inspiration / That had borne office in congregation" to rail against tobacco as "a pagan plant, a profane weed / And a most sinful smoke, that had no warrant / Out of the word; invented sure by Satan."[110] The bombastic tirade against tobacco continues for many lines. D'Olive is invested in lampooning the weaver's argument, but the characterization nonetheless says something about the perception of weavers in the period. Before it came to be associated with a style of inflated rhetoric, the word "bombast" referred to puffed up cotton wool used as padding in doublets and other woven items, and "fustian" originally referred to a thick cloth; in the 1590s these woven products came to refer also to the "blown-up" rhetoric evident in *Monsieur D'Olive*'s tale of the Puritan weaver.[111] A decade later, in *Hengist, King of Kent* (1616–20), Middleton would also satirize the extreme religious outlook of weavers through his character Oliver, self-described "Puritan and Fustian-weaver altogether," who upon being told to bow to the new lord mayor, vaunts, "I was not born to stoop but to my loom" (5.1.156, 164).

Robert Wild's satirical ballad *Alas Poore Scholler, Whither Wilt Thou Goe?* (1641) similarly associates weavers with an overweening Puritanism. Among the speaker's laments about the decay of learning is an anecdote about preaching alongside a weaver:

> Once, I remember,
> I Preached with a *Weaver*,
> I quoted *Austine*,
> He quoted *Dod* and *Cleaver*,
> I nothing got,
> He got a Cloak and Beaver.
> Alas, poor scholar, whither wilt thou go?[112]

The author's point is that learning, signaled by citations of St. Augustine, is devalued in favor of quoting popular Puritan preachers like John Dod and Robert Cleaver. The scholar is outdone by a Puritan Nick Bottom. It is worth noting, however, that although Wild's weaver may be disparaged here, he is also literate, devout, and, most important, willing to audaciously enter into the public sphere. Representations might fall far afield of any lived reality for early modern weavers, but Muggins, like the weaver-poets who came before and after him, also felt the urge to voice his thoughts in the public sphere.[113]

MUGGINS'S READING

Unlike previous generations of weaver-poets, Muggins was born into an early modern England where the Reformation, the spread of humanist learning, and the printing press naturally exposed him to a range of reading beyond the immediate tradition of the weavers' shop. One may presume that Muggins read a selection of the popular literature of the day—ballads, almanacs, a psalmbook. However, the estimation of what was typically read by commoners is often driven by numbers of editions of the particular text coupled with a priori judgments of popular taste. A careful study of *London's Mourning Garment* for echoes of other texts yields concrete and at times surprising results.

It comes as little surprise that Muggins was a dedicated and lively reader of the Bible. The prayer Muggins included in *London's Mourning Garment* alludes to Old and New Testament passages throughout and provides some sense of which passages Muggins read most ardently. For example, in describing the sinfulness of London in its prosperity, the prayer announces, "our Wine is bitter as the Wine of Sodom, and our grapes as the grapes of Gomorrah: wee are become as the seede of the wicked corrupt children, disobedient seruantes, a rebellious people, & now that we are rich, and are waxen fat, we spurne with the heele, like ye vnruly Heifar, we are sicke of long prosperity, & haue surfeited of peace and plentie" (sig. D3v). The prayer moves seamlessly from one biblical allusion to another, from the vineyard imagery of Deuteronomy 32:32 to "the seede of the wicked corrupt children," a direct quote from Isaiah 1:4, to the disobedient and rebellious, an allusion to either Isaiah 30:9 or Psalm 78 (or both), to "waxen fat, we spurne with the heele," a clear echo of Deuteronomy 32:15, to the "unruly heifer" of Hosea 4:16.[114] Muggins's prayer is a creative reassembling of evocative imagery gleaned from his reading. Scarcely a sentence goes by in the prayer without two or three scriptural references. This was not altogether unusual for the period. Prayers were supposed to be heartfelt and even spontaneous, but many worried that they also needed to speak in a language God might understand. Thus, the most effective prayers, some thought, would express genuine zeal while relying heavily on words, phrases, and images from the Bible.[115] As George Herbert would put it some decades later, prayer was—or at least could be—"God's breath in man returning to his birth."[116]

A careful examination of *London's Mourning Garment* reveals that Muggins favored particular books of the Bible. He alludes to the Psalms, Deuteronomy, Isaiah, and Jeremiah far more than all of the New Testament books combined. Favoring the Old over the New Testament, while not peculiar to Muggins, suggests a more radical, even Puritan, mindset, as does the writing of his own prayer rather than merely relying on the state-authorized prayers issued during the plague.[117] Within the books he alludes to most, moreover, Muggins clearly favored the more poetic passages: the Psalms, of course, but also, the first third of Jeremiah and its companion

Lamentations.[118] Taken together, Muggins was keenly interested in the Israelites' exile into Babylon and the hope of reclaiming the promised land. At the same time, for Muggins, Jeremiah's admonishing the Israelites for their lack of faith spoke as much to Londoners in 1603 as it did to the Israelites in 500 BCE. Just as Muggins's poem situated London as the site of epic mourning, the prayer pieced together a biblical narrative of London's hubristic failure to recognize God's grace and the demands of a socioeconomic covenant expressed in Isaiah and Jeremiah in particular. As in so many of the books of the Old Testament, a city's pride and failure to tend to the poor resulted in a devastating plague, but with the hope that through pious devotion the plague might cease and London might really become a new Jerusalem. The weaver-poet was concerned with the day-to-day struggles of the middling sort in London—labor, debt, childrearing—but he also strove for prophetic heights, discussed more fully in chapter 4 of this book.

Without doubt, Muggins drew most of his poetic inspiration from the Bible. As the head of the household he was responsible for the spiritual education of his children and apprentices, and it is probable that like many, he followed some variation of the practice recommended by Lewis Bayly in 1613: "Call euery morning all thy familie to some *conuenient* roome; and first, eyther read thy selfe vnto them a Chapter in the word of *God*, or cause it to be read distinctly by some other. If leasure serve, thou maist *admonish* them of some remarkable good *notes*; and then kneeling downe with them in reverent sort, as is before described, pray with them in this manner."[119] In *London's Mourning Garment*'s eulogy for the child Bess, the bereaved mother recalls the pleasure she took in observing her daughter read (sig. C1r, line 292). This passage and Elizabeth Muggins's probable education is discussed in more detail in chapter 3, but here it is worth noting the value Muggins's poem placed on a young woman's literacy. How Muggins himself learned to read and write is unknown, however. Although literacy places Muggins among the better educated of his craft, his name does not appear in lists of grammar school students, nor is it clear how much Latin he could read.[120] Outside the formal structure of Elizabethan grammar schools and without the extensive resources of the gentry, Muggins's literacy must have involved persistent dedication, literate parents, or a master weaver who saw the ability to read as of significant spiritual or economic value.[121] If *London's Mourning Garment* is at all autobiographical, one can imagine that Muggins similarly dedicated himself to teaching his children to read, perhaps asking that his eldest daughter occasionally read passages from the Bible aloud for the household's edification.

Based on its estimated worth in the inventory of his household goods and on citations in *London's Mourning Garment*, it appears that Muggins owned a Geneva Bible that he consulted with great regularity.[122] The citational style (i.e., the bringing together of disparate phrases from the Bible for his prayer) suggests the use of a commonplace book where Muggins recorded salient lines from his reading under various headings.[123] But what else did Muggins read? The inventory of his household with its "viij sev[er]all english printyd Bokes" assessed at eleven shillings provides only the vaguest of clues. Whereas the inventory assesses the value of "one dozen of shorte White Pynns," "one pound of blew thredd," "iij Pynpillowes," and further in domestic items like "one paire of Tonges" and "ij old yron Potts," the books did not hold enough individual value to be listed by title.[124]

Muggins read the Bible, and he knew Deloney's writing and shared with it a keen interest in representing the concerns of commoners, but Muggins's reading went well beyond scripture and the popular ballad of the day. *London's Mourning Garment* is written in rhyme royal, a seven-line stanza in iambic pentameter rhyming a-b-a-b-b-c-c—a subtle, complex form.[125] As Elizabethan poet George Gascoigne puts it, "The first and third lines do aunswer (acrosse) in like terminations and rime, the second and fourth, and fifth, do likewise answere eache other in terminations, and the two last do combine and shut vp the Sentence."[126] That is, the stanza is made up of both alternating rhymes and couplets, with the fourth line serving as both the end of alternating rhymes and the beginning of the couplets. For Gascoigne the final couplet offers a kind of closure. Muggins exploited this "shut[ting] vp" and the shift to couplets for dramatic effect. For example, in one stanza Muggins describes a marriage cut tragically short by the plague:

> The joyfull Brydegroome married as to day,
> Sicke, weake, and feeble before table layde,
> And the next morrow dead and wrap't in clay,
> Leauing his Bride, a widdow, wife and mayde,
> Which sudden change doth make her so dismayde,
>   That griefes and sorrowes doth perplexe her heart,
>   Within three dayes she takes her husbands part. (sig. C4r, lines 512–18)

The wedding day is taken up by four lines of alternating rhymes that, along with disruptions in the meter at the second and fourth lines, slow the pace of the first death. Whereas the tragedy might end with the bride left both widow and maid, the fifth line introduces the "sudden change" in fate with a rapid rhyme on "mayde." The two couplets sprint across three days, with rhyming couplets quickening the pace of the stanza to emphasize the rapid spread of the plague and its effects. The rhyme scheme is used to emphasize the sudden overwhelming speed with which the plague takes lives. Elsewhere Muggins employs the final couplet to forcefully moralize the stanza's point, as in a passage in which London condemns the city's brothels surmising at the end of the stanza, "Like wicked SODOME, doth my Subburbs lye, / A mighty blemish, to faire LONDONS eye" (sig. D2r, lines 629–30). Throughout Muggins works various effects within the confines of the rhyme royal stanza form.

Muggins had read enough to know that rhyme royal was the stanza form appropriate to the seriousness of his subject matter. Gascoigne describes rhyme royal as "seruing best for graue discourses," and George Puttenham in his *Arte of English Poesy* (1589) declared it as "the chiefe of our ancient proportions" appropriate for a "historical or graue poem."[127] It was the stanza form of Geoffrey Chaucer's *Troilus and Criseyde*, Thomas Wyatt's "They flee from me," John Lydgate's *The Fall of Princes*, and much of its Tudor sequel, William Baldwin's miscellany *Mirror for Magistrates*. Although less often used in the later Elizabethan period, it was also the stanza form for Shakespeare's *The Rape of Lucrece*. Which of these, if any, had Muggins read?

Muggins was familiar with Homer and Ovid, as *London's Mourning Garment* alludes to works by both ancient writers. The poem begins by describing London in its glorious preparations for King James's royal entry, with foreign princes arriving "like to AGAMEMNONS gallant trayne" (sig. B1r, line 15). To help with the pageantry, "PIGMALION foorth his skilfull Caruers sent" (sig. B1v, lines 47), and to fund the festivities, merchant strangers "scattered coyne, like IVPITERS showres of Golde" (sig. B1v, line 41). If Muggins attended one of London's grammar schools before embarking on an apprenticeship, he may have read Ovid in Latin. But both *The Metamorphoses* and Homer's *Iliad* had been translated into English by 1598.[128]

Other allusions in *London's Mourning Garment* are harder to track. Muggins's dedication asserts, "the Vertuous minde, respecteth not so much the valewe of the guift, as the good will of the giuer," a paraphrase of Seneca. Muggins might have read Seneca's *De Beneficiis* or Arthur Golding's 1578 translation of it, but this particular aphorism had been paraphrased so frequently as to be virtually idiomatic.[129] Similarly, Muggins refers to "Cunning APPELLES with his pencill" (sig. B1v, line 48), a reference to the ancient Roman artist whose unmatchable skill was related in several anecdotes in Pliny the Elder's *Natural History*. Maybe Muggins had read *The Natural History*, which had been translated into English in 1601; maybe he found the references to Apelles in Abraham Fleming's translation of Claudius Aelianus, itself largely a summary of anecdotes from Pliny; or maybe he found references to Apelles elsewhere.[130] Still, Pliny the Elder, Seneca, Ovid, Homer—what is significant here is the breadth of Muggins's classical allusions: he knew enough about these classical writers to recognize their currency among early modern readers.

Muggins was also well aware of contemporary texts. *London's Mourning Garment* was not the first "mourning garment" pamphlet. The earliest use of the phrase in a title was Robert Greene's *Greene's Mourning Garment Giuen Him by Repentance at the Funerals of Loue* (1590). This was followed by William Worship's popular devotional work *A Christians Mourning Garment*, which had reached its third edition by 1603. Muggins may have appreciated Worship's pamphlet, with its claim that weeping was the appropriate Christian posture. It seems almost certain, however, that *London's Mourning Garment* was in part a response to Henry Chettle's pamphlet *England's Mourning Garment* (1603), an account of the funeral of Queen Elizabeth along with two pastoral poems: one mourning the death of Elizabeth, the other celebrating the ascension of King James. The pamphlet's shepherds—Collin, Thenot, Dryope, and Chloris—seem blissfully unaware of the plague's spread through London. *London's Mourning Garment*'s polyphony of mourning Londoners rehearsing their hardships and losses provides a stark contrast with Chettle's idyllic countryside shepherds.

The plague did not go unnoticed by Chettle, however. About a month before *London's Mourning Garment* appeared in print, Chettle issued *A True Bill of the Whole Number That Hath Died in the Cittie of London, the City of Westminster, the City of Norwich, and Divers Other Places* (1603). Chettle's bill included a brief history of the plague, beginning with ancient Rome, and emphasized its spread outward from London to Norwich, over one hundred miles away.[131] Regardless of whether he knew of this other publication of Chettle's, Muggins was keenly aware of the bills of mortality issued in London. *London's Mourning Garment* ends with a table listing the numbers of dead by parish between July 14 and November 17. Indeed, for an early reader of the copy of *London's Mourning Garment* held at the Huntington Library, the table of the dead appears to have been of great interest—this individual tallied the total burials for London within the walls and, as the final handwritten note explains, "burialles in all" (sigs. E1v–E2r).[132]

And Muggins had surely read other plague pamphlets. *London's Mourning Garment* refers to a "Most true report" of the plague's spread to the countryside. Throughout the sixteenth and seventeenth centuries every visitation of the plague was immediately followed by an outpouring of plague writing—sermons, medical tracts, pamphlets, and broadsides with debates on the causes, supposed cures, thundering condemnations, prayers, or journalistic "Most true report[s]" of the plague's progress through the city and country.[133] Ernest B. Gilman describes the proliferation of plague texts as a collective effort to fill the traumatic void created by the epidemic.[134] That printers were ever willing to produce these works attests to a readership hungering for solutions or solace.

Muggins, of course, produced his own plague pamphlet, and he seems well aware of its contribution to the field. The same stanza that mentions a "Most true report" describes the suddenness of the plague's effects:

> You see the runner, in his race is tript,
> Well when he went, dead ere his journeyes done:
> You see how soddaine, beauties blase is nipt,
> Which sought all meanes, deaths danger for to shunne,
> You heare what successe, followe them that runne. (sig. D2r, lines 638–52)

The stanza's "You see" and "You heare" gesture to the abundance of plague pamphlets in 1603 and before. In particular the stanza echoes a passage from physician William Bullein's popular *A Dialogue Bothe Pleasaunte and Pietifull Wherein is a Goodly Regimente against the Feuer Pestilence with a Consolacion and Comfort against Death* (1564), where Death brags, "I ouerthrowe the Daunser, and stoppe the breath of the singer, and trippe the runner in his race. I breake wedlockes, and make many widdowes."[135] Bullein's *Dialogue* had been reprinted in 1573 and 1578, a popular work mixing the medical and moral with the stuff of jest and satire.[136] Some of the imagery in this particular passage is echoed in Muggins's tale of the bridegroom who died immediately after his wedding, while Muggins's "runner in his race" is an unmistakable nod to Death's vaunt in *A Dialogue*.

Among the clearest signs of Muggins's reading is revealed in the first sentence of *London's Mourning Garment*'s dedication to Sir John Swinnerton. It draws on Thomas Wilson's dedication to King Edward VI in his *The Rule of Reason, Conteinyng the Arte of Logique*, first printed in 1551 but reprinted several times in the sixteenth century. Wilson begins his dedication, "If my power & habilite were answerable to my good wil, most excellent Prince and sovereign Lord, this token of mine humble dutie which I now offer unto your Majestie, should be as great & preciouse, as by reason of the contrarie, it is base and slender."[137] Muggins echoes Wilson in his own dedication to Swinnerton: "Right Worshipful and graue senator: if my knowledge and learning, were answerable to my good will and affection: this my poore labour now mourning in a sable Weede, should be as great and precious, as to the contrary it is weake, and slender" (sig. A2r). The "sable Weede," "poor labour," and anxiety about levels of education are Muggins's own additions, but the particular rhetorical gesture and the syntax are overtly Wilson's. Having never penned a dedication and worried about the impact of the bold statement the pamphlet made about the failure of magistrates to fulfill their duties, Muggins must have thought it prudent to follow a trusted model very closely.

Beyond cribbing a passage from Wilson, however, Muggins's knowledge of *The Rule of Reason* is not wholly unexpected. Wilson explains that he wrote *The Rule of Reason* in English to make the study of logic available to those "barred, by tongues vnacquainted"—that is, for those with little or no Latin, namely those who had never been to university, where logic comprised one third of the university *trivium* of grammar, logic, and rhetoric (to be followed by the *quadrivium* of arithmetic, geometry, music, and astronomy).[138] While rigorous, Wilson's text was not by any means dull. As an example of a faulty syllogism, Wilson offers up the following Falstaffian logic:

> He that drynkes wel, slepes wel,
> He that slepes well, sinnes not,
> He that sinnes not, shalbe saued.
> Therefore let vs drynk wel, and we shalbe saued.[139]

More often, however, Wilson promotes the logic of the Tudor commonwealth, a combination of humanist thought, reciprocal relations in the political hierarchy, and Protestant theology. The very idea of providing the rules of logic in the vernacular, of course, was a radical humanist project. As a part of his reformist agenda, a "romishe bishop" is made to mouth several faulty syllogisms for Wilson to dissect.[140] And a faulty syllogism praising Nero provides Wilson the chance for a digression on tyranny and right rule.[141] The echoes of *The Rule of Reason* in *London's Mourning Garment* reveal Muggins to have been something of an autodidact, someone keen to take advantage of the expansion of print culture to further his personal education. Muggins could have spent his spare time reading the latest salacious ballad, or not reading at all, but instead he dedicated his time to a treatise on syllogisms and faulty reasoning.

The Bible, poetry, plague pamphlets, popular ballads, treatises on logic—Muggins read widely. His books were among his prized possessions. Just before the Bible and English printed books in the inventory of his goods is a "danske Chest," a box made of spruce or pine in which it seems Muggins kept his books.[142] In addition to his reading and acquaintance with Deloney, Muggins had other points of access to the literary circuit in London. Before moving to St. Olave's, Muggins lived about one block from two print shops, those of Edward Allde and Cuthbert Burby. More than mere workspaces, Elizabeth Eisenstein describes early print shops as sites of lively intellectual exchange.[143] While it is impossible to know how engaged he was with the comings and goings of the nearby shops, Muggins was definitely acquainted with other printers. Along with Deloney, Muggins shared his cell with printer Gabriel Simson, and by 1603 Muggins had teamed up with Blower to print *London's Mourning Garment*.

Whether in consultation with his printer or on his own, the decision to dedicate the pamphlet to Swinnerton hints at a significant knowledge of London's literary scene. At the moment that Muggins wrote his dedication, Swinnerton was a prosperous wine merchant, sheriff of London, and alderman for St. Giles, Cripplegate.[144] Ten years later he would rise to the position of mayor. At the same time, he was a prominent part of a civic patronage system. While most studies of patronage have focused on the court and other titled nobility, London's civic officers—mayors, aldermen, sheriffs, and wardens of livery companies—also contributed to a system of support fostering theater, music, the visual arts, and writing in the city.[145] Thus, carpenter Richard More dedicated *The Carpenters Rule* (1602), a pamphlet about the proper measurement of timber, to alderman and former mayor (and translator of Euclid) Sir Henry Billingsley and "To the Worshipful, the Master, Wardens, and Assistants of the Companie of Carpenters of the citie of London." Richard Robinson dedicated his *Certain Selected Histories for Christian Recreations* (1577) "To the worshipfull maister Symon Roo, nowe Maister of the worshipful Companie of Lethersellers in London and to the Wardens and whole fellowship of the same." And schoolmaster William Averell dedicated his *A Dyall for Dainty Darlings* (1584) to William Wrathe, warden of London's Company of Mercers.[146] In a similar vein, writers might seek patronage from the lord mayor: in 1590 Robert Greene dedicated his translation of Orazio Rinaldi's *The Royal Exchange* to then mayor Sir John Hart and his two sheriffs, Richard Gurney and Stephen Soame (who would go on to be mayor a few years later); Ralph Blower dedicated his printing of *A Rich Store-House of Treasury for the Diseased* to then mayor Sir Thomas Skinner; and in 1600 Henoch Clapham dedicated *A Description of New Jerushalem* to then lord mayor Sir William Ryder.[147]

Among these civic dedicatees, Swinnerton stands out as an especially active figure in London's arts and letters. Indeed, by 1606 Swinnerton had himself entered print with an epistolary pamphlet attempting to persuade a gentlewoman to convert to the Protestant faith.[148] But Swinnerton was more often a significant local patron. Whereas such dedications tend to cluster around the short period an individual dedicatee occupied highest office (mayor or master of his company), Swinnerton emerges as a dedicatee in some twenty or so printed works from 1602 to just before his death in 1616.[149] The pageantry for Swinnerton's lord mayor's show was written by Thomas Dekker.[150] Henry Peacham, Anthony Munday, Joseph Hall, and Michael Drayton all dedicated works to Swinnerton.[151] Thomas Ravenscroft singled out Swinnerton and his fellow alderman, Sir Thomas Hayes, as "most True and honourable affectors of Musicke," and Wentworth Smith described the patron as "the great Fauourer of the Muses."[152]

Dedications in print are only the most immediate evidence of Swinnerton's patronage. In his dedication to Swinnerton, Smith further alludes to "hauing receiued some fauours from you, for priuate things."[153] The indication is that much of Swinnerton's patronage of Smith and others occurred outside of print, in manuscript or performance. Swinnerton hosted a private performance of the lost play *Cardenio* in 1613.[154] And Swinnerton appears to have been close to King's Men actors John Heminges and Henry Condell. Heminges even named one his children Swinnerton, suggesting that the patron served as godfather at the child's christening.[155] Most revealing of Swinnerton's reputation as a prominent patron of London's arts, in 1607 the Merchant Taylor's Company prepared for a banquet in honor of King James; the company decided that they would ask Swinnerton "to conferr with Mr. Benjamin Johnson the Poet, aboute a speech to be made to welcome his Majestie, and for musique and other inventions which maye give likeing and delight to his Majestie."[156] Among all the members of the company, Swinnerton made sense as the man to reach out to Jonson and to arrange the music for the high-profile event.[157]

London's Mourning Garment was among the earliest works to be dedicated to Swinnerton. The mayor in 1603, Sir Robert Lee, was the dedicatee for several printed works that year, including two plague pamphlets: Thomas Thayre's *A Treatise of the Pestilence* and Henry Holland's *Spirituall Preseruatiues against the Pestilence*.[158] Both make mention of the sheriffs, Swinnerton and Sir James Pemberton, but Muggins chose to dedicate his pamphlet to Swinnerton alone. Muggins's choice here is yet another indication of his engagement with London's literary scene. He knew that Swinnerton, more than Lee or Pemberton, was appreciative of poetry and prayer. In addition to echoes and allusions of specific texts in *London's Mourning Garment*, Muggins's knowledge of the local patronage system indicates something about his familiarity with the literary world of London.

SOURCES AND METHOD

Rebecca Totaro has described Muggins as "the man about whom we know so little," while the *Dictionary of Literary Biography* simply lists Muggins as the author of *London's Mourning Garment* and offers no further biographical detail.[159] This book seeks to redress the dearth of knowledge about Muggins as well as the lives of the poorer end of the middling sort more broadly. Tracking the activities of a member of the middling sort is particularly challenging. Most did not leave behind diaries or copious records of their lives. Many scarcely appear in the archives at all. Among the archival sources used in this project, parish registers have proven invaluable. In 1538 Thomas Cromwell ordered that each church in England maintain a parish register, a record of the baptisms, marriages, and burials performed by the church. Not every church immediately complied, and the information recorded varies. The small parish of St. Mildred's in the Poultry, where Muggins lived from

1595 (or earlier) to 1598, felt it important to record not only baptism date but date of birth. The church's leaders apparently thought that the parish register had been instituted to ensure that churches were performing baptisms in a timely fashion. Large parishes like St. Olave's in Southwark, where Muggins lived from 1598 through at least 1603, typically included the trade or status of individuals listed in the register. In this case, the church's leaders felt it was important to be able to distinguish in their records parishioners of the same name, a likelihood for larger parishes.

In addition to aiding in tracking individuals, the parish registers also provide a picture of the parish—who lived and died there, what trades were practiced, who was getting married or giving birth. Two of Muggins's children were baptized at St. Mildred's. The Poultry was about the size of a soccer pitch, and nearly all the residents met weekly for church services. The parishioners are sure to have known one another. St. Olave's in Southwark was a much larger parish, and while many parishioners knew one another, the parish also afforded some anonymity. St. Olave's baptized four of Muggins's children. Often the registers include the names of churchwardens, so one has a sense of who in the neighborhood had risen to significant prominence. The churchwardens accounts and vestry minutes survive for both churches but yielded somewhat less in terms of tracking Muggins and his known associates. Still, various church records allow for one perspective on early modern subjects and their immediate communities.

Wills also provided significant information about Muggins's surrounds. In my research I consulted every extant will to come out of St. Mildred's in the Poultry and St. Olave's in Southwark in the sixteenth and seventeenth centuries. One can find the trade of individuals and their family members, the possessions they held dear, and the people they knew. Muggins did not leave a will and was not named in any of the wills from St. Mildred's or St. Olave's, however. His friends and family members simply did not die with enough goods to have left a will that included him. In and of itself, this tells us something about social networks of the period. Despite the wide range of means among the middling sort, like stuck with like. Prominent tradesmen of St. Mildred's might leave something for the nameless poor, but if they left anything to neighbors by name, those neighbors were invariably of a similar wealth and status.

Like the parish registers, the records of the lay subsidy, an occasional tax of householders assessed at three pounds or more, provide information about Muggins and his neighbors. Organized by ward and parish, the lay subsidies list names and assessed value, and occasionally other details. Muggins's appearances in the lay subsidy of 1598 through 1600 indicate a period of economic stability and even prosperity for the household. Moreover, the lay subsidy provides a window into the relative wealth of Muggins's neighbors, those in similar or far better economic circumstances. A large number of subsidy payers in a small parish suggests a wealthy parish, while the fairly short list of names for St. Olave's in Southwark indicates the general poverty of the parish.

The importance of the Worshipful Company of Weavers to Muggins is pieced together from a variety of sources, especially the Guildhall "Remembrancia" and the records of the company itself. Held by the London Metropolitan Archive, the records of the Company of Weavers detail practices of the company, their governance, and occasionally disputes.[160] The most prominent weavers held office. Muggins was not among them, but as chapter 1 explores more fully, Muggins was involved as a member of the company's Yeomanry and was among a group of silk-weavers who challenged the authority of the company's leadership through the aforementioned co-authored petition. Other company archives similarly shed light on the craftsmen of London, their practices, and their interactions with one another. Muggins even makes a brief appearance in the records of the Drapers' Company.

Traces of individuals from the middling sort are clearest when they were in trouble. The Guildhall "Remembrancia" includes copies of correspondence between the monarch, the lord mayor, aldermen, and other civic authorities from 1579 to 1664. Here one finds Muggins mentioned among the handful of other silk-weavers imprisoned for their petition. A short while later Muggins appeared in Chancery Court for his outstanding debt. Together these documents provide names of Muggins's close associates, his adversaries, and the inventory of everything in his household. The archives of church, livery company, and court thus provide some sense of how Muggins appeared not only in print but before his fellow parishioners, his fellow silk-weavers, the courts, and civic authorities.

The archives have their limitations, however. The many parish registers I have consulted do not yield a record of Muggins's marriage, so his spouse remains nameless in this project. Similarly, there seems to be no record for the birth of Muggins's daughter, Elizabeth. One would want to view the record of Muggins's apprenticeship and the records of those apprenticed to him, but the company's apprentice rolls were lost in the fire of 1666. The petition Muggins co-authored in 1595 has also been lost—but not, fortunately, before it was transcribed by Frances Consitt.[161] One full page of the inventory of Muggins's home has been so damaged that it is illegible. Such is the fragility of early modern manuscripts.

Still, a number of basic facts of Muggins's life can be presented here. Muggins lived in the Poultry until 1598. He may have lived there several years, but the earliest his name appears in the parish register is 1595. At that time the household included Muggins; his wife; their eldest daughter, Elizabeth; and an apprentice named Thomas Stephenson. We know the details surrounding Muggins's imprisonment for his co-authored petition, and because of his problems with debt, we know the location and contents of Muggins's household in the Poultry. In 1598 Muggins moved to St. Olave's in Southwark. He appears in the lay subsidy of 1598, 1599, and 1600, assessed at three pounds. We know the names of Muggins's children, when they were baptized and, in several cases, when they were buried. And we know the names of Muggins's apprentices. In all, the archives provide a fairly detailed record of Muggins from 1595 to 1603.

The lack of such standard data as Muggins's birth, apprenticeship, and marriage makes me reluctant to consider this book a biography. Rather, *A Weaver-Poet and the Plague* is part literary criticism, part microhistory.[162] The years covered in the pages that follow, 1595 to 1603, mark a high point in Elizabethan literature: Sir Philip Sidney's *An Apology for Poetry* was printed for the first time in 1595. In 1596 Edmund Spenser's second installment of *The Faerie Queene* appeared in print. Francis Bacon's essays were printed in 1597. The miscellany *The Passionate Pilgrim* was printed in 1599. In the same year the Globe Theater was built just a mile from Muggins's home in Southwark. The years 1595 through 1603 saw the emergence of a number of early modern England's great dramatists: Ben Jonson, John Marston, and John Webster. And William Shakespeare wrote some of his most enduring plays in these years: *A Midsummer Night's Dream*, *Romeo and Juliet*, *Twelfth Night*, *Henry V*, and *Hamlet*. These were significant years in the establishment of what would come to be the canon of early modern English literature.

London's Mourning Garment is an admittedly marginal text from the period, but that marginality is very much the point. The routine impulse to examine canonical texts necessarily skews our understanding of the literature and culture of the period. Just as Thomas Smith discussed craftsmen as passive objects of rule, so the canonical drama of the period frequently portrayed commoners as clownish objects of ridicule.[163] The importance of examining the working poor on their own terms is readily apparent: Muggins was not illiterate, laughable, or passive. Literate and poor, committed to his reading of the Old Testament prophets, Muggins stands out as a writer very different from the aspiring court poets who dominate the literary canon. Muggins worked a craft to survive and gradually felt the need to use his acquired knowledge and skill to advocate first for his fellow weavers and then for the working poor and economically vulnerable in London.

Thus, this book is a contribution to a literary history from below. Whereas similar projects have surveyed tropes or attempted to reconstruct popular print culture, this book works from the vantage point of a single weaver and his world. That is, I consider this book to be a microhistory. Microhistory is characterized by a reduction in scale of historical study. Rather than nations or "great men," microhistories generally focus on a village, a neighborhood, or an obscure individual. Microhistories often examine what on the surface appears esoteric in the past—the misprisions of an eccentric Italian miller, a young drummer turned prophet, an enslaved woman taking on the role of evangelist—to highlight the important contributions of the marginalized individuals who nonetheless lived lives that complicate our sense of the past.[164] Rather than a history of major developments, microhistories typically investigate localized events—a trial, conversion narrative, or folk tradition—often to get at the lived experience of commoners. Instead of anomalous cases, however, microhistories more often than not uncover complex social networks extending beyond the expected walking distance of the average villager, highlight the individual or collective agency of the non-elite, or pose particular challenges to the grand narratives of a given period.[165]

Some might allege that extrapolating anything from the atypical cases that occupy many microhistories must necessarily distort one's understanding of the past. While quantitative studies are invaluable, Arthur E. Imhof has suggested that notions of "average" and "typical" when applied to the disparate "small worlds of the past" might obscure as much as clarify. In his discussion of the average age of marriage, for instance, Imhof argues that in early modern German towns there were so many deviations as to make the so-called typical age of marriage a meaningless imposition by scholars.[166] Following Edoardo Grendi, Giovanni Levi suggests that microhistory's engagement with the particular and qualitative aims "to furnish more realistic and less mechanistic representations."[167] Or, as Peter Lake puts it in his study of the "odd" and "obsessive" seventeenth-century debate between John Etherington and Stephen Denison, a microhistorical approach "can show us aspects of the period that are all but invisible in other more normal, conventional or typical sources."[168] A microhistorical approach does not preclude generalizations, however. Especially in an anthropological mode, microhistories often provide crucial new understandings of how various groups lived their lives and coped with crises.[169] Moreover, microhistories often show how history's grand narratives and focus on the elite occlude important ways that others—women, the poor, the enslaved—have been significant, if overlooked, actors on the historical stage.

In some sense, the structure of *London's Mourning Garment* itself can be said to reflect the tension between qualitative and quantitative approaches to the past inherent in microhistory's relation to other historiographic methods. The final pages of the pamphlet offer a table of the dead up through November 17, 1603. The table begins:

>   Albones in Woodstreet --------------------- 174
>   Alhallowes Lumbarstr. --------------------- 107
>   Alhallowes the great ---------------------- 278
>   Alhallowes the lesse ---------------------- 220

It continues, parish by parish, enumerating the dead. In the suburbs, the numbers are staggering:

>   Georges in Southwarke ------------------- 895
>   Giles without Creeplegate --------------- 2455
>   Olaues in Southwarke -------------------- 2459
>   Sauiours in Southwarke ------------------ 1858

But the table of the dead works in tandem with the pamphlet's prayer and the poem. While the prayer situates London in a biblical narrative of loss and redemption, the poem offers portraits of individual Londoners. It gives voice to a personified London, but then London listens to the voices of the distressed Londoners. The table of burials in the city gives a broad, impersonal view of deaths during the plague; the poem insists on a close-up picture of what it meant to live during the tragedy. The desperation of the widow or the family in debt, the sorrow of the mother who has lost her children—these tell us things that no numeric table could possibly express.

Microhistorians Carlo Ginzburg and Carlo Poni describe their practice as a "prosopography from below," a careful tracking of names to reveal a complex web of connections.[170] *A Weaver-Poet and the Plague* owes much to that particular method. I have made extensive use of parish registers, records of the lay subsidies, wills, and other documents from the period to track the name William Muggins, to locate his household, and the names of people he knew or likely knew, to trace the contours of his life. *London's Mourning Garment* then ceases to be a text existing like a generic message in a bottle floating through the archives, and instead becomes the product of particular social practices within a complex web of social relations.

A Weaver-Poet and the Plague thus provides a careful reading of *London's Mourning Garment* within a microhistorical study of William Muggins and his social network to highlight the perspective of the lower end of the middling sort in early modern London. The chapters that follow are organized around Muggins's movements from 1595 to 1603, but they also focus on his acquaintances—Thomas Deloney, Gabriel Simson, Humphrey Milward, James Balmford—and his attachment to important institutions in early modern London: his livery company and the two parish churches he attended, St. Mildred's in the Poultry and St. Olave's in Southwark. The book is about how Muggins translated his experiences of poverty, prison, debt, birth, and death into a poetry of social and spiritual reform. But it is also about the Mary Blacks and Henry Bestes of the period, people often lost in statistics or overlooked entirely.

Chapter 1 covers Muggins's relationship to the London Weavers' Company and his fellow weaver-poet Thomas Deloney. As the institution through which most young men received their training and freedom to practice their trade, Muggins's decision to join in collective action at variance with his livery company marks a vital starting point for this book. Muggins and his fellow petitioners found themselves imprisoned at Newgate. Although Muggins seems to have prized an idealized hierarchical order, the experience of joining with his fellow disaffected weavers opened up an ideological fissure from which the weaver-poet and his cellmates could begin to critique the practices of those in positions of authority: the lax enforcement of specific regulations within the weavers' craft, the Elizabethan prison system, and ultimately Muggins's more comprehensive critique of Londoners' rampant acquisitiveness and indifference to the suffering of the city's most vulnerable.

Alongside the livery company, the parish church was without a doubt among the most important institutions in Muggins's life. Chapter 2 follows Muggins to his household in the parish of St. Mildred's in the Poultry. Unlike the livery company, the parish was inclusive of women. Two of Muggins's children were born in the parish and baptized as St. Mildred's by its rector, Thomas Sorocold. Historians have emphasized the marginal role men played in childbirth, but *London's Mourning Garment* offers a surprisingly detailed and sensitive view of labor and infant care. Women were central to birth as midwives, and women of the parish gathered to tend to the infant and the new mother. Birth was a communal event. Muggins and Sorocold's writings give us a sense of the anxieties and celebrations of the parish as new life came to the community. Just as chapter 1 examined the centrality of the livery company but also Muggins's marginal place within it, so chapter 2 focuses on the ways parish communities forged community but also the limits of such communities. A part of the fabric of life in the Poultry, Muggins was soon entangled in a dispute over outstanding debt. Debt was a part of life in early modern London. Writers of the period registered general cultural anxieties and resentment about debt in *The Merchant of Venice* and a number of other plays and poems. Muggins's experiences in the Poultry similarly led the weaver-poet to consider the fragility of new life against the inevitability of debt for those struggling at the bottom of the socioeconomic system of Elizabethan London.

Muggins's financial problems eventually led him to move his family to St. Olave's in Southwark, where a lease could be purchased more cheaply. Here Muggins's finances improved. In the crowded parish he became a subsidy man, someone with sufficient wealth to be taxed. While the subsidy was a burden, it was also a communal measure of wealth and status. But Muggins's time in Southwark was also marked by death. Three of his children and three of his apprentices were buried at St. Olave's. While the state's plague orders limited attendance at funerals, Muggins presents mourning as a necessary and uniquely productive, communal practice. In that sense, *London's Mourning Garment* resists the isolation brought about by the plague as well as the cultural premium on moderate mourning as exemplified by Ben Jonson's "On My First Sonne." Instead, Muggins focuses specifically on the capacity of a community of women to mourn fully and efficaciously. Muggins's London elicits tears from the destitute women of the poem who in turn relate their losses. The shared experiences of women in the poem lead from isolation to collective, communal mourning that in itself protests the self-interested, acquisitive society Muggins saw as the core problem of his city. Chapter 3 thus argues for the ultimately political relationship between local, communal funeral rites and Muggins's experiments in elegy in *London's Mourning Garment*.

Chapter 4 continues to follow Muggins's social network in Southwark. Despite the state's attempts at uniformity, each parish was unique, its own social, economic, and spiritual unit. While St. Olave's parish could once be counted as among the most devoutly Catholic, by the 1590s St. Olave's was decidedly more theologically radical and diverse than the Poultry. This and the parish's much greater concentration of poor craftsmen and laborers amplified Muggins's sympathies with the disenfranchised in London. But it was the plague that led Muggins to enter print. This chapter examines the centrality of women and the poor to Muggins's reading of the Old Testament prophets. Listening to the mourning women, London calls for action. Here the radicalism of St. Olave's seems to have informed Muggins's more prophetic mode as he denounces the acquisitive indifference of Londoners and calls for a new socioeconomic covenant, much like an early modern Jeremiah.

A Weaver-Poet and the Plague thus argues that poorer members of the middling sort were not passively ruled and politically mute, as Smith would have it, nor were their views simply undereducated echoes of the elite. On the contrary, Muggins's focus on women runs counter to much of the misogyny found in the poetry of his courtly contemporaries, and Muggins's ideas about how the city should work is markedly different from the practices of many of England's aristocrats and wealthy merchants.[171] *London's Mourning Garment* is overtly a spiritual meditation on the plague, but that meditation led Muggins directly to an analysis of the socioeconomic problems he experienced from 1595 onward. The longer title of Muggins's pamphlet singled out "wealthy Cittizens," and the pamphlet was dedicated to one such wealthy citizen, but the poem focused on the "other her Inhabitants," too: impoverished families, homeless widows, and grieving mothers unsure of their economic future. The poem insists that the wealthy have a duty to the poor and that the city's magistrates were sworn to protect the livelihoods of those who worked. Smith and others might depict England as stable and orderly, threatened only by those who challenged authority. A study of poetry by a member of the laboring class of the middling sort in early modern London complicates that view. A mix of economic analysis and vatic poetry, *London's Mourning Garment* frames Muggins as a poet of London's most vulnerable, those savaged by the plague of 1603 and kept poor by the growth of acquisitive oligarchic control of the city's institutions. It was on their behalf that Muggins wrote in his poem, "O you of LONDON, now heare LONDON speake" (sig. D1r, line 582).

CHAPTER 1

Company and Complaint
The Limits of Craft Identity

> Mans life is like the Bubble in the Brook,
> Or like a glasse wherein a man doth look,
> Or like a shuttle in a Weavers hand,
> Or like the writing that is in the sand.
>
> The bubble's broke, and soon the looke's forgot.
> The shuttle's flung for and the writing's blot:
> Euen such is man that liueth on the earth,
> Hees always subject for to loose his breath.
> —ANONYMOUS, *A Discourse of Mans Life* (1629)

WEAVER-POETS IN AND OUT OF NEWGATE

William Muggins sat confined to a cell in Newgate Prison one evening in late June 1595. The cell was dark, crowded, and unsanitary, a study in human neglect. Newgate was notorious for its poor conditions. The first-person narrator of *Moll Flanders* (1723) described the prison as "an Emblem of Hell itself, and a kind of an Entrance into it."[1] That reputation was earned much earlier, however, and maintained throughout Muggins's lifetime. Raphael Holinshed recalled Newgate as "a most ugly and loathsome prison," and in 1620 it was still described as "a place of infamy and great distress."[2] The conditions were such that in 1599 a large group of Newgate's prisoners petitioned Robert Cecil, Earl of Salisbury, for relief, describing themselves as "grievously afflicted with hunger, cold, and nakedness."[3]

Like most of the poorer prisoners, Muggins was in irons, with shackles around his neck, wrists, or legs to ensure maximum discomfort.[4] One could pay to have the irons removed, but it is doubtful that Muggins had the resources to upgrade his conditions.[5] Near him sat fellow dejected silk-weaver Thomas Deloney and the printer Gabriel Simson. Also present was another silk-weaver by the name of Willington, probably John Willington, who like Deloney resided in the parish of St. Giles, Cripplegate.[6] Given their economic circumstances, the four men were reliant on whatever meager sustenance family, friends, and charity could provide. The weavers and their printer languished in the dismal, unsanitary conditions of Newgate. The time in prison, I will argue, seems to have led the prisoners from a concern with their own predicament to a broader sense of responsibility for the suffering of those in and out of London's prisons. The general poverty of many weavers coupled with, as noted in the introduction, the way the craft of weaving lent itself to the production of poetry meant that weavers were uniquely prepared to speak out about London's social problems. Going public with their writing landed them in prison, but Deloney, Simson, and Muggins continued to see the public nature of print as a means of drawing attention to society's wrongs and, more important, startling readers out of the passive indifference that empowered wrongdoers.

Deloney was already a well-known writer of popular ballads, some relating recent news, others recounting particularly dramatic moments in the chronicles of England. Within a year there would be another warrant for his arrest, this time for "a certain ballad contanynyng a Complaint of the great want and scarcity of corn within the Realm."[7] The short stint in Newgate in 1595 seems to have led Deloney from ballads on recent events of national interest—a fire in Suffolk, Queen Elizabeth's speech at Tilbury—to a focus on the dire conditions of the middling sort in England.[8] Even a historical ballad like "The Imprisonment of Queene Elenor" appears to have been informed by Deloney's time in prison. The ballad ends with the once imprisoned queen successfully ruling in the king's absence, but the only example of her good rule is its final couplet: "And many a prisoner then in holde, / she set at large from yrons colde."[9] Memories of those cold irons could not have been too distant for Deloney. The Elizabethan pamphleteer Thomas

Nashe observed the change in Deloney's writing in late 1596.[10] Whereas Deloney had previously written ballads appropriate for an alehouse, Nashe noted that since "this deare yeare, together with the silencing of his looms ... not one merrie Dittie will come from him, but *The Thunder-bolt against Swearers, Repent England repent, & The strange judgements of God*."[11] Although the melodramatic, invented titles aim at mocking Deloney, they nonetheless highlight the pronounced turn to serious social critique in Deloney's writing.

In addition to ballads, Deloney would spend his remaining years writing prose fiction dedicated to merchants and craftsmen. A mix of legend, chronicle, and jest book, these publications centered on the middling sort, some struggling, others fantastically successful. In 1597, Deloney's *Jack of Newbury* and *The Gentle Craft, Part I* were entered in the Stationers Register.[12] Dedicated "TO ALL FAMOVS Cloth workers in England," *Jack of Newbury* was about legendary Henrician clothier John Winchombe with several digressions about men and women in the cloth trade.[13] *The Gentle Craft* related a series of tales about shoemakers and was dedicated naturally enough "To all the good Yeomen of the Gentle Craft" of shoemaking.[14] Although difficult to date, Deloney soon followed up with *The Gentle Craft, Part II*, dedicated "To the Master and Wardens of the worshipfull company of the Cordwaynors in London"; and *Thomas of Reading, or The Six Worthy Yeomen of the West*, lacking a formal dedication (at least in its extant version) but again about clothiers.[15] Like *London's Mourning Garment*, these works were dedicated to Londoners, craftsmen, and those who occupied positions in the city's civic institutions, and they demanded that readers attend to the lives of laborers. While Deloney's earlier ballads sometimes displayed his commitment to the middling sort, the shift to an overt and consistent focus on their lives followed his time in Newgate with Willington, Muggins, and Simson.[16]

Simson gained the freedom of the Stationers Company in 1583 along with Thomas Morris and William White, all three apprentices under the widow Joan Jugge.[17] Simson and White worked together for several years in a shop on Fleet Lane, printing and selling primarily religious tracts like Richard Greenham's *Two Learned and Godly Sermons* (1595), Roger Cotton's *A Direction to the Waters of Life* (1591), and several tracts by theologian Hugh Broughton.[18] While in Newgate with Deloney and Muggins, Simson seems to have met another Newgate prisoner, the notorious highwayman Luke

Hutton. By November Simson and White entered their right to print Luke Hutton's *Repentance* (1595) and two months later Hutton's *The Black Dogge of Newgate* (1596).[19] Hutton's *Repentance* is now lost, but *The Black Dogge of Newgate* survives. Focused on the conditions of the prison, the pamphlet comprises two dedications, an eighty-one-stanza poem and an extended dialogue.

Hutton's poem provides an eyewitness account of the horrifying prison. Forty men were crowded in one room to sleep on boards, amid "filthe and noisome smels." Shackled and begging for food, "metamorphosd we were beasts not men," writes Hutton (sig. C4r). Even the simple comfort of a candle is denied the poem's narrator, as a rat snatches the candle from his hands, "And then a hundred Rats all sallie foorth, / As yf they would conuaye their prize of worth" (sig. B4v). The poem goes on to detail a nightmare world where rats triumph and men are treated worse than dogs. The basic human comradery Simson and his silk-weaving associates may have sought would be compromised by the dismal scene as described by Hutton. Hutton laments in gory detail:

> Greefe vpon greefe, did still oppresse my minde,
> Yet had I store compartners in my woe:
> No ease, but anguish, my distresses finde,
> Here lyes a man, his last liues breath dooth blow.
> And ere the sorry man be fully dead,
> The Rats do prey vpon his face and head. (sig. C4r)

Overcrowding in the prison was a physical manifestation of the prisoner's internal "Greefe vpon greefe." Rather than comfort, fellowship in the prison merely amplifies the gruesome misery of the scene—more crowding, more woe, more dead and dying. The poem describes the inhumane conditions of London's prisons, a glaring blot of injustice within early modern London's justice system.

The second half of the pamphlet offers a dialogue between the author and a fellow prisoner, Zawny, who describes the corruption and cruelty of those who run the prison. As Hutton explains in his dedication, the pamphlet was written "to certifie you of the notable abuses dayly committed by a great number of very bad fellowes, who vnder the couller of Office and seruice, doe mightely abuse both Justice and Justices: which in this Booke is largely discouered" (sig. A1r). *The Black Dogge of Newgate* presents the prison as a nightmare of inversions: humans treated like animals, animals preying on men, and the true criminals were those in charge of Newgate. Among those in charge was the titular black dog who sometimes transforms himself into a menacing jailer, sometimes a ruthless con artist behaving no better than the criminals who populated the prison. Depicted on the cover of the pamphlet as a gigantic dog with serpents coming out of its head, the figure of the transforming jailer-dog further blurs the distinction between human and beast and therefore the beastly treatment of prisoners. *The Black Dogge of Newgate* provided a virulent and comprehensive indictment of Newgate and presumably other prisons in London. Upon release from prison Simson would soon resume printing theological texts like John Downame's *Spiritual Physicke to Cure the Diseases of the Soule* (1600) and handy items like *A Table Declaring What Planet Dooth Raigne Euery Day and Houre Enduring for Euer* (1598), but his first order of business was to collaborate with Hutton to protest the conditions of the prison he had just left, to denounce a system that thrived on sadism and bribery.[20] Like Deloney, the experience at Newgate led Simson to feel a sense of urgency about social injustices, a will to enter the public discourse to bring about reform. The early modern prison, as Molly Murray has argued, was a significant site of poetic production, but few works of the period combined the prisoner's petition of complaint with the poetry of prison to wield such a comprehensive critique of the prison itself.[21]

The "scarcity of corn," the successes and failures of craftsmen, the corrupt treatment of prisoners—these are the issues that immediately preoccupied Deloney and Simson once they got out of Newgate. Muggins's name would not appear in print for another eight years, but *London's Mourning Garment* seems similarly motivated by an ethic of empathy, a keen awareness of the suffering of others, and a sense that one could publicly denounce indifference and demand action from those in positions of authority. Many prisoners were simply debtors too poor to pay off their creditors; taken up more fully in chapter 2, Muggins's poem devotes several stanzas to a family sinking deeper and deeper into debt despite their productive labor. Like his fellow cellmates, Muggins sought to speak out about the economic injustices in the city. The weaver-poets Muggins and Deloney came to this broader sense of social responsibility following their experience of the relationship between poorer weavers like themselves and the leadership of the Weavers'

Company, the conflict that led to the imprisonment of Muggins, Deloney, Willington, and Simson with which this chapter started.

WOMEN, STRANGERS, AND THE WORSHIPFUL COMPANY OF WEAVERS IN LONDON

Granted a royal charter in 1155, the Worshipful Company of Weavers was the earliest of London's livery companies, so called because of the livery, or honorary robes, worn by each company's elite.[22] Early on the company was made up of weavers of wool and linen, but by the later sixteenth century a large number of London's weavers, like Muggins and Deloney, worked on silk production, primarily ribbons, lace, and garters, although Muggins also made buttons and gloves, as the inventory of his household makes clear. Despite its long history and vast numbers, the Weavers' Company was among the poorer companies and was never counted among the "Twelve Great Companies" of London that dominated the ranks of the aldermen and mayors of the city over the centuries.[23] Like all the livery companies, the Weavers' Company had been formed primarily as a regulatory body. Their tasks ranged from ensuring the quality of products made by weavers in London to authorizing apprenticeships and monitoring labor practices in individual shops.

The Weavers' Hall was located near Guildhall, in Bassinghall Ward, just south of Moorgate. The hall provided the space for the weavers' annual feast days and sometimes served as the site for theatrical performances and other entertainments.[24] But most of the time, the hall provided the space for the company's officers to conduct its business. The Company of Weavers was led by two bailiffs (the upper bailiff acting as the master of the company), two wardens, and a council of twelve advisers, all selected from the liverymen. The livery itself was made up of the wealthiest of the company's members, those who could afford the entrance fee to join this upper echelon of the company. Those wealthy enough to join the livery were not simply productive weavers; for the most part, liverymen had shifted their priorities away from artisanal labor to retailing cloth and other goods for significant profit.[25] Since the company's inception the bailiffs and wardens were understood to have the right to search shops for infractions of the company's ordinances and impose penalties for the same.[26] Substandard products might be burned; too many apprentices would result in hefty fines; the officers would seize or destroy excess looms.

A few days before his imprisonment at Newgate, William Muggins had hosted a meeting of dissatisfied silk-weavers at his household on the eastern edge of Cheapside Ward in a neighborhood called the Poultry, so named for the poulters who had once occupied the area.[27] Not quite as expensive as Cheapside itself, the neighborhood was home to a wide variety of members of the middling sort—Muggins's household on Conyhope Lane led directly to Grocer's Hall, but in addition to grocers the parish included a number of skinners and haberdashers.[28] Two printshops stood between Muggins's household and the nearby St. Mildred's Church. In all likelihood Muggins had established himself in the Poultry because it was among the cheapest neighborhoods still strategically close to the market in West Cheap, where he could expect to make deals with the mercers who congregated in the area and sell some of his wares directly to high-paying customers.[29] Centrally located, Muggins's modest household provided a meeting place for London's disaffected silk-weavers.

Tensions ran high as the silk-weavers crowded into the household on Conyhope Lane. Deloney and Willington were there, as were twelve other silk-weavers from various parts of the city. Amid several looms and a stock of silk thread, laces, buttons, and bobbins, the household was not really big enough to accommodate such a gathering comfortably. Muggins's wife, then seven months pregnant, and their daughter, Elizabeth, then a toddler, may have retired to the living quarters of the household. The living area included, among other things, "one Table & vj Stooles," where the family ate meals. As the number of stools indicates, at this point the household included Muggins, his wife, their daughter, and three apprentices. Mary Black had not yet joined the household, but one Thomas Stephenson had recently begun his apprenticeship under Muggins following a failed apprenticeship to a goldsmith.[30]

Where Stephenson and his fellow apprentices were for the meeting is unclear. A few weeks earlier an unnamed silk-weaver stood outside Mayor John Spencer's home at Crosby Place in Bishopsgate Ward and used "some hard speeches against the Lord Mayor in dispraise of his government." Spencer ordered his servants to take the disgruntled weaver "to Bedlam as a madman," but as they arrived at Bishopsgate (the city's gate that led to Bedlam, otherwise known as Bethlehem Hospital), the weaver "was rescued by prentices and diverse other to the number of about 200 or 300 persons."[31] The outspoken weaver may have been among those in attendance at Muggins's household. Whether Muggins's apprentices participated in the rescue or not, it seems likely that they watched the proceedings of the meeting with keen interest, an alternative to the apprentice riots that so worried the authorities throughout the period.[32]

The weavers thus gathered in what space they could find at Muggins's household to read the proofs of a petition attempting to right perceived wrongs done to London's silk-weavers. Debate ensued, but the weavers could agree that things were bad for them. As the petition put it, the weavers were "distressed" and in a "lamentable state."[33] While historians have questioned how much of a crisis was experienced in the mid-1590s, Ian Archer judiciously suggests that there was at the very least a perception of crisis among many at the time.[34] In September of 1595 the mayor and aldermen considered the way the city was "pestered with begging poor" thrust to the streets, they observed, by "Couetous Land lordes."[35] Crop failures from the previous year had caused food prices to rise. A reduction in the demand for cloth exports led many workers to shift to other trades, thereby driving down the demand for labor and therefore wages.[36] The demand for labor was further weakened by rapid population growth in London. English "foreigners" (people who had grown up outside of the city) and immigrants from the continent flocked to London making it one of the most populous cities in all of Europe.

For decades England had admitted thousands of Protestant refugees from the continent into England. By the mid-1590s, roughly ten thousand immigrants had settled in London and its immediate surrounds. Immigrants made up about 5 percent of London's rapidly expanding population.[37] Whereas native-born subjects typically served apprenticeships to obtain the right to open their own shops and retail in the city, strangers, mostly from France and the Low Countries, were permitted by the queen to peacefully ply their trades. There would be no point in welcoming refugees to the realm only to deny them the ability to earn a living. In fact, the state hoped that in welcoming strangers from the continent, England would acquire specialized skills that might give the country an edge on the global market and reduce its reliance on imports.[38] At the same time, some trades were hit harder than others by the influx of refugees, and silk-weaving was among them.

Immigrants were an integral part of the history of weaving of linen, wool, and silk in England. The 1340s in particular mark a time of intense competition between Flemish and English weavers.[39] By 1352 English and immigrant weavers were able to strike a temporary accord, no doubt the result of tension between them.[40] In 1441 the English weavers submitted a petition to the mayor and aldermen asserting the company's authority over the activities of their immigrant counterparts, and by 1497 the company was confidently laying out ordinances to ensure that immigrant weavers were integrated in the company.[41] These tensions emerged when England's immigrant population was relatively small, but the influx of Protestant refugees in the later sixteenth century exacerbated the fragile equilibrium between English and immigrant weavers.

Silk-weaving was not within the authority of the Weavers' Company until the mid-sixteenth century, but similar tensions between English and immigrant existed throughout the fourteenth and fifteenth centuries.[42] Initially silk products appeared in England only as imports, but the production of narrow silk wares—lace, ribbons, and the like—was soon mastered by English women, who in turn were reliant on the supply of raw silk imported primarily by merchant strangers.[43] Beginning in the second half of the fourteenth century the London silkwomen were involved in efforts to contain the influence of foreign merchants and weavers on the market for their wares.[44] In 1368, for example, the silkwomen of London banded together to complain to the mayor and aldermen about a merchant stranger who had made significant efforts to inflate the price of raw silk.[45] By 1455 the silkwomen had successfully petitioned for an act of Parliament prohibiting the import of finished silk into the realm, thereby protecting their craft for the time being.[46]

By the mid-sixteenth century silk-weaving had clearly come under the purview of the Company of Weavers: a 1551 ordinance described in the company's "Ancient Book" lists the "Rate of jornamens wagies being silke wevers."[47] Whereas in 1379 the company had asserted that its ordinances applied "to all the bretheren and the sustres of the fraternitie," by the sixteenth century nods to women weavers disappeared as the craft came to be dominated by men.[48] In 1555, in an effort to break with the long history of women in the craft of silk-weaving, the company ordained "that no maner of p[e]rson or p[e]rsones of ye said craft of silke wevers shall take any women to his apprentice in the payne that every p[e]rson doing ye contrary to forfett and paie for everye muneth y^{at} he dothe kepe any suche apprentices iii^s iiii^d."[49] As Mary Black's work at the Muggins household attests, however, women persisted in the craft, though subordinated to the men who had the institutional power of the livery company behind them. The practices of men like Muggins evidently made the company feel it necessary in 1577 to reiterate its prohibition that "no maner of person or personnes usinge or exercisinge the said Arte or Mysterie of Weyvinge shall kepe, teache, instructe or bringe upp in the use, exercisinge or knowledge of the same Arte or Mysterie of Weyvinge any mayden, Damsell or other Woemen whatsoever." The company then doubled the earlier 1555 fine to six shillings, eight pence.[50] In 1596 the company acknowledged what was already likely understood: that widows (and implicitly wives) of silk-weavers could practice the craft, but a new fine structure—five shillings for the first violation and a staggering ten shillings a month thereafter—was introduced for any other women found employed at the craft of silk-weaving.[51] The company seems to have been primarily concerned with keeping women away from the looms. The low-wage job of spinning silk was typically held by women, after all.[52] The impulse behind the many ordinances of the Weavers' Company seems to have been control of the craft, monitoring the dispersion of skills so as to maintain reasonable livings for members of the company, but a patriarchal undercurrent led the Weavers' Company to focus its energy on controlling women and immigrants.

The demand for silk in the sixteenth century was high, and immigrants met that need in ways that clouded the horizon of expectations of English silk-weavers like Muggins. Between 1571 and 1593 the number of immigrants involved in silk-weaving in London doubled. Additionally, immigrant silk-weavers in London were known to sometimes sell products produced by their countrymen in other parts of England, items from Sandwich, Norwich, and Canterbury. By the time Muggins established his own household he needed to compete with not only English weavers but the approximately 1,800 immigrant silk-weavers in the city as well.[53]

For several years the poorer ranks of the weavers had agitated within their company for more thorough enforcement of the company's ordinances regarding limits on the number of apprentices and looms, particularly in the households of immigrant silk-weavers. The growth of the industry, however, had overtaken the managerial capacity of the company's leadership, and it further appears that several of the wealthier members in power were not especially keen to enforce regulations that limited their own ability to expand production or lower costs.[54] Meanwhile poorer weavers, perceiving the ordinances as protections on the labor market, complained about lax enforcement. As a concession to the discontented weavers, in 1594 the company established the Yeomanry of the Company of Weavers, a committee of freemen of the company below the rank of the livery who would be empowered to search households and bring infractions of the company's ordinances before the Court of Assistants, the main governing body for the Company of Weavers.[55] They were, as Alfred Plummer puts it, "the eyes and ears, and sometimes the conscience, of the Court of Assistants."[56] Joseph P. Ward has shown that over time the Yeomanry were crucial in demanding that the company be responsive to the needs of the rank and file and limiting the leadership's impulse to simply exploit their poorer brethren.[57] However, whereas other livery companies maintained a robust Yeomanry (and sometimes used the term to refer to the entirety of the company apart from the elite of the livery), the Weavers' Company limited the committee to twenty young men.[58] Even then, the Yeomanry seems to have rarely exceeded sixteen weavers, a sort of non-elite parallel to the sixteen officers of the company.[59] The Yeomanry were organized into five divisions, with a leader and two deputies per division and one foreman overseeing the committee as a whole. Each individual was to survey weavers in his vicinity and then convene each month at the Weavers' Hall to present infractions and observe the activities of the Court of Assistants.

On this particular night the Yeomanry had decided it would be best to meet at Muggins's household rather than the hall, where the company's leadership might keep an eye on their plans. Evidently, the company's leadership simply refused to enforce its own ordinances with any consistency. Several weeks earlier the Yeomanry had appealed to London's Court of Aldermen to complain about the company's negligence in enforcing its own rules. On paper the Yeomanry had won a victory: the aldermen sided with them, reiterating and highlighting the company's relevant ordinances.[60] The company proceeded to discipline several immigrant weavers who had been found operating too many looms. The effect was only temporary, however, and things quickly went back to the way they were, with several households known to be in violation of the company's ordinances going undisciplined and the wealthy leadership of the company indifferent to rigorous enforcement.

Underlying the specific grievances of the silk-weavers appears a keen awareness that their company's leadership was gradually developing into an oligarchy of men with waning interest in the conditions of their poorer brethren.⁶¹ Those involved in the manufacture of textiles appear to have been particularly vulnerable to exploitation by merchants, so much so that in March of 1593 Elizabeth felt compelled to weigh in on the matter. Several weavers had apparently petitioned the queen for clarification regarding the regulation of prices and wages in the Statute of Artificers; particularly, it was explained, "ambiguities and doubts have bene noted whether the wage and rating of the Spinsters and weavers be within the meaning of the Statute made in the fifth year of our Maj[esty]'s raigne intituled An Act touching and order for artificers, laborers, servants of husbandry and apprentice[s] for the releeving of all."⁶² Elizabeth emphasized that weavers and spinsters were quite definitely part of the Statute of Artificers, and in April of that year the Privy Council issued a new act increasing the wages of weavers while introducing new warnings for those who might try to inflate prices or degrade the quality of cloth.⁶³ Other crafts did not require such intervention.

Despite Elizabeth's revised statutes, the conditions of poorer weavers were such that sometime before 1603 the preacher Thomas Carew devoted an entire sermon, "A Caveat for Craftes-Men and Clothiers," to their plight. Although probably originally preached in Suffolk, the printed version was to be sold in London, at "the sign of the Bible" by Paul's Churchyard.⁶⁴ Carew begins with the basic moral principle that the rich should be magnanimous rather than miserly, citing among other passages from scripture Jeremiah 22:13, "Woe vnto him that buildeth a house by vnrighteousnes, who vseth his neighbour without wages, and giueth him not for his worke."⁶⁵ Carew quickly homes in on the extraordinarily low wages for weavers as his case in point. In London the process of selling silk wares was somewhat scripted by the company: a merchant silkman would bring raw silk or yarn to the master weaver of his choice for the production of lace, ribbon, or other wrought items, and pay for the work "as both parties can agree," or the silkman might sell the raw material to the weaver with the option of purchasing the finished items.⁶⁶ As orderly as this may seem, the silkman held a distinct advantage over the weaver. The former, after all, had the raw material of the weaver's craft; without him, the weaver had no work at all. An increase in the number of weavers with whom to bargain naturally drove down wages. As Carew argues, "The Clothier sets the price, wheras in other trades men set the price of their owne worke, and other men aske their workmen either when they begin or when they haue done, what they shall paye, but Clothiers will set downe what these that worke shall haue, as if one man should beare two persons both of the buyer and seller."[67] Carew then notes that weavers tend to work longer hours than those in other trades, and he addresses various objections that merchants presumably posed—that weaving is a sedentary craft requiring less food and sustenance than other crafts, for instance.[68] These and other objections are handily dismantled as Carew presents a modern-day parable of the impoverished weaver and the hard-hearted merchant. As Carew puts it toward the end of his sermon, the corruption that stemmed from the clothiers was enough that had Jeremiah "seene such a thing as this, he would haue put it among his Lamentations," a book of the Bible that, as chapter 4 shows, had special significance for Muggins.[69] Carew focused primarily on weavers of woolen cloth rather than silk, but the general state of weaving is clear enough: the wealthy and well-connected silk merchant, who might technically belong to the Company of Weavers (or Mercers or Clothiers), lived a significantly different life from that of the poorer weavers who relied on merchants as not only buyers but often as suppliers of the raw material of their trade.

In 1595 the upper bailiff at the head of the company was John Dutton, a man who may not have ever worked a loom in his life.[70] While it is possible that Dutton served an apprenticeship, he is more likely to have acquired the status of freeman of the Company of Weavers through patrimony. Whatever the case, throughout the 1570s and 1580s John Dutton and his brother Laurence were not weavers but actors: first with Sir Robert Lane's Men, then the Earl of Warwick's Men, eventually the Earl of Oxford's Men, and finally the Queen's Men. By the early 1590s John Dutton appears to have abandoned the theater; instead, he ran an inn at Bishopsgate. A player and an innholder, there is little evidence that Dutton had much to do with weaving, but with his connections to the Weavers' Company and the theater men who frequently needed silks for performances he may well have been the ideal middleman. At the same time, he also held various offices in the Weaver's Company. Despite his utter lack of experience as a weaver for the previous two decades, Dutton was elected warden in 1591 and 1592. By 1594 he was second bailiff, and in 1595 he occupied the top office in the company. He held the position of upper bailiff again in 1608, and for almost every year in between he was the auditor of accounts.

This constant holding of one office or another was indicative of an entrenched leadership in control of the company. Livery companies throughout London were going through a similar process. Whereas craftsmen could work as merchants and vice versa, in most cases the Elizabethan era saw a bifurcation among these men of the middling sort with merchants gradually having less to do with the manual trades with which they had traditionally been associated. Sixteenth-century mercers expressed considerable disdain for those members of the company who "occupy manual, hand occupations and crafts, not meet, comely or commendable to be used in this occupation or mistery."[71] Primarily merchants, mercers might seem to be a special case, but even in handicrafts the division between elite and rank and file can be detected. Whereas weaver-poets Muggins and Deloney found themselves at odds with the wealthy in control of their company, their water-poet counterpart, John Taylor, was firmly ensconced among the elite of the Company of Watermen.[72] Serving as clerk of the company, Taylor fiercely defended the status quo the company's leadership had established for themselves against accusations that they had extorted money from some and accepted bribes from others. Some among the disaffected watermen, noting Taylor's vocal opposition to their desire for reform, even called for Taylor to be hanged.

Whether among watermen or weavers, the tensions between elites and the craftsmen they supposedly served provides an apt illustration of how fictional the community built around "the company" might be. Although a company's rhetoric might appeal to order and the welfare of all, at moments of tension the commonalty's resentment and the elite's disdain might come to the fore. As Joshua Phillips points out, belonging to a community is inextricably caught up in ownership—not just belonging, but belongings.[73] The breakdown of the communal feeling among weavers (and later watermen) appears to be precisely around this issue of access to wealth and resources. The entrenchment of an oligarchy within the livery company created two communities: a privileged, well-connected elite and a neglected class of artisans and poor laborers.

Dutton's opportunistic disposition as upper bailiff can perhaps be gleaned from a libelous verse from the decade before he took to holding office in the Weavers' Company. Around 1580 a number of gentlemen ridiculed Dutton and his fellow actors for "forsakyng the Erle of Warwycke" in favor of the earl of Oxford. The actors had newly unfurled themselves as Oxford's "COMOEDIANS." The gentlemen in question, disapproving of the actors' lack of loyalty to Warwick, defaced the *D* to look like an *L*, rendering the new title "COMOELIANS"—ever-changing, and therefore untrustworthy, reptilian clients to their patron. The Dutton brothers were incensed and reportedly "compared themselves to any gentlemen." This sparked their critics to compose a series of rhyming couplets describing the Duttons' supposed coat of arms:

> The field, a fart durty, a gybbet crosse-corded,
> A dauncing Dame Flurty of alle men abhorred;
> A lyther lad scampant, a roge in his rages,
> A whore that is rampant, astride with her legges,
> A woodcocke displayed, a calfe and a sheepe,
> A bitch that is splayed, a dormouse asleepe;
> A vyper in stynche, *la part de la drut*,
> Spell backwarde this Frenche and cracke me that nut.[74]

The screed goes on for another twenty lines lambasting the brothers for abandoning their patron and asserting a status above their birth. The insults display a form of class antipathy toward the weaver-players, but something of Dutton's character nonetheless comes through in the episode. Dutton was a social climber who would willingly abandon his obligations if it meant some sort of advancement. He may have been out of his depths as upper bailiff, but he also had exactly what he wanted: a position that placed him among the elite of his company, affording him connections and control without any manual labor.

At least some of the unresponsiveness of the company to the concerns of the Yeomanry was a result of men like Dutton reaping the benefits of office without necessarily understanding or even caring about the lives of ordinary weavers in an increasingly crowded market. Every year in August the bailiffs of the company were to take their oath. In the fifteenth century the oath stated, "Ye shall swere that alle the ordinaunces maad . . . ye shull trewely execute," and "Ye shal trewely kepe to the wellfare of the comunetie of the crafft."[75] By 1577 the oath had been modified: "You shall endeavor yourselves the best you can justlye and indifferentlye to execute and cause to be executed your office in every respect, and all the good and laufull ordunaunces in this booke of our ordynances expressed."[76] It may be that Dutton and his cohort took "the best you can" and the specifying of "all the good ordinances" to be loopholes for enforcing the ordinances they found onerous or inconvenient to enforce—after all, what constituted "the *good* ordinances"? Some ordinances—those establishing the minimum pay for journeymen, for instance—were good for journeymen but disliked by the elites of the company. Whatever the case, years later Muggins questioned whether civic leaders upheld the ideals of their oaths. As his personified London tells those in civic office to attend to the needs of the poor, she exhorts leaders:

> Remember rulers, of each publycke charge,
> The seuerall branches, of your priuate oath:
> Remember them, that vse a conscience large,
> And on themselues the needyes stocke bestow'th,
> He robbes his God, and his poore neighbours both.

For Muggins the economic and the religious were of one cloth: oaths to uphold the laws and serve the commonwealth were sacred as well as civic. Using one's office for private gain was not only harmful to one's "poore neighbours" but also an affront to God.

Having appealed to their own company and the city's aldermen, the Yeomanry considered petitioning directly to the French and Dutch churches of London where the vast majority of immigrants congregated. The French Church in particular kept strict discipline of its members. A wide range of misbehaviors—adultery, public altercations, outstanding debt, public intoxication—resulted in strict punishment with fines, temporary suspension from communion, or, occasionally, excommunication.[77] The English silk-weavers—some of whom had been trained by or at least worked alongside immigrant weavers—knew this and presumed that direct communication with the church elders might be a way of impressing on the larger community of immigrants the tensions that had been building among English and immigrant weavers. Indeed, on June 26, 1595, as the silk-weavers sat in Newgate, a street brawl broke out between two Englishmen and two Frenchmen. Even though it seems evident that the Englishmen provoked the fight, the French consistory suspended the two Frenchmen from taking communion.[78]

Still, the Yeomanry seem to have been aware that their petition might be perceived as scapegoating the immigrant weavers. Certainly, Elizabethan England had its share of xenophobia. In May 1593 a libel was posted to the door of the Dutch Church in London threatening the strangers as follows:

"Weele cut your throtes, in your temples praying" and "We will doe just vengeance on you all."[79] Such vitriolic statements are only the most overt expressions of xenophobia in a period riddled with subtler forms of discrimination. Although lengthy and forceful in its description of the problems with strangers violating the company's ordinances, the petition sought to appeal to the leaders of the French and Dutch churches as coreligionists. The weavers addressed the petition "To the Minister and Elders of the French Church in London. Grace and peace in Christ Jesus," and more specifically in the salutation to the "Right reverend Pastor and grave Elders."[80] Although one might allege that the petition's moments of flattery were merely artifice, the actual request was fairly modest. After detailing their grievances, the weavers explained, "We thought it good to write theis our Letters unto you, that according as it becometh the Minister and Elders of soe Christian [a] Congregacon, we might intreate you to call those men before you and exhort them to be obedient to good Orders, which are made for a generall benefitt to all men that use this trade."[81] The weavers truly thought of the company's ordinances as regulating the craft for the good of weavers and imagined that where admonishment of the violators from the company had failed, pressure from their own community might succeed. The weavers insisted, "It is not our intentes to drive aways or expell any distressed Straungers out of our land, but to have them live here, that wee might be able to live with them."[82] The weavers asserted that the immigrants had been "Christianly entertayned amongst us, even as the Members of the misticall body of Jesus Christ, and Cittizens with us of that heavenly and celestiall kingdome."[83] While the elders of the French and Dutch churches (and the English weavers themselves) could point to instances in recent memory when strangers had not been treated nearly so well, the Yeomanry at least recognized the way in which a shared Protestantism might bridge differences with their immigrant counterparts.

One of the petition's paragraphs in particular attempted to leverage scripture to argue for compliance with the company's ordinances. Paraphrasing Leviticus 23:22, the petition explains, "Wee reade in Scripture that the gleanings onely of the Corne, the Fruites and the vineyard weare reserved for the Stranger and the Poore, but our Straungers have not had the Gleanings of our Field but the full and fatt sheaves, while we have ben constrayned to gather their leavinges, and yet have they bin not Contented, but have reached unto their Neighbours store and taken from them their proper right." Much like Muggins's prayer in *London's Mourning Garment*, the passage draws from several books of the Bible in quick succession, moving from Leviticus to citations of Deuteronomy 24:9–14 (on neighbors) and then Judges 1:28 (on Canaanites living in Israel). Here the petition implies that the violations of ordinances and the general economic dominance by the strangers was not only a matter of poverty and law but religion. Hospitality, both a cultural practice and a spiritual mandate, required reciprocal roles for host and guest. The petition suggests that the preeminence of foreign silk-weavers and their willingness to violate their host city's ordinances amounted to not simply indecorous behavior but a failure to uphold the standards of a Christian commonwealth.[84]

The petition breaks down the weavers' complaint into five specific grievances. First, specific immigrant weavers were maintaining more apprentices and looms than allowed by law. Second, they were known to have taught the trade to other strangers without entering into formal apprenticeship. Third, they trained women who then went on to marry into families who in turn learned the craft without paying their dues as apprentices. Fourth, they exposed secrets of the craft to merchants, thus weakening the bargaining position of weavers. And fifth, the immigrant weavers engaged in selling the wares of their counterparts from other cities.[85] The fifth grievance is presented almost as an afterthought, but the main tenor of the complaint can be found in the first four: specific crafts in London were sometimes referred to as "mysteries" primarily because the skills required were to be carefully guarded by the members of the livery company. The livery company had passed ordinances to protect the craft and maintain its numbers, and the first four grievances are about the ways particular practices violated these provisions and compromised the integrity of the company. If the skills were taught without regulation, there was little point in the livery company at all.

There had long been a cap on the number of apprentices and looms one could maintain depending on one's status in the company: while householders could keep three apprentices, bailiffs might contract with up to six.[86] Formal apprenticeship was the bedrock of the company, the way skills were transferred to the next generation. Apprentices entered formal contracts, usually paying a premium up front and gradually becoming more skilled and therefore increasingly more important to the household's income. In that sense, a successful apprenticeship led to cheap labor until the apprentice was presented to the company where he paid his fees and offered "a masterpiece" for appraisal.⁸⁷ The limit on the number of apprentices one could keep had several functions. The unequal number based on one's status in the company was clearly designed to provide the liverymen with an edge over others in the company, in order to perpetuate disparities in wealth. Still, this hierarchy seems to have been acceptable to the rank and file of the company; at the least, there appears to have been no strong protest of the advantage liverymen had over their poorer counterparts. The Yeomanry sought out violations of the number of apprentices one could train because they thought of the cap on apprentices as a way of limiting the number of skilled individuals entering the workforce and therefore the volume of production of any given household. And the Yeomanry were not focused exclusively on strangers. Around this time London silk-weaver and buttonmaker Robert Whyte complained that he was being harassed by the Yeomanry "only of malice toward" him. He had nine apprentices, three times the number permitted.⁸⁸

The Weavers' Company attempted to deal with the number of immigrant weavers in London by encouraging them to be admitted to the company as "foreign brethren."⁸⁹ Although some immigrant weavers joined the company, many did not. The continued presence of weavers independent of the company only compounded the problem of too many apprentices, since it meant that the apprentices under these weavers had never been enrolled in a formal contract through any company. Unenrolled apprentices, although not entirely uncommon, posed a problem to the Yeomanry and the company as a whole. The Weavers' Company, already among the poorer companies, lost revenue from the various fees associated with enrollment of apprentices and payment for their freedom at the end of the apprenticeship. Without formal enrollment both apprentice and master might more easily abandon their obligations to one another; while some masters and apprentices may have seen this freedom as a benefit, significant protections to the apprentice were surrendered in the process.⁹⁰ Whether completing their apprenticeship or not, unenrolled apprentices naturally added to the ranks of highly skilled cheap labor undercutting the wages of English weavers.

Wives were considered partners in the craft, and when husbands passed away the widows often succeeded in managing the household with all the rights previously afforded to the husband.⁹¹ Women did in fact work as spinners and some even operated looms. Unlike the company's various ordinances, which sought the utter banishment from the craft once exclusively practiced by women, the petition of the Yeomanry focused on the specific danger of skills being dispersed outside the company by marrying trained weavers to men of other crafts. By 1603, Muggins had at least one young girl, Mary Black, in his employ, and he may also have had his eldest daughter working lace or doing other essential tasks in the preparation of silk. Indeed, women continued in the silk trade throughout the early modern period, albeit typically in a subservient position to male weavers, who had seized the craft from them. Carew's sermon, for instance, includes a substantial discussion of the deplorable state of women's wages as spinners, arguing that "when the woman spendes as much time, takes asmuch paines, and dooth as profitable worke as men of other trades," the difference in pay should be negligible.[92] The records of the Weavers' Company reveal several instances of weavers fined for defying ordinances against the employment of women.[93] The petition's specific objection seems carefully worded—the Yeomanry and the weavers they represented probably employed women, but they did so in a way that maintained regulatory control of the craft, or so they told themselves. The various grievances enumerated in the petition fit a pattern, however: long-standing ordinances designed to protect the earning power of individual households were being left unenforced, and this threatened the livelihoods of the vast majority of weavers.

To modern sensibilities the tensions between the liverymen and the rank and file of the company appears as a debate between a regulated economy and a free market of labor. This has been reflected in historians' views of London's livery companies. A pioneer in the field, George Unwin saw in the livery companies the forerunners of modern trade unions.[94] Steven A. Epstein has more recently described the livery company as "an association of employers who banded together to foster their self-interest," about as far from the modern trade union as one could get.[95] Between the liverymen and the Yeomanry both views seem sustainable. To the Yeomanry the central problem was the disintegration of the system into which they had paid their dues. According to the petition, the result of the various violations of the company's ordinances was that "the poore Freemen can get noe worke at all, or very little, and that he must doe soe good Cheape that the gaine thereof will not finde his people bread."[96] Work was scarce and paid little. The Yeomanry claimed that they had obeyed the ordinances and that this had put them at a disadvantage, so much so that it had "growne to be a proverbe amongst them—That if Silkeweavers will kepe themselves true, the Silkemen will kepe them poore enough."[97] The liverymen, because of their general success, saw the system as working rather well and had no real interest in elevating the lot of those weavers who might compete with them. Consciously or not, the lax liverymen and the immigrant weavers aimed at creating a small number of masters who could employ a vast number of laborers, thereby gaining a larger share in the profits of the industry. Conversely, the Yeomanry and the many poorer weavers they represented aimed at a large number of masters with a small number of apprentices and journeymen under them, a commonwealth of small producers.

The extensive detail and rhetorical flourishes of the Yeomanry's petition meant that it was long, too long to copy out by hand for each of the French and Dutch church's ministers and elders as well as the mayor and all the city's aldermen. One weaver recommended having a printer make copies of the petition. For just five schillings the entire petition, weighing in at around eight folio pages, could be printed in an edition of forty copies.[98] Printing the petition, however, was not without risk. Richard W. Hoyle notes that petitions purporting to represent a craft or whole town already carried with them a hint of rebellion.[99] In submitting the petition to the elders of the stranger churches, moreover, the weavers were planning to go outside the normal channels of petitioning. Printing a petition might further smack of an attempt to make a grievance more public than necessary, to rally apprentices and others on the petition's behalf—and that in a month of considerable unrest in the city.

According to the mayor, who later made an inquiry into the meeting, "the greater parte to the number of xii shewed their mislike to have the same proceed into print."[100] The twelve dissenters here feared appearing unruly to the authorities, but they may also have worried about running afoul of their own livery company. They had already pressed their case before the court of aldermen. Making their grievances more public might result in subtle or overt retaliation. The liverymen chose those who could enter their ranks, and they would certainly remember those involved in repeatedly exposing the company's leadership to public scrutiny.

It should be noted that the hope of entering the ranks of the livery was not altogether unrealistic for the Yeomanry. Although the weavers described themselves as "poore" and "distressed," they do not seem to have always or constantly been in such a dire economic situation. Muggins's own household was not devoid of comforts. Among the household's more prized possessions was "one Carpett ymbrodered with the falkon" estimated to be worth just over three pounds.[101] And the parlor of the household featured a "staind wainscott" worth around five pounds. That the large wood panel was "staind" indicates that it featured some painted image. The hall and chamber of the household were lined with "paintyd Clothes," wall hangings that, like the wainscot, featured some imagery.[102] Given Muggins's intensive reading of the Bible, it is reasonable to guess that these wall hangings, like many such hangings, depicted biblical scenes.[103] The wainscot and painted cloths thus insulated the household from drafts while decoratively adding to the moral instruction of the household. Although the "paintyd Clothes" were not extravagantly expensive (the wall hangings in the chamber were estimated to be worth three shillings, four pence), they were comforts not all could afford.[104] Similarly, among the bedding in the household was "one featherbedd ij bolsters & ij Pillowes." Certainly, featherbeds were among the more comfortable bedding of the period, and while the estimated value was not outrageous, featherbeds were generally valuable enough to make frequent appearances as significant legacies in wills.[105] It may well be that some of these items had been inherited or purchased at moments when the household income appeared stable. Regardless, assuming that Muggins's fellow yeomen lived in similar circumstances, any or all of them could have imagined that under the right economic conditions they, too, might join the prestigious livery. They may well have seen membership in the recently established Yeomanry of the Company of Weavers as placing them at the threshold of the elite of their company. Such expectations were shaped at an early age among the middling sort, who were raised on stories of such figures as Dick Whittington and Simon Eyre, poor boys who rose up the ranks of their craft to achieve legendary status.[106]

Whether the weavers saw such legends as realistic possibilities or hollow promises, the livery companies nonetheless formed a significant part of how individuals of the middling sort saw themselves. One might identify with one's kinship bonds, neighborhood, or parish church, but the livery companies also constituted an important communal identity for craftsmen and merchants.[107] Young men were inducted into the craft and its culture at an early age.[108] The promotion from apprentice to freeman of the city was in many respects a coming-of-age ritual grounded in the company, and craft or guild identity was reinforced at the company's annual feast.[109] The companies regulated not only labor and products but also at times the behavior of members.[110] While the courts of assistants of various companies appear to have preferred that matters of moral behavior be handled by the ecclesiastical courts, the livery companies were active parts of individuals' lives. They provided charity and helped fund funerals.[111] Prominent members sought to be memorialized in the hall of their respective company.[112] More important than his standing as mayor or member of Parliament, Swinnerton, Muggins's eventual dedicatee, commissioned a portrait of himself to hang in the Merchant Taylor's Hall, where it seems he most wanted to be remembered.[113]

While texts from the period invite us to see the community established through the livery companies as indisputably positive, such communities always call for a degree of conformity—they paradoxically enable particular identities even as they tacitly discourage any outspoken individuality that might question their hierarchical foundations.[114] The twelve weavers who "shewed their mislike" of printing the petition may have felt the implicit communal pressure to not expose the company as failing to fulfill its purpose as a regulatory body. By the same token, the weavers may have approved of the petition but not wanted to expose themselves as at such striking variance with the company's leadership. Leaving their names off the petition provided a degree of deniability and therefore safety within the company.

Whatever the case may have been, the petition was printed, and Willington, Deloney, and Muggins were willing to risk attaching their names to it. According to the mayor, "The principall men that have bin doers in this busyness are one Willington, Muggins and Delonye, whereof Willington was cheife devisor."[115] That Muggins hosted the meeting of the Yeomanry suggests a less hierarchical organization than the mayor was willing to imagine, however. The petition was the product of collective knowledge and experience and a shared need to bring order to the market for silk. In any case, the three silk-weavers commissioned the stationer Gabriel Simson to print at least twenty-two copies of the petition.

It is not clear how Simson came to be the printer. Around the corner from Muggins's household was the Long Shop, run by printer Edward Allde, who had printed Deloney's 1586 ballad on the execution of the men involved in the Babington Plot against Queen Elizabeth.[116] John Wolfe and Thomas Orwin had both printed some of Deloney's ballads in the 1580s, and both were, like Allde, geographically closer to Muggins's household than was Simson. It may be that Willington or one of the other weavers knew Simson, or perhaps one of Deloney's printers had referred the weavers to Simson.

Whatever the case, Muggins and Deloney were soon to be well acquainted with Simson.

According to the weavers, when they presented their petition to the ministers of the French and Dutch churches, it was "most gentlie by them accepted." Despite the rhetoric of shared religion and the meager request that the church simply confront the violators, the church elders did in fact take offence. Among its more forceful moments, the petition described the immigrant weavers as "a most obstinate and perverse kinde of people," who "onely seeke their owne private Lucre."[117] The ministers alerted the mayor, and the mayor promptly had all fifteen weavers arrested. Upon investigation, he released on bond the twelve who denied approving the petition for print, while Muggins, Deloney, Willington, and Simson were held at Newgate Prison for several days. Generally, prisoners were charged for their stay in prison, and Newgate keepers had a reputation, confirmed by Hutton, for overcharging prisoners, soliciting bribes, and otherwise extorting money from the inmates.[118] While wealthier prisoners might purchase tolerable conditions, the weavers' complaints of poverty indicate that they suffered some of the worst conditions Newgate could offer. The four cellmates could expect to be shackled and confined to a small space in an overcrowded cell.

Muggins and Deloney promptly petitioned Chief Justice Sir John Popham for redress of their grievances and release from prison. The printing of the first petition was not, they insisted, an act of sedition, but "that the writing of said letters seemed burdenous."[119] They referred Popham to the previous decision of the aldermen to uphold the position of the Yeomanry; they were therefore only requesting that the ministers "exhort their Countrymen to ... conformitie of Orders" already established. Unfortunately, they explained, the ministers had taken the weavers' "simple meaninges in the worste sence." In addition to reiterating the demands of the initial petition, the letter to Popham pled for release from prison, where they languished "at great Charges, restrayned from their occupacions and their families in great distress." The stay in prison was no doubt exacerbating their economic woes. Popham sided with the Yeomanry, writing that they were "greatly decayed and injured by the negligence or oversighte of some former Governors or Masters of the said Company" who had allowed strangers "Such priveledges and Apprentices as by the provisions and Ordynaunces of their Guyld have not ben suffered or permitted amonge the Freemen of the said Company."[120]

Popham referred the matter to the Privy Council, who demanded that London's aldermen address the issues raised by the Yeomanry.

Ordinances were reiterated, clarified, and modified in favor of the poorer weavers, but like the aldermen's previous support, this did little to effect lasting changes for the impoverished silk-weavers. It appears that intermittent agitation of the Yeomanry was necessary to keep the company's elite focused on the concerns of the poorer weavers. In June 1611 the king was in receipt of a petition requesting the establishment of a new livery company, "The Corporation of Silkmen," to include merchants as well as silk-weavers and spinners. The city's authorities objected. To establish a company that overlapped so significantly with other long-standing companies would be "a strange innovation" and "would in short time worke an alteration of the whole frame and politique constitution of the cittie." The mayor argued that grievances that gave rise to the petition could be remedied by the existing civic structures, among them that the Weavers' Company already had "the search, viewe and correction" of silk-weavers and their products.[121] This may have been a ploy by the silk merchants to gain greater control over production, but the pressure on the Weavers' Company to enforce its ordinances was evidently felt as the coming years saw the company's Court of Assistants approaching their job with greater rigor.[122] Still, by the early 1620s the Yeomanry had many of the same complaints they had had thirty years earlier. Indeed, they found themselves frequently avoided, at times retaliated against, and at least one time locked out of the proceedings of the Court of Assistants of the company.[123] In 1630 a group of weavers submitted a petition to the mayor of London complaining that the company failed to enforce its own statutes, and in 1635 English silk-weavers again petitioned the French and Dutch churches in London with grievances virtually identical to those of 1595.[124]

FROM PETITION OF THE YEOMANRY TO POETRY OF THE CITY

In 1595 Muggins, Deloney, Willington, and Simson had every reason to feel optimistic that complaints might be respected and even addressed. On Popham's urging, the Privy Council recommended that the silk-weavers and their printer be released from prison. Simson and his new acquaintance Luke Hutton went on to protest the conditions at the prison. Although Hutton was careful to avoid naming names, *The Black Dogge of Newgate* laid special blame on the keepers of Newgate. Simson and Hutton decided to dedicate the pamphlet to Sir John Popham himself, and beneath the title on the cover of the pamphlet, Simson made sure to print a Latin inscription especially for his dedicatee: "Vide, Lege, Caue"—See, Read, Do.[125]

Deloney would soon complain on behalf of the commons regarding the price of grain in the realm. London's mayor, Stephen Slaney, described the ballad as including "certain vaine & presumptuous matter bringing in her highness to speak with her people in dialogue wise in very fond and indecent sort & prescribeth orders for the remedying of the dearth of corn."[126] As Roze Hentschell points out, although the ballad has not survived, one can surmise from the mayor's description of it that Deloney had developed a "distrust of official inaction" like that of the Weavers' Company.[127] As with the printed petition, this ballad ran the risk of agitating citizens and apprentices to riot. Indeed, in his letter to the lord treasurer, Slaney recalled Deloney as "an idle fellow and one noted with the like before in printing a Book for the Silkweavers wherein was found some like foolish & disordered matter."[128] Criticizing the unequal distribution of grain and the system of imprisonment in London—as Nick Bottom might say of Deloney and Simson, "This was lofty."

In 1603 Muggins would take up the task left by his sometime cellmates. *London's Mourning Garment* displays none of the animosity toward strangers that the petition had, however. Indeed, the poem makes a point of including merchant strangers in the description of London's inhabitants coming together to celebrate the imminent royal entry of King James. Although the petition risked his place in the larger community of weavers, *London's Mourning Garment* expresses a special admiration for the work of London's artisans generally. The poem's description of the preparations for James's entry to the city especially focuses on the productive labor of the city's artisans: "My wealthy Free-men also wrought their best, / Preparing Pageants in each famous street" (sig. B1v, lines 38–39). As a weaver of, among other things, ribbons, Muggins may well have been among those freemen who, as the poem explains, "to worke were ready bent" to decorate the city's streets for the royal entry (sig. B1v, line 46).

Muggins's personified London further recalls moments of great prosperity, namely, the marvelous wares a merchant could purchase in the city: "The finest shagges, wrought stuffes, and purest glasse, / Rare cloth of gold, and silkes of euery dye" (sig. C3r, lines 423–24). Muggins's own products—silk, lace, and ribbon—make a cameo appearance in this catalog of luxurious items. The quality of the goods was such, argues the poem, that a merchant could expect to triple his profits. But once the plague strikes, the fragility of the economy is laid bare. In brutal contrast to the ultimately frivolous items for sale during London's prosperity, London laments:

> But most of all my sorrowing heart doth grieue,
> For such as worke and take exceeding care,
> And by their labour knowe not how to liue,
> Going poore soules in garments thinne and bare,
> The bellie hungry, of flesh leane and spare. (sig. C4v, lines 533–37)

The 1595 petition provides the picture of a weaver unable to earn enough to "finde his people bread," a weaver "quite undone with his wife and poore Children, and brought to such miserye as is lamentable to rehearse."[129] In *London's Mourning Garment*, no sooner have the working poor stayed their hunger than

> The day insuing brings the like distresse:
> The painefull Parents working all their trade
> For new supply, fell famine to suppresse,
> But all in vaine, their woes are nere the lesse. (sig. C4v, lines 541–44)

The rapid cycle of struggle against need is here emphasized by the movement to the couplet as well as internal rhymes on "-ing" and "-aine." Just as Deloney and Simson broadened their political sympathies, so by 1603 Muggins had turned from the distressed silk-weavers of his company to the distressed families of the entire city.

Throughout the poem, Muggins blames the problems of the city on the indifference of the wealthy and powerful. London describes the poor workers going "Vnto such Trades-men as haue small pittie," who "like NABALS, will not with them mell, / Vnlesse for halfe the worth they may it buy: / The rich man laughs, the poore in heart doth cry" (sig. C4v, lines 548–51). Knowing that commerce has slowed, the merchants attempt to drive down the costs of goods so that they can make more money at resale, leaving the poor man desperately underselling his household's labor. There is here an echo of the desperation of the craftsman from the 1595 petition who, having been undersold at the market by immigrant weavers, returns "home, with a heavye and a sorrowfull harte."¹³⁰ Lurking in both these images is an objection to a market driven solely by supply and demand and the wealthy's ability to manipulate both. Although some negotiation was no doubt expected at market, the poem and the petition express a mixture of sorrow and outrage at the opportunism of those who feel free to ignore what the community might deem fair prices for labor and goods.¹³¹ Indeed, *London's Mourning Garment* hints that hubris and ruthless economic self-interest were the causes of the plague itself. Muggins's description of opportunistic merchants is not without foreboding, however. The extortionate merchants are likened to Nabal, the rich miser struck down by God for begrudging David and his servants any relief.

Just as Deloney prescribed remedies for the scarcity of grain in London, so Muggins offers his own radical proposal. London addresses the city's leaders and declares:

> When in the senate, house with counsell graue,
> You sit debating, causes how to end.
> Make some decree, poore working trades to mend.
>   At least set downe, some order for their good,
>   That each man may, with labour earne his foode. (sig. D1v, lines 612–16)

Framed as a modest request with the words "At least," London asserts that there should be something like a living wage law in early modern London, a standard of living for all laborers. Labor should be compensated sufficiently for families to be able to eat each day. London's remedy for poverty thus reaches beyond the immediate crisis brought about by the plague to address the more sustained problem of underpaid labor, the problem Muggins observed among his fellow weavers in 1595, a problem he had no doubt observed in the years between the petition and his poem. The urgency of both the petition and the poem rests on the basic necessity of food. The radicalism of Muggins's unrealized proposal should not be underestimated. Even now there are those who object to the idea that a full day's work should necessarily result in basic sustenance. Muggins's experiences in the mid-1590s led to a kind of class consciousness, an insight into the workings of the city's economy that cut through appeals to community and the promises of advancement to engender in him an affinity not just with his fellow weavers but with the working poor throughout London.

Upon release from prison in 1595, however, Muggins did not, as far as anyone knows, join with Simson or Deloney in their immediate efforts. The fees for staying in prison surely made a bad situation worse. If the petition's depiction of a famished family at all represented the state of Muggins's household, he needed to get back to weaving. The time in prison had compromised his household's productivity, and therefore his ability to immediately ensure food for himself, his daughter, and his pregnant wife. In early July 1595 Muggins instead made his way from Newgate to his household in the Poultry and the support he could find among his neighbors there. The petition described the misery of weavers' families as "lamentable to be rehearsed."[132] Muggins was not yet ready to rehearse his own lament.

CHAPTER 2

Life and Debt in the Poultry

The Communal Bonds of the Parish

> The year revolves, and I again explore
> The simple Annals of my Parish poor;
> What infant-members in my flock appear,
> What pairs I bless'd in the departed year;
> And who, of old or young, or nymphs or swains,
> Are lost to Life, its pleasures and its pains.
> No Muse I ask, before my view to bring
> The humble actions of the swains I sing.
> —GEORGE CRABBE, "THE PARISH REGISTER" (1807)

NEW LIFE IN THE POULTRY

On September 29, 1595, just three months after his release from prison, William Muggins was to make his way to the Weavers' Hall to pay his quarterage to the company, six shillings due four times a year.[1] It was difficult to afford following the fines for his stay at Newgate. The Muggins household was getting by on credit. The city buzzed with news of the election of a new lord mayor, Stephen Slaney. It was also Michaelmas, a day of official feasting throughout England.[2] At their livery company's hall, weavers—including many of the men who had met at Muggins's household in June—socialized. Muggins would have a more recent gathering at his home on his mind. On

September 23, Muggins's wife had given birth to a daughter, and on the twenty-eighth the infant was christened at St. Mildred's Church, a short walk from Muggins's home in the Poultry.³ Michaelmas eve was an auspicious day for a christening.⁴ On Michaelmas Day, before heading out to pay his quarterage, Muggins and his neighbors went to church to hear a reading of Mark 18:1, in which Jesus gestures to a child and declares, "Whosoever therefore humbleth himself as this childe, the same is the greatest in the kingdome of heaven."⁵ The newborn would serve as a model, an embodiment of the day's lesson. Rather than the city's leadership or his company's failures, Muggins would be preoccupied with the care of his household, as well the comradery and support he could find in his parish, St. Mildred's in the Poultry. Unlike the male-dominated realm of the livery company, women were much more involved in the parish, especially surrounding matters of childbirth but also in negotiating market prices and the maintenance of the household. Bonds among women were especially strong at the level of the parish: women were seated together at church and relied on one another for aid during pregnancy and childbirth. Far from idyllic, however, the parish was also a significant site for the working out of social rank and economic struggles that threatened the cohesion of social bonds. Unlike Shakespeare, who set his exploration of credit and community in a distant Venice, Muggins gives an all too "local habitation" to the problems of debt in London. This chapter is about middling-sort men and women and the social bonds of neighborhood and parish in early modern London—and how Muggins translated his experience of the parish into his poetry.

WOMEN, CHILDBIRTH, AND THE BONDS OF THE PARISH

The late summer and early autumn months in sixteenth-century London were unusually difficult, with burials typically at their peak from August through October.⁶ With a mortality rate for women in childbirth in London hovering around 1 to 2.6 percent, anxieties about the mother's health were understandably high.⁷ Muggins's pastor at St. Mildred's, Thomas Sorocold, would later describe labor as "those terrors, horrors, and pangs which accompany that houre."⁸ First printed in 1608, Sorocold's best-selling prayer book, *The Supplications of Saints*, devotes several prayers to the various stages of childbearing: pregnancy and fears of "an untimely birth," the calling of the midwife, childbirth itself, and the mother's postnatal recovery.⁹ Sorocold's first wife, Susan Sorocold, died in March of 1604.[10] Sorocold's prayers reflect the personal trauma of losing a wife or infant in childbirth. The prayers meticulously meditate on each moment from pregnancy through recovery, emphasizing the apprehension felt about the mortal danger posed to the mother throughout pregnancy and the weeks after birth.

Infants themselves faced far worse odds. The infant mortality rate for females born in England between 1550 and 1599 was around 127 in 1,000. And London's infant mortality rate was higher still.[11] Not without reason were early modern subjects preoccupied by infant mortality. Sorocold's "Prayer after the Deliverance of Women" includes a blessing for the infant, but notes in the margin "Leave out all this, if the child be not born alive."[12] In the three months before Susan Sorocold's death, Thomas Sorocold oversaw the burials of two children "dead borne": an infant who died shortly after being born and a child just two months old.[13] Hannah Cleugh has drawn attention to the way provisions for private baptism, often used because the infant's death seemed imminent, ran counter to the church's theology of predestination, but the practice seems also to acknowledge the fragility of infant life and the parents' desperate need to provide some form of comfort and spiritual connection to their newborns.[14] That Muggins's wife and child had both survived the first few days beyond childbirth in September, when infant mortality was highest, constituted a significant triumph for the household. Two years earlier plague had devastated the parish, with a mere fourteen baptisms compared to more than fifty burials. This birth contributed to the parish's return to equilibrium, a testament to the community's resilience following the plague.[15]

Still, Muggins was keenly aware of dangers in childbirth. In his 1603 poem, as his personified London battles against indifference by inspiring a deeper sense of common humanity, she implores mothers:

Againe bethinke you, at that instant hower,
The little difference, was twixt life and death:
When as the infant, with his naked power,
Laboured for life, to have his rightfull birth,
And with the sickly, Mother gaspt for breath,
   The one nere dead, as nigh to death the other,
   Sore to the babe, worse Trauell for the Mother. (sig. B3v, lines 190–96)

The tiny infant expends "his naked power" in a struggle with mortality waged on the body of the mother as both labor, or travail, to bring about new life. For Muggins one of the defining features of birth is how the beginning of life brings mother and infant close to death. The lines express a deep anxiety about mother and child wavering "twixt life and death."

Sorocold's "Prayer in Time of Womens Travell" asks God to show mercy on the mother, and to "mitigate the judgement which thou hast laid upon her, and all Women for sin."[16] This almost requisite allusion to Eve is absent from Muggins's description of the pain of childbirth, however. Rather than dwelling on shame or just penance for original sin, the poem describes the dangers of childbirth as occasion for recognizing a shared humanity and the fragility of human life.[17] Original sin may be a part of that sense of shared humanity for early modern subjects, but Muggins focuses instead on the immediate experience of childbirth, the physical exertion, its risks, and the delicate relationship of mother and infant.[18] Indeed, although generally viewed as an event exclusive of men, *London's Mourning Garment* suggests Muggins's intimate knowledge of and appreciation for the birthing experience and the bond between mother and infant.[19]

After a successful confrontation with death, the next step would be to secure the infant's spiritual life through baptism. Although the state, through the prescriptions of the *Booke of Common Prayer*, sought uniformity in church rituals like baptism, each baptism, marriage, and feast day also reinforced the bonds of the local community—namely, the specific parish church as focal point of the unique neighborhoods that made up the parish. In addition to providing for the spiritual life of the local community, the parish was a fundamental unit of social organization in the period: local governance was largely carried out through church vestries made up of lay members of the parish; the parish church often offered basic education in reading and was responsible for the upkeep of roads and bridges; the parish was charged with keeping the peace and maintaining neighborliness (in fact, disputes among parishioners were often settled through the parish church); and the parish church was generally in charge of providing poor relief.[20]

The communal nature of the parish church was visible in the materiality of the church itself. Most structures of the church were the result of donations from parishioners. Stow records that in 1505, draper Richard Shore contributed fifteen pounds to the construction of a porch for St. Mildred's and that the window of the east wall, facing the baptismal font, featured "the Armes of divers Gentlemen, as Benefactors." Similarly, Thomas Ashehill supplied the funds to make substantial repairs to the church in the fifteenth century.[21] The church cared for the spiritual well-being of parishioners, but it was parishioners themselves who were responsible for the well-being of the church.

Parishioners contributed to the textual world of the church as well. Despite needing to provide for his children and wife (who was pregnant when he passed away), Thomas Iken, London skinner and sometime churchwarden at St. Mildred's, left to the Hodnet church where he was born a copy of Foxe's *Acts and Monuments* as well as money for a desk and chain for the book. Additionally, he left "to the poore of Saint Mildred's parishe Twentie shillings," and he or his wife and siblings who also attended St. Mildred's further arranged for an epitaph to be put up on a pillar near the altar of the church:

> In Hodnet and London
> >   God blessed my life
> Till forty and sixe yeeres,
> >   with children and wife:
> And God will raise me
> >   up to life againe,
> Therefore have I thought
> >   my death no paine.
> >   Thomas Iken, qui obiit 10. die Martii, 1590.[22]

The epitaph, like the long opening to Iken's will, expresses a kind of optimistic Calvinism.[23] Inside the church and throughout the grounds one could read other epitaphs dedicated to the memory of the community's more prosperous parishioners from the fifteenth century onward.

In the chancel of the church, Muggins would note the gravestone of poet Thomas Tusser. Born around 1524, Tusser had been a musician serving Lord William Paget during the reigns of Henry VIII and Edward VI. Tusser left the turmoil of the mid-Tudor court to start a farm first in Suffolk and then in Essex. At the same time, Tusser began writing georgic verse. His *Fiue Hundreth Points of Good Husbandry* provided advice on farming along with a number of topical poems and experiments within the georgic mode:

poems on right religion, others on the importance of service, even one about the qualities of good cheese.[24] Tusser's most repeated advice, however, was about the importance of thrift, expressed periodically throughout the book and amplified in individual poems like "The Ladder to Thrift" and "Comparing Good Husband, with Vnthrift His Brother." Indeed, Tusser defines the eponymous "good" of *Good Husbandry* as virtually synonymous with thrift:

> The husband is he, that to labour doth fall,
> the labour of him, I do husbandry call:
> If thrift by that labour, be any way caught,
> then is it good husbandry, else is it naught.[25]

But Tusser was never a parishioner of St. Mildred's. Just west of the church was the Poultry Compter, a small prison primarily used for vagrants and debtors. Among the prison's more famous inmates was religious dissenter John Penry as well as the dramatists turned debtors Thomas Dekker and Ben Jonson.[26] Somewhat ironically, Tusser, the poet of thrift, was also held in the Poultry Compter for debt, where he died in 1580. As with many other prisoners who died in the Poultry Compter, Tusser's burial was managed by St. Mildred's. Unlike the other prisoners buried by St. Mildred's, Tusser was given a modest place of honor. *Fiue Hundreth Points of Good Husbandry* was among the most popular books of the Elizabethan era, reprinted in sixteenth-century England more than any other volume of secular poetry, so it merited some recognition.[27] His gravestone included the following inscription:

> Here Thomas Tusser,
> clad in earth doth lye,
>   That sometime made
> the pointes of husbandrie,
>   By him then learne thou maist;
> here learne we must,
>   When all is done, we sleepe,
> and turne to dust:
>   And yet, through Christ,
> to Heaven we hope to goe;

Who reades his books,
shall find his faith was so.[28]

Appropriately enough, the epitaph emphasizes Tusser's occasional forays into devotional poetry. That the grave was a prominent feature in the Poultry is attested to in the church's parish register. When Sorocold took on his position at St. Mildred's, he took it upon himself to make the church's records uniform, arranging to have the older records copied into a single volume, the extant copy of St. Mildred's parish register. The clerk in charge of copying out the older entries thought it important to refer to the inscription: "[1580, May] The ix. Was buried Thomas Tusser gentlema[n], prisoner about the age of lxiiij yeares[.] He made the booke called the points of husbandry, as appeareth by the supscription of the stone upon his grave, in the Chauncell."[29] The clerk may or may not have known Tusser's poetry, but he had evidently noted the epitaph in the chancel, a significant place of honor for a prisoner. Tusser's poetry, like *London's Mourning Garment*, was populist in nature and focused on the lives of the middling sort in England.[30] Even if he had not read *Fiue Hundreth Points of Good Husbandry*, Muggins, like the parish clerk, had surely taken note of the epitaph: Stow recorded it in his *Survey of London* as among the most notable monuments in St. Mildred's.

While Tusser's epitaph provides traces of the parish's literary life, others, like those of John Hildie (1416) and Simon Lee (1487), both poulters, attest to the historical significance of the parish's name. Other monuments chart the gradual demographic change in the sixteenth century from poulters to haberdashers and grocers.[31] A monument to haberdasher William Hobson was perhaps of special significance. The Hobson family had played an integral role in the life of the Poultry—under Henry VIII, haberdasher Thomas Hobson purchased the chapel at St. Mildred's and converted it to a line of shops adjacent to Conyhope Lane, and William Hobson had owned a significant tenement on Conyhope Lane, including perhaps the very household that Muggins leased.[32] Buried in 1581, William Hobson had a reputation as a local wit, a trickster of the middling sort. Thomas Heywood portrayed him and his antics in the second part of *If You Know Not Me, You Know No One* (1605), and Richard Johnson made Hobson the central figure of *The Pleasant Conceites of Old Hobson the Merry Londoner* (1607).[33] Johnson drew on stock jests but also included elements that were clearly part of an oral tradition memorializing Hobson's wit.[34] Together the epitaphs on St. Mildred's funeral monuments and the lore around them served as a veritable anthology of the neighborhood's historic residents, a chorus of the community's past.[35]

The importance of St. Mildred's to the neighborhood was especially apparent when the church was under attack. In 1592 one former parishioner, John Haselden—described by sometime resident of the Poultry Anthony Munday as "an evill minded man"—alleged that St. Mildred's churchyard, parson's chamber, and several tenements attached to the church were really "concealed lands," property hidden from the state or otherwise overlooked following the dissolution of the monasteries.[36] Elizabeth had long sought to lay hold of such property, granting patents to various low-level courtiers to oversee the discovery and seizure of said lands. The holder of one such patent, the sometime poet Sir Edward Dyer, employed William Tipper and Robert Dawe, particularly thorough and ruthless agents, to manage the seizure of the property attached to St. Mildred's and to auction it off to the highest bidder.[37] Sorocold and several other parishioners filed suit to prove that the lands were not in fact "concealed." A compromise seems to have been struck: rather than lose the lands to an outsider, the property was conveyed to four prominent parishioners, who then held the property collectively for the use of the parish.[38]

Collective ownership of the lands was seen as desirable for the maintenance of the parish. Years later, when most of the original neighbors had passed away, arrangements were made to transfer the property to a larger group of parishioners to hold collectively for the parish. Such efforts underline the role of the parish church as both spiritual and communal center, a place that neighbors saw as their responsibility to maintain and defend. Thus, baptisms inducted infants into the spiritual life of the church but also began the child's integration into the social world and collective responsibilities of the neighborhood. Such rituals reaffirmed the family's place in the local community. While the livery company informed Muggins's identity as a weaver, the parish established his place as father, husband, householder, and neighbor, and both institutions informed his role as a poet.

Thus, the christening of Muggins's daughter was not a private matter between priest and parents—in fact, parents rarely attended their children's christenings. Instead, the midwife and three godparents along with some neighbors and nearby family and friends took the infant to the church while the mother rested and the father prepared for a modest celebration following the christening.[39] Although there was some Puritan resistance to the particulars of the Church of England's ceremony of baptism, an unusually detailed entry in the parish register of St. Mildred's reveals that Sorocold followed to the *Booke of Common Prayer* precisely. In 1611, Sorocold baptized "Dederj Jaquoaoh about the age of 20 yeares, the sonne of Caddibiah king of the river of Cetras or Cestus in the cuntrey of Guinny."[40] Although the African prince Dederj, newly christened "John," recited the Lord's Prayer himself, the register's description of the use of a baptismal font, the sign of the cross, and number and gender of the witnesses was very much in keeping with directions in the *Booke of Common Prayer*.

One can be fairly certain, then, that on September 28, 1595, the midwife and infant daughter of Muggins along with two godmothers and a godfather met Sorocold at the door of St. Mildred's and proceeded to the baptismal font at the west end of the church.[41] Sorocold would ask if the infant had already been baptized. Upon being told that the answer was no, he would read from the *Booke of Common Prayer*, emphasizing the need for all to "bee baptized with water and the holy Ghost, and receiued into Christes holy Church, and be made liuely members of the same."[42] Sorocold would then recite the *Booke of Common Prayer*'s version of Luther's Flood Prayer, a typological meditation on biblical waters from Noah's ark and the parting of the Red Sea to the New Testament baptism of Jesus whereby water was sanctified "with the mysticall washing away of sinne."[43] Sorocold would implore God to "open the gate unto us that knocke, that these infantes may enjoy the euerlasting benediction of thy heauenly washing, and may come to the eternall kingdome which thou has promised by Christ our Lorde."[44] In many respects, the service at the entrance to the church presented a spatial metaphor for baptism itself: just as the participants made their way into the sacred space of the church, so baptism provided the infant a way to enter the mystical body of Christ and the spiritual life of the community.

Sorocold would recite Mark 10, in which Jesus implores his followers to "suffer little children to come unto mee, and forbid them not, for to such belongeth the kingdome of God." He would then reflect on the passage and its relation to baptism. At this point, Sorocold would ask a series of questions of the infant to be answered by the godparents, culminating with "Wilt thou be baptized in this faith?" and the godparents answering for the infant "That is my desire." Before dipping the infant in the font water and blessing her "in the name of the Father and of the Sonne, and of the holy Ghost,"

Sorocold would ask the name of the infant, to which one or perhaps all three godparents in unison would have answered, "Anne Muggins."[45]

Sorocold would make the sign of the cross on the infant's forehead and pronounce, "We receive this childe into the congregation of Christes flocke." The gesture was not without controversy, and suggests, as Matthew Dimmock notes, what would come to be described as a "Jacobean high Anglicanism" in Sorocold.[46] After reciting the Lord's Prayer, Sorocold would counsel the godparents on their responsibilities in instructing Anne in the faith.[47] Although the emphasis throughout was on the spiritual nature of baptism, the ceremony was also quite literally an introduction to the parish church and the local community beyond the walls of the birthing room. The *Booke of Common Prayer* encouraged baptism on Sundays, "when the most number of people may come together" so that "every man present may be put in the remembrance of his owne profession made unto God."[48] At the same time, the gathering of the neighborhood and lay participation in the ceremony put those present in remembrance of the social unit of the parish, the reciprocal bonds of neighbor to neighbor. The christening was a religious ceremony, but it was also a ritual of community.[49]

After the baptism, the crowd would join the mother and father, and their first daughter, Elizabeth, for a celebration that might range from modest fare to a lavish feast. Given Muggins's circumstances just a few months earlier, the celebration was probably humble while still providing a scene for greater integration of the neighborhood in communal feelings of goodwill. In his 1603 prayer, Muggins would bemoan the way the crisis of the plague had divided the community and prevented neighbors from coming together to comfort or celebrate (sig. D3v). For the moment, however, Muggins likely enjoyed the brief gathering and its articulation of the social bonds in his neighborhood.

The role of the laity in the parish church and the diverse resources and skills of parishioners meant that each parish comprised its own unique and dynamic community even as the *Booke of Common Prayer* sought a more homogenous national culture of reform by imposing uniformity in baptism and other ceremonies.[50] Every parish had its own epitaphs, generically similar, but also announcing the parish's distinct history. Parish priests might range from staunchly conservative to zealous nonconformist. And parishioners sometimes rejected the precisely scripted baptism described in the *Booke of Common Prayer* or interpreted for themselves the meaning of particular traditions. A case in point: another spiritual ceremony would take place about a month or so later, when Muggins's wife, accompanied by at least two other women from the parish, would leave the isolation of recovery, or "lying in," for the first time since going into labor. Known as "churching" or "the thanksgiving of women after childbirth," the new mother would go to the church to receive blessings and prayers and give thanks to God for having spared her from the worst of what the *Booke of Common Prayer* described as "the great paine and perill of child birth."[51]

The 1549 printing of the *Booke of Common Prayer* retained the pre-Reformation notion of churching as "purification" of the mother, and this idea (though made less explicit in the liturgy) persisted well into the seventeenth century and beyond. As some scholars have suggested, churching might well be seen as ritualized misogyny, a ceremony focusing communal energy on the imagined impurity of the mother. Several sixteenth-century churches included in the ceremony a special "churching seat," putting the new mother on display for the congregation as the purification rite proceeded.[52] Such an interpretation effaces the varying attitudes of distinct parishes and individuals. Parishioners had complex and divergent interpretations of the ritual: a "churching seat" near the pulpit might reasonably be interpreted as a place of honor rather than shame, for instance. Kathryn R. McPherson has shown how seventeenth-century women actively engaged in reinterpreting the ritual to their own ends, as a way of coming to terms with their own suffering in childbirth, for instance. David Cressy and Adrian Wilson suggest that for many new mothers, churching was an opportunity for female solidarity and a solemn prequel to the churching feast—a communal celebration of motherhood.[53]

If Sorocold's *Supplications of Saints* is any indication of how the ritual was carried out at St. Mildred's, the churching was primarily an occasion of thanksgiving. His "Prayer after the Deliverance of Women," the text most closely corresponding to the *Booke of Common Prayer*'s churching ceremony, begins "O Lord God, by whom all men and women are wonderfully & fearefully made, we give thee most humble thankes, that in thy judgement towards this our Sister, thou hast remembred mercie, in giving her safe deliverance, together with a comely fruit of her body."[54] This is a far cry from John Donne's view of childbirth in Lady Doncaster's 1618 churching sermon, which focused on the need for spiritual cleansing, an extended discussion of Canticles 5:3, "I have washed my feet."[55] Donne declares, "our

Mothers conceived us in sin; and being wrapped up in uncleannesse there, *can any Man bring a cleane thing out of filthinesse?*"[56] To be sure, Donne turns this "filthinesse" into metaphoric dung and therefore the well-manured soil of the soul, but the association of motherhood with impurity, and thus the necessity for baptism and churching, is at the forefront of Donne's sermon. Sorocold instead focuses on the health of the mother and the "comely," rather than filthy, "fruit of her body."

Despite Muggins's commitment to scripture, his depiction of motherhood does not appear to be informed by notions of impurity either. Following the description of childbirth, London continues her appeal to mothers by describing the interactions of a mother and infant:

> The Child new borne, the Mother some deale well
> Are all the griefes, and sorrows at an end:
> No cares and troubles, yet I haue to tell,
> Though Child be swath'de, and sickly Mother mende,
> The feeble Infant, many a fret doth send.
>   Which grieves the Mother, till she weepe againe,
>   To heare and see, the Infant in such paine. (sig. B4r, lines 211–17)

The "infant, with his naked power" in birth has given way to "The feeble Infant," as mother and infant recuperate. This intimate description of mother and child focuses on the mother's capacity for empathy and sacrifice, and the infant's dependence on the mother. Moreover, the infant here appears to be very recently born, only recently swaddled.[57] In the early modern period, a baby was referred to as "the infant" until it was christened with a name, and the emphasis here is on the child "*new* borne." The "sickly Mother," by the same token, is only "some deale well," not fully recuperated and churched.

The portrait of mother and child continues in the next stanza, emphasizing the mother's only-partial recovery from childbirth. Despite fatigue and exhaustion, the mother tends to the infant's needs: "And with her feeble, hand and weakely strength / She playes and dallyes, for the babyes good." She then breastfeeds the infant:

> And to her milke-white, brestes doth lay at length
> The pretty foole, who learnes to take his foode.
> His onely meanes, to nourish life and bloud,

> He fed, she paynd, he drawes, poore Mother yeelds,
> Whose loving brests both shutes and prickings feeles. (sig. B4r, lines 218–24)

The fact that the child here "learnes to take his foode" indicates again that this is to be understood as one of the infant's first feedings. Regardless of whether the nameless child has been baptized, it is clear that the mother has not been well enough to be churched, but there is no indication that "purification" is needed. Indeed, Rebecca Totaro finds that whereas some plague pamphlets might represent nursing mothers as a source of contagion (perhaps an extension of the idea of the pre-churched mother), this passage hints at an allegorical image of Charity.[58] The mother appears as a symbol of selfless abundance rather than death and impurity. The allusion to Charity would seem to complement the realistic detail of the passage: *London's Mourning Garment* emphasizes intimate knowledge of breastfeeding—the sensation of "shutes and prickings," the discomfort and pain involved in nursing. In any case, between Muggins's and Sorocold's descriptions, one may reasonably speculate that at St. Mildred's churching was less about impurity and more about the care of new mothers. Laypeople may fully integrate in the local community and happily participate in rituals like churching without giving up their own convictions about birth, motherhood, or spiritual well-being.

Neither Sorocold nor Muggins seems to have thought of new mothers as especially impure. Rather, both focus on the care for and physical recovery of the mother. Although Muggins's associate, Thomas Deloney, never wrote directly about churching, he does describe a churching feast. In Deloney's *Thomas of Reading* several clothiers' wives gather at the household of Sutton of Salisbury, where they had "prepared great cheare." The women sit and talk while male servants attend on them. Deloney emphasizes the extensive, wide-ranging conversation that ensues: "Some talkt of their husbands frowardnes, some shewed their maids sluttishnes, othersome desciphered the costlines of their garments, some told many tales of their neighbors: and to be briefe, there was none of them but would haue talke for a whole day."[59] When the servant Crabbe attempts to outdo one of the women, they prove the sharper wits. Deloney depicts the churching feast as a communal event where women triumph. Although Deloney's depiction of churching is shaped by the generic constraints of *Thomas of Reading*, it fits a view of churching not as a shaming ritual but as a celebration of maternity and the centrality of women. Indeed, although lighthearted, the dominance of women's wit in Deloney's proto-novel reinforces Adrian Wilson's sense that churching and the heavy involvement of women in events around pregnancy and childbirth more generally constituted a "counter-power against male control" and an important aspect of a "collective culture of women" that included family members, neighbors, and local midwives.[60]

There were at least two midwives in St. Mildred's parish, Anne King (née Saiwell), wife to William King, and Dorothy Waterstone, wife to tailor William Waterstone.[61] Anne King was married in 1591 and had two daughters by 1595, when Anne Muggins was born.[62] Anne King and Muggins's wife would have been about the same age, and Elizabeth Muggins would have been close in age to one of Anne King's daughter's. Dorothy Waterstone, widowed in 1591, had more time to devote to midwifery and more need of the income that might go along with tending to childbirths in the neighborhood.[63]

In addition to family and midwives, pregnancy and childbirth brought together women of the parish to look after one another and share their experience and knowledge. The size of the Poultry meant that bonds among pregnant women and new mothers in the parish were particularly strong. At its widest point, the parish of St. Mildred's in the Poultry was only around three hundred feet wide and five hundred feet long. Each parishioner knew nearly every other parishioner—they met on the streets, at the market, and frequently at church. On the same day that Anne Muggins was baptized, John Kirby's daughter Elizabeth was also baptized. A merchant tailor by trade, Kirby was among the larger group of parishioners to whom the nearly confiscated church grounds were transferred in 1606.[64] His wife, Susan (née Lewen), who had previously been married to one John Palmer, seems to have been pregnant nearly every year from the mid-1580s on through the 1590s.[65] She would have been a neighbor to turn to if one had any questions about pregnancy. When she died in 1624, a monument to her was erected on the north aisle of St. Mildred's.[66] Other women of the parish required comfort and advice from Susan Kirby, Muggins's wife, and others. Alice Clowes (née Butcher), for example, was roughly seven months pregnant when Anne Muggins was born. The wife of saddler Antony Clowes, she had given birth to a daughter the previous year, on September 22, but the infant was buried the next day.[67] The mothers in the neighborhood would need to calm fears that she might lose another infant.

By the summer of 1597, Muggins's wife was pregnant again, this time with a son, Henrie, who was baptized on February 26, 1598.[68] Elizabeth, Anne, Henrie—was it a coincidence that the children bore the names of the monarch and her parents? Henrie's birth sheds light on further connections among parishioners. Sara de Prill, daughter of Joos and Margaret de Prill, was baptized on the same day as Henrie. Joos de Prill had come to St. Mildred's following conflicts he had with the elders of the Dutch church, Austin Friar's, not far away.[69] De Prill worked as a throwster, preparing raw silk for weavers like Muggins. Just below the entry for Henrie Muggins and Sara de Prill, two weeks after their christenings, the parish register lists in large, bold letters the birth of "Susan daughter of Thomas Sorocold."[70] Sorocold's wife (also named Susan, née Smith) hailed from the neighboring parish of St. Benet Sherehog and had married Thomas Sorocold in 1592. Susan Smith was listed as a "spinster," probably involved in the spinning of silk or, less likely, wool. Her family did business with the silk-weavers in the area. Her father, grocer Robert Smith, would have walked past Muggins's household many times to get to the Grocer's Hall further up Conyhope Lane.[71] Pregnant at the same time, Susan Sorocold and Muggins's wife likely shared some degree of friendship, a common bond that intersected with both church and craft within the confines of the neighborhood.

Thomas Sorocold himself probably also felt some affinity for the bookish silk-weaver who had his Bible at the ready. Born in Manchester, as a boy Sorocold distinguished himself by his commitment to study, earning him the recommendation of several in his hometown of Lancashire as well as Oliver Carter, fellow of the Collegiate Church in Manchester. Sorocold went on to Oxford, where he was listed in the register as "pleb. f.," or of common birth.[72] He received his master of arts in 1585 and went on to be a preacher in Lancashire, where he again distinguished himself: in 1587, based on his reputation for compelling sermons, he was invited to preach at the private chapel of Lord Stanley, Earl of Derby.[73] Shortly thereafter he was assigned to his post at St. Mildred's. Despite his education and reputation, Sorocold was guarded about abandoning his humble roots. Thus in his *Supplications of Saints* he penned "The Schollers Prayer," in which the speaker begs God, "Lord, when I shall haue attained vnto any measure of knowledge, let it not puffe me up to stand high in mine owne conceit, or be proude of thy gifts; but let mee be wise vnto sobrietie, and cary my selfe humbly, lowly, and modestly."[74] Sorocold's caution around pride contributed to a surprisingly participatory governace of St. Mildred's. While most parish churches were managed by a vestry of select, usually fairly wealthy parishioners, St. Mildred's seems to have allowed for the voices of the poorer parishioners as well. In 1594 Thomas Lane, scrivener and sometime churchwarden at St. Mildred's, complained that in terms of church governance, individuals "be he never so Base or quarrelling a man ... hathe had equall voice and hearing and borne lyke swaye as the chiefest man of the parrishe and some time overtaunted the chiefest man of the parishe." Lane was clearly bothered by the way the church allowed "Base" men like Muggins to dispute with the wealthiest grocers of the parish. In his will Lane asked that the vestry be limited to "onely twelve of the sufficientest, and Discreetest men" of the parish and that they alone be empowered to "order and decyde matters" of the church.[75] Muggins's experience in St. Mildred's more democratic church governance set part of the foundation for his polyvocal poem that gave voice to the poor and needy, those Lane would exclude from the vestry.

Supplications of Saints was dedicated to Princess Elizabeth and included three prayers by Queen Elizabeth, but the book is in many respects aimed at the middling sort that made up much of St. Mildred's in the Poultry. The prayer book includes "The Housholders Two Prayers," "The Souldiers Prayer," "The Fatherles Childe, or Orphanes Prayer," but no "gentleman's prayer" or "landlord's prayer."[76] Even "The Wiues Praier for Her Husband, in Absence, or Otherwise" assumes that the husband is away "to prosper in his businesse," a decidedly merchant-class view of travel.[77] In each of these, Sorocold attempts to inhabit the mind and cares of the individual, constructing what might be termed devotional dramatic monologues. Sorocold naturally had a relationship with nearly everyone in the small, tight-knit parish, and he may have been thinking of specific parishioners as he wrote *Supplications* with its several prayers about pregnancy and childbirth.

More explicit in revealing the social networks of parishioners at St. Mildred's, in 1593 Sorocold's kinsman Alexander Sorocold of Manchester sought an apprenticeship in London. Thomas Sorocold arranged for the young man to serve under William Crowche, a haberdasher living in the parish.[78] Like Susan Kirby, Crowche's wife was pregnant most of the time from 1586 to 1598.[79] The Crowches had eleven children in all. She was thus pregnant at the same time as Muggins's wife, giving birth to John Crowche two months before Anne Muggins was born, and to Joan Crowche one month prior to Henrie's birth. With eight children in tow before 1595, Crowche's wife was another woman of the parish to turn to during pregnancy, and no doubt had a significant role in the circle of mothers and mothers-to-be including Susan Sorocold, Susan Kirby, Anne King, and Muggins's wife.

Paralleling the circle of female parishioners, a community of mothers is at the center of *London's Mourning Garment*. As she seeks Londoners to share in her woe, Muggins's personified London seeks men because, she supposes, "Men mourne for men, where friendship long hath bred." But she finds instead that "The liuing Friend deceiues the friend that's dead" by attempting to swindle his friend's orphaned children out of their inheritance (sig. B2r, lines 79–81). Eventually London turns to "Olde Widdowes and yong wiues," appealing to their shared pain in childbirth and their deep attachment to their children: "And now a fresh," implores London, "remember all your throwes, / Your gripes your panges, your bodies pincht with paine, / As if this instant, you did them sustaine" (sig. B3v, lines 148, 180–82). And London recounts the more emotionally painful stories of childbirth and the loss of children, of "Seauen hundred Widdowes, wounded to the Hart, / With their sweet Babes, which they full dearly bought, / Some dead new borne, some neuer forth were brought" (sig. B3r, lines 164–67). The women then share their stories of loss during the plague. This community of women mourners is discussed in greater detail in chapter 3, but the centrality of the women's shared experience is surely reflective of Muggins's understanding of the bonds among women in the parish and the foundation of social life in his neighborhood.

DEBT IN THE POULTRY

In addition to the spiritual and personal bonds of the parish, Muggins's neighborhood, like all parishes in early modern England, was held together economically through a complex system of interdependent debts and credits. The sixteenth century saw a significant coin shortage. In fact, between 1540 and 1600, while population growth and an expanding economy led to an estimated 500 to 600 percent increase in the demand for coin, foreign trade deficits and military efforts in Ireland and the Low Countries meant that actual money in circulation had scarcely increased during those same years.[80] By the 1590s, then, networks of credit and debt were even more important than they had been in centuries past. Such networks were essential components of daily life, especially for those of the middling sort, like

Muggins and his neighbors.[81] At any given moment a member of the middling sort might be indebted to some neighbors while extending credit to others. Eventually individuals or groups of neighbors would have a reckoning in which debts and credits might be cancelled out, shifted, renegotiated, or paid off. Failure to make good on one's debts generally meant a loss of reputation in the credit system, while consistent paying of one's debts signaled an unusually solvent household and dependable neighbor.[82] Because of the harsh treatment of debtors by the law and the way credit and debt relations overlaid spiritual and personal relations, neighbors were reluctant to take one another to court over unpaid debts; however, beginning in the 1580s, the number of such cases steadily increased. In 1560 the King's Bench and Common Pleas saw 3,161 suits over debt; by 1606 that number had risen to 16,260.[83] The rate of increase in such suits far exceeded that of population growth. Lawsuits over outstanding debts naturally put a strain on social relations within parishes. While the parish continued to play a crucial role in the formation of local community, the increase in lawsuits posed a serious threat to the parish's social networks. The formal credit system's obligatory bonds threatened the largely voluntary social bonds of the parish.

So prevalent was the early modern preoccupation with credit and debt that Sorocold among many others preferred the translation of the fifth petition of the Lord's Prayer as not "forgive us our trespasses," but rather "forgive us our debts, as we forgive our debtors."[84] Sorocold explicated the phrasing thus:

And forgiue vs our debts	$\left\{\vphantom{\begin{array}{c}a\\a\\a\end{array}}\right.$	Whereby thou are dishonoured. Our Neighbour wronged, or, Our selues indangered.
As we forgiue our debtors.	$\left\{\vphantom{\begin{array}{c}a\\a\\a\end{array}}\right.$	That haue hurt vs in our bodies, Hindred vs in our goods. Wronged vs in our good Name.[85]

While the lines might be extended to sin as a metaphoric debt to God, Sorocold's focus on harm to body, property, and reputation rather than soul suggests that for him and many others, the fifth petition was very much about worldly debt. Sorocold emphasizes the wrong to neighbors stemming from outstanding debt, a sense that the bonds of credit might tear apart bonds of community among his parishioners. Londoners could see their anxieties about debt dramatized on the stage, too, in plays like Robert Wilson's *The Three Ladies of London* (1584), William Haughton's *Englishmen for My Money*, Robert Tailor's *The Hog Hath Lost His Pearl* (1613), and Shakespeare's *The Merchant of Venice* (1598).[86] Debt was on people's minds in early modern England.

Most economic transactions involved credit, usually of an informal or semiformal sort. Idealistically put in one of his sermons, Edwin Sandys declared, "Euerie man is to his neighbor a debtor not onely of that which himself boroweth, but of whatsoeuer his neighboour needeth, a debtor not oneley to pay that he oweth, but also to lende that he hath and may conueniently spare."[87] Neighbors were more shrewd and practical than Sandys would have them be, however. Agreements were struck orally, generally before trusted neighbors or friends who served as witnesses.[88] The system relied on individuals knowing one another. One needed to have a fairly thorough knowledge of how much credit might be reasonably extended to any given neighbor—or, in other words, how much one could trust a fellow parishioner to repay debts.[89]

Seating arrangements in the parish church likely facilitated such knowledge. Most churchwardens separated the congregation by gender, with women on one side and men on the other, and they further ordered the seating by social standing with the wealthiest, most prominent parishioners seated in the front and the poorest in the back.[90] During Muggins's time in the Poultry, the front of the church would be occupied by the few gentlemen in the parish and the wealthiest of the middling sort, men like grocer Robert Tudnam (who had been warden of his company in 1593), upholder (upholsterer) John Hodgson, haberdasher Richard Rudde, vintner William Crosse, and merchant Robert Nicholson. Behind them one would find grocer Daniel Winche and skinner Richard Ware. Crowche and Kirby sat somewhere behind these men in a crowd of prosperous but not spectacularly wealthy men: goldsmith Alexander Coxe, skinners William Singleton and Richard Iken, grocer William Besse, and others.[91] It is from this well-to-do group that St. Mildred's drew its churchwardens, including Hodgson, Singleton, Cowche, Coxe, and Iken.[92] Toward the back sat William King, William Muggins, and many others on the lower end of the middling sort. Every gathering at church, then, provided a ritualized *tableau vivant* of the neighborhood's most and least credit worthy. Less formal methods—casual observation, direct inquiries, and gossip—further informed what

Alexandra Shepard has described as the early modern neighborhood's "calculus of esteem."[93]

Whereas this largely informal system of credit counted on trust, interdependence, and knowledge about the individual's reputation, moneylenders, pawnbrokers, and an increasingly less trustful number of wealthy neighbors relied on contracts to ensure a profit for letting their money out for use. They used bills of exchange, bonds, or mortgages.[94] Usurious interest had been illegal and stigmatized, but beginning in 1571 the state approved an interest rate of not more than 10 percent. In practice the rates could be much higher; a moneylender might factor in an additional fee for the loan itself or establish a nearly inescapable penalty.[95] Unlike the neighborly, oral system, this more formal and impersonal system of credit tended to utilize the courts, where the penalties for unpaid debt were severe: the state would seize all of the debtor's property until a sufficient amount of goods had been auctioned off to repay the debt as well as the expenses of the court (generally a nominal stipend to the panel of men compiling an inventory of the debtor's goods). Meanwhile, the debtor would be held in prison until the debts were cancelled: the debtor was paradoxically prevented from earning until the debt was paid in full.[96] The penalties were such that often simply starting the lawsuit was enough to encourage debtors to find the means to pay their creditors. Whereas few had been willing to so devastate their neighbors earlier in the century, the scarcity of coin and the increased reliance on moneylending further and further outside of one's immediate neighborhood contributed to the rise of lawsuits over unpaid debt.

Lawsuits over debt might involve either the formal and impersonal debt or the more informal oral contracts. The difference between these systems of credit are caricatured in *The Merchant of Venice*, with one character who "lends out money gratis" and the other demanding a "pound of flesh" as the penalty for an unpaid debt. Antonio enters as a perpetual font of coin and credit for Bassanio, and their relationship appears more like that of lovers than of creditor and debtor.[97] A temporary lack of coin leads Antonio and Bassanio to Shylock, whose practices are characterized as utterly alien. Even the language of impersonal loans is rendered foreign to Bassanio, as Shylock finds himself needing to explain the meaning of the phrase "Antonio is a good man" as referring not to Antonio's moral but rather his economic worth. Of course, like Shylock, Shakespeare's own society conflated moral and financial standing. In addition to status, trustworthiness, integrity, honesty, generosity, and ultimately sociability itself were caught up with ideas of real or imagined wealth.[98] Thus, while the final sentence leveled on Shylock—that he convert to Christianity—may have felt vindicating to the many debtors in the audience, it also served as an uncanny reminder that most debtors were undone not by foreigners but by their fellow churchgoing Englishmen. The English system may not have called for a slicing away of human flesh for outstanding debts, but debtors' prison was still very much an attack on the debtor's body.[99]

The prevalence of day-to-day debts that made up the bulk of transactions throughout early modern English society is evident in wills from the period. Nearly all wills included a vaguely worded clause regarding the payment of any outstanding debts before itemizing personal property, but occasionally wills included details about specific debts. The will of St. Mildred's grocer Thomas Childe, who died in January of 1598, displays how even a wealthy member of the middling sort could feel racked with anxiety about debt. Childe was part of the elite of the middling sort, a liveryman and sometime clerk of his company.[100] Childe had substantial land holdings in Worcester, where he was born, as well as a valuable strip of land in Surrey along the Thames. Among various other items, Childe's will lists some £200 owed to him. Thomas Childe was no doubt one of the privileged men who sat near the front of St. Mildred's Church. His reputation was such that in 1596 and 1597 he served as churchwarden.[101] Despite all this, in his will Childe frets over a potential lawsuit that might be brought against his executor. Childe explains, "I stood charged for the debtes of my cozin Haywarde to divers personnes above the summe of three hundred poundes."[102] Childe and his cousin needed money immediately, so they took out a loan from one Hugh Morrall, a prosperous London merchant free of the Company of Clothworkers, but also evidently an occasional moneylender.[103] As security for the loan, Hayward delivered to "the saide Morrall clothes and other things which amounted to a farre greater summe" than they would borrow. Childe describes "the hardnes of the saide Morrall," for Morrall further insisted that Childe "enter into absolute bondes for the repayment of the same which I was forced for want of monie to doe." Childe felt "forced." He was, as he puts it, "driven to seale the same." There is something of a desperate, confessional quality to this section of Childe's will, a frustrated shame, and a deep concern that his executor might be charged for the outstanding debt despite his cousin's best attempt to settle the matter. Childe appeals to "all conscience and equitie" in the hopes that Morrall might settle the matter without taking Childe's executor to court. Such a suit might lead to the imprisonment of Childe's executor and compromise the creditworthiness of Childe's wife. As he neared death, anxiety about debt gripped Childe's imagination. Even the very wealthy of the parish were vulnerable to the scarcity of coin. Indeed, two years later, Robert Nicholson, arguably the richest merchant in the Poultry, was imprisoned for debt for which he ultimately declared bankruptcy.[104]

If the wealthy could find themselves subject to devastating debt, the less well-to-do of the middling sort were even more susceptible to what Childe called the "hardnes" of moneylenders. Muggins's stay in prison in the summer of 1595, although not for debt, may have compromised his reputation in his parish's ranking of creditworthiness. Muggins had already counted himself among the "distressed weavers" of the city, so his family probably had to pawn items to get the cash to pay for the stay in prison. This, of course, nearly coincided with the birth of Anne Muggins, another mouth to feed, and a temporary reduction in the mother's contribution to household income during the period of lying in. The celebrations around christening and churching also incurred additional expenses. If Muggins's stay in Newgate diminished his standing in the community, his access to credit would be further limited. Increased consumption, decreased production, and less access to credit—the household economy of members of the middling sort was fragile; a minor change in circumstances could lead to destitution. What appeared to Muggins as distressing in the summer of 1595, however, quickly led to much worse in the fall.

At some point in 1594 or 1595, Muggins, like Childe and so many others in London, had need of actual money. This may have been required to secure his lease in the Poultry, to pay off mounting debts, or for some other unknown reason: unlike Childe, Muggins did not leave a will detailing the circumstances of his liabilities. What is known is that at some point he reached out to Humphrey Milward, a vintner from St. Christopher Le Stocks, a parish just east of the Poultry.[105] Milward was a prominent citizen, owner of the Red Lion, the defunct theater in the area of Whitechapel and Stepney.[106] Whereas Childe worried about the representation of his outstanding debts, Milward's 1608 will focuses on making a magnificent show at his funeral with payment for a sermon to be preached, purchases of mourning gowns and cloaks for family and friends as well as gowns for ten poor men, the dispersal of money to the poor who attend his funeral, bread for the children at Christ's Hospital on the day of the service, numerous rings "in my remembraunce," and assurances that alderman and sometime mayor Sir John Spencer would attend.[107] Milward lived near enough to Muggins to be a part of the informal credit system of the neighborhood; however, despite his significant wealth, he was reluctant to loan the money outright. Instead he referred Muggins to his cousin, George Maunsell, a fishmonger living in St. Magnus parish near London Bridge.[108]

Maunsell was even wealthier than Milward, with property holdings in Southwark, Berkshire, and Shropshire. Maunsell counted Milward as his closest friend: while Maunsell's 1596 will leaves modest gifts to several friends and family members, he bequeathed forty pounds and his "best gowne and a cloake" to Humphrey Milward, whom he described as "my verie loveinge frende and cosen."[109] Only Maunsell's wife received a greater portion of Maunsell's wealth. And Milward along with Maunsell's brother Robert were entrusted to help Maunsell's wife with executing the will. Maunsell and Milward together provided the loan to Muggins, and Muggins was to pay them fifty pounds on All Saints' Day—November 1, 1595, just a few weeks after Muggins's wife's churching.[110] The specified day of repayment suggests that the loan was not a bond but rather a bill obligatory—Muggins probably borrowed much less, as the penalty for nonpayment of such bills by the deadline was often equal to the amount borrowed.[111] Predictably, Muggins was unable to repay the loan—even if he had sold more goods than in previous years, the shortage of coin virtually guaranteed that only extraordinary measures would enable him to cancel the debt. Maunsell and Milward, perhaps concerned about repayment following news of Muggins's arrest over the summer, appeared at the Common Bench to demand repayment before Chief Justice Edmund Anderson. Anderson ordered that Muggins be arrested and held in debtors' prison until Maunsell and Milward were paid in full. He then arranged for a panel of "p[ro]bor[um] & leg[alium] ho[m]i[nu]m," "honest & law-worthy men," to compile an inventory of all of Muggins's goods.[112]

The composition of the panel dramatizes the tensions between the more informal neighborly credit system founded on trust and the impersonal credit system reliant on bonds and the bench. Nine of the men—David Floud, Roger Walrond, Ralph Betts, Richard Horne, Richard Morris, James Leather, Valentine Mercer, John Allen, and John Butler—hailed from St.

Stephen's, Coleman Street; two more men—John Symondes and Edward Gassley—were from the neighboring parish of St. Margaret, Lothbury.[113] Both parishes were wealthier on the whole than St. Mildred's. A twelfth man, saddler Thomas Dunwell, was a parishioner of St. Botolph's, Bishopsgate, considerably farther away from the Poultry than Coleman Street or Lothbury.[114] Dunwell may have been selected because of his experience—his name appears on a number of such panels, and it is possible that he then served as a kind of foreman, ensuring an orderly inventory of Muggins's goods.[115] Some of the men had served as churchwardens in their respective parishes, and nearly all of them would soon be rated wealthy enough to be required to pay the lay subsidy. They were, as Anderson had requested, well-respected men; indeed, the previous year Roger Walrond had been made London marshal along with two other men.[116] Despite their reputations, Maunsell must have been distrustful that so many of the men lived near the Poultry and might therefore be friends or acquaintances of Muggins. Although typically such panels were made up of just twelve citizens, Anderson added a thirteenth member, Simon Houghton, a mercer from Maunsell's own parish.[117] Presumably Houghton was there to look after Maunsell's interests.

And so sometime in early November, the thirteen men made their way to Conyhope Lane to knock on the door of the Muggins household. The men worked through the inventory of the household, appraising each item: six dozen silk points, several pounds of silk of various colors, thread, thimbles, ribbons, lace, velvet gloves—the things one expects in the household of a silk-weaver. Work in progress was evident as well: some "grene Checkerd Ribbyn" was found on one loom, and one pound of "silke coloryd greene in another loome to make greene curreld lace." Further in the men tabulated the household stuff: some pewter, a brass pot, a spice mortar, a frying pan, a table with six stools provided a space where the members of the household ate meals. There were also several beds ranging from a more luxurious featherbed to three humbler flock beds, and one straw bed.[118] The Muggins household included the silk-weaver himself, his wife, their two children, and by this time probably two or three apprentices.

The jurors' arrival, the prying into each corner, the financial doom the inventory seemed to presage all must have mortified the Muggins household. Still but a baby, Anne Muggins would have only sensed the turmoil in the household. Others had more precise anxieties. The apprentices would worry about their fates: In the short term, would they eat that night? In the long term, would they be able to complete their apprenticeships? Would they need to be transferred to a different master? Was crushing debt a glimpse of their own fates once they completed their apprenticeships? Elizabeth Muggins probably worried that her father would once again be imprisoned, that her family would continue to spiral into destitution. Muggins's wife no doubt shared these concerns, but with a broader sense of the family's finances as she necessarily focused on the infant Anne rather than the household's production and sale of goods. A helpless panic probably hovered in the air.

The panel of men compiling the inventory of Muggins's goods assessed the total worth at £179 5s. 5d., with the remainder of the lease on the household worth twenty pounds. While most of the items in the inventory were worth less than a pound, some held significant value: one batch of silk was valued at thirty-nine pounds, and a large batch of satin was thought to be worth some forty-eight pounds. Muggins's household was productive, and this was why Maunsell and Milward were ready to give him a loan, but Muggins was evidently not able to sell his goods quickly enough to repay the loan in coin. Even if Muggins could have sold the more substantial amounts of silk and satin, London's reliance on a credit system, combined with the lack of coin circulating in the economy, virtually ensured that Muggins would be unable to get the money needed to repay his debt. Instead, some of his goods were auctioned off by the state to pay for the debt as well as fees to the panel compiling the inventory and to the two sheriffs involved, merchant taylor Leonard Halliday and haberdasher Thomas Lowe (both of whom would go on to be lord mayors of London).[119]

Plate, pewter, and other household objects found in Muggins's household were not mere creature comforts. Material possessions were a form of savings in an era when coin was hard to come by. Unlike coin, goods were not devalued by inflation, and pewter and brass objects did not generally depreciate.[120] If needed, a selection of goods could be quickly converted to coin by a pawnbroker. And such objects stood as visible markers of one's creditworthiness in the neighborhood. The loss of more than fifty pounds in goods struck a significant blow to Muggins's household. They were left with not only fewer things, but only the most fragile of safety nets: there was very little left to pawn should times get harder still.

Although *London's Mourning Garment* was primarily about the spiritual and economic crisis surrounding the plague of 1603, it also recalls the poignancy of Muggins's problems with debt in the mid-1590s. After the poem's personified London listens to the laments of mothers bereft of children and of widows who have lost all, she overhears a family trying to make ends meet:

> The Wife doth weepe, the needy seruantes play,
> The Children cry for foode where none is bought:
> The Father saith, I cannot sell to day,
> One jot of worke, that all of vs haue wrought;
> In euery shoppe, I haue for money sought.
>   And can take none, our hunger to sustaine,
>   Teares part from him, the Children cry amaine. (sig. D1r, lines 554–60)

The focus of the stanza is on a basic necessity: food. The household's collective efforts (the work "that *all of vs* haue wrought") come up short as the father can find no buyers for the household's wares. Studies of the middling sort frequently focus on upward mobility, the merchant class whose wealth at times surpassed that of the nobility; these stanzas emphasize the fragile position of the middling sort, that most were in some degree of debt and in constant danger of slipping into abject poverty. One slight change in the household's economy—a new mouth to feed, a death, or economic slowdown due to plague—could plummet the family's finances.[121] With no way to get food, this first stanza about the impoverished family begins and ends with weeping.

London's Mourning Garment's devotes three more stanzas to the family in crisis. The weeping that began with the wife spreads to the father, and then the children with the intensifier "amaine." In the next stanzas the family discusses the only solution available given the household's meager resources:

> What shall we doe? a counsell straight they take,
> Meate must be had, our people must not starue,
> Wife, take such thinges, & goe without A LOATE,
> In HOWNDES DITCH, pawne them, our great neede to serue,
> They wil make sure, if that a day we swarue;
>   All will be lost, our garments are their owne,
>   Though for a pound we giue a shilling lone. (sig. D1r, lines 561–67)

When all else failed, one could go to London's pawnbrokers. The stanza illustrates the idea of domestic items—"such things" as brass, linen, and tapestries as a kind of savings—at hand for pawning when needed. Although pawning goods was common throughout the city, Houndsditch, just north of the city's walls, was a street notorious for its pawnbrokers, especially those who were willing to deal in used clothing. According to Stow, the street was so named because the stretch of land had at one time been a ditch for "filth (conveyed forth of the Citie) especially dead dogs."[122] That the brokers were willing to exploit the poor out of such basic needs as clothing suggested other sources for the name, however. The water-poet John Taylor asserted instead that the street was named for the inhumane brokers themselves:

> *Was Houndsditch Houndsditch calld can any tell,*
> *Before the Broakers that street did dwell?*
> *No sure it was not, it hath got that name*
> *From them, and since the Time they thither came:*
>   *And well it now may be called Houndsditch,*
> *For there are Hounds will giue vengeance twitch:*
> *These are the Gulphes, that swallow all by lending*
> *Like my old shoes, quite past all hope of mending.*[123]

For Taylor the street was occupied by pawnbrokers who were more like vicious dogs in human form (not unlike the jailer in Hutton's *The Black Dogge of Newgate*), and the ditch was really a massive, unfathomable gulf into which debtors' goods were easily lost. Along similar lines, in the late Jacobean play *A Match at Mid-Night* (1622), William Rowley named his family of Houndsditch pawnbrokers the Bloodhounds.[124] Clergyman Donald Lupton builds on this notion, providing a false etymology for the brokers as "Broke Currs" because "most of them were broke before they set vp, & Currs for biting so sore euer since they set vp."[125] *The Merchant of Venice* channels this antipathy onto Shylock, who is repeatedly insulted with the word "dog" and "cur," the latter invective providing the moneylender with a pun as he refers to Antonio's epithets as "these curtesies."[126] The alleged viciousness of the pawnbrokers and the usurers with whom they were associated was a common trope in early modern London. In the plague pamphlet *A Rod for Run-Awayes* (1625) Thomas Dekker (himself imprisoned in the Poultry Compter for debt in 1599) appears to relish the story of a tanner who, during the plague, refused to provide shelter to his own brother for being a Houndsditch broker. If one wonders what family might be left to the brokers, in Jonson's *Everyman in His Humor*, Brayne-worme describes a Houndsditch broker as "one of the deuil's neere kinsmen."[127]

Muggins lingers on the distraught state of the family in debt and the economic system that seemed designed to keep them in poverty. The father laments:

> Besides the Bill a powling groat will cost,
> And euery Moneth our pawne must be renew'd,
> So was my Lease to griping vsurie lost,
> The first beginner of my sorrowes brew'd,
> And euer since want vpon want insew'd.
>   My bedding forfeite for a thing of nought,
>   My brasse and Pewter, want of conscience bought. (sig. D1r, lines 568–74)

The use of the phrase "powling groat" here suggests an extortionate fee for the drafting of the loan.[128] The mere acquisition of a bond or bill obligatory cost the debtor money she or he did not have, introducing a new need for money in addition to the needs that prompted the loan in the first place. The crisis for Muggins's family in debt goes well beyond the specific instance of plague—poverty appears in the poem as an effect of the system itself: one must pay up front for the bill, and pay again and again to renew the pawn until one can no longer afford to do so, resulting in the forfeiture of the goods pawned. The downward spiral is described thoroughly by former Poultry resident Anthony Munday in his additions to Stow's *Survey of London*:

> These men, or rather monsters in the shape of men, professe to liue by lending, and yet will lend nothing but upon pawns; neither to any, but unto poore people onely, and for no lesse gaine, then after fifty or threescore pounds in the hundred. The pawne of the poore borrower, must needs be more than double worth the money lent upon it, and the time of limitation is no longer than a moneth: albeit they well know, that the money needs not be repayed backe, untill a tweluemoneths end. By which time, the interest growes to be so great, that the pawne, which (at the first) was better than

twice worth the money borrowed on it, doth not (in the end) prove to be valuable to the debt, which must be payed, before the poore party can redeeme it. By which extorting meanes of proceeding, the poore borrower is quite cheated of his pawne, and for lesse then the third part, which it was truly worth indeed.[129]

Munday—who had begun an apprenticeship in 1576 under John Allde at the Longshop in the Poultry and went on to reside in Thomas Deloney's neighborhood of St. Giles, Cripplegate—shares Muggins's view of pawnbrokers: the need for coin was so great that the poor were often compelled (or as Childe put it, "forced" or "driven") to part with their goods at a far lower than reasonable rate. Muggins and Munday similarly agree that the pawnbroker's use of money as a commodity in and of itself amounted to a kind of extortion. And Munday echoes the various etymologies for Houndsditch in asserting that the brokers were merely "monsters in the shape of men."

Muggins, however, moves beyond the isolated instance of unequal exchange to present the system of impersonal credit over the long term as one that puts the poor into an inextricable cycle of debt, losing one thing after another until they have nothing left to pawn but the clothes on their backs. Just as the previous stanza had been organized around weeping, so this stanza is structured by "want," or lack, beginning with the lack of funds to procure the bill and ending with "want of conscience" on the part of the lender. Each lack requires yet another run through the cycle of impersonal credit gradually siphoning off goods until "want vpon want," debt heaped on debt, leads to a forfeit of one's possessions and shelter. The stanza ends with a brief list of items (bedding, pewter, and brass) lost to "want of conscience" and "griping vsurie," epithets for the system of impersonal credit that devastated so many. "Griping" especially emphasizes the brokers grasping for pawned items as well as the relentless clutch that brokers had on the debtors themselves. For Muggins, lack of conscience is the defining feature of the impersonal system of credit—the usurer or pawnbroker necessarily operates outside considerations of impact on the individual or the neighborhood. That is, the Houndsditch broker was not a part of the moral economy of the parish, where self-interest was generally tempered by a sense of communal obligations and reciprocity among neighbors.[130] Linked to other stanzas on callous indifference, *London's Mourning Garment* suggests that the impersonal system of credit's lack of conscience is at the root of its voracious appetite for the goods of the poor. It is as if usury is always waiting for the slightest opportunity to lay hold of bedding, brass, and persons in a vain effort fill a lack of conscience that is paradoxically expanded with each new acquisition.

Houndsditch brokers were especially reviled for their willingness to accept clothing for pawn. Clothes were a significant sign of status, and those who pawned them were generally thought to be so poor as to have no other goods left to exchange.[131] At least one commentary on the 1563 Statute of Artificers warned against dismissing a servant before his term had been completed because he was likely to sell his clothes to survive, "and beinge once oute of apparell, fewe will after take him into service, and so he becometh a Rogge or a vagabound."[132] Charity rather than predatory loans was the appropriate response to those in such a desperate state of poverty. Still, if Philip Henslowe's diary is any indication, the pawning of clothes was not uncommon. The majority of his loans used clothing as a surety. And Henslowe's diary similarly reveals that Muggins's allusion to the wife being sent to arrange the pawn was not unusual either.[133] What makes the case of Muggins's family in debt so desperate is that the taking of the loan is to provide for subsistence living without any sense that the market will change so that the loan can be repaid. Thus, as Muggins's family in debt assesses its situation, the father declares:

> If now our clothes which clad out naked skinne,
> Should thus be lost, as was our other good,
> Alas, (poore Wife) what case are we then in,
> Such shamefast Beggers neuer asked food.
> If honest labour could this griefe withstood,
>   We would haue reckoned day and night as one
>   To worke for meate, rather then make such mone. (sig. D1r, lines 575–81)

In this, the final stanza of the family in debt, the father confronts the cycle of impersonal credit amid the economic crisis of the plague as it threatens to strip the family of clothing, reducing them all to begging. The stanza thus points to a central problem in London: families and individuals were willing and able to work, but the economy seemed to be designed to render them all vagrants.

Muggins's use of the word "reckoned" in this stanza is especially apt. The household would work nonstop, reckoning or considering "day and night as one" to make ends meet. But "reckon" also recalls accounting and the cancellation of debts, the theme of this sequence in *London's Mourning Garment*. The family would work constantly to meet its financial obligations, to cancel debts, if only labor translated to actual coin. But the immediate circumstances of the plague along with the long-term problems of impersonal credit made labor futile. This, then, is the motive for Muggins's demand "That each man may, with labour earn his foode" (sig. D1v, line 616), discussed in chapter 1.

The Muggins household had its allies, however. Their proximity to the Poultry Compter ensured that Muggins's neighbors were all too familiar with the suffering of debtors. Many in the Poultry could identify with Philip Stubbes's remarks on the plight of debtors in prison: "Beleeue mee, it greeueth mee to heare (walking in the streats) the pitiful cryes, and miserable complaints of poore prisoners in durance for debt, and like so to continue all their life, destitute of libertie, meat, drink, (though of the meanest sorte) and clothing to their backs, lying in filthie strawe, and lothsome dung, wursse then anie Dogge, voide of all charitable consolation, and brotherly comfort in this World, wishing and thyrsting after death, to let them at libertie, and loose them from their shackles, giues and yron bands."[134] So moved by the suffering of imprisoned debtors, Stubbes, addressing ruthless moneylenders, declares, "The very stones of the prison walles shall rise up against thee, and condemne thee for thy crueltie."[135] Fellow parishioners Childe and Robertson knew or would soon know what it was like to be unable to repay a substantial debt. Did Muggins's other neighbors feel the same? Like Stubbes, they had at least heard "the pitiful cryes" of the Poultry Compter's prisoners, and many had experienced inescapable penalties for debt themselves. A few years later, in 1601, a libel containing "very odious and seditious matter" was posted at the Poultry Compter and Newgate. Although the contents of the libel have not been preserved, the locations where the libel was retrieved suggest that they were aimed at the conditions in the prisons. Tellingly, the libel in the Poultry was left up until a servant from the neighboring parish reported it to his master. It may be that the servant was the first to notice the libel, but it is also probable that people of the Poultry quietly approved of the complaint.[136]

Similarly, when Leonard Halliday and Thomas Lowe, the sheriffs tasked with arresting Muggins for his outstanding debt, inquired after the whereabouts of the silk-weaver, they were met with a wall of silence. The sheriffs' written response to Justice Anderson stated in the highly abbreviated Latin typical of such documents, "Quod Wills Movggings in pd bres noiatus laicus est & non est invent in ballia nra"—"That William Muggins is a layman and could not be found in our bailiwick."[137] Runaway debtors were common enough, but Muggins's whereabouts should have been easily discovered. The proceedings were completed in late November. Muggins's wife would have been churched just a few weeks earlier, and it is unlikely that she and the infant also went into hiding.

Records show that the family continued to live in the Poultry for another two years—Muggins had not vacated the neighborhood permanently, if at all. Muggins seems to have gone into temporary hiding, but many neighbors surely knew something about his whereabouts. When questioned by authorities, it seems that they refused to cooperate. They were unwilling to expose their neighbor to further incarceration and humiliation. The situation again illustrates the tension between the two systems of credit: in an attempt to enforce the impersonal bond drawn up by Maunsell and Milward, the sheriffs ran up against another, stronger bond, that of the neighborhood and its sense of what was just in enforcing the payment of debts. "Forgiue vs our debts as we would forgiue our debtors," they had heard their preacher expound upon, or perhaps they had taught him how to understand the line. In any case, Halliday and Lowe were turned away empty-handed. For the moment, the personal bonds of the parish triumphed over the impersonal bonds of credit and debt.

NEW LIFE IN THE PARISH

For the time being the Muggins household survived. Two years went by relatively quietly. Muggins's imprisonment in the summer and charges of unpaid debt in the fall of 1595 very likely demoted the household's standing in the neighborhood's system of credit, but the family evidently got by. On February 17, 1598, Muggins's wife gave birth to Henrie, which may have been a particularly difficult labor: whereas christenings typically occurred three to seven days after birth, this infant was not christened until February 26, a week and a half later.[138] Whatever the circumstances of the delay, the community once again came together to celebrate new life in the neighborhood. Mother and child's survival of a difficult labor helped the family focus for a while on life rather than debt, but soon living in the Poultry would prove untenable. The cost of renewing a lease, the inability to sell a volume of silk wares at a rate that would satisfy the needs of the growing household, and the neighborhood's doubts about the household's creditworthiness—all may have contributed to the decision to leave the Poultry.

It appears that the turmoil of 1595 proved too much for at least one member of the household. Thomas Stephenson, the recently arrived apprentice who had originally been working under goldsmith James Prince, soon changed masters again.[139] The precise timing and circumstances of Stephenson's changes of master are unclear, but it seems reasonable to suspect that watching Muggins—impoverished, imprisoned, and then in hiding—may have led the young man to draw on whatever resources he might have had to find a more stable household. He completed his apprenticeship under draper Lodowicke Rosser in 1602.[140] In the end, however, Stephenson does not seem to have been aiming at a life as a goldsmith, weaver, or draper. Although he regularly paid his quarterage to the Company of Drapers, he is listed in their records as a musician.[141] Around the time of Henrie's birth Muggins may already have begun working out the details of relocating to St. Olave's in Southwark. This, too, may have been the factor that led Stephenson to switch masters.[142] It is possible that Stephenson had been heard practicing his instrument in the household on Conyhope Lane, but by the time the family had relocated to Southwark, Stephenson had transferred his apprenticeship to Rosser. The Muggins family would have to make its own music.

Moving was common in the period, but not easy. Simply hauling what remained of the household goods—looms, bedding, chairs, painted cloths, and the remaining products of their labor—from the Poultry to St. Olave's in Southwark, a one-mile walk, would have taken considerable effort given that Muggins's wife would still be recovering from childbirth and tending to the newborn as well as the toddler Anne Muggins. Once they arrived in St. Olave's, the Muggins household would have to establish itself in a new neighborhood's system of informal credit, acquaint itself with a different parish church, and adapt to the rhythms and character of the parish and the local market. Although leases in St. Olave's were more affordable, the household would need to continue to guard against the ever-present danger of slipping into vagrancy at the slightest fluctuation in the economy. At the same time, the Muggins household would add apprentices and children—James,

William, Mary, and Robert Muggins were all born in St. Olave's parish. Their christenings would provide a significant ritual of integration into the church and the neighborhood. The parish would remain among the most significant social, economic, and spiritual structures in their lives.

CHAPTER 3

Grief and Grievance

Communal Elegy in St. Olave's Parish

> Weep Cloudy Suburbs, Widow'd Flood,
> Now Corn grows there where Troy once Stood.
> —ANONYMOUS (1680)

THE MOVE TO SOUTHWARK

Within months of Henrie Muggins's birth, the Muggins household moved from the Poultry to St. Olave's parish in Southwark. A suburb of London across the Thames River, St. Olave's was just east of London Bridge. Unlike St. Mildred's, St. Olave's was large and crowded. In 1603 the population of St. Olave's is estimated to have been 8,418, with another 7,123 in the neighboring parish of St. Saviour's.[1] Although the parish covered roughly 116 acres, much of that land was devoted to the open fields of Horseley Down and the Maze.[2] Households were thus clustered close together, so much so that many complained of failure to regulate the unauthorized construction of buildings in St. Olave's and other suburban parishes.[3] John Stow described the main streets of the parish as "hauing continuall building on both sides," with numerous makeshift alleys and lanes similarly packed with households.[4] The newly transplanted Muggins household was just one of some two thousand or so households in the parish.[5] If Muggins was fleeing a reputation as an agitator among weavers or an unreasonable credit risk in the Poultry, here he might find some anonymity.

The move was undoubtedly hard on the household. At a time when they had run low on resources, the household was abandoning whatever neighborhood support they might have built up over the years to help them with their newborn or to connect them to potential customers. Now they would begin again in a more densely populated, less comfortable parish. They would need to learn the ins and outs of the new neighborhood, adapt to a new church, find a place in the Southwark market, and fit themselves into the neighborhood's credit network.

St. Olave's parish in Southwark occupies this and the next chapter. Muggins and his wife had survived the plague ten years earlier, but little could prepare them for the devastation of the plague of 1603 as it decimated the crowded parish where they had made a new home. The parish's literary, theological, economic, and social world made it distinct from St. Mildred's. Whereas St. Mildred's included some extremely wealthy parishioners, St. Olave's was dominated by struggling craftsmen like Muggins himself. It was from St. Olave's that Muggins wrote his plague epic, with its focus on the poor and middling-sort men and women around him.

In particular, this chapter is dedicated to the personal experience of death and grieving. Between 1598 and 1603 Muggins buried three children and three apprentices at St. Olave's. Friends and neighbors also died during those years, especially during the plague. Like birth and baptism, death and burial were supposed to be communal events. Parishioners often joined family and friends in mourning, and during the plague complete strangers might join a funeral procession to prove their faith in God's protection by exposing themselves to infection despite plague orders that sought to keep funeral attendance to a minimum. Prominent citizens left epitaphs on funeral monuments for posterity in order to contemplate their own mortality. Poets channeled their grief into verse that mixed a belief in salvation with struggles to cope with loss. Like Muggins, Ben Jonson lost a child to the plague; his poem "On My First Sonne" expresses grief and anguish steeled by a stoic commitment to the consolations of the church.

For Muggins death was a matter of faith, but it was also a matter of material conditions. The table of the dead at the end of *London's Mourning Garment* made this clear—anyone familiar with London's parishes could see that while the plague might feed on rich and poor alike, it clearly preferred to glut itself on poorer parishes. With thousands dying within weeks, the cries of the lone mourner of many elegies seemed inadequate. Whereas poets like Ben Jonson dwelled on their private losses, *London's Mourning Garment* moves from the individual mourner to the communal losses of London's citizens, from isolation to collective action. Muggins thus filled his poem with those often excluded from political discourse, mourning women who cry for the dead while testifying to the miserable conditions of the poor. Southwark provided a setting for the tragedy; however, through a personified London and her chorus of women mourners, Muggins aimed at moving through grief and despair to address the ongoing suffering of the poor.

THE THEATERS

As the Muggins household established itself in St. Olave's, carpenter Peter Street was busy overseeing the building of the Globe Theater less than a mile away, near the already popular Rose and Swan theaters.[6] Many of the theater men lived in the various Southwark parishes, especially St. Saviour's. Philip Henslowe, owner of the Rose Theater, and his son-in-law, former lead actor of the Admiral's Men Edward Alleyn, were churchwardens at St. Saviour's.[7] Of the twenty-six actors named in Shakespeare's First Folio, exactly half lived in Southwark at one time or another.[8] William Shakespeare's brother, Edmund, was buried at St. Saviour's.[9] Southwark was likewise home to several actors from the Admiral's Men, not only Edward Alleyn but also his brother Richard, John Day, Thomas Downton, Edward Dutton, Edward Juby, Richard Juby, Robert Shaw, John Singer, and Thomas Towne.[10] And then there were Southwark residents like Robert Pallant and Martin Slater, whose careers spanned several acting companies.[11] Southwark would provide the stages for Shakespeare's *Hamlet, Julius Caesar,* and *Henry V*; Ben Jonson's *Everyman out of His Humour;* the anonymous *The London Prodigal;* and numerous other plays. In a study of John Resonable, a black silk-weaver in St. Olave's, Imtiaz Habib and Duncan Salkeld have drawn attention to the reliance of theaters on the silk industry, suggesting that there was significant commerce between the theaters and silk-weavers like Resonable—and, one might add, like Muggins.[12]

The Puritan leanings of most of the ministers of Southwark's parish churches, however, suggests that parishioners were generally cautioned against the trappings of the theater. In fact, Thomas Sutton, lecturer at St.

Saviour's and sometime preacher at the nearby St. Mary Overy's, routinely railed against the theaters. In print, he lamented that Londoners had continued to "flocke vnto such wanton Theatres, and there to spend their goods to no other purpose but to set their owne lusts on fire, to vphold schooles of lewdnesse and of sin, to maintain men of a corrupt life, and dissolute behauior in a calling no way warranted from God?"[13] Nathan Field, a member of the King's Men and parishioner of St. Saviour's, complained that Sutton had "bene of late pleased (and that many tymes) from the holy hill of Sion the pulpitt" to condemn actors.[14] Of course, Sutton's sermons on the evils of the theater presuppose that at least some in his congregation made the short walk to see plays or other entertainments, but there was clearly some institutional pressure to shun plays and players. It is unknown whether Muggins or any in his household enjoyed the nearby theaters, but they surely knew about such activities as Londoners made their way across London Bridge to see Richard Burbage or Robert Armin perform some of their most memorable roles.

Regardless of whether Muggins or any in his household attended the theater, a number of plays performed in Southwark must have piqued the silk-weaver's curiosity. In 1602 and 1603 the Rose Theater provided the stage for parts 1 and 2 of *The Blacke Dogge of Newgate*, plays evidently based on the pamphlet of the same name by Muggins's former cellmate.[15] And earlier, in 1599, Thomas Dekker's *The Shoemaker's Holiday*, based in part on Deloney's *The Gentle Craft*, was also performed at the Rose.[16] Around this time, Muggins must have gotten word that Deloney had died. There is no official extant record of Deloney's burial, but in 1600, comedian and Southwark resident William Kempe published his *Kemps Nine Daies Wonder*, featuring "Kemps humble request to the impudent generation of Ballad-makers and their coherents . . . to the tune of Thomas Delonies epitaph." Kempe complained that his antic journey from London to Norwich was being misrepresented by balladeers. "I was told," he explains, "it was the great ballet-maker T.D. alias Tho. Deloney, Chronicler of the memorable liues of the 6 yeomen of the west, Jack of Newbery, the Gentle-craft, & such like honest men: omitted by Stow, Hollinshed, Grafton, Hal, froysart, & the rest of the those wel deseruing writers: but I was giuen since to vnderstand, your late general Tho. dyed poorely, as ye all must do, and was honestly buried."[17] Even as he disparages the unknown author of the ballad in question, Kempe praises Deloney for championing honest craftsmen and merchants otherwise marginalized in

English chronicles. Muggins's own chronicle of the plague similarly sought to prioritize the marginalized—the countless dead and the destitute craftsmen, poor widows, and bereaved mothers who survived, people he was familiar with in the overpopulated parish of St. Olave's. Kempe's claim that Deloney died poor, "as ye all must do," would no doubt ring true with Muggins, who had struggled to stay out of abject poverty. The move to Southwark might improve finances; however, as Muggins knew, they could take a downward turn at the slightest change in the market.

STATUS AND THE ECONOMICS OF ST. OLAVE'S PARISH

Although St. Olave's had its prominent merchants, it primarily consisted of craftsmen like Muggins. Indeed, Muggins was part of a significant migration of craftsmen and poor laborers to Southwark at the end of the sixteenth and beginning of the seventeenth century. The proximity to the Thames was a draw for some trades—brewers, dyers, and woolworkers in St. Olave's and watermen for the most part in St. Saviour's to the west.[18] While the pages of St. Olave's parish register feature some grocers and fishmongers, not a page goes by without listing joiners, dyers, feltmakers, and a large number of individuals simply listed as "laborer," a growing class of working poor in and around London.[19] This latter category accounts for John Stow's impression that for the most part the parish was made up "of Aliens or Straungers, and poore people."[20] Southwark had long been host to a significant immigrant population; in fact, the guild of Saint Barbara at St. Olave's largely, if not exclusively, comprised strangers.[21] By Muggins's time in St. Olave's, the immigrant population was not any higher than that of the rest of London; however, because many attended St. Olave's rather than trek to the stranger churches in the center of the city, their presence was more immediately observable. In the capacious church of St. Olave's, Muggins would have encountered Dutch and French weavers in Southwark as fellow parishioners rather than harsh competitors. Indeed, Muggins may well have come to recognize a certain affinity with his Dutch and French counterparts. The cheap rent in Southwark attracted immigrants, poor laborers, and the roughly 30 percent of the parish who, like Muggins, struggled to make ends meet in the textile industry.[22]

Muggins thus found himself in competition with many of his fellow silk-weavers, but the large population and its notoriety for textiles meant more potential buyers, too. Southwark was a nexus for trade connecting London to Kent, Sussex, and the rest of Surrey.[23] In this context the Muggins household thrived. Whereas in previous years Muggins had counted himself among the "distressed," deep in debt and in danger of imprisonment, by the end of 1598 Muggins was one of the few parishioners in St. Olave's to be assessed as having sufficient wealth to be taxed in the lay subsidy, and this would hold true for years to come.[24] The lay subsidy was a periodic tax on an individual household's wealth and income.[25] The tax was carried out by local commissions, so while it was a state tax, assessment and collection were of local importance; the local commission would come to know the worth of each household, and that information might affect one's standing in neighbors' estimates of creditworthiness.[26]

Although the tax was a burden, to be a subsidy payer elevated one's status. Subsidy men made up only 13 percent of the parishioners in St. Olave's.[27] While local offices were held by a wide array of parishioners, payment of the subsidy was a significant qualification. Paying the subsidy made one eligible to serve on the parish's vestry (although in practice one had to be among the wealthiest of the subsidy payers).[28] When some sought to expand the number of vestrymen in the neighboring parish of St. Saviour's, where only the wealthiest of subsidy men held office, a survey of all subsidy men in the parish was implemented to assess the proposal's popularity.[29] That is, payment of the lay subsidy, while a hardship, also bought some local political influence—the opinion of subsidy payers like Muggins held importance at the level of the parish. Beyond the formal privileges afforded to subsidy men, Muggins enjoyed the enhanced credit and respect that came with the status of subsidy payer.

"FUNERALL TEARES"

Despite some financial success for the household, the move to Southwark was especially hard on Henrie Muggins, who was not yet one year old. Shortly after arriving in St. Olave's parish, Henrie—like roughly 25 percent of all children in early modern London under the age of ten—died.[30] He had fallen ill, or some accident had occurred—parish registers rarely listed the cause of death. He was buried at St. Olave's on October 9, 1598. Burial involved private and public rituals. In the household Henrie Muggins's body would need to be washed and laid out in repose. Household members likely stayed up all night to watch the body and to comfort one another. Friends and extended family would do their best to participate in the overnight vigil.[31] New neighbors may have made an appearance, as well. Like birth, death was a communal event in sixteenth-century parishes.

The household's formal introduction to the parish was a solemn one, then. Within a day or two of Henrie's death, the burial would occur. Henrie's body would be winded in a sheet, essentially swaddled as he had been after birth only a few months earlier. Soon after, Henrie's body was carried to the graveyard of St. Olave's parish where family, friends, and some neighbors met the parish priest, who, following the *Booke of Common Prayer*, would offer a number of theological consolations for the living: that life is short and "full of miserie"; that death is merely the end of "our uile body"; that the elect "shall not die for euer." There might have been some singing and a short lecture on the resurrection of the dead in Corinthians 15:26, that "the last enemie that shall be destroyed is death," lines that Donne would rework into Holy Sonnet 10.[32]

Describing funeral sermons, James Balmford, who around 1600 became one of St. Olave's ministers, cited Isaiah, Revelations, and Luke: "That as the wicked are reserued for a further mischief, so the righteous is taken away from the euill to come: besides, that he resteth in glorie from mo[re] and greater labors, then the wicked are commonly subjected to."[33] Death was thus framed as a mercy, an alleviation of the suffering of earthly life. The priest would end with a prayer thanking God "for that it hath pleased thee to deliuer this, Henrie Muggins, our brother out of the miseries of this sinfull world" and expressing the hope that God will hasten the apocalypse so "that wee with this our brother, and all other departed in the true faith of thy holy name, may haue our perfect consummation and blisse, both in body and soule in thy eternall and euerlasting glorie. Amen."[34]

The somewhat scripted nature of burial was in part an attempt to do away with lingering Catholic beliefs about death. The service, at least as prescribed in the *Booke of Common Prayer*, was significantly shorter than it had been in the fifteenth and early sixteenth centuries.[35] Prior to the Reformation, English funerals focused on the care of the soul of the deceased. In 1528, leather-seller and St. Olave's parishioner John Crowle arranged for his burial to be accompanied by "a prest to singe for my soule and the soules of my father and mother."[36] St. Olave's was a large church featuring four aisles, each with its own altar. Many pre-Reformation testators from St. Olave's included in their wills payment to the fraternities associated with the church's various altars—the fraternity of Saint Clement, Saint Anne, Saint Barbara, and Our Blessed Lady. Suppressed under Edward VI, these were medieval religious guilds dedicated to the maintenance of their respective altars, the care of the needy, and prayers for the souls of the deceased.[37] In 1504, skinner and St. Olave's parishioner John Skylborne willed payments to all four fraternities "that my soule may be praied for among the prayers of the brethren and sistren of the same."[38] The soul needed bells, singing, and prayers to help it on its journey.

Whereas previous generations had focused their resources on the well-being of the souls of the deceased, after the Reformation the focus was on the living. In 1561, for instance, St. Olave's parishioner Edward Vaughan's will asked that his wife arrange for his funeral to be conducted "withoute any pompe or any solemnitie savinge that I will she cause a sermon to be made at my burial by the w[h]iche the herers may be made to understand that they must passe the same passage that I have past before them and so to be edified by the same as after the hering thereof they may the better lerne to lyue and gouerne themselves in the feare and lawes of god duringe their lives."[39] Although the sermon would no doubt announce its own kind of muted pomp and solemnity, Vaughan's expressed purpose was for hearers to think on their own salvation rather than his. The emphasis of the funeral had shifted from saving the souls of the dead to caring for the souls of the living, creating a time for communal meditation on mortality and the comfort of the bereaved.

Payments for funerals had once been made for prayers to hurry the deceased's soul out of purgatory; now such payments were for the living—gifts, charity, and the maintenance of the parish church.[40] Church bells would still ring—they were objects of regular maintenance in the records of St. Olave's—but many priests emphasized that these were not of any benefit to the deceased's soul, that they should perhaps be limited to ringing out at the moment of dying.[41] As preacher Thomas Adams put it, "Now (though we be all seruants of one familie of God, yet) because of particular families on earth; and those so remoued, that one member cannot condole anothers griefe, that it feels not: *non dolet cor, quod non nouit*. The Bell, like a speedie Messenger, runnes from house to house, from eare to eare, on the soules errand, and begges the assistance of their Prayers" for the dying, not the dead.[42] Bells were no longer a sonic assist to the soul or defense against evil spirits; they were merely an efficient signal to the community.

Funeral services, then, were aimed at the living within a neighborhood—the "herers," as Edward Vaughan put it. Richard Hooker explained, "The end of Funeral duties is, first, to shew that love towards the party deceased, which Nature requireth; then to do him that honor which is fit both generally for man, and particularly for the quality of his person: Last of all, to testifie the care which the Church hath to comfort the living, and the hope which we all have concerning the Resurrection of the dead."[43] Honor for the dead, but ultimately care for the living. In all, this was very much the introduction of the Muggins household to its neighborhood. The transition to their new life in Southwark was marked with grief, lamenting a life cut short, a boyhood that would never be.

As in St. Mildred's in the Poultry, St. Olave's in Southwark featured a number of funeral monuments offering words as though from the dead themselves. On one wall was a prominent monument from around 1575, the image of a husband and wife kneeling and facing each other in devotional pose with two books before them. Beneath the image an inscription explains that these figures represent Helayne Maledge and her husband, Thomas Maledge, "cetyzen and a cutler free / And a wardyn of the same, so worthy thought to be." The epitaph begins, "To yow that lyffe posses great trobles do befalle / Where we that sleape by Deathe, do feele no harme at all." With no special acts to be carried out on behalf of the deceased's soul, the Maledges' epitaph simply asserts, "An honest Lyffe dothe bringe a joyfull Dethe at last."[44] A similar sentiment could be found on the east wall of the church, on the monumental brass for the wife of John Nycolls, Crystian Nycolls, who passed away in 1580:

> Tossy'd wyth Waves as a Ship on the Sea
> Wyth Sorrowes and Cares both nyght and Daye
> And weery I was of this Worlde thralle
> That lyved in Synne, as Men do all
> I harde the Lordes Voyce unto me saye
> Repent and come to me away.
> Then I consyderyd the Woorkes of Man
> After Dethe to be all vayne,
> I dyd repent all was amyss,
> Praysyng my God who made all hys.[45]

Like many of the monuments in the church, the epitaph emphasized that life was full of "Sorrowes and Cares," but that looked at from the perspective of the hereafter such toil appeared "all vayne." On nearly every wall and pillar in the church, the community of the parish's dead assured the living that life, not death, was the burden.[46] While this comforted some, the loss of a loved one was still difficult, another sorrow, another care that made daily living an even greater burden.

Parents were advised to moderate their mourning and to recall the theological consolations offered at burial.[47] In 1625, at the funeral sermon for the eldest daughter of Christopher Villiers, the earl of Anglesey (the earl of Buckingham's brother), preacher George Jay cited Saint Augustine: "I will allow that the floud-gates of your eyes may be open, but not too wide, nor too long; and I will give you leave to sigh from the bottom of your hearts, but not too often, nor too much." Put more bluntly, he surmised, "'tis stupiditie and dulnesse, not to lament at all; as the excesse is madnesse, the meane is safest, and will gaine you the opinion of a discreet, and well-tempered mourner."[48] Again, the focus was on the living: the bereaved parents could mourn their loss, but they also needed to be mindful of how others perceived them; they needed to perform moderation to "gaine . . . the opinion" of those around them.

G. W. Pigman charts a change in seventeenth-century English formularies away from purely consoling the bereaved out of mourning and toward grieving with the bereaved, offering condolences before insisting on consolation.[49] Despite this development, moderation was still the prevailing advice to mourners. By the end of the seventeenth century, Thomas Doolittle would devote a whole treatise to the issue of moderating sorrow, alleging, "If we sorrow not at all we are unworthy the name of men, because without the workings of those natural Affections in the Principle common to all men. If we sorrow with turbulent Passion, vexatious, fretting Grief, we sorrow as sinful men."[50] Doolittle and others encouraged mourners to convert their grief away from the deceased to a "godly sorrow" aimed at repentance and salvation for themselves.[51] Death was an occasion for individual introspection, while funeral rites involved the community in support of the living.

The death of a spouse or child was singled out as a particular challenge to moderate mourning. The period saw hundreds of epitaphs to dead children, often expressing a struggle between profound grief and the lessons of the church.[52] Five years after Henrie's burial, as the plague took young and old alike, Muggins would describe a succession of grieving mothers whose cries and gestures signal shock and sorrow that advice on moderation could not contain and that words could not immediately convey: one "cryeth loude and shrill, / Wringing her hands"; another wishes she had died as well, "Casting her handes, abroade, as shee were wood" (sigs. C1r–v, lines 281–82, 324). Presumably these were scenes familiar to Muggins in the wake of the plague, but they may also hark back to the anguish expressed in his household at Henrie's passing. In all, these descriptions remind us that advice is always prompted by contrary behavior—pamphlets and sermons encouraged moderation precisely because many people mourned intensely.

Despite their extreme grief, the Muggins family would strive to embrace the church's consolations and moderate their mourning to focus on making ends meet and ensuring the health of their other children. At the time of Henrie Muggins's burial, Muggins's wife was already pregnant with their next child, James Muggins, born in May 1599.[53] Another son, William, was baptized on January 11, 1601, but buried five days later, another occasion for sorrow, and one that makes sense of *London's Mourning Garment*'s description of the fragility of life at the moment of birth.[54] A daughter, Mary Muggins, was born in May 1602, and in the hot summer of 1603 Muggins's wife gave birth to Robert Muggins.[55] By 1603, but probably much earlier, the household also included the apprentices Henry Beste, Robert Redman, and Mary Black.[56]

Between 1598 and 1603, the Muggins household grew not only in size but also in status and notoriety. This is in part measured in Muggins's status as a subsidy man, but the parish register also suggests that Muggins was increasingly well-known in the community. When Henrie Muggins was buried, the parish clerk listed William Muggins as a "haberdasher."[57] The misattribution in 1598 is perhaps indicative of the parish clerk's confusion between the grief-stricken silk-weaver and his kinsman, James Muggins, a haberdasher from the London parish of St. Mary Magdalen, Old Fish Street.[58] James Muggins had lost four children between 1595 and 1598 and would offer in his mere presence at the funeral a sense of perseverance following such a loss.[59] James Muggins would later offer yet another link to the printer Ralph Blower. Both men were parishioners at the relatively small and tight-knit St. Mary Magdalen's.[60] William Muggins's next son was given the same first name as the haberdasher from St. Mary Magdalen's, and Muggins's daughter Mary Muggins was perhaps named for James Muggins's wife, Mary

Muggins (née Wrighte).[61] At any rate, when James Muggins was christened in 1599, William Muggins was known to the parish clerk as a "silkman," and by the time William and Mary were christened more precisely as a "silkweaver."[62] In 1603, when the parish clerk was overburdened with twenty to thirty plague burials a day, Muggins's occupation was shortened to simply "weaver."[63] Various and interchangeable occupational titles were indicative of the poorer sort in the parish, but the pattern here is of the parish clerk's increasing familiarity with the well-read silk-weaver William Muggins.[64]

PLAGUE COMES TO SOUTHWARK

Above all, for the Muggins household the years 1598 through 1603 were punctuated by death. Henrie Muggins was buried on October 9, 1598. Thomas Deloney died in 1599. The infant William Muggins died in 1601.[65] And then, in the summer of 1603, Southwark became notorious not for its theaters but for the plague. The plague of 1603 allegedly started in Southwark, and with its dense population the neighborhood was hit harder than most other areas of the city. One bill of mortality covering the eight-week span of July 14 through September 8 listed St. Olave's parish in Southwark as having buried 1,818 victims of the plague, more than seven hundred more burials than any other parish in and around the city.[66] Thomas Dekker joked that the plague was making parish clerks rich from the enormous number of burials, and that the sextons of "Saint Gyles, Saint Sepulchres, and Saint Olaues, ruled the roaste more hotly, than euer did the Triumuiri of Rome."[67] Dekker's macabre humor was a cover for the sorrow and pain that overwhelmed Londoners during the plague. In 1604, observing that crowded, poorer neighborhoods had been the hardest hit by the plague, physician Francis Herring wrote more somberly, "Remember the hideous and lamentable crie in Olives parish in Southwarke."[68] Those cries were all the more lamentable as plague orders limited the size and nature of funerals, and members of households where the plague had struck were prohibited from roaming freely. The degree to which parishioners might comfort one another in their losses was thus severely restricted.

More than most parishes, signs of loss surrounded the inhabitants of St. Olave's. As St. Olave's minister, James Balmford, put it in October of 1603, it was difficult for even the most godly to maintain the faith when he or she "heareth nothing but crying of wiues and children, mourning of husbands and parents, sorrowing of friends and kinfolke, and withal seeth the plague weekely to increase from tens to hundreds, from hundreds to thousands, and to draw nearer and nearer to himself, and that God in uisiting him may justly take hold of this feare."[69] Each week the death toll in St. Olave's rose: 98 plague victims were buried between July 14 and July 21. The next week the parish buried 143 of the plague, and the week after that 234. From August 4 through August 11, St. Olave's recorded 228 plague interments, a slight dip, but the parish buried an additional 124 individuals evidently not of the plague; the next week saw the highest number of burials for the parish for a single week—301.[70] The numbers verify Balmford's vision of parishioners terrorized as the plague took more and more people "nearer and nearer" to one's self.

Muggins's household must have experienced something like this in July and August 1603. In late July Thomas Deloney's son, also named Thomas, had been buried at St. Giles parish. The younger Deloney had been apprenticed to George Avery, a fellow weaver, who along with his five-year-old daughter had succumbed to the plague a week earlier.[71] Meanwhile, the church bells at St. Olave's tolled for the dead every evening. One heard about the losses. They were mentioned in church services and talked about on the streets. If the names of the deceased were unfamiliar at first, it would only be a matter of time before the names of acquaintances, friends, and neighbors joined the parish register's list of daily burials.

By August 29, the Muggins household was struck by the plague. The dread began several days earlier when Muggins's apprentice, Mary Black, began to show signs of the sickness. It is difficult to learn much about an early modern member of the poorer end of the middling sort who died so young, but Mary Black appears to have been just ten years old when she died.[72] As Muggins's London put it, "none dwelling in my Cittie / Should thinke themselues more safer then the rest" (sig. C3v, lines 449–50). Numerous preventatives were prescribed—wearing a bag of arsenic, burning various herbs, imbibing concoctions that included such ingredients as gun powder.[73] But still the plague would infect even the most cautious.

Mary Black was one of forty-eight burials in the parish on August 29, one of 270 plague burials in the parish for that week, but for the household her death was not simply a statistic or the loss of a laborer. She was a young person entrusted to the care of the household; Muggins and his wife would have been in charge of not only her vocational training, but her upbringing as well, offering her not just room and board but spiritual and moral guidance. The family ate and prayed with Mary Black. She was about the same age as Elizabeth Muggins. Now the Muggins household would be responsible for her burial with whatever family she had left kept far from the infected household.

Mary Black's death, moreover, meant that others in the household were in danger of soon following her to the grave. In accordance with the plague orders, the household would have to be under quarantine for six weeks after the last plague death in the house. If fleeing the plague was ever an option, it was no longer, and their home was probably not large enough for the well to adequately avoid the infirm.[74] In the heat of the summer, the surviving members of the household—William Muggins; his wife; their children, Elizabeth, Anne, James, Mary, and the newborn Robert; as well as two apprentices, Henry Beste and Robert Redman—found themselves confined to a dwelling where contact with the infected was almost inevitable.[75]

Fears must have run especially high regarding Muggins's wife, who had given birth to Robert Muggins just a week earlier. The lying-in that mothers went through may have supplied a sanctuary from infection for the mother, infant, and the other young children, but the traditional care visited on a new mother by neighbors and friends would have to stop immediately. The plague thus disrupted the mutual aid and communal feeling of the parish. That lack of care might in turn further endanger the infant and the mother. *London's Mourning Garment*'s new mother, discussed in chapter 2, pauses for a moment to speak of her fears for her newborn: "Shall Death haue thee, and lay thee in the grasse, / Ile rather goe, to Earth from whence I was" (sig. B4v, lines 256–57). She then addresses Death:

> Of this sweete Babe, which cost my life almost:
> I pray thee grimme Death, doe not him annoy,
> Goe get thee further, to some other Coast.
> To kill an Infant giues small cause of boast.
>   Theres many liuing, that would gladly dye,
>   Take them away, but spare my Childe and I. (sig. B4v, lines 261–66)

Having only recently escaped death during labor, the mother bargains that she might lay down her own life for that of her newborn's, or that Death might be ashamed to take the life of a defenseless infant, or that the personified plague might travel elsewhere, or that there might be other more willing victims. The stanza's rapid options offered to Death reflect the desperate mood of Londoners, quarantined or not, amid the plague.

The Muggins household could expect daily provisions brought to them, but not much else. In October 1603, as the plague decimated his congregation at St. Olave's, Balmford's *A Short Dialogue concerning the Plagves Infection* (1603) argued for strictly upholding the state's plague orders, including provisions for quarantining infected households and prohibitions against visiting the sick. Balmford asserted that the state's plague orders extended not from cruelty but rather "fatherly care." Following Isaiah 49:23, explained Balmford, "Kings and Queenes ought to be nurcing fathers and nurcing mothers to the Church," and that the orders to avoid the infected aimed at saving lives.[76] Dedicated to his own parishioners at St. Olave's, Balmford's pamphlet presents a conversation between a "professor" of the faith and a "preacher" (the mouthpiece for Balmford's views). That the preacher frequently addresses the professor as "neighbor" suggests that Balmford thought of his pamphlet as a conversation he might have with one of his own parishioners.

Balmford was in part countering Henoch Clapham's pamphlet *An Epistle Discoursing vpon the Present Pestilence* (1603), which reasoned that fear of infection, a sure sign of a lack of faith in God's protection, actually spread the plague.[77] Balmford's professor ventriloquizes Clapham's providential understanding of disease. The professor alleges, "If I go where the plague is a thousand times, I shall not die of the plague, if God haue not appointed me to dy thereof: and if he haue, I shall die thereof though I come not neare it by a thousand miles."[78] Balmford's preacher counters that just as "it is impossible to liue a yeare without meate and drinke, except God worke a miracle," so one ought to protect oneself against the plague by avoiding the infected.[79] One must have faith, but one must also take reasonable precautions against the plague—namely, avoiding the infected if at all possible. For individuals to do otherwise is "wantonly and vnnecessarily to put God to manifest his power and speciall prouidence in preseruing them from the Plague: therefore to runne into danger of the plague without necessary cause, as they do, who resort as boldly, &c. is a tempting of the Almighty."[80] Failing to avoid infection was for Balmford trifling with God's will, in essence demanding that God work miracles on behalf of the elect. Despite its focus on saving lives, *A Short Dialogue concerning the Plagves Infection* was not without controversy. One W. T. sneeringly responded to Balmford, "All your reason in your books laid downe for your opinion touching the Pestilence, fauours more of a natural feare, then a spirituall faith."[81]

Fearful or not, Balmford remained in Southwark even as weekly burials reached three hundred. Reflecting on the experience of quarantine, Balmford's professor complained, "They thinke it an hell to be so long shut vp from companie and their businesse: the neglecting whereof is the decay of their state."[82] The "hell" was more than isolation, boredom, and a decline in income, however. Muggins and his people necessarily relied on the system of poor relief provided by the plague orders, offering meager sustenance for such a large household, especially at the height of the plague—the plague deaths in the parish remained over two hundred per week until the second half of September, straining the system of relief. By the time Mary Black was buried, apprentice Robert Redman was surely showing signs of infection. By September 2 he, too, was dead. On September 8 Elizabeth Muggins, the eldest daughter of William Muggins, was listed in the burials for St. Olave's. And two days later, apprentice Henry Beste passed away. Each individual required care as their health waned. Each member of the household must have been gripped by fear about who would be next. A quarantined household was in effect sentenced to weeks of anguish in the face of the epidemic, weeks of helplessness as loved ones suffered and died.

Unable to leave the household, Muggins and his family no doubt prayed often. *The Booke of Common Prayer* included several short prayers on the plague, and as in previous years, the state required church attendance three times a week during the plague so that community members could recite additional prayers for deliverance.[83] After several weeks of attending church service, family members may well have memorized some of the prayers, a small comfort when they could no longer go to church.[84] Muggins's own prayer appended to *London's Mourning Garment* provides some clues to the emotional state in the household: "O LORD God Almightie, the Father of mercies and God of all consolation, we miserable distressed creatures, wounded with the multitude of our grieuous sins, repayre vnto thee (the Phisition of our soules) for Balme to cure our Sores. O Lord, we acknowledge and confesse our owne vnworthinesse: great is thy goodnesse towards vs, and great is our ingratitude towardes thee" (sig. D3r). The prayer frames its speakers as "miserable distressed creatures" (with a faint echo of Muggins's 1595 petition). There is a sense of desperate submission in the prayer: it did not really matter if the family had been pious in its devotion; they must confess a "multitude of grieuous sins"—original sin, individual moments of pride, as well as lapses in charity—but the prayer takes on the faults of others, the sins of the city, and Londoners' pursuit of wealth and pleasure in the face of poverty and suffering. As Melissa Smith argues, Muggins's prayer depicts all Londoners as "implicated in the spectacle that displeases God."[85] In his prayer Muggins explains, "Often times while one prayeth in the bitternesse and anguish of his spirit, another blasphemeth in the pride and presumption of his heart. Heare one groueleth on ye ground, gasping & gaping after life, there another walloweth in the sincke of sin, and puddle of iniquitie" (sigs. D3v–D4r). One Londoner basks in pride, avarice, and concupiscence; another writhes in pain rendered audible in Muggins's guttural alliteration and possible pun on here/hear.[86] Indeed, the "here" of Muggins's prayer emphasizes how very near death each member of his household was. For weeks in the summer of 1603, Muggins and his family could not escape the sound of those desperate gasps for life, the pain and sorrow of losing those closest to them.

ELEGY

While *London's Mourning Garment* is both contemporary chronicle and plague epic, it also owes a great deal to funeral elegy, as its complete title attests: *London's Mourning Garment, or Funerall Teares: Worne and Shed for the Death of Her Wealthy Cittizens, and Other Her Inhabitants.* Funeral elegies allowed for expression that had been curtailed in Protestant funeral rites and even more severely limited by the plague orders.[87] Elegies—and even epigrams in an elegiac mode—afforded an opportunity to linger on honoring the dead, publicly bemoaning their loss, and thereby reconciling oneself to the living. Where moderation was advocated, elegies opened up a space for indulging in a broader range of emotional responses to death—elegies and funeral epigrams commemorate the dead while registering moments of guilt, anger, remorse, and despair as well as love and faith.[88]

Even Ben Jonson's famously stoic "On My First Sonne," with its attempt to contain parental grief within the genre of the epigram, nevertheless displays a range of emotions. Jonson's seven-year-old son died during the plague of 1603 while the poet was visiting William Camden and Robert Cotton in Huntingdonshire.[89] Matthew Greenfield argues that the poem is largely a "refusal to mourn," a funerary poem that resists lamentation, but underlying the measured diction of the poem is a tumult of conflicting emotions.⁹⁰ Jonson writes:

> Farewell, thou child of my right hand, and joy;
>   My sinne was too much hope of thee, lou'd boy,
> Seuen yeeres tho'wert lent to me, and I thee pay,
>   Exacted by thy fate, on the just day.
> O, I could loose all father, now. For why
>   Will man lament the state he should enuie?
> To haue so soone scap'd worlds, and fleshes rage,
>   And, if no other miserie, yet age?
> Rest in soft peace, and, ask'd say here doth lye
>   BEN. JONSON his best piece of *poetrie*.
> For whose sake, hence-forth, all his vowes be such,
>   As what he loues may neuer like too much.⁹¹

The ceremonial "here doth lye" works in tandem with the epigram to offer a kind of formal closure: it begins with a confession, the sin of "too much hope" presumably resolved by the final renunciation of ever liking "too much" again, penance for the sin. However, what ought to be a conclusion—"Rest in soft peace"—only leads the speaker to continue and disturb that rest with instructions on how to answer others, a last bit of fatherly advice to an absent child.

    Suppressed in this epitaph is a profound mix of loss and guilt, as Jonson was safely absent from his family as they suffered the same kind of quarantine Muggins's family had to endure in 1603.⁹² The smooth surface of the church's consolations, here framed as rhetorical questions, is disturbed by irregular caesuras. The enjambment of the first question, "For why / Will man lament the state he should enuie?" coupled with its lack of clear caesura requires a long, drawn-out breath. "To haue so soone scap'd worlds, and fleshes rage," provides a more regular rhythm, with a caesura and a pause at the end, but even here the stress on "scap'd" throws off the highly wrought iambs of the poem. The controlled breathing of these lines then gives way to the stifling punctuation of the next line, each demanding a momentary pause: "And, if no other miserie, yet age?" The frequency of pause or breath here parallels the way the speaker strains under the weight of the church's teaching. That life is merely borrowed, that death is a state to be envied, that the dead are spared further earthly miseries—all seem inadequate to the occasion. The state Jonson should envy might lend itself not so much to consoled resignation as to an aggressive desire to change places with the younger Ben Jonson.[93] And the short life of the child is precisely what makes parental grief so poignant.

By the same token, the poem's puns suggest a kind of linguistic control but hint at how fragile that control might be. The opening pun "child of my right hand," a translation of the name "Benjamin," allows the speaker to keep the name of the dead child hidden until the penultimate couplet. As soon as the name is uttered, the speaker of the poem offers another pun, "poetrie" as another word for making, intellectualizing and again distancing the deceased from the bereaved (not "my sonne" but "my poem"). Here paronomasia displaces the child for the text, the biological heir for the poetic legacy. An additional pun might be detected in the emotional snap of "I could loose all father, now." Readers rightly interpret this as a futile wish to cease feeling like a father, to relinquish the bond to the dead child; and this reading is highlighted in modern editions, which render "loose" as "lose." But the line might also suggest setting loose the fatherly love the poem tries so hard to restrain.[94] Even as Jonson's work seems invested in containing emotional outbursts, it nevertheless tests the limits of moderate mourning.[95] Only the formal nature of the epitaph's "here doth lye" seems to hold back the unspeakable grief.[96]

As Andrea Brady has shown, most early modern elegies were inextricably caught up in ritual, and in that sense the genre was at once both deeply personal and crucially civic in nature.[97] The plague troubled the public outlet for mourning, however. It separated the living from the dying, and the dying from the dead. Thus, Muggins has his personified London search for Londoners capable of genuine collective expressions of grief. London singles out parents, asking:

> Art thou a Father, or a Mother deare?
> Hadst thou a Sonne, or Daughter of thy side:
> Were not their voice, sweete musicke in thy Eare,
> Or from their smiles, could'st thou thy countnance hide.
> Nay, were they not, the glories of thy pride?
>   I doubt too much, thy loue on them were set,
>   That whilst thou liuest, thou canst not them forget. (sig. B3r, lines 134–40)

A smile, a voice—amid the greed and indifference Muggins's London encounters in her search for mourners, the death of a child emerges as the most significant and enduring loss. It is as if the intensity of the parent-child relationship lives on as a lasting bond among the bereaved, an incomparable emotional distress only parents can fully grasp.

Noting several verbal similarities, Ernest B. Gilman suggests that Jonson and Muggins "mirror" each other in their treatment of parental mourning.[98] Given that *London's Mourning Garment* entered print years before Jonson's "On My First Sonne," it seems likely that the grieving Jonson had read Muggins's poem upon arriving in London and, consciously or not, echoed Muggins's poem in his own. But where Jonson staves off emotion, Muggins depicts the range of reactions of parents bemoaning the fate of their children. Immediately following the fears of the new mother, London calls on her "Chast LONDON wiues . . . Each seuerall Mother, hauing greefes to shewe" to unburden themselves, to relate their losses, the beginning of a seventeen-stanza section of the plague epic dedicated to eulogizing dead children. The tears evoked, says London, are a kind of cure, "The onely Phisicke, women can bestow" (sig. B4v, lines 267–68, 270). Patricia Phillippy rightly takes issue with the limiting nature of London's "onely."[99] After all, this is a poem in which mothers not only weep but also give birth, nurse, comfort, and manage household finances.[100]

The tears evoked appear to be essential elements in the progression of the poem. When London began her search for mourners, she found only self-interested individuals. She bemoans, "Is there none then, that will take Londons part? / And help to sing, a welcome vnto wo?" London expresses a need for condoling voices to strengthen her resolve: "Two mourne together, swage ech others grief" (sig. B2v, lines 99–100, 104). But after addressing mothers and reminding them of the pains of childbirth, London renews each mother's grief:

> But I a skilfull Surgeons part will play,
> First search the sore, then minister things meete:
> Vnto your memories, I your plants will lay,
> Causing a fresh, your heauie eyes to greete. (sig. C1r, lines 274–77)

Muggins's personified London transforms herself from maid, bride, and mourner to metaphoric surgeon. The mothers are mournful, but it is London reminding them of their plaints that introduces the specifically elegiac movement of the poem. In doing so, Muggins follows George Puttenham, who in the *Arte of English Poesy* (1589) described elegy thus: "Lamenting is altogether contrary to rejoising, euery man saith so, and yet is it a peece of joy to be able to lament with ease, and freely to poure forth a mans inward sorrowes and the greefs wherewith his minde is surcharged. This was a very necessary deuise of the Poet and a fine, besides his poetrie to play also the Phisitian, and not onely by applying a medicine to the ordinary sicknes of mankind, but by making the very greef it selfe (in part) cure of the disease."[101] Like the tears of mourning mothers in *London's Mourning Garment*, poetry is a kind of medicine. Puttenham continues with his medical model for elegy. Poets do not, like Galenists, introduce "a contrary temper ... but as the Paracelsians, who cure [*simila simibilus*] making one dolour to expel another, and in this case, one short sorrowing the remedie of a long and grieuous sorrow." Such "Poeticall mournings," explains Puttenham, arose primarily at burials as "funeral songs" sung by one or many to commemorate the dead.[102]

Although Muggins's elegies involve intimate renderings of his own losses, the poem aims at a cure for the whole city as mourners gradually expose London's failings. As Alison Thorne points out in her study of female complaint in Shakespeare, Muggins's poem connects the loss of children "with other, more overtly politicized, kinds of loss."[103] The poem moves from private grief to collective grievance. Following Puttenham, Muggins thus offers an "epicedium," an elegy in several voices, to collectively overcome callous indifference, stoic restraint, and paralyzing grief. Each mourner speaks in turn as though in a public procession, but the first mourner, described as "One tender mother," seems especially personal to Muggins and his circumstances. She laments:

> my children both are dead:
> Sweet louing Henry, and my eldest gyrle,
> Ah Besse, my wench thou hadst thy mother sped
> With sorrowes, that will neuer from my head. (sig. C1r, lines 282–85)

With the appearance of Henry and Besse, the names of Muggins's deceased children, the polyvocal poem becomes for a moment much more personal. Elizabeth's burial had occurred only a few weeks before Muggins wrote this, but the experience, as London-as-surgeon had warned, seems to have caused afresh the pain of losing Henrie as well. The mother thus endorses London's initial claim that parents can never forget or fully get over the death of a child. *London's Mourning Garment* addresses the moral, social, and economic failings of the city, but it is also a deeply personal testament. Like the portrait of the family in debt, here a glimpse of the Muggins family's loss provides an intimate version of the emotional turmoil felt throughout the city; one mother's loss works as a synecdoche for the collective pain of the city.

The "tender mother" eulogizes each child. Elizabeth was ten years old with "flaxen haire." She was tall with "manners milde," and a "countnance smilling, neither sad nor light" (sig. C1r, lines 288–90). Above all, she was intelligent. The mother extols her daughter's "forward wit to learning and to awe" and her "reading best of all" (sig. C1r, lines, 286, 292). Whether the focus on education was motivated by religious, humanist, or economic concerns, one of the mother's fondest memories is connected with her daughter's intellectual curiosity, her capacity for awe. The silk-weaver who derived so much from his reading seems to have been keen to impart his knowledge to his daughter. The elegy for his daughter in turn subtly promotes the value of literacy among young women of the middling sort.[104]

The mother further recalls Elizabeth "With needle pregnant, as thy Sampler shewes" (sig. C1r, line 293). Samplers were pieces of cloth with pictures or designs for young girls to practice embroidery. Practically speaking, samplers were used as decorative covers for cushions, cabinetry, or books. Such skill was a clear asset in a household dealing in silk and silk goods, and certainly a ten-year-old would be expected to make some contributions to the household's labor.[105] The upwardly mobile longed for skilled needlework to clothe themselves and furnish their homes.[106] But samplers were also an integral part of a young girl's education.[107] Samplers typically featured images from Old Testament stories, patterns, and sometimes words. In addition to the practical skill of embroidery, they taught literacy and were thought to impart moral lessons. At the same time, Susan Frye has noted the ways in which the practice of needlework reveals a limited but by no means insignificant agency among young women.[108] Women chose particular subjects and at times reworked the images to express their own perspectives on the material. One can only guess at how Elizabeth Muggins approached her samplers, but it is surely significant that much of William Muggins's elegy to his daughter emphasizes her intellectual and creative potential.

The "tender mother" who voices this elegy, over the course of four lines beginning with an emphatic "To see . . . ," then imagines the life that her daughter could have lived. She had hoped, she explains, to eventually see her daughter married, to see her have children of her own, and to watch them "in the streete haue playde." She had hoped, in short, that Bess had survived "To cheere my age, as should a louing daughter, / But thou art gone, and I must follow after" (sig. C1r, lines 299–301). The potential joys expressed in the life not lived leave the mother with only one solemn conclusion: to follow her daughter to the grave.

As if this sentiment were not enough, the mother then turns to her dead son, "My little HENRIE," in some sense a memorial to the boy who had died five years before the plague of 1603. But here Muggins curiously describes not a baby from 1598 but a boy who had often uplifted the spirits of the family. The mother describes Henrie as follows:

>   that prety foole;
> That oft hath made my sorrowing heart full glad,
> His words were Mamma: sit, here is a stoole,
> Some bread and butter I haue nothing had;
> Ile busse you well, (good Mamma) be not sad,
>   Vp on cock-high, I will sit in your lappe,
>   Where oft (poore sweeting) he hath caught a nappe.
>
> And if sometimes, he hearde his Father chide,
> As housholde wordes, may passe twixt man and wife:
> Vnto my Husbande, presently he hyed
> As he should say, I will appease the strife;
> And with his Childish mirth, and pleasvres rife.
>   Abates the heat, and makes vs both to ioy:
>   To see such nature, in the little Boy. (sigs. C1r–v, lines 302–15)

The nearly eight-month-old Henrie Muggins had not grown enough to speak any words much less to intercede between his parents. Curiously, Jonson, too, imagined his son older. Before knowing of his son's death, Jonson claimed to have had a vision of his son in "a manlie shape" with "the mark of a bloodie crosse on his forehead." Jonson interprets his apprehensive dream, complete with the cross that might appear outside a quarantined household, as presenting his son "of that grouth that he thinks he shall be at the resurrection."[109] The interpretation was perhaps a way of consoling himself after his loss.

Of course, Muggins was under no obligation to accurately represent his own family in the poem, but the choice of names is uncanny. It is as though Henrie had kept growing in Muggins's imagination. Muggins writes not of a dead baby but of Henrie, a boy of around four or five years of age who should never have died. The boy talks with his mother. If Muggins and his wife ever had tense "householde words," it was because Henrie was not there to remind them of his "Childish mirth, and pleasvres rife." While at some level the Henrie of the poem is simply a generic child for readers to imagine as their own, there is also a sense that this elegiac moment in the poem led Muggins to consider what his son's life might have been had he survived to see the plague of 1603. Here the theological consolations that an early death spared one further agony may have rang true. However Henrie Muggins died, he did not have to endure the blisters and sores, the fever and nausea, the slow, painful death of the plague. The mother ends her lament, "With the eternall I beleue they rest, / Oh, happy Babes, for euer they are blest" (sig. C1v, lines 321–22).

Recounting her losses leads the first mourner to reconciliation with her faith. But the tenderness of a parent's "too much . . . loue" could give rise to an outburst of rage and helplessness. The next mourning mother of *London's Mourning Garment* is a widow "olde and withered," whose losses have left her weak and impoverished. She describes herself as "Feeble and weake of yeeres, three score and ten," alluding to Psalm 90:10 that for the elderly near the end of life "strength is but labour and sorowe" (sig. C1v, line 357, 331).[110] Her daughters were married; having given all she had to them, she would spend three months at a time with each household. She then details the coming of the plague:

> But now alas, a heauy Tale to tell,
> As with my Chickins, I at pleasure slept:
> Comes the great Puttocke, with his Tallantes fel,
> And from me quite, my youngest Chicken swept;
> Then to the other, he full nimbly leapt,
>   Seazing on her, as hee had done the other,
>   Oh greedy Death, could'st thou not take their Mother? (sig. C2r, lines 344–50)

The near bathos of the elderly woman framing herself as a mother hen is juxtaposed with the tragic nature of the action being described—not the far remove of a bird of prey swooping down on a pastoral scene, but the plague infecting more victims, spreading through each body, and adding more names to the bills of mortality. The simile itself appears to have been borrowed from Robert Cawdry's *A Treasurie or Store-House of Similies* (1600), a sort of printed commonplace book. Cawdry placed his description of "yong Chickens . . . in safetie from the Hauke and Puttocke" (itself borrowed from Lyly's *Euphues*), under the heading "Gods fauour the safest refuge." Cawdry further explicated the passage as relating to the dangers one faced for failing to live by the church's precepts: like unguarded chicks, "by their sinnes and iniquities, they must needs fall into the talons and jawes of that tyrannicall Hauke and hound of hell, from whence there is no deliuerie."[111] The simile's theological trappings, along with the widow's addition that she "at pleasure slept," hint at a sense of self-reproach for the deaths of her daughters.

This sense of responsibility for the passing of one's children leads the elderly widow to wish for death for herself: "My age is fitter for the yawning Graue," she declares, a proposition she develops in a point-by-point comparison of how her aged limbs, bones, and blood are better suited for death than are her daughters' youthful features. In addition to their youthful limbs, her children "were matched, & fruite might bring foorth store," she explains. As though offering sound advice on husbandry, the widow proffers Death ought to leave the young alone so they can continue to provide "store" for Death's appetite (sig. C2r, lines 351, 356).

The next stanza expands on the widow's wish to die in place of her daughters as she rails against death:

Thou cruel leane, and ill deformed Death,
Thou great intruder, and vn-welcomde guest:
Thou palefac't hog, thou shortner of long breath,
Thou mighty murdrer, of both man & beast:
Why doest thou not, inuite me to thy feast?
    And on my body, shew thy fury great
    That lackes house, lodging, sight, & what to eate. (sig. C2r, lines 358–64)

The liturgy might frame death as a sign of God's mercy—in George Herbert's "Time," Death is a gardener and usher of souls—but faced with the premature death of her children, the widow of *London's Mourning Garment* sees death as an outrage, an unnatural, homicidal trespasser on the lives of Londoners.[112] The emotional loss is only compounded by the widow's former reliance on her grown children; homeless and without anything to eat, she offers herself up as food for Death's feast. The widow's tirade against Death comes close to an overt questioning of God's will, an energetic despair that contrasts with the resigned sorrow one was to adopt from the church's consoling words. And yet, in the presence of so much untimely death, the feelings of guilt, frustration, anger, and despair seem as natural as the first mother's gentle longing.

The elegiac stanzas of *London's Mourning Garment* offer a wide range of emotional responses to counter the rigid indifference London initially finds among her citizens. A younger widow speaks next, having lost "As well her Children, as her Husbande good, / With labouring seruantes that did earne their foode." She begins by fondly recalling the hard work and sacrifices of mothering:

> Ah my sweet Babes, what woulde not I haue done?
> To yeelde you comfort, & maintaine you heer:
> Early and late, no labour woulde I shun,
> To feede your mouthes, though hunger pincht me neere;
> All three at once, I woulde your bodies cheere.
>   Twaine in my lappe, shoulde sucke their tender Mother,
>   And with my foot, I woulde haue rockt the other. (sig. C2r, lines 370–78)

This stanza's portrait of a mother comforting three small children at once may well have been drawn from life in the Muggins household. When the plague came to Southwark, James was four, Mary one, and Robert only a few weeks old. The importance of childrearing as labor was not lost on Muggins. Like the description of childbirth discussed in chapter 2, the emphasis here is on the sacrifices of motherhood, on the selfless and exhausting nature of domestic work and childcare.

The vivid picture of the mother caring for several children at once is contrasted with the next stanza's emphasis on the children's sudden absence. The mother explains:

Me thinkes I see them still, and heare their cryes
Chiefly a nights when I on bed am layde,
Which make fresh teares goe from my watry eyes,
When I awake and find I am deceived;
Sweet pretie Babes, Christ hath your souls received. (sig. C2v, lines 379–83)

While this mother had worked "early and late," feeding two children while appeasing a third, their deaths afford her no rest. The souls of children might be in heaven, but the loss is still real for the living, as the misery is renewed nightly despite the promise of salvation. The lines strike a painful balance between profound loss and the teachings of the church. Heavenly design might console, but it nevertheless cannot remove earthly grief.

Although reconciled to her losses, the mother nonetheless continues to envy the passing of her husband. She recalls:

Your louing father tooke a great delight,
Often in Armes to haue those children small,
And now he hath them euer in his sight,
Not one or two, the heauens possesse them all,
Father and Babes obayde when Christ did call.
    They all are gone, I onely left with breath,
        To byde more sorrowes in this wretched earth. (sig. C2v, lines 386–92)

The flow of couplets in the stanza is here thrown off by the off rhyme of breath/earth, just as surely as the tender scene of mother with children was disrupted by the plague. The mother's confusion and longing for her children is evident in the shifting pronouns. She addresses the children in the second person as though they were present—"*Your* louing father"—and then shifts instantly to the third person and their absence—"*those* children," and "*them* all." The oscillating presence and absence of the deceased parallels the previous stanza's "Me thinkes I see them still," while the description of the father's affection for his children prompts an expression of envy for the dead with nothing for the living to do but "byde more sorrowes in this wretched earth."

Although the wretchedness of the earth hints at the disposition of the older widow in despair, the phrase is closer to an enduring notion of *contemptus mundi* extending from medieval tracts well into the Reformation.¹¹³ The phrase is evoked not only in early modern translations of Boethius and Saint Augustine, but also by John Foxe and John Jewel.¹¹⁴ One should not love life among the living, but rather always keep in mind that life on earth is transitory; one must focus on the hereafter, taught generations of theologians. After describing her future hardships—poor and without family or friends—she surmises, "Onely I trust God will increase my health, / That I may worke and hate dishonest wealth" (sig. C2v, lines 398–99). As Amy M. Froide asserts, single working women in early modern England were increasingly conflated with prostitutes.¹¹⁵ In addition to a potential imputation of wealth itself, then, there is here a dread of the means left to impoverished women at the time. With few options, one might feel compelled to beg or work in the sex trade. It is worth observing that twice in 1602 a Suzan Muggins was arrested for vagrancy. Whether she was related to William Muggins is unknown, but if she was, her predicament might well echo in these lines' anxiety about honest work and "dishonest wealth."¹¹⁶ At the same time, the lines strike a balance between the first, faithfully consoled mother and the second, despairing widow. Life goes on in all its misery, but it still must be lived through honest labor.

London's Mourning Garment was deeply personal, eulogizing the deaths of the author's children and depicting his family's fears about sickness and prospects for the future, but the pamphlet was also committed to the social and the larger polity. The Reformation led mourners to consider the fate of the souls of the living rather than the dead; *London's Mourning Garment* moved beyond consoling the individual mourner to a concern for the well-being of society as a whole. The poem focuses on not only the emotional and spiritual but also the social and economic woes of the city—poverty, homelessness, and exploitation. Isolated in his household, Muggins populated his poem with average Londoners devastated by the plague. Outside, Muggins's social landscape changed radically. Friends and family had died. Thousands in Southwark were buried in the summer months of 1603. The poem's tales of bereavement—just three standing in for thousands—voiced the experience of loss that could not be captured in weekly bills of mortality. Like the collective petition on behalf of impoverished weavers, the polyvocal nature of *London's Mourning Garment* challenges complacency and mere self-interest in early modern London. It is at this point that London intervenes:

> Many more sorrowes might I here repeate,
> Of grieued Mothers for their children deare,
> But times are precious and worke too great
> For my hoarse voice to shew and vtter here. (sig. C2v, lines 400–403)

The fears about debt, homelessness, and exploitation expressed by the pamphlet's mourners were outcomes of the plague; however, as will be seen in the next chapter, they were also for Muggins symptoms of the sinfully acquisitive system that led to the plague. As with other parts of the poem, labor is central—"worke too great" remained, as London puts it—but, as will be seen in chapter 4, the depiction of the mourning women in these elegiac stanzas plays an integral, importantly scriptural role in Muggins's shift from mourning the dead to a vision of social change for the living, a vision that was grounded in private losses but motivated by collective experience.

CHAPTER 4

The Jeremiah of Southwark

The Prophetic Poetry of William Muggins

> Wee are to consider the workman, and his Worke.
> The Workeman is the Prophet Jeremy, His work are Lamentations.
> —JOHN HULL (1618)

MUGGINS AMONG THE NONCONFORMISTS

In the weeks before the quarantine of the Muggins household, the family along with apprentices and other parishioners were to attend St. Olave's Church at least three times a week as part of the state's spiritual effort to combat the plague. The regular assemblies at church also allowed for the dissemination of further plague orders and news, part of a bureaucratic fight against the epidemic. St. Olave's Church was near the river on Tooley Street (a compression of its earlier name, St. Olave's Street). Although many shops and tenements would be erected around it in the next two decades, judging by its depiction in the 1560s Agas Map, it was already buttressed in by numerous buildings on every side. Across the street was a priory that had been converted to an inn and St. Olave's Grammar School. A few doors down was another inn as well as Bridge House, a major granary for the city.

During the plague, the state required the clergy to "exhort their Parishioners to endeauour themselues to come to the Church with so many of their families as may be spared from their necessarie businesse . . . not onely on the Sundayes and Holydayes: but also on Wednesdayes and Frydayes during the time of these present afflictions."[1] In addition to the liturgy provided by the *Booke of Common Prayer*, ministers were to follow the directions in *Certaine Prayers Collected out of a Forme of Godly Meditations*, a collection of prayers and readings revised and reprinted whenever an outbreak of the plague appeared. As a subsidy man, Muggins would find a place not far from the front of the church to listen to the day's lecture and participate in the church's prayers.

By 1603 Southwark, once a fervently Catholic parish, had become an equally zealous site of establishment and nonconformist Protestantism. Whatever Muggins's inclinations while at St. Mildred's, the radical Protestants of Southwark had an impact on the weaver-poet. One can see the influence in Muggins's decision to compose his own plague prayer for his pamphlet as well as in his preference for the Old Testament prophets. Whereas earlier chapters addressed the plaintive, social, and elegiac elements of *London's Mourning Garment*, this chapter focuses on the poem's visionary mode. Like Spenser before him and Milton after, Muggins ultimately aims at producing vatic poetry, but his was a unique combination of radical Protestantism and class consciousness leading to a vision of the laboring poor and middling sort's perfect commonwealth.

James Balmford applauded his parishioners at St. Olave's for their zeal and consistent church attendance during the plague: "Ye frequent Friday Lecture as diligently (euer since the Plague was kindled) as in winter nights: wheras many in & about London are winter hearers, attending the word when they haue nothing else to do: and ye fill Gods house vpon the daies of humiliation, & holy rest, notwithstanding there haue died in our parish from the 7 of May to this day 2640."[2] Despite fears of infection, parishioners of St. Olave's dutifully ventured forth three times a week. Wednesdays were official days of fasting, or "humiliation," during the plague, and unless absolutely necessary, individuals were encouraged to abstain from work and instead set their minds on religious devotion with prayer and reading from the Bible. Fridays, as Balmford indicates, were for lectures. Balmford's pamphlet, *A Short Dialogve concerning the Plagves Infection*, arguing that the plague was contagious even to the godly, was based on what he had, he claims, "publickly taught." One may assume that alongside readings of scripture Balmford frequently offered his "warning of that bloudy errour, which denieth the Pestilence to be contagious."[3]

Whereas St. Mildred's Sorocold appears to have been a reserved moderate, Balmford was an outspoken Puritan-leaning polemicist. All of Balmford's surviving pamphlets were printed by Richard Boyle, who specialized in religious tracts often more radical than that of the mainstream of the Church of England. In the late 1580s Balmford was an associate of radical Puritan John Udall.[4] And by 1600 Balmford was removed from his ministry in Newcastle for his dissenting views.[5] Under the protection of Puritan sympathizer Henry Hastings, Earl of Huntingdon, Balmford was assigned to serve at St. Olave's in Southwark, where his unflinching Puritanism found a welcome audience.[6]

Balmford's earliest pamphlet, *A Short and Plaine Dialogue concerning the Vnlawfulnes of Playing at Cards or Tables, or Any Other Game Consisting in Chance* (1594), argued that games of chance, even cards, exploited God's providence, a position of a piece with his later argument that risking infection of the plague unnecessarily tested predestination.[7] In this earlier pamphlet Balmford reasoned that because the Bible offered serious instances of deciding matters based on the drawing of lots, to engage in games of chance for diversion or profit was an offence to God just as "to pray or sweare in sport" might offend God.[8] Unlike his position on the plague, Balmford's extreme position on games of chance was out of step with the state: Queen Elizabeth had already weighed in on the lawfulness of playing cards, and in *Basilikon Doron* King James similarly took up the matter, arguing (from the very same passages Balmford cited) that the Bible's positive depiction of lots implicitly authorized games of chance.[9] Nevertheless, Balmford's pamphlet was still widely read more than two decades later when, in 1619, fellow Puritan Thomas Gataker revived the debate over games of chance with a direct attack on Balmford's early pamphlet.[10] By 1623, Balmford reprinted his 1594 pamphlet, to which he appended a lengthy response to Gataker.[11] Gataker quickly responded that same year, sometime in late September or October.[12] The plague of 1625 appears to have prevented Balmford from further response, however, as he was buried at St. Olave's on July 20, 1625.[13] Balmford's early pamphlet on games of chance, including cards, remained controversial throughout his life.

The inventory of Muggins's household in the Poultry, it will be recalled, included two entries for "playing cardes," possibly for personal use, but given the number of cards ("fyve dozen & x paire" and "iii dozen & a half playing cards"), more likely for sale. How might Muggins have felt coming under the spiritual guidance of someone who described games of dice and cards as "Heathenish pastimes"?[14] It may be that Muggins abandoned cards by the time he arrived in Southwark or in response to Balmford. Given the premium *London's Mourning Garment* places on the value of labor against idleness, Balmford's argument that "Gamesters worke not with their hands the thing that is good, to be free from stealing," may have at least had some appeal to Muggins, who in *London's Mourning Garment* held in disdain "dishonest wealth."[15]

Echoes of Balmford's plague pamphlet or his preaching at St. Olave's on the same can be heard in Muggins's poem.[16] Just as Balmford alludes to Isaiah 49:23 in describing rulers as "nurcing mothers and nurcing fathers," so Muggins's personified London admonishes magistrates "To be as nursing, fathers to the poore" (sig. D1v, line 604).[17] Balmford suggests that the wealthy "may go and abide in the countrey, sith the good they can do (as they be rich men) is to releeue the sicke and needy: which they may do well inough, without their residence," that "they are to be no lesse liberall in releeuing their afflicted neighbours, then they should be, by order from authority or otherwise, if they were resident."[18] Similarly, Muggins has London assert:

> And wealthy Citizens, whose store is great,
> I gently wooe you to haue good fore-sight,
> And cast your eyes vpon the needy wight,
> > Though feare of sicknesse driue you hence as men,
> > Yet leaue your purse, and feeling heart with them. (sig. D1v, lines 584–88)

For both Balmford and Muggins, escaping the plague did not free one from communal responsibilities—not only material aid but also compassion for one's fellow Londoners. How much Muggins had learned from Balmford is impossible to fully ascertain, but by the time he sat down to write *London's Mourning Garment* he had acquired a stance not out of keeping with the more radical elements of the London suburb.

Indeed, in Balmford Muggins may have found a kindred spirit, someone who, like Deloney, focused on England's poor and middling sort. Just as Muggins dedicated *London's Mourning Garment* to sheriff John Swinnerton, so Balmford, while in Newcastle, dedicated his early pamphlet on games of chance "to the right worshipfvll master, Lionel Maddison, Maior, the Aldermen his Brethren, and the godly Burgesses of Newcastle upon Tine."[19] Moreover, rather than emphasize his credentials as a minister educated at Oxford, Balmford often asserted that he was "a Carpenters sonne." He was free of the Company of Carpenters, apparently by patrimony. While at Oxford the company made regular payments of support to Balmford, a scholarship of sorts and an investment in promising children of the company.[20] Just as his father had done for him, in 1611 James Balmford presented his son, Samuel, to the company to attain the freedom of the city through patrimony.[21] Like his father, Samuel Balmford and one other member's son received regular funding from the company to attend university.[22] Balmford preached at the Carpenter's Hall upon the election of new wardens in 1602 and appears to have maintained a positive relationship with the company throughout his life.[23]

Two of Balmford's pamphlets, *Carpenters Chippes* and *A Short Catechisme*, featured the coat of arms of the Worshipful Company of Carpenters of London, a shield with a chevron, presumably symbolizing a roof. The chevron divided the shield in three, and in each of the three spaces was a compass, an important tool of the trade. *Carpenters Chippes* brought together three essays, one for each of the coat of arms' compasses: one on the sabbath, one on the errors of the Roman Catholic Church, and the third a reprinting of an earlier pamphlet on the execution of Catholic priests for treason rather than heresy.[24] The full title of the pamphlet emphasized the importance of carpenters for Balmford: *Carpenters Chippes: or Simple Tokens of Vnfeined Good Will, to the Christian Friends of James Balmford, the Unworthie Seruant of Jesus Christ, a Poore Carpenters Sonne.* The words of the pamphlet were like woodchips, while the final phrase—"a poore Carpenters sonne"—ambiguously points to both Balmford and Jesus, reminding readers of the central role of the craft in the New Testament.

While *Carpenters Chippes* was dedicated to the Countess of Cumberland, Margaret Clifford, the other pamphlet featuring the coat of arms of the Company of Carpenters, *A Short Catechisme, Svmmarily Comprizing the Principall Points of Christian Faith*, was dedicated to "the Right Worshipfvll, the Masters, Wardens, Assistants, and whole company of Carpenters in London." In the dedication, Balmford recalls the debt he owed the company for their "charitable exhibition, when I was a poore student in Oxford."[25] It is doubtful that Balmford or his son could have afforded university without the company's support.

As with *Carpenters Chippes*, Balmford is keen to draw parallels between carpentry and piety. Where some ministers might evoke the labors of the priest as shepherd or fisherman, Balmford, the "Carpenters sonne," instead writes that he is "a builder, according to his calling and gifts." Continuing the woodworking conceit, Balmford wishes London's carpenters "the continuall edification of their godly faith."[26] Expanding on the theme, Balmford explains, "Vnderstanding that *Edification*, so much commended and commanded in *Holy Writ*, doth signify *Building*. Of which spiritual building, your temporall building should daylie put you in mind."[27] Whereas a Puritan artisan like Nehemiah Wallington appears to have been troubled by trade, for Balmford the labor of craftsmen becomes an extended metaphor for understanding the mysteries of the spirit.[28] Balmford's vision of labor as a mediator for spirituality seems to have become part of the culture of St. Olave's. S. Bryn Roberts argues that nonconformist Ralph Venning (Balmford's mid-seventeenth-century successor at St. Olave's) developed a theology that saw labor not as an impediment to but rather as an integral aspect of godliness based in large part on his experience of worshiping with the middling sort that made up most of St. Olave's parish at the time.[29] Muggins was an outspoken craftsman with a decidedly nonconformist view of the world; Balmford was an outspoken nonconformist preacher with a decidedly craftsmanlike view of the world.

Balmford was not a lone voice of Puritan or nonconformist thought in St. Olave's parish. In 1561, with a bequest from the Dutch refugee and local brewer Henry Leke, St. Olave's established a free grammar school. In 1586, after a high turnover of schoolmasters, the vestry chose Robert Browne to head the school. Infamous for his insistence that even Puritan reformers were not radical enough in their theology, Browne had been arrested the previous year for the publication of *An Answere to Master Carwright His Letter for Joyning with the English Churches* (1585), a pamphlet that, like several of Browne's tracts, denied the authority of the Church of England's bishops to appoint ministers. Browne was committed to a covenant theology incompatible with a state church, instead insisting that each congregation be empowered to appoint its own minister.[30] Browne was soon compelled to sign a "submission" to the Church of England, and upon appointment as schoolmaster to St. Olave's Grammar School he was further required to sign an agreement requiring him to avoid meddling with the church and its parishioners or keeping any conventicles, to take his children to church, to conform to the doctrine of the church, and to read only the authorized catechism to the students of the school.[31]

The appointment had to do with powerful family connections, but it could not have happened without the support of at least some of the vestry of St. Olave's. Whereas the stipulations to the appointment reveal considerable anxiety about bringing controversy into the parish, Browne signed the agreement "Subscribed by me Robert Browne according to my answeres before all the gouernours, & the distinctions & exceptions before them named."[32] Although not recorded, Browne's exceptions were clearly intended to weaken the degree of submission entailed in the agreement. Browne was not beyond careful quibbling. When in prison he was compelled to submit to "my Lord of Cant[erbury's] commandement, whose authority vnder her Ma[jesty] I wil neuer resist." A few years later it was reported that he claimed this to mean that he submitted only to the archbishop's "ciuill authoritie," and that the godly were not necessarily beholden to the word of the archbishop in spiritual matters.[33] This interpretation was understandable, as in the end it was very much in keeping with the Separatist movement of which Browne was an integral part. If his "exceptions" to the vestry were anything like this, he must have had several vestrymen on his side to overlook his various objections, qualifications, and equivocations.

Unsurprisingly, then, Browne by no means settled into the role of meek schoolmaster. Contemporary physician Stephen Bredwell reports that during Browne's time in St. Olave's parish he had converted one woman to his "sottish separation, so as at this day in respect of inferior meanes, we see vtterly no hope of her recouerie."[34] In Kent, Browne "railed openly" against the minister there, successfully drawing away some of the congregation. And he reportedly held conventicles in several homes throughout London.[35] Some in St. Olave's were no doubt persuaded by Browne, or at the very least were introduced to a decidedly radical way of thinking about scripture and the authority of the church. In the early 1590s several parishioners of St. Olave's and St. Saviour's were imprisoned for their involvement in a Separatist congregation led by the Brownist Francis Johnson.[36] Among them was shipwright Roger Rippon, who occasionally hosted the congregation in his house in St. Olave's parish.[37] When Rippon passed away in Newgate, a group of his fellow separatists, including a St. Olave's weaver named Christopher Diggins, carried the coffin to Justice Richard Younge's home in protest. Diggins would later declare that he did not recognize the authority of the English church and had ceased to attend for some two years.[38]

Much of what is known about Johnson's separatist congregation comes from the interrogation of scrivener and St. Olave's resident Daniel Bucke. Bucke not only named many of those present but also detailed the congregation's baptism and communion practices, both stripped of the ceremony prescribed by the *Booke of Common Prayer*.[39] Bucke eventually left Johnson's congregation, evidently persuaded by preacher Henry Jacob. In 1599 one "D. B.," identified by Francis Johnson as Bucke himself, provided a preface to Jacob's anti-Johnson, anti-Brownist tract, *A Defence of the Churches and Ministry of Englande* (1599). Bucke described a series of debates between Johnson and Jacob while Johnson was imprisoned in Southwark.[40] Despite his break with Johnson, Bucke maintained some connections to the congregation. In fact, he married the widow of Roger Rippon.[41]

In October 1603, while Muggins was finishing *London's Mourning Garment*, Bucke wrote his will, in which he left his volumes of Johannes Piscator to his "very loving friend maister Henry Jacob preacher in London." Bucke credited Jacob with helping save him "from a most fearfull schisme unto the truth of salvason now professed and practized in the churche of England."[42] Bucke further commended his "deare frend maister Anthony Wotton, preacher at Barking in London." Despite Bucke's praise of Jacob and Wotton for their role in the Church of England, they were not strictly establishment figures. Both held unorthodox views that were tied in part to St. Olave's parish. In 1614, Wotton was accused of promoting various nonconformist points of view, that he was an early supporter of Socinianism, a significant theological challenge to not only the establishment but also the mainstream of Puritan reform.[43] It was agreed that Wotton and his accuser would each select four ministers to review the evidence and arbitrate the dispute. Wotton chose St. Olave's James Balmford to be among his four panelists. The eight theologians found Wotton to have opinions at variance with their own, but not so egregious as to warrant claims of heresy or Socinianism.[44] Balmford was not a Socinian, but he did embrace a Protestantism that had room for radical departures from orthodoxy. Meanwhile although he had disputed with Johnson, Jacob was now developing a "semi-Separatist" theology founded on much the same covenant theology that motivated Browne and Johnson. By 1616 Jacob decided to put his ideas into practice by establishing his own church made up of Separatists and non-Separatists, those dissatisfied with the established Church of England but unwilling to risk fully breaking with it.⁴⁵ He set the church up in St. Olave's parish in Southwark, where he imagined he could draw on the tolerance of ministers like Balmford and the parish's tradition of nonconformity.

Southwark, and St. Olave's in particular, seems to have provided a milieu for Separatists, Independents, nonconformists, and a more radical wing among Puritans. James Balmford was not uniformly out of step with the establishment, however. His pamphlet on avoiding the plague was precisely in keeping with the state's plague orders, but the influence of Southwark's radicals like Browne, Bucke, and Rippon can be found in Balmford's son, Samuel Balmford, who in many respects followed in Browne's and Jacob's footsteps, gaining a reputation as a nonconformist Puritan preacher in the 1620s and eventually leading a congregation in exile on the continent.⁴⁶

LONDON THROUGH THE SCRIPTURAL LENS

In moving to St. Olave's, Muggins had placed himself and his family in a parish where nonconformist ideas circulated, a context likely to encourage lay engagement with scripture independent of church authority. This is not to say that the parishioners of St. Olave's were uniformly in line with Brownism or Puritanism. Christopher Haigh has shown how divisive the more radical wing of preachers could be in early modern parishes.⁴⁷ Still, Balmford continued at St. Olave's for two decades, until his death, and must have had some impact on the parishioners' understanding of Reformed theology.⁴⁸ For such a large parish, moreover, there were guaranteed to be nonconformist enclaves where laypeople could read and discuss scripture on their own. Indeed, Muggins's decision to pen his own prayer for *London's Mourning Garment* puts him in line with Puritans as well as more extreme thinkers like Udall and Browne, who strongly supported lay reading and lay preaching. In his prayer Muggins expressed a longing for "solemne meetings, and frequent assemblies" (sig. D3v). Were these conventicles or formal chuch assemblies?⁴⁹ Muggins owned a Bible and seems to have immersed himself in scripture.

As the suppression of conventicles demonstrates, while reading the Bible was encouraged, authorities felt considerable anxiety about how lay readers interpreted scripture.⁵⁰ In a 1591 sermon at Paul's Cross, Thomas Barne complained, "Laymen haue in their nocturnal couenticles presumed to interpret the same [scripture], and the weaker sort likewise, whom Saint Paul in any wise would not permit to teach haue peruerted the ordinarie meanes of saluation to their owne destruction."[51] In *The Course of Christianitie* (1579), Flemish theologian Andreas Hyperius similarly worried that readers might see fit "to hunt after subtil and straunge interpretations, to muse vppon allegories wythout cause why." Rather than do so, Hyperius suggests rereading the puzzling passage, consulting others, reading commentaries, or, if all else fails, accepting that not fully understanding a passage may also be a meaningful experience. Above all, Hyperius warned one must not "crake continuallye of mysticall meanings."[52] In the early seventeenth century, Elnathan Parr warned readers to "take heed, that we feigne not a meaning of our owne, and thrust it vpon the word; lest we proue Hereticke," while Richard Rogers and John Downame advised lay readers on how to engage with scripture but ultimately cautioned them to consult their minister on difficult passages.[53] Muggins appears to have been an exceptionally astute reader, but if he consulted with his Southwark neighbors or his own minister on scripture he may well have encountered unorthodox opinions. Whether directly or not, the nonconformist context of early modern Southwark seems to have led Muggins to work with scripture in his own way. Reading the Bible was a way of thinking through what he perceived as both a spiritual and a socioeconomic crisis in London. *London's Mourning Garment* uses scripture to not only understand the failings of London's citizens, but to imagine something like a Christian utopia, a commonwealth that while hierarchical nonetheless prizes compassion over indifference, labor over idleness, and mutual aid over exploitation, all as though these ideals were God's will. Muggins delved into the covenants of the Old Testament to find a model for social reform, and while his thinking about covenants is not Separatist in nature, his will to offer criticism and advice from below participates in the spirit of much of the more radical Puritanism of late Elizabethan Southwark.

After the "tender mother" of *London's Mourning Garment* dwells with loving detail on her daughter's features, Besse's "pleasant eyes" and "hands with fingers small," she concludes with a brief description of how her daughter died, a simple line that conveys a muted anguish at the passing of the child: "Patient in death like sucking Lambe she goes" (sig. C1r, line 294). The comparison of Besse to a "sucking Lambe" emphasizes her youth and innocence, but it also frames the daughter's death as a kind of sacrifice. The phrase "sucking Lambe" is an allusion to 1 Samuel 7. Samuel gathers the Israelites to repent their previous idolatry, and they "drewe water and powred it out" in prayer; that is, as the gloss to the Geneva Bible explains, they "wept abundantly." When the Philistines learn of the gathering, they attack, and Samuel is implored "to crye vnto the Lord our God for vs," at which point Samuel offers a "sucking lambe" and "cryed vnto the Lord for Israel."[54] The sacrifice and collective prayers prove successful as the Philistines are vanquished. While the Israelites are saved by the prayers over their "sucking lambe," Besse's death and her mother's laments, unfortunately, fall short of halting the plague.

Muggins's simile of the "sucking lambe" juxtaposes efficacious prayer and sacrifice with the senseless, seemingly random death meted out by the plague. Whereas Samuel's sacrifice follows the collective tearful prayers of the Israelites, the "tender mother" is only the first of the mourners. Her elegy cries out for more tears from more mothers. Of a piece with the poem, the prayer that Muggins included in *London's Mourning Garment* asserts that one of the central sins of Londoners was rendered manifest during the plague—people were indifferent to the suffering of others. As the prayer puts it, "We haue not had that sympathy, and fellow-felling of each others miserie, which ought to bee in the members of Christ" (sig. D3v). In 1595 Muggins and his silk-weaving cohort appealed to their French competitors as "Cittizens with us of that heavenly and celestiall kingdome."[55] Eight years later Muggins was again taking Reformed Christianity as a given for London, presuming a Christian commonwealth of shared ethics and natural empathy even when he saw it threatened by vice and an overweening self-interest. Muggins had seen that troubling lack of empathy before: in his own livery company's refusal to act on poorer members' concerns, in the disregard of the problems faced by debtors, in the callous treatment of prisoners, in the indifference of office holders. Each Londoner needed to mourn not only his or her particular losses but also the collective losses of the city; each Londoner needed to repent for the sins of all. Apathy coupled with unrelenting self-interest had allowed, as Muggins put it, "a people that doe leawdly liue" to thrive, and all this had brought God's wrath on the city (sig. C4r, line 491).

As discussed in the introduction, Muggins packed his prayer with biblical allusions, often borrowing phrases or images from three or more sections of the Bible for one sentence. When Muggins prays, "Then will we offer vp w^t the calues of our lips a sacrifice of prayse and thankesgiuing, when thou hast raised vs vp, out of the pit of our grieued desolation, then shalt thou put myrth and gladnesse into our heartes," he quickly compresses Old and New Testament allusions: Hosea 14:2 ("calues of our lips"), Psalm 40 ("pit of our grieued desolation"), and Jeremiah 33:11 ("a sacrifice of prayse" connected to "myrth and gladnesse") with echoes of Ephesians 2:6 ("raised vs vp") and perhaps Hebrews 13:15 ("sacrifice of prayse"), itself an echo of Hosea 14.2–3 (sig. D4r).[56] The prayer gives some sense of Muggins's intensive reading of the Bible, especially in how he inventively thought about one passage in terms of another, and how he reconfigured all the passages to understand the present.

The Psalms, Exodus, Deuteronomy, Hosea, and Jeremiah were somewhat commonplace in plague writing of the period, presenting clear examples of the predominant belief that the plague was a result of God's wrath, even as the plague was treated more and more as a contagion.[57] Gilman suggests that early modern engagement with these books (to which he adds 2 Samuel and Numbers) provided a "mode of grafting sacred history onto the history of the nation."[58] But specific chapters and books of the Bible seem to have held a special importance for Muggins. The Psalms were a mainstay for early modern readers and a favored text for translation, but in addition to the Psalms, Muggins was drawn to the other especially poetic passages of the Bible.[59] Whereas most plague pamphlets show a preference for Deuteronomy 28 and its many curses for failing to obey God, Muggins alludes to that chapter only twice, relying instead on Deuteronomy 32, the "Song of Moses," which he refers to at least seven times in his prayer. In Deuteronomy 32 Moses describes how despite God's favor, the chosen people come to neglect their devotions: "But he that shulde haue bene vpright when he waxed fat, spurned with his hele."[60] As a result, God is provoked to "spend plagues vpon them."[61] After detailing the woes of the people, the song ends with Moses assuring his listeners that God will ultimately protect and favor the faithful.[62] One can discern here the contours of *London's Mourning Garment*: London was favored but its people failed to humble themselves by acknowledging God and were oblivious to the suffering of the city's most vulnerable, so personified London implores magistrates to institute changes that will return the city to its former glory and God's protection. Although Muggins was drawn to the poetry of the Bible, scripture also provided a structure through which he understood himself, his city, and their relation to the plague of 1603.

More than any other book of the Bible, however, Muggins attended to Jeremiah and its continuation in Lamentations. Muggins alludes to these books more than twenty times in his prayer and, along with Deuteronomy 32, embedded elements of them in his poem.[63] The book of Jeremiah oscillates between poetry and prose, and Lamentations, which Raymond-Jean Frontaine describes as a "poet's poem," attracted the likes of Francis Quarles and John Donne to try their hand at translation.[64] While a stray line from Malachi or Philippians might hint at recourse to a commonplace book, Muggins's frequent citation of Jeremiah and Lamentations suggests that he read and reread those books while under quarantine in 1603. He made a conscious effort to organize his poem as a modern-day Lamentations. Indeed, the failure of Besse's death to fulfill the role of Samuel's "sucking lambe" seems to have been intended as an allusion to Jeremiah 15:1, in which God declares that he will not relent in his anger even if "Moses or Samuel stode before me."[65] Mid-seventeenth-century minister John Trapp similarly understood the passage from 1 Samuel in terms of the people's failure to listen to Jeremiah and other prophets.[66] Much of Jeremiah's laments, after all, are concerned with either the people failing to heed his prophecies or God shunning their prayers.

Certainly, many read Jeremiah and Jeremiah's Lamentations during plagues and other catastrophes.[67] Both books spoke to a state of intense collective sorrow, so much so that in the seventeenth century Jeremiah came to be known as "the weeping prophet" or the "mourning prophet."[68] Jeremiah offered an entry point to thinking about tragedy on a grand scale. Balmford's professor cites Jeremiah throughout *A Short Dialogve*, and at one point describes the book as "now so much vrged," presumably by ministers and lay readers throughout London.[69] As plague deaths mounted, it made sense to search the Bible for precedent and an emotional register that matched the misery of those who struggled to survive what at the time could only be imagined as God's wrath.

At Paul's Cross and throughout the city, Londoners were admonished for their sins and exhorted to lend tears to their prayers, to weep like Jeremiah. Thus, amid the plague of 1603 Christopher Hooke preached the following at Paul's Cross:

> Oh let it be far from us, that this complaint that the Prophet Jeremie taketh up against Jerusalem, should be taken up against us.

> *O Lord, thou hast stricken them, but they haue not sorrowed, thou hast consumed them, but they haue refused correction, they haue made their faces harder then a stone, and haue refused to returne.* For if notwithstanding these judgements of God, we continue still in those sins which haue thus sore kindled his wrath, if in this day of our visitation wherein the Lorde calleth to weeping & mourning, to sackcloth & ashes, we fal to eating & drinking, that is, to our wonted gluttonie & drunkenness, & other abhominations. Let vs assure our selues that the wrath of God will still burne, and his arme be stretched out still, vntil hee hath laide our land waste, and this Citie without an inhabitant.[70]

Like Muggins, Hooke weaves descriptions of present-day London with lines from Jeremiah—not only the lines attributed to him at the outset of the passage (5:3) but also the "kindled" and still burning wrath of God (17:4), God's outstretched arm (21:5), the "weeping & mourning" and "sackcloth & ashes" (6:26), and the wasted city without an inhabitant (9:11).[71] Londoners were to understand that Jeremiah's warnings were not bound by time and place; they may have been written in and near Jerusalem around 600 BCE, but they clearly applied to London in 1603 CE.

At Hanwell, Oxfordshire, around the time of Hooke's sermon, nonconformists John Dod and Robert Cleaver (the weaver's favored theologians in Robert Wild's ballad discussed in chapter 1) each preached on the third chapter of Lamentations and went on to print the two sermons in a single pamphlet a few years later.[72] Dod led a call for widespread, heartfelt weeping, what he calls "holy mourning," the appropriate emotional state for any Christian in the face of the plague.[73] He anticipates an objection: "Oh, but to weepe and lament, it is not manhood: it argues that men want courage and fortitude and is altogether vnbeseeming the person of a man: they will trust in God (they say) and neuer mourne for the matter." The culture's premium on moderating mourning, it would seem, conspired with models of early modern masculinity in a way that might potentially compromise Dod's call for national mourning.[74] Dod counters the objection by pointing to the weeping of Jacob, David, and Jesus, each with the rhetorical refrain "Was he a coward?" Dod thus challenged the dominant idea of masculinity of the period.[75] Pious, heartfelt tears were not a sign of effeminacy, but rather a salve for the nation. Dod's reading of Lamentations leads him to surmise rather forcibly, "There is no danger in Christian sorrow, but the more of it, the better."[76] For Dod, tears lent prayer a special force to cleanse individual, household, municipal, and national sins.

Whereas Dod spoke to concerns about masculinity, Cleaver addressed widespread anxieties as the plague spread from London to other cities and towns. After asserting that Jeremiah's Lamentations showed that fervent, collective prayer would alleviate suffering, Cleaver ventriloquizes an objection: "Oh, but what if the pestilence should enter into the familie, and the house should be shut vp, that no body could come to me? What of that?"[77] That is, if intensive collective prayer is the key to being spared from the plague, then quarantine is especially cruel, the isolation weakening the efficacy of national prayer and acting as almost a preemptive condemnation of the household. For Cleaver this came down to the "different carriage of the faithful and of infidels." Judas, reasons Cleaver, "sorroweth desperately" and commits suicide while Peter "confesseth this fault, weeps bitterlie, and gaines exceedingly by it."[78] Cleaver and so many others argued that one must avoid the hard-heartedness of the indifferent as well as the sorrow of despair in favor of the productive "holie teares" modeled by Jeremiah.

Such sermons, retroactively referred to by scholars as jeremiads, were a staple during times of plague or other adversity.[79] The books of the prophets, argued preachers, showed again and again that a failure to comply with God's laws always ran the risk of God's retribution, what Michael McGiffert calls the "Israelite paradigm" in English preaching.[80] These sermons exhorted hearers to repent and reorient themselves to pious worship and communal responsibility lest they suffer some awful national calamity as had been faced at Nineveh, Sodom, and above all Israel. As Patrick Collinson puts it, "Jeremiah and Hosea were so many cassettes, to be inserted into the tape-deck of the present."[81] Or, to use the prevailing metaphor of the period, the Bible was not so much a depiction of a distant past as it was a "looking glass" in which England might view itself.[82]

Putting aside for a moment the national implications of the mirror metaphor, Muggins may well have seen something of himself in Jeremiah. Under quarantine and mourning the loss of friends and family, Muggins probably identified with the many exclamations about mourning in Jeremiah and Lamentations, such as the frequently cited "Oh, that mine head were ful of water and mine eyes a fountaine of teares, that I might wepe day and night for the slaine of the daughter of my people"; or "For these things

I weepe: mine eye, euen mine eye casteth out water, because the comforter that shulde refesh my soule, is farre from me: my children are desolate."[83] Between relaying God's warnings of famine and plague, Jeremiah objected to economic exploitation and demanded that the enslaved be freed. And whenever the authorities disapproved of his prophecies, Jeremiah found himself imprisoned.[84] Jeremiah surmised, "I am the man, that hathe sene affliction."[85] Economic protest, prison, plague—it is possible that Muggins saw in Jeremiah's convictions, isolation, and mourning a reflection of his own predicament as a highly literate, insightful, and compassionate member of the poor-to-middling sort in early modern London.

THE SOCIOECONOMIC VISIONS OF WILLIAM MUGGINS

London's Mourning Garment, then, stands apart from the courtly style of English poetry that had been nurtured under Elizabeth, drawing instead from sermons and the English tradition of radical Protestant prophetic verse (where prophecy generally refers to speaking God's will rather than specifically predicting future events). An offshoot of pre-Reformation poems like William Langland's *Piers Plowman*, such poetry, especially in its heyday of the mid-sixteenth century, typically used a plain style to call for not only religious but social reform, in contrast with an ornate courtly style focused on ostentatious displays of wit and the adaptation of Italian courtly forms.[86] Robert Crowley's apocalyptically titled mid-Tudor poem *The Voyce of the Laste Trumpet* (1549), for instance, addressed "lessons" to each member of the commonwealth. Crowley (who by 1569 worked as schoolmaster at St. Saviour's Grammar School down the road from St. Olave's) instructs yeomen to be sure to share their earnings with the poor, and merchants are told to sell their goods "Vpon a price reasonable." Gentlemen are advised to avoid leisure and pomp, and magistrates are reminded, "thou madest therto a vowe / At the takeynge of thyne offyce" to enforce the laws, especially against "them that do oppresse."[87] The tradition carried on more or less overtly from mid-Tudor "gospelling poets" like Crowley to Edmund Spenser and George Wither, whose own plague epic, *Britain's Remembrancer* (1628), owes a generic debt to *London's Mourning Garment*.[88]

As he wrote his poem and prayer, carefully consulting his Bible and probably a commonplace book full of lines that had struck him as particularly poignant, Muggins sought to bring about reform. Moving deftly from

Isaiah to Romans, Muggins wrote, "Wee are one afraid of another[. . . .] We haue not comforted the weake and feeble knees, we haue not wept with them that weepe" (sig. D3v). Muggins's poem gives voice to a personified London and then adds to that voice a chorus of mourning mothers and a family in debt. Muggins did not write a personal prayer about his singular plight, his personal losses, and private hopes, what he thought he alone should do; he insisted that his poem be polyvocal and that his prayer be collective, speaking for the city as a whole, taking up the role of spokesperson, lay minister, vatic poet, a voice from the streets of London's crowded suburbs, a Jeremiah of sorts.

Lamentations begins, "How doeth the citie remaine solitarie that was ful of people? She is as a widdow: she that was great among the nacions and princesse among the prouinces, is made tributarie. She wepeth continually in the night, & her teares runne down by her chekes."[89] Early modern commentators were struck by the abruptness of the opening lines of Lamentations and their compressed expression of a desolate city in the figure of a solitary, distraught widow.[90] Some two decades after the publication of *London's Mourning Garment*, amid the plague of 1625, the anonymous author of *Lachrymae Londinenses* would quote the lines and recommend, "It is worth your reading, to read ouer that first chapter of the Lamentations, when you thinke vpon the present estate of desolate London."[91] Muggins appropriated the opening of Lamentations to draw a bleak comparison between desolate Jerusalem and the desperate condition of London in 1603:

> With heauy heart, and sighes of inward Cares,
> With wringing hands explayning sorrows wo,
> With blubbered cheekes, bedewde with trickling teares
> With minde opprest lamenting griefs that flowe,
> London lament, and all thy losses showe. (sig. B1r, lines 1–5)

Muggins's readers would immediately recognize the image of the city as weeping woman as a nod to the oft-cited weeping prophet's opening lines to Lamentations. Muggins builds anticipation with the anaphoric prepositional phrases describing signs of grief, withholding for the moment the subject of the mourning, announced with the imperative initial trochee of "London lament." Muggins evokes London in part as muse who speaks through him, in part as spokesperson for his and really all of the city's "inward Cares."

The poem's induction is one that invites readers to think in terms of their own personal losses, their own "minde opprest," but also to consider themselves collectively suffering as part of an as-yet-unwritten chapter of the godly. Jerusalem wept, and now London laments.

To the command to relate all her losses, London speaks her first lines, "What al? nay some, all were too much to tell, / The learned Homer could not penne it well" (sig. B1r, lines 6–7). The tragic fall of Troy—for early modern readers the iconic downfall of a city—is an inadequate touchstone for the cataclysmic plight of London, and while Muggins draws on Lamentations, London speaks of her own particular downfall as well. With echoes of Jerusalem's triumphs in Lamentations ("great among the nacions and princesse among the prouinces"), London begins by boasting of days of prosperity:

> That I in MAIE, was calde a famous thing,
> Yea Townes and Cities did my glory ring:
>   Nay thorowe the worlde my golden fame so grewe,
>   That Princes high, crost Seas, my seate to viewe. (sig. B1r, lines 11–14)

London prepares for the coronation celebrations for King James, "as a Bryde, against her Nuptiall day," when the plague strikes with "Vnwelcome death" declaring, "oh, LONDON, thou must yeeld to mee" (sig. B1v, lines 29, 52–53). In place of the king, a personified death enters London. Death, later berated by the elderly widow, turns the nuptial to funeral, the raucous celebration to doleful lament. "Drown'd in deepe seas (poore Lady) thus I lye," bemoans London, "Vnlesse some speedie helpe a comfort yeeld," a counter to Death's demand that London "yeeld" to him (sig. B1v, lines 57–58). London's losses are compounded by indifference and isolation. As Muggins put it in his prayer, "men stand a farre off" and fail to come to one another's aid (sig. D3v).[92]

As discussed in chapter 3, London gathers mourning mothers because, as she says, "For Parents loue, vnto their Children deare, / In iudgment sounde, nothing can come more neare" (sig. B2v, lines 111–12). The elegies that constitute this section of the poem articulate personal, intimate losses perhaps stemming from Muggins's immediate surrounds but also emblematic of pain felt throughout the city during the plague. Taken collectively, the mourning mothers of *London's Mourning Garment* are an allusion to

Jeremiah 9:17–20. In this chapter of Jeremiah, the solitary prophet complains of the duplicity and callousness of the people; God explains that he will punish them and says, "Take hede, & call for the mourning women, that thei may come, & send for skilful women that thei may come, And let them make haste, & let them take vp a lamentation for vs, that our eyes may cast out teares & our eye liddes gush out of water." Jeremiah interjects, "Therefore heare the worde of the Lord, ô ye women, and let your eares regarde the wordes of his mouth, and teache your daughters to mourne, and euerie one her neighbour to lament. For death is come vp into our windowes & is entred into our palaces, to destroye the children without, and the yong men in the stretes."[93] Death sneaking through windows and leaving the dead in the streets was not too far from what was actually happening during the plague of 1603, where bodies were carried out nightly for burial, not far at all from Muggins's personification of death "with his darts" demanding that London submit to his will.

That the "skilful women" referred to in Jeremiah were professional mourners led some early modern commentators to read the lines as a scornful attack on mere shows of repentance. Daniel Tossanus imagined the words "vttered as it were scoffingly, to awaken the people, and to depaint out [highlight] the wonderfull hardnesse of their heartes, which was such as that they were faine to hire, and cause come, all the mourning men and women of the worlde, to make them shed teares."[94] John Trapp, on the other hand, suggested that the mourning women were skilled musicians with "the chief hand in funeral mournings," who were called upon "so as to wring teares from the beholders."[95] For Trapp, the "skilful women" were an integral part of bringing about collective expressions of grief. Muggins's mourning mothers perform much the same function: Muggins's appropriation of the mourning women of Jeremiah avoids the issue of disingenuous mourning by presenting the procession of bereaved mothers whose genuine grief is not in question but whose elegies are nonetheless "skilful" in evoking tears from others.

The mourning women are essential to the ethical, spiritual, and political project of *London's Mourning Garment*. While one might see in them an image of static, excessive mourning, in her reading of the weeping women of Jeremiah, L. Juliana M. Claassens argues that "the act of wailing and calling others to join in public grief transforms the wailing woman from a state of invisibility to a position of vivacity, authority, and significance; from a woman-as-object to a woman-as-subject whose actions . . . have a powerful effect in a community in crisis."⁹⁶ London's initial search for condoling mourners results in finding only widows and widowers already seeking new spouses, children too busy enjoying the inheritance from their deceased parents, trusted friends using "wresting Law" to extract the inheritance of their friends' children, and apprentices focused on taking over their masters' shops (sigs. B2r–v, lines 71–84). London encounters the very sins of pure self-interest that Muggins would attribute as the cause of the plague, or at least its continuation. The mourning mothers are important in moving readers out of complacency and into an active sense of communal suffering—or, as the prayer would have it, a "fellow-felling of each others miserie," an appropriate affect for "the members of Christ" (sig. D3v).

London ultimately dubs this idealized community the "blessed Common-weale," and it is important to note that the poem's mourning mothers evoke the affect, the mutual sympathy that Muggins imagines as the foundation of such a commonwealth (sig. D2v, line 672). "Common-weale" itself was a contested term in the period. The term could signal an orderly political community, but as Keith Wrightson notes, "common-weale" was also "the watchword of most of the major conflagrations and rebellions between 1450 and 1650."⁹⁷ When used by commoners like Muggins, the term was disruptive, one of the marginalized insisting that their perspective was essential to governance. This is at the radical heart of *London's Mourning Garment*. When London turns to the city's leaders, she asks that they in essence model themselves not on some ruling class elsewhere but rather on the mourning mothers of the poem and "for mercy pray. / Desiring pardon, with a contryte heart" (sig. D2r, lines 649–50). But first London demands a number of reforms to set the commonwealth right. As intimately autobiographical as some of the poem is, *London's Mourning Garment* aims throughout to be a public statement, and Muggins's poem is ultimately prophetic in nature, decrying the plague as a sign of the city's failure to live up to God's covenant. That covenant included an individual's genuine worship and sincere repentance, especially in prayer, but more often than not Muggins appealed to an economic covenant grounded in scripture as the basis for his "blessed Common-weale" (sig. D2v, line 672).⁹⁸

Having chronicled the plague of 1603—its devastation of families, of households, and of trade, its indiscriminate infection of young and old, rich and poor, sinner and zealous minister—London declares, "O you of LONDON, now heare LONDON speake" (sig. D1r, line 582). Although London has ostensibly been speaking throughout the poem, the line announces a turn from past triumphs and present woes to future-oriented reform, from chronicle, complaint, and elegy to prophecy. London announces the main economic theme almost immediately. Singling out "you Magistrates of might, / And wealthy Citizens, whose store is great," London insists, "cast your eyes vpon the needy wight" (sig. D1r, lines 583–84, 586). In the next stanza London hammers the message home, repeating "Remember" at the start of almost every line as she articulates an economic amplification of the pamphlet's memento mori woodcut of the hourglass, skull, and scales:

> Remember all, your riches are but lent,
> Though in this world, you beare such power and sway:
> Remember too, how soone your yeares are spent,
> Remember eke, your bodies are but clay,
> Remember death, that rangeth at this day.
>   Remember when, poore Lazers woes did end,
>   The full fed glutton, to hell, did discend. (sig. D1v, lines 589–96)

Remember—the core concept of memento mori—here repeated to urge the sharing of wealth because the trappings of the world are temporary and death might come after "yeares are spent" or sooner, "at this day" as the plague spread from Southwark outward. And wealth, argues the stanza, may well be a hindrance to salvation: London ends the stanza with a paraphrase of Luke 16 in which the impoverished, sore-covered Lazarus unsuccessfully begs at a rich man's gate; when the two die, Lazarus "was caried by the Angels into Abrahams bosome," while the rich man was buried and tormented.[99] The rich man then begs that Lazarus visit his brothers to warn them of their possible damnation, but Abraham insists that they already have the words of "Moses and the Prophets" from which they should already have derived the lesson. Muggins uses extraordinary rhetorical force for ideas that were at least in theory widely accepted in Christian societies for centuries but clearly forgotten by the acquisitive Londoners around him. The anaphora of "Remember" emphasizes that the ideas are known but not practiced, that wealth had been sinfully hoarded rather than righteously shared.

Having spoken directly to the issue of unequal wealth, London next aims specifically at the city's magistrates. London repeats "Remember" a sixth and seventh time to remind rulers of their responsibilities. Following the Geneva Bible's gloss of Matthew 25:14–30, that the parable of the five talents is a message that "the graces of God shalbe taken away from him that doeth not bestowe them to Gods glorie and his neighbours profite,"[100] London declares,

> Giue much and be, no niggards of your store:
> God in his wisedome, gaue it you therefore.
>   Put foorth your tallents, and gaine ten for fiue,
>   so shall you in, the heauenly Cittie thriue. (sig. D1v, lines 606–9)

Reducing the gap between the wealthy and the poor of the earthly city is an investment in "the heauenly Citie," argues Muggins. London adds yet another "Remember" to this, emphasizing that magistrates must be like "nursing fathers" to the needy, echoing Isaiah 49:23 and perhaps Balmford. And, London warns, the magistrate who uses his office to enrich himself "robbes his God, and his poore neighbours both" (sig. D1v, line 600). London urges, "Let then your kindnes, now to them appeare" (sig. D1v, line 605), for each act of economic self-interest, argues the poem, is a spiritual affront. Just a few blocks away from St. Olave's was the Bridge House, a massive store of grain for the city. As craftsmen struggled to survive under the economic freeze brought about by the plague, were the aldermen perceived as miserly with the grain, not unlike the senators of *Coriolanus*, performed at the Globe just a few years later? Whatever the case, Muggins implies some failure on the part of the city's government to adequately fulfill its duties to the poor. Citing Isaiah and Matthew, Muggins took scripture as a guide to the economy and the proper functioning of the commonwealth.

At this point London turns to more concrete demands, asking that the rulers pass the decree discussed in chapter 1, "That each man may, with labour earne his foode." While almsgiving preoccupied the first of London's demands, at this point Muggins seems to reflect on his own lot and the lot of the working poor around him. As Patricia Fumerton has shown, the years roughly corresponding to Muggins's lifetime saw migrant workers and even poor householders "living in an unstable state of subsistence poverty in which they had to hustle in multiple, shifting by-employments to just get by."[101] Muggins was keenly aware of the state of affairs; he had seen the wealthy consume, and the poor consumed. Somehow products were bought and sold but the poor were poorer. At the very least a nation that routinely recited the Lord's Prayer should do more than lip service to the idea of "our daily bread." Muggins's personified London goes further, however, rebuking those who live off the labor of others, describing them as "deuouring drones" in contrast to "laboring bees" (sig. D1v, lines 617–18). Whereas early modern analogies between bee and human society typically describe drones as "lazy," Muggins draws attention to their consumption, the way they live off the labor of others.[102] These "drones" relate directly to the pawnbrokers discussed in chapter 2, but London interestingly singles out not only loans but bribes as well, powerbrokers manipulating the market and cornering monopolies and thereby devaluing the labor of others. Although the extended title of *London's Mourning Garment* promises a lament for "her wealthy Cittizens," Muggins only really focuses on the wealthy to remind them that their wealth is "but lent," not theirs at all in the vast scheme of things, and best put to charity for those in need. The real focus of the poem is the laboring poor against the idle rich.

Whereas St. Olave's and St. Saviour's were populated primarily by craftsmen, the area to the west of these parishes conjured up images of idleness and vice for contemporaries. John Stow felt compelled to include a special subsection in his description of Southwark devoted to bear gardens and "the Stewes" or brothels. Stow recounts the signs painted on the sides of these houses: "a Boares head, the Crosse keyes, the Gunne, the Castle, the Crane, the Cardinals Hat, the Bell, the Swanne, &c." And he describes the various rules for the bawdy houses and the exclusion of prostitutes from "Christian buriall" and "the rights of the Church." Stow summarizes a long history of attempts at regulating brothels in Southwark, from reducing the number of houses from eighteen to twelve early in the sixteenth century until 1546, when "this row of Stewes in Southwarke was put downe by the Kings commandement, which was proclaimed by sound of Trumpet, no more to be priviledged, and used as a common Brothel, but the inhabitants of the same to keepe good and honest rule as in other places of this Realm, &c."[103]

Despite Stow's triumphant tone, the putting down of brothels in Southwark simply dispersed prostitution throughout the city, often under the guise of alehouses or inns. For this reason, Gustav Ungerer cautions against overestimating the prevalence of brothels in the suburbs of London. Indeed, Ian Archer has shown that by the 1570s, while many brothels still operated outside the city's walls, some were within, nestled surprisingly close to respectable neighborhoods and centers of power.[104] Thus, in a sermon printed in 1614, Thomas Adams observed, "Whoredome, scornes to liue obscurely in the Suburbs: She hath friends to admit her within the walles."[105] Still, whether based on reality or popular perception, as late as 1606 the anonymous author of *The Returne of the Knight of the Poste from Hell* could write with confidence that his readers would understand his references to "shorditch Curtezans" and "Southwarke brothels," while other early seventeenth-century writers referred to "the strumpetrie of the Suburbes," "The Suburbs pandors," and the generally "sinfully-polluted Suburbes."[106]

The proliferation of brothels and their continued conspicuousness in the suburbs did not go unnoticed by Muggins. London's last demand denounces them:

> The number, numberlesse of houses vaine,
> Which beere and ale, forsooth make shewe to sell:
> Vnder which couller, doth such vyces rayne
> My cheeke doth glowe, my toongue refraines to tell,
> Offending God, and pleasing Sathan well,
>   Like wicked SODOME, doth my Subburbs lye,
>   A mighty blemish, to faire LONDONS eye. (sig. D2r, lines 624–30)

Stow could recall by name the Southwark brothels of the early sixteenth century, but Muggins's impression, or at least rhetorical stance, was that by the seventeenth century such houses of prostitution were innumerable. Here the "couller" or disguise under which brothels operated is matched by the blushing cheek of London at the sight of illicit sexuality. Plague pamphlets often evoked the story of Sodom as a biblical precedent for renewed rigor in the enforcement of Christian morality, but the concern here, following as it does stanzas about ensuring that labor results in a living wage and restraining idle exploiters, may be as much economic as it is moral. The "Subburbs lye," they recline in sexual repose but also in idleness and deceit, like the "deuouring drones" of the stanza just preceding this one.[107] And one must recall the last of the mourning mothers' worries about how the difficulty of making ends meet might lead to sexual exploitation. Here and throughout Muggins's writing, the moral and the economic seem inseparable.

London's insistence in these stanzas stems directly from the individual voices the poem brings forth. To the widow who "lackes house, lodging, sight, & what to eate," the wealthy are urged to "Giue much and be, no niggards of your store." To the forlorn mother who wishes "That I may worke and hate dishonest wealth," each laborer will be fed, and brothels will be taken down. To the family in debt, those who "in their bribes and lones" seize "Mens whole estates" will be restrained (sig. D1v, lines 619–20). Drawn from Muggins's life in the Poultry and St. Olave's, the many voices of the poem present a plurality, a chorus of the city in need.

Although prophetic poetry is often associated with visual tropes, the ethical demand of hearing and being heard is equally important to the work.[108] Certainly this is a major theme of Jeremiah: the people refuse to hear Jeremiah's prophecies, and God in turn refuses to hear their prayers. Thus, after uttering another prophecy, Jeremiah pleads, "Heare and giue eare, be not proude, for the Lord hathe spoken it."[109] London similarly asks that readers listen: "Ymmagin now, you heare a Mothers griefe" (sig. C2r, line 366). Mothers in turn weep "To heare and see, the Infant in such paine" (sig. B4r, line 217). And most important, London demands to be heard as a representative: She begins gently, echoing Jeremiah: "Onely I pray you listen and giue eare / To LONDONS sorrowes" and "Excuse me then, and heare me too, a while" (sig. C2v, lines 404–5; sig. C3r, line 414); but this gives way to greater force as London begins her program for reform bluntly stating, "now heare LONDON speake" (sig. D1r, line 582). London acts as an advocate, but as a modern-day figure from Lamentations, she is also grounded in scripture, citing chapter and verse to present the will of London's poor as the will of God, building on the early modern proverb that equated *vox populi* with *vox Dei*.[110] Muggins brings together the many voices of desperate Londoners to protest more loudly the indifference many encountered in the city.

The visual, too, has a place in *London's Mourning Garment*. As she calls for mourning mothers, London announces, "Chast LONDON wiues me thinkes I see you all" (sig. B4v, line 267). In fact, the elegies discussed in chapter 3 are narrated as visions. London sees the tears, and after one speaks, she declares, "Step after Step, I see an other come" (sig. C1v, line 323). And the visual trope leads to the visionary aim of the poem. Toward the end, London asserts that if the "heads of LONDON Citie" implement the reforms demanded by London, the plague will cease: "Yf this you will, incontinently doe, / The Lorde in pittie, will his judgments cease" (sig. D2r, lines 631, 652–53). Sounding rather like Jeremiah pleading with the Israelites, Muggins reiterates his understanding of the covenant, that if people are pious and the economic reforms are in place, God will bestow his blessings:

> Health and long life, Honour & happie peace,
> Your Foes shal quaile, your friendes shall still increase,
>> Your Wiues shall flourish like a fruitfull Vine,
>> Your Children prosper, and your griefes decline (sig. D2r, lines 655–58)

As vague as these blessings may sound, Muggins pulled them from Psalm 128. Again, the Geneva Bible's gloss is helpful in understanding how Muggins likely understood these lines: "The worlde estemeth them happie which liue in welth, and ydleness: but the holie Gost approueth them best that liue of the meane p[ro]fit of their labours." Even, or perhaps especially, in a vatic mode, Muggins spoke to the economic injustices around him, a sense that exploitation and indifference were not simply matters of an individual's lack of empathy—one of the hazards of the marketplace—but public issues of salvation for the entire city. Condemning idleness, Muggins repeatedly promotes the importance of labor.

In the next stanza, London announces that the city's "men of Worth shall stay," and merchants will be enriched, but the remaining five lines of the stanza are devoted to London's laborers:

> Your Trades-mens sorrows shall bee done away,
> True loyall seruants shall with them remaine:
> Your Artisants shall neuer more complaine,
>> Their honest labour so shall thriue and speede,
>> That they shall giue to others that haue neede. (sig. D2v, line 661–65)

Muggins's vision still has a ruling class, a middling sort, and people in need, but with reform—ending prostitution and extortionist loans, sharing wealth, and ensuring that labor is sufficiently compensated—the ideal commonwealth could be seen on the horizon of possibilities. The complaints Muggins lodged in 1595 would be unnecessary; no one would need to turn to the pawnbrokers of Houndsditch; the middling sort could join the wealthy in supporting the needy; and the plague would not strike the city, if everyone fulfilled the mandates of a "blessed Common-weale."

The poem ends with one final vision: King James's royal entry into London. The poem had begun with London recounting the excitement around preparations for the celebration of the new king's coronation, traditionally beginning with a procession through London and ending with the king's formal coronation at Windsor. In place of James's tour of the city, London herself searches the devastated city for genuine mourners to energize her vision of reform. Early in the poem London reflects on the preparations for the royal entry; she recalls magistrates pulling out their scarlet robes, artisans preparing pageants to entertain the king, and merchant-strangers funding many of the celebrations, scattering "coyne, like IVPITERS showres of Golde, / Hoping with ioy this CESAR to behold" (sig. B1v, lines 41–42). The stanzas about preparing for the royal entry draw most conspicuously from classical sources. Visitors arrive "like to AGAMEMNONS gallant trayne" (sig. B1r, line 15), artisans are Pygmalions (sig. B1v, line 47), merchants like Jupiter, London startlingly like Icarus:

With ICARVS, I soring then aloft,
Bathing my limbes in heat of highest sonne,
Till waxen wings with melting heate were soft,
And had no power me from the waues to shunne,
Downe must I fall, my glorie quite vndone. (sigs. C3r, lines 435–39)

Here the heights of classical allusion appear to be as doubtful as Icarus's waxen wings. They serve to glorify London, but for Muggins they also presage the plague. Depictions of London as a new Troy were commonplace in the period.[111] King James's entry into London was to begin with the invitation, "Dread King, our hearts make good, what words do want, / To bid thee boldly enter Troynouant."[112] Rather than the triumph of Troynovant, Muggins reads Troy typologically, its downfall not unlike the several grand biblical cities that failed to temper success with prayer and humility. This is perhaps another reason London doubts Homer's ability to chronicle the city's suffering.

The poem thus shifts from classical to biblical allusion, rooted in England's native tradition of visionary poetry. Imagining her reforms already implemented, London envisions its new state. Whereas earlier London described herself as "poore LONDON," in the penultimate stanza London declares:

Renowned Lady, now must be my name,
O famous LONDON, who is like to thee;

> Thy God is serude by men of each degree,
>   Thy Churches filde, thy Preachers burne with zeale,
>   Thy glory shines, O blessed Common-weale. (sig. B1r, line 8; D2v, lines 668–72)

Allusions to Ovid and Homer are shed as the molten wings of Icarus give way to the shining glory and burning zeal of Muggins's ideal commonwealth. And it is at this point that London envisions King James's arrival:

> My crowned CESAR and his Peerlesse Queene,
> Comes now tryumphing with their princely sonne,
> Deckt with rich robes the like was neuer seene,
> Nor neuer none more welcome to LONDON,
> Me thinkes I see the people how they runne,
>   To get them roome this happy sight to see,
>   That this may come say all Amen, with mee. (sig. D2v, lines 673–79)

A vision "the like was neuer seene," observes London. Londoners like Muggins were evidently aware of James's interest in imperial Roman iconography, but Muggins nonetheless ends with "Amen," revealing that like the text that follows the poem, this, too, was a kind of prayer.[113] After some anxiety about the succession of Elizabeth, the image of the royal family complete with heir apparent lent some sense of added stability to the realm, but James would not actually enter London for five more months. The vision of filled churches and throngs on the streets to view "this happy sight" stands in stark contrast with the quarantined households and neighbors reluctant to contact one another that surrounded Muggins as he wrote *London's Mourning Garment*. The vision of the king's as yet unfulfilled entry signals an imaginary restoration of order and, more important, since the delay was due to the plague, an end to God's wrath. The final two stanzas thus anticipate London's reforms enacted and envision the people of Muggins's ideal commonwealth attending church and, afterward, the coronation celebration. In place of the self-interest with which the poem began, Londoners in the final vision collectively focus outward, on charity, on piety, and on the celebration of an orderly body politic.

In the October eclogue of Edmund Spenser's *The Shepheardes Calender* (1579), the shepherd Cuddie reflects on Spenser's pastoral persona, Colin

Clout: "He, were he not so ill with love bedight, / Would mount as high, and sing as soote as Swanne," says Cuddie.[114] EK, the puzzling glossator of the poem, muses, "As soote as Swanne) [sic] The comparison seemeth to be strange: for the swanne hath euer wonne small commendation for her swete singing: but it is sayd of the learned that the swan a little before hir death singeth most pleasantly, as prophecying by a secrete instinct her neere destinie."[115] As Kevin Pask argues, *The Shepheardes Calender* asserts and forestalls Spenser's own entry into the vatic mode, and frames prophetic poetry as a kind of final act.[116] *London's Mourning Garment* is both Muggins's first and last work known to appear in print. By the time he brought the pages of *London's Mourning Garment* to Ralph Blower for publication, Muggins had lost his apprentices and his eldest daughter to the plague. Other losses were not recorded, or the records may have been lost. After 1603 Muggins disappears from the historical record as well. A William Muggins was buried at St. Bride's Church in 1636, but with no profession or next of kin listed, one cannot say for certain that this was the aged silk-weaver.[117] If it was, he lived out the remainder of his days quietly—there is no record of further controversial petitions signed by Muggins, no more warrants for arrest or suits for debt. Perhaps he printed something else anonymously, but it seems doubtful. *London's Mourning Garment* recorded his deepest fears and highest hopes for his own life and the lives of his fellow Londoners. It described London as he saw it and as he would like to have seen it. He called for an economy that rewarded labor, a society that tended to the neediest, a godly city focused on mutual aid. Was there anything else Muggins wanted to say about the way the city could have been? Like Cuddie's prophetic "soote Swanne," Muggins's song was sung.

Epilogue

The Horizon of the Past

> Lord giue vnto the Nobles, & Senators of this Land, the spirit of wisedome, counsell and vnderstanding.
> —WILLIAM MUGGINS (1603)

The inner leaf of the Bodleian Library's copy of *London's Mourning Garment* features the signature of its former owner, "Thomas Adamson."[1] Adamson was a soldier eventually serving as a master gunner to Charles II. In 1673, concerned that France might invade England with the help of English Catholics, Adamson arranged to print an Elizabethan manuscript by Thomas Digges, *Englands Defence. A Treatise concerning INVASION* (1680). Adamson added his own preface, notes, and tables working out the logistics of organizing a defense force against what seemed to him a likely invasion. While the pamphlet is of interest primarily to military historians, in his preface "To the Reader" Adamson makes some startling assertions. Imagining a governor who might allow an enemy force entry, Adamson asserts, "The Inhabitants and Souldiers may justify the killing of him, and defend themselves. Which Position I hope neither Divine nor Lawyer will deny, seeing the end of Government is to preserve the People (Salus Populi suprema Lex)."[2] Despite his role as soldier to the king, Adamson appears as something of a radical, doing away with the divine right of rulers and insisting on the accountability of government to the governed. The Latin summation comes from Cicero, but Adamson may well have appropriated it from New

Model Army officer William Rainborowe, who for some time used it as a motto.[3] Whatever the case may be, Adamson would have found some confirmation of his own politics in Muggins's demands on magistrates in *London's Mourning Garment*. He may have shared Muggins's sense that on the horizon was the possibility of a commonwealth responsive to the needs of the most vulnerable. Muggins may even have seemed to anticipate the years of the English Commonwealth that left such a profound stamp on Adamson.

Just after the inscription of his name in *London's Mourning Garment*, Adamson wrote "1665–1666," the year of the Great Plague that took the lives of nearly seventy thousand Londoners.[4] Daniel Defoe, only a boy at the time of the plague, would write of it:

> London might well be said to be all in Tears; the Mourners did not go about the Streets indeed, for no Body put on black, or made a formal Dress of Mourning for their nearest Friends; but the Voice of Mourning was truly heard in the Streets; the shrieks of Women and Children at the Windows, and Doors of their Houses, where their dearest Relations were, perhaps dying, or just dead, were so frequent to be heard, as we passed the Streets, that it was enough to pierce the stoutest Heart in the World, to hear them. Tears and Lamentations were seen almost in every House, especially in the first Part of the Visitation; for toward the latter End, Mens Hearts were hardened, and Death was so always before their Eyes, that they did not so much concern themselves for the Loss of their Friends, expecting, that themselves should be summoned the next Hour.[5]

Defoe captures in novelistic detail the horrors of the plague that Adamson likely experienced, the anguish and fear of being quarantined, the despair at losing so many loved ones, the dread that one might be next to die. Although the images are common to many texts about the plague, here Defoe imagines little room for the callous indifference against which Muggins strove. Instead, any Londoners who failed to mourn were merely resigned to their own death. According to Defoe there was no need to search for genuine mourners—"the Voice of Mourning" was everywhere. Despite advances in understanding the contagion and more organized efforts to contain the spread of the plague, Adamson still evidently found comfort in Muggins's pamphlet, with its elegies for dead children and its prophetic vision of a "blessed Common-weale" bolstered by a flourishing economy and magistrates serving the needs of citizens.

I have suggested that Ben Jonson probably read *London's Mourning Garment* before writing "On My First Sonne." Patrick Phillips hears echoes of Muggins in John Davies's poem recollecting the plague of 1603, "The Triumph of Death."[6] And George Wither would seem to have at least consulted Muggins's poem in the 1620s as he prepared to write *Britain's Remembrancer* (1628). The future mayor and member of Parliament John Swinnerton certainly read the pamphlet, and he may have recommended it to members of his circle; indeed, this may have been the route the poem took to Jonson.

While one might find Muggins and his poem to be esoteric, a footnote at the tail end of the Elizabethan era, it is telling that sixty years after its publication in 1603, early modern readers were still finding *London's Mourning Garment* relevant. In this sense Muggins fits what microhistorian Edoardo Grendi describes as the "exceptional normal," the archival figure who in his eccentricity reflects unspoken norms.[7] Struggles with debt and with the grief of burying one's children, living through poverty and the plague, all this makes Muggins all too typical of early modern London's middling sort. Even translating his experiences into a pamphlet might not make Muggins exceptional. The petition discussed at Muggins's household in the summer of 1595 was the product of lively debate among the weavers. The Yeomanry compared their experiences at the market and their economic woes, discussed the law and scripture, and then drafted the petition discussed in chapter 1 of this book. Petitions are not, strictly speaking, "literary," but Muggins's fellow weavers and their neighbors surely made songs, poems, and stories out of their daily struggles as well. Muggins stands in a long line of laboring poets who reflected on the conditions of their lives and how they could be improved. After finding himself in prison for his involvement in the printing of the weavers' petition, it is perhaps most exceptional that Muggins was willing to risk entering print again in 1603, especially since *London's Mourning Garment* included complaints about the city's leaders. The decision to publish and the subsequent individual and institutional efforts to preserve copies of *London's Mourning Garment* over the centuries are really the only things that make Muggins's experience of his world visible to us at all.

Taken from another perspective, however, everything about Muggins might be deemed exceptional. His connection to Deloney, his problems with debt within the tight-knit community at the Poultry, his encounters with Puritans and nonconformists, the fact that he happened to move to the parish hardest hit by the plague of 1603—each of these and other countless undiscovered details about Muggins compose a singular constellation of contingent experiences and beliefs that make *London's Mourning Garment* a unique work of vatic poetry. And we might in our own way take up the prophetic message of *London's Mourning Garment*. Just as Muggins read the Bible in terms of his present, we might think about our present moment in terms of *London's Mourning Garment*. While modern readers will have varied reactions to Muggins's call for a more zealous commonwealth, his personified London's proposal that "each man may, with labour earne his foode" still seems as vitally relevant today as it was in Muggins's lifetime. As Muggins knew, change requires the voices of the disenfranchised speaking of their experiences, and it requires those in power to listen and act. To take my own place of birth as an example, the United States of America has the highest maternal mortality rate among so-called developed nations, and it has the highest incarceration rate in the world, both disproportionally affecting the lives of African Americans. CEO pay has increased by 937 percent since 1978, whereas the real wages of average workers have stayed the same even as hours of productivity have increased. Half a million people in the United States are homeless, and forty million live in poverty.[8] Modern versions of Muggins's "Remember all, your riches are but lent. . . . Remember rulers, of each publycke charge . . ." ought to resound through every street and alleyway of the United States. Muggins's vision of a commonwealth founded on labor, charity, and mutual aid, where no one faces homelessness or hunger, has yet to be fulfilled. He could envision a better, more equitable world, but he also knew there was much to be done. The horizon of the past may be our horizon, too.

APPENDIX: *LONDON'S MOURNING GARMENT*

Four copies of *London's Mourning Garment* have survived and are held in the following archives: the Bodleian Library, the British Library, The Huntington Library, and University of Oxford.

The complete pamphlet appears here transcribed and annotated with original spelling and punctuation. I have taken the liberty of changing VV/vv to W/w where appropriate, however. I have also indicated the original signatures in brackets. I have provided line numbers for the verse and glosses for uncommon words or spelling. More extensive annotations appear in endnotes. For Muggins's prayer I have not indicated every allusion but rather annotated what seem to me the most salient scriptural allusions.

For a modern-spelling edition of the poem, readers are directed to Rebecca Totaro's *The Plague Epic in Early Modern England*, pages 53–70.

LONDONS
Mourning garment, or Funerall
Teares: worne and shed for the death
of her wealthy Cittizens, and other her
inhabitants.
To which is added, a zealous and feruent
Prayer, with a true relation how many haue dyed of all diseases, in euery particuler
parish within London, the liberties, and out
parishes neere adjoyning from the 14 of
July 1603. to the 17 of Nouember.
Following.

At London printed by Raph Blower.
1603. (. ˙ .)

To the Right Worshipfull, Sir Iohn
Swinnerton Knight: one of the worshipfull Aldermen, of the honorable Citty of London:
W. M. wisheth Earths Happines, and Heauens Blessednes.[1]

Right Worshipful and graue Senator: if my knowledge and learning, were answerable to my good will and affection: this my poore labour now mourning in a sable Weede, should be as great and precious, as to the contrary it is weake, and slender. And knowing that the Vertuous minde, respecteth not so much the valewe of the guift, as the good will of the giuer, emboldeneth me to present this smal Pamphlet to your Worships view;[2] most humbly crauing pardon for my rash attempt, which if to your wonted clemmencie I doe obtaine. I shall liken my selfe to a poore Debtor owing much, freely forgiuen of all his large reckonings and dangerous accounts, and bound in duty to pray for your Worships long life, with increase of honor.

Your Worships at Commaund,
    WILLIAM MVGGINS

¶ Londons mourning garment, and Funerall Teares.

With heauy heart, and sighes of inward Cares,
With wringing hands explayning sorrows wo,
With blubbered cheekes, bedewde with trickling teares
With minde opprest lamenting griefs that flowe,
London lament, and all thy losses showe: [5]
    What al? nay some, all were too much to tell,
    The learned Homer could not penne it well.

Ay me poore London, which of late did florish,
With springing MARCH, the tidings of a King:[3]
And APRILL showers, my blossomes so did nourishe, [10]
That I in MAIE, was calde a famous thing,
Yea Townes and Cities did my glory ring:
    Nay thorowe the worlde my golden fame so grewe,
    That Princes high, crost Seas, my seate to viewe.

And like to AGAMEMNONS gallant trayne,[4] [15]
Throughout my streetes, with stately steps did goe,
Where them with welcomes, I did entertaine;
Pleasing their liking, with each seuerall showe,
Where they in me, much treasure did bestowe,
    Honouring the Church with Prayers, the Change with golde,[5] [20]
    Where Princes bought, and beauteous Virgins solde.

To adde more glory to my prosperous state,
My Soueraigne Lord, most high and mighty King,
Made oft repayre, both Morning, Eu'en and late,
To me both gainefull, and a pleasant thing: [25]
My heart was glad, my voice SOL, FA, did sing,[6]
    My head did muse, not strucke with sorrowes sad,
    But how to make, my crowned Soueraigne glad.

[B1r]

And as a Bryde, against her Nuptiall day,
Doth deck her selfe, with fayre and rich attyre, [30]
Accompanide with Damsells fresh and gay,
To plight her faith, to him she did desire
Euen so did I with zeale as hot as fyer.
  Prepare my selfe against this day of ioye,
  To giue him welcome, with VIVE LE ROYE.[7] [35]

My Magistrates were all so ready prest
In skarlet rich, this potent Prince to greet:[8]
My wealthy Free-men also wrought their best,[9]
Preparing Pageants in each famous street
My Marchant-strangers laboured hands and feete,[10] [40]
  And scattered coyne, like IVPITERS showres of Golde,
  Hoping with ioy this CESAR to behold.[11]

And as those men the wealthiest in my Bower,
Was neuer sparing in this good intent,
So did my Artisants with all their power, [45]
For loue or gaine, to worke were ready bent.
PIGMALION foorth his skilfull Caruers sent?
  Cunning APPELLES with his pencill drew
  Prospectious* strange, for King and Peeres to veiw.[12]

But oh, a sudden qualme doth crosse my heart [50]
twixt cup and lip are dangers oft we see,
Vnwelcome death approcheth with his dart,
Yelping, oh, LONDON, thou must yeeld to mee:
I must haue rootes and branches for my fee.
  The fruits full ripe and blossomes that might grow [55]
  Are mine, not thine, the Fates decree'd it so.

Drown'd in deepe seas (poore Lady) thus I lye,
Vnlesse some speedie helpe a comfort yeeld:
Is there no wife nor widdow that will hye,

Perspectives

And reach a hand that hath some sorrowes felt, [60]
My griefes are more then I my selfe can welde,
    Helpe some good woman with your soules-sigh deepe,
    For you are tender hearted and can weepe.

[B1v]

What none? nay, then I see the Prouerbe old is true,
The widdowes care is studious where to loue, [65]
Sith women are so fickle, men to you,
LONDON laments, will ye her plaints remoue.
I heare no Eccho; men like women proue,
    Widowers for wiues, widdowes for husbands seeke,
    Before the teares are dryed from their cheekes. [70]

To children then I will my sorrowes shew,
Whose Parents lately in the graue were layde;
Their hearts with sighs will cause fresh teares to flow,
And reach a hand for sorrowing LONDONS ayde.
Come children mourne, I cry but am denayde, [75]
    Their Parents riches so inflames their brest,
    That they long since did wish them at their rest.

Where, or to whom, may I my voyce set forth?
Men mourne for men, where friendship long hath bred:
Fye no (good Lady) there is found small troth, [80]
The liuing Friend deceiues the friend that's dead,
Robbing his children with a subtill head:
    By reason he executor, made the† drowne
    By wresting Law, the riches are his owne.

Oh (helplesse Lady) whither shall I flye, [85]
To find true mourners in this sad lament?
To aged people; no, their heads are dry,
They cannot weepe, long since their teares were spent:

---

† *them*

To middle age? (alas) their wits are bent
    To purchase lands and liuings for their heires,   [90]
    Or by long life, to gaine which other spares.

The louing seruant may yet helpe at neede,
That now hath lost his Master and his stay,
Sending foorth sithings‡ till the heart doth bleed:
Oh, LONDON, thou in vaine to him doest pray,   [95]
His power and wits he bends another way:
    His Masters custome, shoppe, and trade to get,
    Is all the teares, the blithe yong man can let.

[B2r]

Is there none then, that will take Londons part?
And help to sing, a welcome vnto wo?   [100]
Is there none founde, that feeles a present smart?
Nor none aliue, that can cause Teares to flow?
If any be? then freely them bestow.
    Two mourne together, swage§ ech others grief,
    Weepe on a while, and I will be the chiefe.   [105]

I heare no answere yet in these estates,
Let me but study, where, and whom to seeke,
Oh, now I haue bethought me, come on mates,
For you and I, must mourne it by the weeke:
And neuer will, new teares, be long to seeke   [110]
    For Parents loue, vnto their Children deare,
    In iudgment sounde, nothing can come more neare.

The loue of Parents, are like Graftes that grow,
Euer encreasing, till it proue a tree:
The loue of Children, like the melting Snow,   [115]
Euer decreasing, till an ende there be,
Dayly experience, proues this true we see,

---
‡ *sighings*
§ *assuage*

Loue to the Children, euermore dependes:
But to the Parents, seldome re-discendes.

And now I haue, with trauel, griefe and paine, [120]
Founde foorth two mourners, that will Agents be:
Choose which of vs, shal settle to complaine,
Or if you will, leaue all the chardge to me:
Onely I with you, to abandon glee.
    And to my voice, prepare your glowing Eares, [125]
    With sighes and groanes, and sometimes scalding Teares.

And if to high my warbling notes ascendes,
Iudge me not bolde but zealous in my loue:
If that too lowe, thinke that with sighes for friendes,
My voice is hoarse, yet I againe will proue, [130]
The vtmost power, I can for to remoue,
    Your too forgetfull, sorrowes which are drye,
    And place them now, a fresh in memory,

[B2v]

Art thou a Father, or a Mother deare?
Hadst thou a Sonne, or Daughter of thy side: [135]
Were not their voice, sweete musicke in thy Eare,
Or from their smiles, could'st thou thy countnance hide.
Nay, were they not, the glories of thy pride?
    I doubt too much, thy loue on them were set,
    That whilst thou liuest, thou canst not them forget. [140]

Remember well, you Dames of London Cittie,
As for you men, ile leaue you for a while,
Because small paines, deserues the lesser pity,
And you are stronger, sorrowes to begyle:
A space we will, your company exile, [145]
    And bid you farewell, till another day,
    When time and place, will giue you cause of stay.

And now my harts, olde Widdowes and yong wiues,
You that in silence, sit so sad and mute:
You that wring hands, as weary of your liues, [150]
Heare London speake, she wil expresse your suite.
I know your sighes, is for your tender fruite.
    Fruite in the budde, in blossome ripe and growne,
    All deare to you, now death hath made his owne.

And as the greedy Wolfe, from harmeles Ewes, [155]
Robbs them of Lambes, sucking their tender Tett:
And in his Rigour, no compassion shewes,
But gormondizing, kils them for his meate.
Euen so deaths fury, now is growne so great,
    The tender Lambe, will not his fury stay. [160]
    Both Lambes and Ewes, he swalowes for his pray.

Witnes I can, poore LONDON for my part,
What palefac't Death, within fiue Monthes hath wrought
Seauen hundred Widdowes, wounded to the Hart,
With their sweet Babes, which they full dearely bought [165]
Some dead new borne, some neuer forth were brought,
    You Mothers weepe, if euer you bore any,
    To thinke how sore, Death did perplexe so many.

[B3r]

Not yet content, he Rageth vp and downe,
And secretly, his heauy visage shewes: [170]
In euery streete, and corner of the Towne,
Emptyeing whole houses, soone whereas he goes,
Taking away, both olde and young God knowes,
    The weeping Mother, and the Infant cleare,
    The louing Brother, and the Sister deare. [175]

Oh, mothers sigh, sit and shed teares a while,
Expell your idle pleasures, thinke on woes:
Make not so much as countenance of a smile

But with downe lookes, which inward sorrow showes,
And now a fresh, remember all your throwes, [180]
    Your gripes your panges, your bodies pincht with paine,
    As if this instant, you did them sustaine

Let not so much, forgotten be of you,
As the least qualme, that then your harts opprest:
No nor the smallest, dolor did ensue, [185]
As heauy wincks and too too little rest;
Remember al, the sorrowes of thy breast,
    Which in the breeding, bearing and deliuery,
    You did indure, with paine yet willing

Againe bethinke you, at that instant hower, [190]
The little difference, was twixt life and death:
When as the infant, with his naked power,
Laboured for life, to haue his rightfull birth,
And with the sickly, Mother gaspt for breath,
    The one nere dead, as nigh to death the other, [195]
    Sore to the babe, worse Trauell¶ for the Mother.

If any Mother, can forget this smart,
Her for a woman, I will neuer take:
And out of Londons, fauor may she part,
And all such brutish, strumpets for her sake: [200]
For such light hus-wiues, I a wish will make,
    That neuer any, may approch my Citty,
    Euer to want, and no hart them to pittie.

[B3v]

And now returne I, to you honest wiues,
Who grieuing sits, and sighing send forth Teares, [205]
Which to your Husbands, lyue chast and true liues,
And with your Children, passeth forth your yeares,

¶ Travail

To you that Londons, Lamentations heares.
    And are true parteners, in my plaints and mones,
    Experience shewes it, by your inward grones. [210]

The Child new borne, the Mother some deale well
Are all the griefes, and sorrows at an end:
No cares and troubles, yet I haue to tell,
Though Child be swath'de,** and sickly Mother mende,
The feeble Infant, many a fret doth send. [215]
    Which grieues the Mother, till she weepe againe,
    To heare and see, the Infant in such paine.

And with her feeble, hand and weakely strength,
She playes and dallyes, for the babyes good:
And to her milke-white, brestes doth lay at length [220]
The prety foole, who learnes to take his foode.
His onely meanes, to nourish life and bloud,
    He fed, she paynd, he drawes, poore Mother yeelds,
    Whose louing brests both shutes and prickings feeles,

And when the Babe doth gather strength a maine, [225]
Most strongly labouring at his mothers dugge.
She patiently endureth all the paine,
Suffering his lippes her nipple still to lugge,
And with her armes most closely doth it hugge,
    As she should say, draw childe and spare not mee, [230]
    My brests are thine, I feele no paine with thee.

Though that poore heart her brest doth ake full sore,
And inwardly fell prickings shee indures,
Till eyes gush teares, and lippes reach kisses store;
Which in true mothers gladsome ioyes procures, [235]
And to more ardent loue them still allures:
    That toares†† and kisses greet the Babe together,
    Like to sunne-shine when it is dropping weather,

** *swathed/swaddled*
†† *tears*

[B4r]

Ymmagin heere, the pretty Lambe doth cry,
The Mother strong, and times of Custome past:[13] [240]
Will, she then leaue it, to the worldes broad Eye,
No, whilst her life, and vitall powers last,
The Mothers loue, to Child is fixte so fast.
    She stills it straight, and layes it to her brest,
    With kisses more, then VENVS could disgest [245]

And with her Armes, she heaues it high and lowe,
As if a cradle, it sweete foole lay in:
Doubt you not to, she kisses did bestow,
And if it smile, a fresh she doth begin.
On prety looke, a hundred kisses winne [250]
    My more then sweete, vnto her Child she saith,
    I would not for, a Kingdome wish thy Death.

Now is her minde, full straight with inward ioy
As if all things, she thought should come to passe:
Vttering forth Sighes, vnto her prety boy, [255]
Shall Death haue thee, and lay thee in the grasse,
Ile rather goe, to Earth from whence I was,
    Fell Death goe seeke, for crooked age and olde,
    My Child is fayre, vnfitting for the molde.

I hope to see, more comfort and more ioy, [260]
Of this sweete Babe, which cost my life almost:
I pray thee grimme Death, doe not him annoy,
Goe get thee further, to some other Coast.
To kill an Infant giues small cause of boast.
    Theres many liuing, that would gladly dye, [265]
    Take them away, but spare my Childe and I.

Chast LONDON wiues me thinkes I see you all,
Each seuerall Mother, hauing greefes to shewe,
And with your greefes, I see the Teares doe fall,

The onely Phisicke, women can bestow, [270]
Oh, that I could, but ease your hart sicke woe,
    LONDON would spare, no labour cost nor time,
    To wipe the water, from your blubbered Eyen.

[B4v]

But I a skilfull Surgeons part will play,
First search the sore, then minister things meete: [275]
Vnto yovr memories, I your plants‡‡ will lay,
Causing a fresh your heauie eyes to greet.
Then gentler salues, I meane perswasions sweete;
    This is the surgery wounded LONDON layes
    To all her Patients, that her hests obayes. [280]

One tender mother cryeth loude and shrill,
Wringing her hands, my children both are dead:
Sweet louing Henry, and my eldest gyrle,
Ah Besse, my wench thou hadst thy mother sped[14]
With sorrowes, that will neuer from my head. [285]
    Thy forward wit to learning and to awe,
    A sweeter daughter neuer woman sawe.

Thy flaxen haire, thy collour red and white,
Thy yeeres full ten, thy body straight and tall,
Thy countnance smilling, neither sad nor light, [290]
Thy pleasant eyes, thy hands with fingers small,
Thy manners milde, thy reading best of all,
    With needle pregnant, as thy Sampler shewes,[15]
    Patient in death like sucking Lambe she goes.

My hopes were that I might haue kept thy life [295]
To see more yeeres, and be a beutious Mayde;
To see thee match't, and be a LONDON wife,
To see thy childe-bed, and be safely layde,

---

‡‡ *complaints*

To see thy children in the streete haue playde:
> To cheere my age, as should a louing daughter, [300]
> But thou art gone, and I must follow after.

My little HENRIE, oh, that prety foole;
That oft hath made my sorrowing heart full glad,
His words were Mamma: sit, here is a stoole,
Some bread and butter I haue nothing had; [305]
Ile busse you well, (good Mamma) be not sad,
> Vp on cock-high, I will sit in your lappe,
> Where oft (poore sweeting) he hath caught a nappe.

[C1r]

And if sometimes, he hearde his Father chide,
As housholde wordes, may passe twixt man and wife: [310]
Vnto my Husbande, presently he hyed
As he should say, I will appease the strife;
And with his Childish mirth, and pleasvres rife.
> Abates the heat, and makes vs both to ioy:
> To see such nature, in the little Boy. [315]

But Death, oh Death, that hater of my wealth
Hath slaine my Daughter, and my little Sonne:
Both of them proppes, vnto my wished health
Both to haue kept I woulde barefoote haue runne:
Fel ATROPOS, her fatall stroke hath done;[16] [320]
> With the eternall I beleue they rest,
> Oh, happy Babes, for euer they are blest.

Step after Step, I see an other come,
Casting her handes, abroade, as shee were wood:
Seeming to tell a heauy tale to some, [325]
But silly Dame, thou art not vnderstoode;
Speake mildely, lowly, not with chafing bloude:
> For hastie speach, hath seldome reason showne,
> When soft deliuerance, makes the matter knowne.

I am a Widdow poore, Christ shew me pittie, [330]
Feeble and weake of yeeres, three score and ten:
I had two Daughters, married in the Cittie,
Both of them well, & vnto honest men;
They had my loues, and I had heirs againe:
  With them I hop't to spend my aged yeeres, [335]
  And to be buried, with their funerall teares.

To them I gaue, that little I possest,
With them to dwel, as long as life ensured:
Three Monthes with one, my Custome was to rest,
Then, with the other, I like space endured: [340]
With vs the Diuel, no iarres nor brawles procured.
  But liued and lou'de, as quiet as might be,
  I bore with them, they dayly honouring me.

[C1v]

But now alas, a heauy Tale to tell,
As with my Chickins, I at pleasure slept: [345]
Comes the great Puttocke, with his Tallantes fel,
And from me quite, my youngest Chicken swept;
Then to the other, he full nimbly leapt,
  Seazing on her, as hee had done the other,
  Oh greedy Death, could'st thou not take their Mother? [350]

My age is fitter for the yawning Graue,
Their yeeres more tender in the worlde to stay:
My bones are dry, and would their porcions haue,
Their Lymmes were nimble, and a while might play;
My bloude is colde, theires hote, mine weares away. [355]
  They both were matched, & fruite might bring foorth store
  I olde and withered, and can yeelde no more.

Thou cruel leane, and ill deformed Death,
Thou great intruder, and vn-welcomde guest:
Thou palefac't hog, thou shortner of long breath, [360]

Thou mighty murdrer, of both man & beast:
Why doest thou not, inuite me to thy feast?
 And on my body, shew thy fury great
 That lackes house, lodging, sight, & what to eate.

With lamentations, and with Teares good store,   [365]
Ymmagin now, you heare a Mothers griefe:
Shee most of all, her sorrowes doth deplore,
Vttring foorth woordes, as helples of reliefe,
She is depriu'de, of all, both lesse and chiefe;
 As well her Children, as her Husbande good,   [370]
 With labouring seruantes that did earne their foode.

Ah my sweet Babes, what woulde not I haue done?
To yeelde you comfort, & maintaine you heer:
Early and late, no labour woulde I shun,
To feede your mouthes, though hunger pincht me neere;   [375]
All three at once, I woulde your bodies cheere.
 Twaine in my lappe, shoulde sucke their tender Mother,
 And with my foot, I woulde haue rockt the other.

[C2r]

Me thinkes I see them still, and heare their cryes
Chiefly a nights when I on bed am layde,   [380]
Which make fresh teares goe from my watry eyes,
When I awake and finde I am deceiued;
Sweet pretie Babes, Christ hath your souls receiued;
 Faire Babes to mee, you nere shall come againe,
 But where you are, I trust aye to remaine.   [385]

Your louing father tooke a great delight,
Often in Armes to haue those children small,
And now he hath them euer in his sight,
Not one or two, the heauens possesse them all,
Father and Babes obayde when Christ did call.   [390]
 They all are gone, I onely left with breath,
 To byde more sorrowes in this wretched earth.

Poore and in want yong widddow left am I,
Kindles and friendlesse, lacking meanes to liue,
Had but my seruants stayde their worke to plye [395]
Their labour, would some comfort to me giue,
My hopes are like to water powrde in syue
    Onely I trust God will increase my health,
    That I may worke and hate dishonest wealth.[17]

Many more sorrowes might I here repeate, [400]
Of grieued Mothers for their children deare,
But times are precious and worke too great
For my hoarse voice to shew and vtter here,
Onely I pray you listen and giue eare
    To LONDONS sorrowes, which so many are, [405]
    My clacking tongue cannot them halfe declare.

And as with paine I did endure to tell
Your too too heauie and vnwelcom'd woes,
Wherein poore LONDON labour'd to do well,
But wanting giftes, the best she can she showes [410]
The willing minde, that all she hath bestowes,
    Must needes be reconed[§§] for a friendly part,
    Deseruing thankes, with as cheerefull a heart,

[C2v]

Excuse me then, and heare me too, a while,
For many sorrowes compasse me throughout: [415]
Neuer since BRVTE set footing in this Isle,[18]
Nor nere since it was walled round about:
More blessed newes, nor happy spring cold sprout;
    Then did to LONDON, in this present yeere,
    When Englands CESAR came this Citie neere. [420]

---

§§ *reckoned*

All went aslaunt, happy that Marchant was
Which had rich wares to please his Chapmans eyes
The finest shagges, wrought stuffes, and purest glasse,
Rare cloth of gold, and silkes of euery dye:
Who for his money could know where to buy, [425]
    Both went and sent to fetch in wares good store,
    Not doubting sale for that and three times more.

And as they thought a while it did continue,
Doings waxt quicke, and wares a pace did sell,
Great men of honours with their retinue, [430]
Approch't my Citie minding here to dwell,
Houses and Chambers were let deare and well,
    There was no corner in me did remaine,
    But the true Owner might imploy to gaine,

With ICARVS, I soring then aloft,[19] [435]
Bathing my limbes in heat of highest sonne,
Till waxen wings with melting heate were soft,
And had no power me from the waues to shunne,
Downe must I fall, my glorie quite vndone,
    He sits aboue that looketh downe below, [440]
    Commanding powers his iustice here to show.

And with King DAVIDS chance doth me correct,[20]
Spreading his Plague, where pleaseth him to strike;
Because in health his lawes I did reject,
Trusting in menes,¶¶ in man, in horse, and pike: [445]
Boasting of riches, beautie and such like.
    Neuer redeeming of swift passing times,
    But still committing new and vgly crimes.

[C3r]
And to the ende, none dwelling in my Cittie
Should thinke themselues more safer then the rest, [450]

¶¶ *means*

Judging their slights and not Gods lasting pittie,
To be the cause why they with health are blest;
Gods judgement vpon all degrees are prest,
    From poorest begger, to the wealthiest Squire,
    From yongest infant, to the oldest Syre. [455]

For if the aged people hee should spare,
They would attribute to themselues too much,
And say their bloudes are drye, their bones so bare,
The Pestilence their bodies cannot touch.
If middle age should scape, their wits are such, [460]
    That through their dyet or by letting blood,
    They wonne the victorie, and the Plague with-stood.

The frolicke youths would judge the strengths the meane,
Boasting of joyntes, armes, legges and sinewes strong,
The little infant being weake and leane, [465]
Wants substance for the Plague to worke vpon.
These are excuses, but effects haue none;
    Gods Messenger (the Plague) doth feare no States,[***]
    But strikes both lowest and the highest Mates.

Now for the rich which haue of golde such store, [470]
Feeding their bodyes with dilicious fare,
Keeping great fires, stirre not out of doore,
Vsing perfumes, shunning infected ayre;
Shall they escape? No, the Plague will them not spare:
    Because they shall not thinke their heaped treasure, [475]
    Can keepe them longer then it is Gods pleasure.

If rich men dye, and poorer people stay,
They will exclame with hate and deadly ire,
Saying with surfeits[†††] they cousume[‡‡‡] the day,

[***] *Estates*

[†††] *surfeits*
[‡‡‡] *consume*

Wallowing in ease like dirtie Swyne in myre, [480]
Judging their scarcitie and their thinne atyre
    The onely Phisicke, poysons to with stand,
    But they like others haue giuen death their hand.

[C3v]

If any then should scape deathes heauie sight,
And claime a pardon for a longer day; [485]
The zealous Preacher and the godly wight,
Which for themselues, and for their hearers pray,
Might haue some fauour in this world to stay:
    But God saith no, they shall yeeld to their kinde,
    Lest they prooue haughtie which remaine behinde. [490]

There are a people that doe leawdly liue,
Swaggering and swearing, prone to euery sinne,
Shall those men scape? No, they account shall giue
Of all the vices they haue wallowed in.
Such wretched Caytiffes,§§§ made the Lord beginne, [495]
    To strike poore LONDON with thy heauie rod,
    For pleasing Sathan, and offending God.

What should I say my sorrowes are so many,
One for a thousand I cannot repeate,
Within my liberties scarce any, [500]
Which haue not felt Gods wrath and mightie threate,
Either by death, or sicknesse fell and great,
    If Parents scap'de, the children had their part,
    If both remaine, their seruants felt some smart.

The sicke bequeather of his wealth by Will, [505]
Not onely dead, but his executors too,
And eke the Scriuener that did make the Bill,
All in one fort-night haue payde death their due,

---

§§§ *base persons*

The like vnto the Landlord doth ensue,
>   Both wealthy father, and succeeding heire, [510]
>   With their poore tenants ended haue their care.

The joyfull Brydegroome married as to day,
Sicke, weake, and feeble before table layde,
And the next morrow dead and wrap't in clay,
Leauing his Bride, a widdow, wife and mayde. [515]
Which sudden change doth make her so dismayde,
>   That griefes and sorrowes doth perplexe her heart,
>   Within three dayes she takes her husbands part.

[C4r]

Much might I speake of other sad laments,
And fill your eares with new and seuerall woes, [520]
Spending a weeke, repeating discontents,
Which needlesse is, where all both sees and knowes,
How many thousands death and graues inclose:
>   Making me (LONDON) which long time hath flowrish't
>   Scorned of those which I both fed and nourish't. [525]

And those that haue my glory most set forth,
Boasting that I for beautie did excell;
Now to approch vnto me are so loath,
As if my presence were a swallowing hell:
Within their houses they refuse to dwell, [530]
>   And to the Countrey flye like swarmes of Bees,
>   Where wealth and credite many of them leese.

But most of all my sorrowing heart doth grieue,
For such as worke and take exceeding care,
And by their labour knowe not how to liue, [535]
Going poore soules in garments thinne and bare,
The bellie hungry, of flesh leane and spare.
>   Pawning and selling clothes, and what they haue,
>   To feed their children which for foode doe craue.

And when poore hearts their hunger once is stayed, [540]
The day insuing brings the like distresse:
The painefull Parents working all their trade
For new supply, fell famine to suppresse,
But all in vaine their woes are nere the lesse.
  Their worke being made, abroade poore soules they trott, [545]
  From Morne to Noone, from Noone to Night, God wott.

Offering their wares, and what they haue to sell,
Vnto such Trades-men as haue small pittie,
But they like NABALS,²¹ will not with them mell,¶¶¶
Vnlesse for halfe the worth they may it buy: [550]
The rich man laughs, the poore in heart doth cry,
  Shedding foorth teares in sorrow to his wife,
  This world doth make me wearie of my life.

[C4v]

The Wife doth weepe, the needy seruantes play,
The Children cry for foode where none is bought: [555]
The Father saith, I cannot sell to day,
One jot of worke, that all of vs haue wrought;
In euery shoppe, I haue for money sought.
  And can take none, your hunger to sustaine,
  Teares part from him, the Children cry amaine.**** [560]

What shall we doe? a counsell straight they take,
Meate must be had, our people must not starue,
Wife, take such thinges, & goe without A LOATE,²²
In HOWNDES DITCH,²³ pawne them, our great neede to serue,
They wil make sure, if that a day we swarue; [565]
  All will be lost, our garments are their owne,
  Though for a pound we giue a shilling lone.

¶¶¶ *deal or mix with*
**** *with speed/force*

Besides the Bill a powling groat[24] will cost,
And euery Moneth our pawne must be renew'd,
So was my Lease to griping vsurie lost, [570]
The first beginner of my sorrowes brew'd,
And euer since want[††††] vpon want insew'd.
    My bedding forfeite for a thing of nought,
    My brasse and Pewter, want of conscience bought.

If now our clothes which clad out naked skinne, [575]
Should thus be lost, as was our other good,
Alas, (poore Wife) what case are we then in,
Such shamefast Beggers neuer asked food.
If honest labour could this griefe withstood,
    We would haue reckoned day and night as one, [580]
    To worke for meate, rather then make such mone.

O you of LONDON, now heare LONDON speake,
Especially you Magistrates of might,
And wealthy Citizens, whose store is great,
I gently wooe you to haue good fore-sight, [585]
And cast your eyes vpon the needy wight,
    Though feare of sicknesse driue you hence as men,
    Yet leaue your purse, and feeling heart with them.

[D1r]

Remember all, your riches are but lent,
Though in this world, you beare such power and sway: [590]
Remember too, how soone your yeares are spent,
Remember eke, your bodies are but clay,
Remember death, that rangeth at this day.
    Remember when, poore Lazers woes did end,
    The full fed glutton, to hell, did discend.[25] [595]

---

††††   lack

Remember rulers, of each publycke charge,
The seuerall branches, of your priuate oath:[26]
Remember them, that vse a conscience large,
And on themselues, the needyes stocke bestow'th,
He robbes his God, and his poore neighbours both. [600]
    He that graunts blessings, to the poore that lends,
    Giues treble cursings, to those it miss-spends.

Remember likewise, God hath plac't you heere,
To be as nursing, fathers[27] to the poore,
Let then your kindnes, now to them appeare, [605]
Giue much and be, no niggards of your store:
God in his wisedome, gaue it you therefore.
    Put foorth your tallents,[28] and gaine ten for fiue,
    so shall you in, the heauenly Cittie thriue.

One other boone, doth mournefull LONDON craue, [610]
Of you on whom, her weale and woes depende
When in the senate, house with counsell graue,
You sit debating, causes how to end.
Make some decree, poore working trades to mend,
    At least set downe, some order for their good, [615]
    That each man may, with labour earne his foode.

Restraine the number, of deuouring drones,
That sucks the hunny, from the laboring bees.
Catching by peece-meale, in their bribes and lones,
Mens whole estates, which are of poore degrees: [620]
And brings them quickly, on their naked knees,
    Fower groates a month, for twenty shillings lent,
    Ys like windes tempest, till the house be rent.‡‡‡‡

---

‡‡‡‡ *destroyed*

[D1v]

The number, numberlesse of houses vaine,
Which beere and ale, forsooth make shewe to sell: [625]

Vnder which couller, doth such vyces rayne
My cheeke doth glowe, my toongue refraines to tell,
Offending God, and pleasing Sathan well,
    Like wicked SODOME, doth my Subburbs lye,
    A mighty blemish, to faire LONDONS eye.[29]   [630]

Reforme these things, you heads of LONDON Citie,
Punnish lewd vice, let vertue spring and grow:
Then Gods just wrath, now hot will turne to pittie,
And for his children, you againe doe know:
Your former health, on you he will bestow,   [635]
    The Plague and Pestilence, wherewith he visites still,
    To end or send, are in his holy will.

You see the runner, in his race is tript,
Well when he went, dead ere his journeyes done:
You see how soddaine, beauties blase is nipt,   [640]
Which sought all meanes, deaths danger for to shunne,
You heare what successe, followe them that runne:
    Most true report, doth tell vs where and how,
    The Countreys plauge,§§§§ exceedes the Citties now.

Sith then it resteth, in Gods mighty power,   [645]
Who when he please, can bid his Angell stay:
Or if he will, destroy you in an hower
A thousand yeares, being with him as one day,
Why should you not, to him for mercy pray.
    Desiring pardon, with a contryte heart,   [650]
    And from your former, wickednes depart.

Yf this you will, incontinently doe,
The Lorde in pittie, will his judgments cease,
And many blessings will he powre on you:
Health and long life, Honour & happie peace,   [655]
Your Foes shal quaile, your friendes shall still increase,

---

§§§§ plague

Your Wiues shall flourish like a fruitfull Vine,
Your Children prosper, and your griefes decline.[30]

[D2r]

Your Termes shall holde, your men of Worth shall stay,
Your Marchants trafficke, and great riches gaine, [660]
Your Trades-mens sorrows shall bee done away,
True loyall seruants shall with them remaine:
Your Artisants shall neuer more complaine,
    Their honest labour so shall thriue and speede,
    That they shall giue to others that haue neede. [665]

And I that long haue beene a loathed Dame,
shall frolicke then with myrth and inward glee,
Renowned Lady, now must be my name,
O famous LONDON, who is like to thee;
Thy God is serude by men of each degree, [670]
    Thy Churches filde, thy Preachers burne with zeale,
    Thy glory shines, O blessed Common-weale.

My crowned CESAR and his Peerlesse Queene,
Comes now tryumphing with their princely sonne,[31]
Deckt with rich robes the like was neuer seene, [675]
Nor neuer none more welcome to LONDON,
Me thinkes I see the people how they runne,
    To get them roome this happy sight to see,
    That this may come say all Amen, with mee.

FINIS.

[D2v]

A godly and zealous Prayer vnto God, for the surceasing of his irefull Plague, and grieuous Pestilence.

O LORD God Almightie, the Father of mercies and God of all consolation, we miserable distressed creatures, wounded with the multitude of our grieuous sins, repayre vnto thee (the Phisition of our soules) for Balme to cure our Sores.[32] O Lord, we acknowledge and confesse our owne vnworthinesse: great is thy goodnesse towards vs, and great is our ingratitude towardes thee.[33] Thou hast opened the Windowes of Heauen, and powred out thy blessings vpon vs, as out of a store-house or treasurie:[34] thou hast giuen vs of the fatte of the earth, and fed vs with the dewe of heauen:[35] peace and plentie haue beene our portion, and inheritance these many yeeres: the sword hath not deuoured vs, hunger and famine haue not come neere vs: the knowledge of thy word hath florished amongst vs:[36] And whereas other Nations sit in darkenesse, and grope at Noone day, being ouerwhelmed with the fogges & mystes of error and supersticion, wee still injoy the fruition of thy glorious Gospell, and the sunne of righteousnes still shineth cleerely in our climate:[37] whose sweete influence might haue caused vs (had we not bene barren trees) to haue brought foorth much fruite. But alas, in vaine hath the doctrine of thy sonne Christ Jesus, dropped as the deaw: in vaine haue the sweet distilling showres of thy mercies beene powred out vpon this Land.[38] For we haue not yet brought forth the first fruites of the spirit: we haue had the first, and the latter raine; but we bring foorth ye fruit of righteousnes, neither [D3r] first nor last:[39] our Wine is bitter as the Wine of Sodom, and our grapes as the grapes of Gomorrah:[40] wee are become as the seede of the wicked corrupt children, disobedient seruantes, a rebellious people, & now that we are rich, and are waxen fat, we spurne with the heele, like ye vnruly Heifar, we are sicke of long prosperity, & haue surfeited of peace and plentie:[41] fulnes of bread hath caused vs to sin against thee, & we haue wearied thee w^t our iniquities, they are too sore and heauy a burthen for vs to beare.[42] Therfore is thy visitation come amongst vs, & thine hand is sore against vs: therefore hast thou armed thy selfe with displeasure, like a man of warre, thou hast prepared thy instruments of wrath, thou hast whet thy sword, thou hast bent thy bow, thou hast put thine hand to the quiuer, thou hast shot out thine arrowes of indignation against vs, like a Gyaunt refreshed with wine, hast smitten vs, and wee are wounded at the heart.[43]

Woe vnto vs, for the voyce of lamentation and mourning is heard in our Cities, as when thou slewest the first borne of Egypt.[44] Our houses are left desolate, and men abhorre their owne inheritance.[45] Wee are one afraid of another, men hardly trust themselues, yea, scarcely the clothes of their backes. Where are our solemne meetings, and frequent assemblies: men stand a farre off: the Streates and high wayes mourne:[46] trafficke ceaseth: marchandize decayeth: the craftes-man and cunning artificer is ashamed of his pouertie. These things doe we justly suffer for our sinnes, at thy hands; O God, and yet still we goe forwards in our sinnes, like the swift Dromedorie in his course:[47] Or like the Asse in the mountaines, which draweth in the ayre at her pleasure, we haue not comforted the weake and feeble knees, we haue not wept with them that weepe.[48] We haue not had that sympathy, and fellow-felling of each others miserie, which ought to bee in the members of Christ, Nay, often times while one prayeth in the bitternesse and anguish of his spirit, another blasphemeth in the pride and presumption of his heart.[49] Heare one groueleth on ye ground, [D3v] gasping & gaping after life, there another walloweth in the sincke of sin, and puddle of iniquitie, vomiting vp his own shame. O God, how displeasing a spectacle is this to thine eyes: how harsh musicke (and distempered harmony) is it to thine eares. Therefore thine hand is stretched out, to smite off the withered branches of those trees which are corrupt.[50] O Lord, thou knowest that it is not in man to direct his owne wayes. Turne vs vnto thee, and we shall be turned.[51] Draw thou vs, and we wil run after the smell of thine oyntments.[52] Touch our flinty hearts, and our eyes shall gush out with water, as the stonie Rocke which Moses smote:[53] Then wilt thou repent thee of this euill, when wee haue repented vs of our sinnes: then wilt thou turne from vs thy fierce wrath, when wee haue turned from our iniquities: Then will we offer vp w^t the calues of our lips a sacrifice of prayse and thankesgiuing, when thou hast raised vs vp, out of the pit of our grieued desolation, then shalt thou put myrth and gladnesse into our heartes.[54] Most mercifull Father, let it be ynough that we haue hitherto borne the stormes of thy displeasure, now let thy angry Angell hold his destroying hand: let vs not all dye in our sinnes for whom Christ dyed, that wee might liue vnto thee, take away thy cup of indignation from vs, and let vs drinke no more of the dregs of thy furie;[55] saue the remnant that are left with thy preseruatiues of grace, Send thy good Angell vnto the Kings Court, and giue him charge ouer his Majestie, that the arrowes y^t flye by night touch not his sacred person, nor come nere his

princely Progeny. Let treacherie, and conspiracie blush and be ashamed and confounded at their presence:[56] let prosperitie attend them on the right hand and on the left: Lord giue vnto the Nobles, & Senators of this Land, the spirit of wisedome, counsell and vnderstanding: the spirit of true fortitiude, courage and magnanimitie.[57] Inspire the Ministers of thy Gospel with knowledge of thy word, inflame their hearts with a feruent zeale for thy glory: giue vnto all Superiors, discretion & moderation: vnto all inferiors, loyalty and obdedience. More perticulerly, for our selues, Wee pray thee blesse our downe sitting and our vprising, [D4r] blesse our going foorth, and our comming in:[58] saue vs from the noysome Plague and pestilence, which is the rod of thy furie, and the hammer of thine indignation, which breakest in peices like a Potters vessell irrepentant sinners, therefore suffer vs not, we beseech thee, to walke any longer in the stubburnesse of our owne hearts, least we hoard vp vengeance for our selues in the day of wrath.[59] O Lord illuminate our vnderstandings, reforme oure irreguler disordered affections, mortifie our sinnes, let them dye in this nights rest, that tomorrow when we awake, we may shake off sinnes, and liue vnto righteousnesse, neuer fearing to goe
foreward from grace to grace, from vertue to vertue,
vntill we haue arriued at the hauen of rest: whither
Christ bring vs, which bought vs for his mercies sake: To whom with the Father
and the holy Ghost, be all honour, power, and domini-
on, for euermore.[60]
Amen.

FINIS.
[D4v]

A true Relation of al that haue bin buried of all diseases, in euery seuerall Parish; aswell within the Cittie of London, & liberties

thereof, as also in the out parishes neere there-
vnto adioyning, from the 14 of Iuly last past,
1603, to the 17. of Nouember following.

Albones in Woodstreet[61] ------- 174	Christ Church parish ---------- 323
Alhallowes Lumbarstr.[62] ------ 107	Christophers parish ----------- 36
Alhallowes the great ---------- 278	Clements by East-cheape ------- 46
Alhallowes the lesse ---------- 220	Dennis Back-church[63] --------- 105
Alhallowes Bredstreet --------- 27	Dunstones in the East --------- 222
Alhallowes staynings ---------- 121	Edmunds in Lumbard.st --------- 72
Alhallowes the wall ----------- 211	Ethelborow within Bishopsg.[64] - 156
Alhallowes Hony-lane ---------- 14	S. Faithes -------------------- 101
Alhallowes Barking ------------ 411	S. Fosters in Foster-lane ----- 93
Alphage at Cripplegate -------- 168	Gabriel Fan-Church[65] --------- 66
Androwes by the Wardrope ------ 282	Georges Buttolph-lane --------- 35
Androwes Eastcheape ----------- 104	Gregories by Paules ----------- 260
Androwes vndershaft ----------- 159	Hellens within Bishopsg ------- 95
Annes at Aldersgate ----------- 140	James by Garlick-hith --------- 136
Annes Black Fryers ------------ 240	John Euangelist --------------- 9
Auntlins parish[66] ------------ 34	John Zacharies ---------------- 131
Austines Parish --------------- 91	Johns in the Walbrooke -------- 133
Bartholmew at the Exch -------- 76	Katherines Cree-Church -------- 391
Bennets at Pauls-wharf -------- 190	Katherines Colemans ----------- 180
Bennets Grace-Church ---------- 39	Laurence in the Jury ---------- 86
Bennets Finck ----------------- 93	Laurence Pountney ------------- 157
Bennets Sherhogg -------------- 26	Leonards Foster-lane ---------- 239
Buttols Billinsgate[67] -------- 18	Leonards Eastcheape ----------- 50

[E1r]

Magnus parish by the Bridge[68] - 107	Nicholas Olaue ---------------- 80
Margrets New fishstreet ------- 81	Olaues in the Iury ------------ 40
Margrets Pattens -------------- 51	Olaues in Hartstreet ---------- 186

Margrets Moyses	67	Olaues in Siluer-street	111
Margrets Lothbery	99	Pancras by Soperlane	18
Martins in the Vintry	242	Peters in Cornehill	132
Martins Orgars	89	Peters in Cheape	45
Martins Iremonger lane	25	Peters the poore in broadstr	44
Martins at Ludgate	192	Peters at Pauls-wharfe	95
Martins Outwich	38	Steuens in Colman-street[69]	339
Mary le Booe[70]	26	Steuens in the Walbrok	22
Mary Bothaw	39	Swithins at London-stone	116
Mary at the hill	139	Thomas Apostles	83
Mary Abchurch	120	Trinitie Parish	116
Mary Woolchurch	48		
Mary Colchurch	10		

Without the Wals of London.

Mary Woolnoth	85		
Mary Aldermary	75		
Mary Aldermanbery	78		
Mary Stayning	49		
Mary Mountawe[71]	47		
Mary Sommersets	193	Androwes in Holborn	1178
Mathew Friday-street	16	Barthelmew the lesse Smithf	84
Maudlins in Milke-street[72]	32	Barthelmew the great Smit	200
Maudlins by oldfishstreet	128	Brides Parish	907
Mighels Bassie shaw[73]	135	Buttols Algate	1465
Mighels Cornehill	119	Buttols Bishopsgate	1202
Mighels in Woodstreet	151	Buttols without Aldersg	556
Mighel in the Ryall	99	Dunstones in the West	484
Mighels in the Querne	59	Georges in Southwarke	895
Mighels Queene-hith	128	Giles without Creeplegate	2455
Mighel Crooked lane	139	Olaues in Southwarke[74]	2459
Mildreds Poultry[75]	79	Sauiours in Southwarke	1858
Mildreds Bredstreet	39	Sepulchers parish	2219
Nicholas Acons	32	Thomas in Southwark	245
Nicholas Cole-Abbay	139	Trinitie in the Minories	39

[E1v]

Clements without Templeb.[76] ------------ 624
Giles in the Fields ---------------------- 439
James at Clarkenwell -------------------- 716
Katherines by the Tower ----------------- 639
Leonards Shoredich --------------------- 856
Martins in the Fields -------------------- 458

Mary Whitechappel --------------------- 1534
Magdalens in Barmondsey---------------
streete ---------------------------------- 578
Bridewel precinct ------------------------ 103
At the Pest-house[77]--------------------------134

The true Number of al that haue bin buried, aswel within ye Cittie of London: as also within the liberties and Subburbes thereof, of all diseases, since the first beginning of this Uisitation, is 37717.[78]

FINIS.

NOTES

INTRODUCTION

The epigraph for this chapter comes from Petowe, *Londoners Their Entertainment in the Countrie* (STC 19807), sig. C3r.

1. On the symptoms of the plague and the disease's progress, see Totaro, *Suffering in Paradise*, 26–30; Cohn and Alfani, "Households and Plague in Early Modern Italy," 179–81; Theilmann and Cate, "Plague of Plagues"; and Slack, *Impact of Plague*, 8–9.

2. London Metropolitan Archives (hereafter LMA), Parish Registers, St. Olave, Bermondsey, Southwark, fol. 137r.

3. Ibid., fol. 75r.

4. Under burials for the month, the parish register of St. Olave's describes her as apprentice to William Muggins, weaver: "ß wth Wm Moggens, weaver." "ß wth" was the parish clerk's abbreviation for "servant in the household of," but more often than not in the parish made up primarily of artisans and day laborers—and especially in the case of weavers—the term denoted "apprentice to." The London Company of Weavers, which regulated the craft, forbade apprenticing women. In a craft once dominated by women, claiming that a female apprentice was really a household servant was a frequent cover for the violation. See Plummer, *London Weavers' Company*, 61–63. Even if Black was more servant than apprentice, Jane Whittle has cautioned against bracketing "domestic labor" as distinct from other forms of labor. Given that Muggins's living quarters and workspace significantly overlapped, it is likely that Black was involved in both weaving and various household chores. See Whittle, "Critique of Approaches to 'Domestic Work.'"

5. See Dale, "London Silkwomen of the Fifteenth Century"; Korda, *Labors Lost*, 41–45; Plummer, *London Weavers' Company*, 61–64; Consitt, *London Weavers' Company*, 192–94; Clark, *Working Life of Women in the Seventeenth Century*, 138–43; McIntsoh, *Working Women in English Society*, 210–33, esp. 223–25; Kowaleski and Bennett, "Crafts, Gilds, and Women in the Middle Ages"; Prior, "Women and the Urban Economy"; Collins, "Jane Holt, Milliner, and Other Women in Business"; Gowing, "Girls on Forms"; Muldrew, "'Th'ancient Distaff' and 'Whirling Spindle'"; and Ben-Amos, "Women Apprentices in the Trades and Crafts of Early Modern Bristol." Although it is focused on Paris, one should also consult Farmer, *Silk Industries of Medieval Paris*, 106–64.

6. See Munkhoff, "Searchers of the Dead."

7. See Wilson, *Plague in Shakespeare's London*, 45–47.

8. See Newman, "Shutt Up"; and Achinstein, "Plagues and Publication," 33.

9. Webbe, *Rare and Most Wonderfull Things* (STC 25153); Hawkins, *Salade for the Simple* (STC 12960); and Barley, *Deligtful History* (STC 4910). See Syme, "Thomas Creede, William Barley, and the Venture of Printing Plays"; Murray, *Thomas Morley*, 89–97, 110–23; Lavin, "William Barley, Draper and Stationer"; and Lievsay,

"William Barley, Elizabethan Printer and Bookseller."

10. Totaro, *Plague Epic in Early Modern England*, 15.

11. Gleed, "'I lov'de thee best,'" 7.

12. Muggins, *Londons Mourning Garment, or Funerall Teares* (STC 18248). For early books that lack modern pagination, I refer to the printers' signatures to identify pages. For *London's Mourning Garment*, I have also included line numbers for the verse. A complete edition of Muggins's *London's Mourning Garment* appears in the appendix with printer signatures in brackets.

13. See Taylor, *Mourning Dress*, 80–100.

14. Ant. Rivers to Giacomo Creleto, March 9, 1603, National Archives (hereafter NA), State Papers Domestic, Edward VI to Charles I, Elizabeth I, 1603 Jan.-Mar. and undated, fol. 74; see Martin and Finnis, "The Secret Sharers"; and Marchant, "Rivers, Antony (*fl.* 1601–1606)."

15. Guildhall Library (hereafter GL), "Remembrancia," vol. 2, fol. 118r–v (#234). All references to "Remembrancia" include folio page references and item numbers.

16. Godskall, *Arke of Noah* (STC 11935), sig. A4v.

17. Dekker, *1603. The Wonderfull Yeare* (STC 6535), sig. C3r.

18. Hanson, *Time Is a Turne-Coate* (STC 12750).

19. See Cummins, Kelly, and Ó Gráda, "Living Standards and Plague in London"; Cohn, *Cultures of Plague*, 208–37.

20. LMA, Parish Registers, St. Mary le Bow, fols. 60r–66r.

21. LMA, Parish Registers, St. Benet, Gracechurch, fols. 90v–94r.

22. LMA, Parish Registers, St. Giles, Cripplegate, fols. 155v–156r, 161v–162r, 167r–v, 172v–173r, 178r–v, 184r–185, 192v–195v.

23. LMA, Parish Registers, St. Olave, Bermondsey, Southwark, fols. 95v–96r, 101v–102r, 107v–108r, 113v–114r, 119v–120r, 124v–125r, 132r–134r.

24. See Appleby, "Nutrition and Disease"; Twigg, "Plague in London"; Robertson, "Reckoning with London"; and Bellhouse, "London Plague Statistics."

25. LMA, Parish Registers, St. Olave, Bermondsey, Southwark, fol. 139r.

26. On the dread of the plague, see Wrightson, *Ralph Tailor's Summer*, 57–60.

27. On the epic elements of *London's Mourning Garment*, see Totaro, "Mother London," 161; see also Totaro, *Plague Epic in Early Modern England*, 1–49.

28. Totaro, *Plague Epic in Early Modern England*, 15–16; see also Totaro, "Mother London."

29. Lines 90–93; subsequent line numbers for this and other of Middleton's works are cited parenthetically in the text. Unless otherwise noted, all citations of Thomas Middleton are drawn from Middleton, *Collected Works*. On the lord mayor's show, see Hill, *Pageantry and Power*; Bergeron, *English Civic Pageantry*, 125–235; Ellinghausen, "'Their labour doth returne rich golden gaine'"; Lobanov-Rostovsky, "Triumphes of Golde"; and Finlayson, "Jacobean Foreign Policy."

30. Phillippy, *Women, Death and Literature*, 138; and Phillippy, "London's Mourning Garment."

31. Smith, *De Republica Anglorum* (STC 22857), 33.

32. Ibid., 29.

33. Munday, *Metropolis Coronata* (STC 18275), sig. B2v. For an overview of the varied functions of guilds or livery companies over time, see Thrupp, "The Gilds"; and Epstein, "Craft Guilds."

34. On labor in the mayor's shows, see Ellinghausen, "'Their labor doth returne rich golden gaine'"; and Northway, "'To kindle an industrious desire.'"

35. On the importance of lace in the period, see Jones and Stallybrass, *Renaissance Clothing*, 24–26, 190–91.

36. NA, Records of the Chancery ... Wm. Mouggings.

37. See Cressy, "Describing the Social Order"; French, *Middle Sort of People*, esp. 1–30; Shepard, *Accounting for Oneself*, 4–6; Wrightson, "'Sorts of People'"; and Wrightson, "Estates, Degrees, and Sorts."

38. Stow, *Survey of London* (STC 23345.5), 697–98. Note that this printing of Stow includes Munday's additions.

39. Wrightson, "Estates, Degrees, and Sorts," 32.
40. See Stone, *Crisis of the Aristocracy*, 589–671.
41. Smith, *De Republica Anglorum* (STC 22857), 33.
42. Rollison, *Commonwealth of the People*, 1–30.
43. Holstun, "The Spider, the Fly, and the Commonwealth," 55–66. See also Wood, "Fear, Hatred, and the Hidden Injuries of Class."
44. Taylor, "Price of the Poor's Words."
45. Hamling and Richardson, *Day at Home in Early Modern England*; Tittler, *Townspeople and Nation*.
46. Shepard, *Accounting for Oneself*; Griffiths, *Lost Londons*.
47. Consitt, *London Weavers' Company*, 147, 316–18.
48. On the freedom of the city (or citizenship), see Rappaport, *Worlds within Worlds*, 23–60; and Pearl, "Change and Stability."
49. Consitt, *London Weavers' Company*, 314.
50. This is not to say that the dramatists of the period were mere lackeys to the ruling class. On the contrary, Chris Fitter, in *Radical Shakespeare*, has provided a compelling account of Shakespeare's engagement with popular politics.
51. In that sense, this book is very much in line with Paul S. Seaver's *Wallington's World*, a study of one London turner's diary entries, which, as Seaver explains, "offer a unique opportunity to gain some insight into the thought and attitudes of one such artisan toward himself and his world, his family and friends, toward the process of getting and spending" (13). Muggins, unfortunately, did not leave behind anything close to the 2,600-plus pages Nehemiah Wallington supplied posterity.
52. Nashe, *Haue with You to Saffron-Walden* (STC 18369), sig. N3v.
53. Blower's last name has appeared variously as Blower, Blore, Bloure, and Bloore, and occasionally the printer simply used the initial R. B.
54. *Transcript of the Registers of the Company of Stationers*, fol. 25a.

55. Deloney, *Thomas of Reading* (STC 6569).
56. Deloney, *Strange Histories* (STC 6568).
57. Ellinghausen, *Labor and Writing*, 1.
58. The humility conveyed in Muggins's dedication is indicative of an authorial strategy referred to as the humility or modesty topos. Although not exclusively gendered, the modesty topos as a strategy has been most fully analyzed in the context of early women writers. See Heller, *Mother's Legacy*, 11, 38–39; Pender, *Early Modern Women's Writing*; Wiesner, *Women and Gender in Early Modern Europe*, 189–91.
59. Unless otherwise noted, all citations for Shakespeare are from Shakespeare, *Norton Shakespeare*. 1.2.24–31; subsequent line numbers are cited parenthetically in the text.
60. James Biester argues that there was a rivalry between Deloney and Kempe. While this may be true, I agree with David Wiles that Kempe appears to praise rather than denigrate Deloney. If there was a rivalry, it was not a bitter one. Biester, "Shaming the Fool"; Wiles, *Shakespeare's Clown*, 25.
61. On this broader connection in *A Midsummer Night's Dream*, see Witte, "Bottom's Tangled Web."
62. There are many studies of the relationship between *A Midsummer Night's Dream* and Ovid's *Metamorphosis* (especially Arthur Golding's translation). See Staton, "Ovidian Elements in *A Midsummer Night's Dream*"; Lamb, "*A Midsummer Night's Dream*"; Forey, "'Bless thee, Bottom, bless thee! Thou art translated!'"; and Rudd, "Pyramus and Thisbe in Shakespeare and Ovid."
63. In 1606 James issued a patent for the importation of white mulberry trees (those bearing the white fruit typically resulting in raw silk of higher quality). *Calendar of the Manuscripts of the Most Honourable the Marquess of Salisbury*, vol. 18, *1606*, 422. See also, Hertz, "English Silk Industry."
64. Moffett, *Silkewormes and Their Flies* (STC 17994), esp. 71–75.
65. NA, State Papers Domestic, Edward VI to Charles I, James I, 1607 Jan.–Mar., fols. 16r–17r.

66. Witte, "Bottom's Tangled Web," 26.
67. On Careless's correspondence with women, see Freeman, "'Good Ministrye of Godlye and Vertuouse Women.'"
68. Careless was taken into custody due to a public dispute with dissenter Henry Hart. See Martin, "English Protestant Separatism at Its Beginnings."
69. Coverdale, *Certain Most Godly* (STC 5886), 613; Foxe, *Actes and Monuments* (STC 11225), 1919–34. Tom Betteridge reads Careless's correspondence in terms of a poetics of friendship. See Betteridge, *Literature and Politics in the English Reformation*, 201–4.
70. Coverdale, *Certain Most Godly* (STC 5886), 233.
71. Ibid., 566, my emphasis.
72. Ibid., 561–62, my emphasis.
73. King, *Foxe's Book of Martyrs*, 50. Careless's use of "bite-sheeps" for bishops appears in Foxe, but the gloss is not necessarily original to Careless. John Bradford also uses the term in one of his letters. See Foxe, *Actes and Monuments* (STC 11225), 172; Coverdale, *Certain Most Godly* (STC 5886), 407.
74. Coverdale, *Certain Most Godly* (STC 5886), 567; Foxe, *Actes and Monuments* (STC 11225), 164.
75. Coverdale, *Certain Most Godly* (STC 5886), 229.
76. Ibid., 624, 638. Ryan McDermott compellingly argues that Careless was thus framing himself as a Christlike figure who embraces martyrdom. See McDermott, *Tropologies*, 278–90.
77. On the print history of the poem, see Watt, *Cheap Print and Popular Piety*, 95. See also Collinson, *This England*, 234.
78. Coverdale, *Certain Most Godly* (STC 5886), 634–35.
79. Gilbart, *Declaration of the Death of John Lewes* (ESTC S923693).
80. *Confession of a Paenitent Sinner* (STC 5627).
81. Nashe, *Haue with You to Saffron-Walden* (STC 18369), sig. Q3v.
82. Bownd, *Medicines for the Plague* (STC 3439), 212–14.
83. The song appears in both Q and F, 1.4.160–63, or 1.4.144–47, respectively (with a plural "fooles" in Q). On Shakespeare's use of the song, see Rollins, "'King Lear' and the Ballad of 'John Careless'"; Kirsch, "'Twixt Two Extremes of Passion, Joy and Grief,'" 28–29.
84. Heywood, *Rape of Lucrece* (STC 13360), sig. C1v.
85. Deloney, *Works of Thomas Deloney*, 323–26. Falstaff sings the first line of this ballad in *Henry IV, Part 2*.
86. Deloney, *Works of Thomas Deloney*, 323.
87. By the same token, one might observe that Nashe's *Haue with You to Saffron-Walden* passes judgment on Careless and Deloney. Nashe's main object of scorn, however, was Gabriel Harvey, whom Nashe ridicules in part for his humble birth as "the eldest sonne of the halter-maker." Harvey, Deloney, Careless, and others are perhaps lumped together as writers with strong middling-sort connections.
88. A few years earlier Nashe had similarly singled out weavers as among the "unlearned lots" who wrote popular verse: "some stitcher, Weauer, spendthrift, or fidler, hath shuffled or slubberd up a few ragged Rimes" that tell some truth, but "they enterlace it with a lye or two to make the meter." Nashe, *Anatomie of Absurditie* (STC 18364), sigs. B4r–v. On Nashe's disdain for handicrafts as opposed to scholarly labor, see Ellinghausen, *Labor and Writing*, 35–62.
89. Snyder, "Web of Song."
90. Tuck, "Stories at the Loom."
91. This latter simile, moreover, is an allusion to Samuel 17:7. *Geneva Bible*, fol. 128v.
92. On the gendered nature of spinning, see Jones and Stallybrass, *Renaissance Clothing*, 104–33.
93. There are numerous variations of this ballad: in place of the earl of Northumberland's daughter, one features a provost's daughter, another a bailiff's, and so forth. The same ballad appears as "The Fair Flower of Northumberland" in Francis Child's collection of ballads, itself derived from an edition of *Jack of Newbury*. It may be that Deloney simply included a

well-known ballad in his book; or it may be Deloney's most widely sung ballad.

94. Several songs related to the textile industry have been found to include such devices. See Robertson, Pickering, and Korczynski, "'And Spinning with Voices Meet.'"

95. See Quitslund, *Reformation in Rhyme*, 268–71.

96. Phillips, *Play of Patient Grissel*, line 1836. On Phillips's play, see Potter, "Tales of Patient Griselda and Henry VIII."

97. Byron, *Works of Lord Byron*, 361. On working-class poetry of the eighteenth and nineteenth centuries, see Christmas, *Lab'ring Muses*; Loose, *Chartist Imaginary*; Landry, *Muses of Resistance*; Murphy, *Toward a Working-Class Canon*; and the essays collected in Blair and Gorji, *Class and Canon*.

98. On the relation between artisans and poets in this period, see Prothero, *Radical Artisans in England and France*, 241–46. On Irish weaver-poets, see Hewitt, *Rhyming Weavers*.

99. Thom, *Rhymes and Recollections*, 14.

100. Ibid., 16.

101. Ibid., 18.

102. Kathman, "Rise of Commercial Playing," 18–20; and Lancashire, *London Civic Theatre*, 69–117.

103. See Reuter, "Some Notes on Thomas Deloney's Indebtedness to Shakespeare."

104. White, "Reforming Mysteries' End."

105. Collinson, *Archbishop Grindal*, 114.

106. Nicholas, *Pleasant Dialogue betweene a Lady Called Listra* (STC 18335.5), sigs. A6v–A7r.

107. Deloney, *Garland of Good Will* (STC 6553.5), sigs. f2v–f5v; Deloney, *Strange Histories* (STC 6566), sigs. A5v–A8r. On Deloney's Calvinism, see Stevenson, *Praise and Paradox*, 153–54; and Dorsinville, "Design in Deloney's *Jack of Newbury*."

108. Shakespeare, *Historie of Henrie the Fourth* (STC 22280), sig. D3v.

109. LMA, Worshipful Company of Weavers, Constitutional Records: Ordinance, Oath and Memorandum Book, Known as the "Ancient Book," fols. 10–11, 14; Consitt, *London Weavers' Company*, 191.

110. Chapman, *Plays and Poems of George Chapman*, 2.2.171–236. Precious little has been written about this play. See Netzloff, "Public Diplomacy and the Comedy of State"; Tricomi, "Focus of Satire and the Date of *Monsieur D'Olive*"; and Hogan, "Thematic Unity in Chapman's *Monsieur D'Olive*."

111. See "bombast, n."; and "fustian, n. and adj," *OED Online*.

112. Wild, *Alas Poore Scholler* (STC 25632).

113. On the radicalism of eighteenth-century weaver-poets, see Whatley, "'It Is Said That Burns Was a Radical,'" 655–62.

114. All Bible quotations are taken from *The Geneva Bible*. The passages referred to here are from fols. 95r–v, 251v, 283r, 292v, and 366r.

115. Alec Ryrie describes such prayers as "soaked in Scriptural quotation, half-quotation, paraphrase, and allusion: Biblical 'patchworks,' 'mosaics,' or 'collages' assembled into distinctive creations." Ryrie, *Being Protestant in Reformation Britain*, 224–32.

116. Herbert, "Prayer (1)," *The Complete English Poems*, 45, line 2.

117. Green, *Print and Protestantism*, 240–41, 274–77; Kaufmann, "'Much in Prayer'"; Branch, "Rejection of Liturgy, the Rise of Free Prayer, and Modern Religious Subjectivity." On the status of the Old Testament among Puritans, see Hill, *Bible in Seventeenth-Century English Politics*, 87–107; and Tyacke, "Puritan Paradigm of English Politics," 546.

118. The prayer includes six allusions to Jeremiah, six to Isaiah, four to Deuteronomy, four to the Psalms, and three to Exodus. The prayer alludes less frequently to the books of Genesis, Malachi, Ezekiel, Job, Hosea, Amos, Numbers, and Romans.

119. Bayly, *Practise of Pietie* (STC 1602), sig. V3r.

120. On rates of literacy among weavers and craftsmen overall, see Cressy, *Literacy and the Social Order*, 134–35, 143–74.

121. On the challenges to acquiring literacy in the period, see ibid., 19–41.

122. The inventory assesses the Bible to be worth six shillings, eight pence. On the

price of a Bible, see Green, *Print and Protestantism*, 58–60, 84.

123. On commonplace books among the middling sort, see Burke, "Ann Bowyer's Commonplace Book."

124. NA, Records of the Chancery . . . Wm. Mouggings.

125. On the history and complexity of rhyme royal, see Addison, "Little Boxes," 133–37; Cummings, "The Province of Verse"; and Stevens, "The Royal Stanza in Early English Poetry."

126. Gascoigne, *Poesies of George Gascoigne* (STC 11636), sig. U1v.

127. Ibid., sigs. U1v, U2v; Puttenham, *Arte of English Poesie* (STC 20519.5), 54.

128. Both George Chapman and Arthur Hall tried their hands at *The Iliad*; Golding's translation of Ovid had gone through several printings by 1603. See Homer, *Ten Books of Homer's Iliades* (STC 13630); Homer, *Seaven Bookes of the Iliades of Homere* (STC 13632); Ovid, *The .XV. Bookes of P. Ouidius Naso, Entytuled Metamorphosis* (STC 18956).

129. Seneca, *Woorke of the Excellent Philosopher* (STC 22215), sig. B1r. Muggins's particular phrasing comes close to Christopher Fetherston's in *Dialogve agaynst Light, Lewde, and Lasciuouus Daunting* (STC 10835), no sig., two sheets before sig. A1r.

130. Aelian, *Registre of Hystories Conteining Martiall Exploites* (STC 164), sigs. 12r, 133r.

131. Chettle, *True Bill of the Whole Number That Hath Died in the Cittie of London* (STC 16743.2). On the bills of mortality see Wilson, *Plague in Shakespeare's London*, 189–208; Slack, *Impact of the Plague*, 240–45; Totaro, *Plague in Print*, 197–204; Greenberg, "Plague, the Printing Press, and Public Health in Seventeenth-Century England"; Munkhoff, "Reckoning with Death."

132. The Huntington's copy of *London's Mourning Garment* is the same as that scanned for Early English Books Online. The early reader of that copy seems to have been puzzling over the fact that the total dead listed on the table does not match the numbers of dead by parish.

133. On the diversity of plague writing, see Totaro, *Plague in Print*.

134. Gilman, *Plague Writing in Early Modern England*, 54–70.

135. Bullein, *Dialogue Bothe Pleasaunte and Pietifull* (STC 4036.5), sig. L2r.

136. On Bullein, see Totaro, *Plague in Print*, 49–178; Healy, *Fictions of Disease in Early Modern England*, 64–65, 71, 83; and Maslen, "Healing Dialogues of William Bullein."

137. Wilson, *Rule of Reason* (STC 25809), sig. A2r.

138. Ibid., sig. A2v.

139. Ibid., sigs. H5v–I1r.

140. Ibid., sig. I2r.

141. On Wilson as a commonwealthsman, see Schmidt, "Thomas Wilson and the Tudor Commonwealth"; and Shrank, *Writing the Nation in Reformation England*, 182–219.

142. On Elizabethan chests of this sort, see Hart, "Old Chests"; and Thornton, "Two Problems," 66–69.

143. Eisenstein, *Printing Press as an Agent of Change*, 18–19, 399–403.

144. For an overview of Swinnerton's life, see Archer, "Swinnerton, John"; and Peck, "Problems in Jacobean Administration," 844–54.

145. On the urban/civic patronage I discuss here, see Sullivan, "Early Modern Creative Industrialists"; and Kilburn-Toppin, "Gifting Cultures and Artisanal Guilds," 877. See also Hill, *Anthony Munday and Civic Culture*, 83–97; Bergeron, *Textual Patronage in English Drama*, 49–72; White, "Biographical Sketch of Dorcas Martin"; Seaver, "Puritan Preachers and Their Patrons"; Davies, "Monuments of Honour'"; and Bishop, "'Utopia' and Civic Politics in Mid-Sixteenth-Century London."

146. More, *Carpenters Rule* (STC 18075), sigs. A2r–A3r; Averell, *Dyall for Dainty Darlings* (STC 978), sig. A2r; Robinson, *Certain Selected Histories for Christian Recreations* (STC 21118), sig. A2r.

147. Rinaldi, *Royal Exchange* (STC 12307), sig. Q2r; A. T., *Rich Store-House or Treasury for the Diseased* (STC 23606), sigs. A2r–v;

Clapham, *Description of New Jerushalem* (STC 5336.5), sig. A3r.

148. Swynnerton, *Christian Loue-Letter* (STC 23558). On this pamphlet see Childs, *God's Traitors*, 318–20. See also Swinnerton's letter to Salisbury (the work's dedicatee) confirming his receipt of the pamphlet: *Calendar of the Cecil Papers in Hatfield House*, vol. 18, *1606*, 447. Finally, one should note that as mayor, Swinnerton took a much harsher approach to Catholicism, actively rounding up recusants in the city.

149. Archer, "Swinnerton."

150. Dekker, *Troia Nova Triumphans* (STC 6530).

151. Peacham, *Period of Mourning Disposed into Sixe Visions* (STC 19513.5), sig. A3r; Munday, *Third and Last Part of Palmerin* (STC 19165), sig. A2r; de Mornay, *True Knowledge of a Mans Owne Selfe*, (STC 18163), sig. A3r; Hall, *Holy Panegyrick* (STC 12673), sig. A3r; Drayton, *Poems* (STC 7216), sig. R1v.

152. Ravenscroft, *Briefe Discourse of the True (but Neglected) Vse of Charact'ring* (STC 20756), sig. Q2r; Smith, *Hector of Germanie* (STC 22871), sig. A2r.

153. Smith, *Hector of Germanie*, sig. A2r.

154. Taylor, "The Embassy, the City, the Text." Swinnerton's involvement in the theater also includes the distinct possibility that he is satirized in the play *The Hog Hath Lost His Pearl* (1614). See Kermode, *Three Renaissance Usury Plays*, 47–53.

155. Archer, "Swinnerton."

156. Clode, *Memorials of the Guild of Merchant Taylors of the Fraternity of St. John the Baptist*, 149.

157. See Duffin, "To Entertain a King"; and Heaton and Knowles, "'Entertainment Perfect.'"

158. Holland, *Spirituall Preseruatiues against the Pestilence* (STC 13589), sig. A3r; Thayre, *Treatise of the Pestilence* (STC 23929), sig. A2r. See also Thomas, *Anglorum Lachrimae* (STC 14671), sig. A2r.

159. Totaro, "Mother London," 147. The name William Muggins rarely appears in the historical record. During the years in question, there were Muggins households in the parishes of St. Mary Magdalen, Old Fish Street and in St. Giles, Cripplegate, as well as one household in Middlesex; the only William Muggins in these parishes, however, was christened on July 22, 1584, and buried nine days later. A young man by the name of William Markcome would sometimes go by the surname Muggins, but his apprenticeship to goldsmith and schoolmaster Ra[l]p[h] Robinsonne began in 1606, suggesting that in 1603 Markcome was probably too young to have written *London's Mourning Garment*. Markcome, moreover, was a member of the gentry, while the author of *London's Mourning Garment* makes no claims to a status above citizen. Apart from the silk-weaver, one does not find an adult William Muggins in the records until 1636. Not only is the silk-weaver William Muggins the only figure of the right age, details of his life point to the authorship of *London's Mourning Garment*. LMA, Parish Register, St. Giles, Cripplegate, fols. 83r–v; see also fols. 200r, 203v. On the Muggins household on Old Fish Street see LMA, Parish Registers, St. Mary Magdalen, Old Fish Street, fols. 108v–110v. On the Muggins household in Middlesex, see LMA, Parish Registers, All Saints, Edmonton, fols. 15r, 16r; Worshipful Company of Goldsmiths, Apprentice Book 1, entry for April 4, 1606; LMA, Parish Registers, St. Dunstan's in the West, entry for August 1, 1636, unnumbered folio; LMA, Parish Registers, St. Bride, Fleet Street, fol. 175r.

160. Many of these have been carefully transcribed by Consitt, but the actual documents (as well as those not transcribed by Consitt) have also been consulted. Wherever relevant, I have listed both the original source and Consitt's transcription.

161. On this document's whereabouts, see Linton, "Jack of Newbery and Drake in California," 46; and Ladd, "Thomas Deloney and the London Weavers' Company," 983.

162. On the relationship between biography and microhistory, see Renders, "Limits of Representativeness."

163. See, for example, Mathur, "Attack of the Clowns," 35.

164. The examples here allude to Ginzburg, *Cheese and the Worms*; Wunderli,

Peasant Fires; and Sensback, *Rebecca's Revival*.

165. On the range and persistent relevance of microhistory, see Robisheaux, Cohen, and Sijártó, *Microhistory and the Historical Imagination*.

166. Imhof, *Lost Worlds*, 36–38.

167. Levi, "On Microhistory," 113. See also Ginzburg and Poni, "Name of the Game", 7–8; and Robisheaux, "Microhistory Today," 22.

168. Lake, *Boxmaker's Revenge*, 9.

169. Gray, "Microhistory as Universal History."

170. Ginzburg and Poni, "Name of the Game," 7. One might also consult articles in the journal *Medieval Prosopography*.

171. While courtly poetry is obviously complex and varied, one barely scratches the surface before encountering misogynist tropes in abundance. See Heale, "Misogyny and the Complete Gentleman."

CHAPTER 1

This chapter's epigraph is drawn from *A Discourse on Mans Life* (STC 6907).

1. Defoe, *Life and Action of Moll Flanders* (ESTC T070316), 146–47. Note that the 1722 printing makes a similar point but without this particular wording.

2. Holinshed, *Third Volume of the Chronicle* (STC 13319), 540; NA, State Papers Domestic, Charles II to George III, Secretaries of State, Letters and Papers, fol. 30.

3. Griffiths, *Chronicles of Newgate*, 181; *Calendar of the Manuscripts of the Most Honourable the Marquess of Salisbury*, vol. 9, 422. On the conditions in the early modern English prison system and Newgate specifically, see Bassett, "Newgate Prison in the Middle Ages"; Babington, *English Bastille*; Halliday, *Newgate*; Ackroyd, *London*, 247–57; and Linebaugh, *London Hanged*, 333–56. On early English prisons more generally, see Dobb, "London's Prisons."

4. On the use of irons, see Babington, *English Bastille*, 5–6.

5. Even in the upgraded conditions afforded by the wealthy, Newgate could prove volatile if not lethal. Thomas Freeman notes the case of Edward Underhill, who after just two short weeks in 1554 was so ill he could not walk out of the prison. Freeman, "Rise of Prison Literature," 144.

6. LMA, Parish Register, St. Giles, Cripplegate, fol. 213v. Willington is a common name. Having searched parish registers, lay subsidies, and wills, the only Willington designated as a weaver is the said John Willington of St. Giles, Cripplegate. Some caution is necessary, however: not all parish registers list parishioners' trade. Still, the surname, trade, year, and association with Deloney conspire to make John Willington the likely weaver named in the mayor's report on this incident.

7. British Library (hereafter BL), Lansdowne MS 81.30, fol. 76.

8. Deloney, *Proper New Sonet Declaring the Lamentation [of Beckles in] Suffolke* (STC 6564); Deloney, *Queenes Visiting of the Campe at Tilsburie* (STC 6565).

9. Deloney, *Strange Histories* (STC 6566), sigs. B2v–C3v.

10. On the date (September or October 1596), see Mackerness, "Thomas Nashe and William Cotton," 343; and Nicholl, *Cup of News*, 239–40.

11. Nashe, *Haue with You to Saffron-Walden* (STC 18369), sig. N3v.

12. *Jack of Newbury* was registered on March 7, 1598, by Thomas Millington; *The Gentle Craft* was registered by Ralph Blower (Blore) on October 19, 1597; see *Transcript of the Registers of the Company of Stationers*, fols. 19a, 93a.

13. Deloney, *Novels*, 3.

14. Ibid., 91.

15. Ibid., 173. On the dating of *Thomas of Reading*, see Rollins, "Deloney's Sources for Euphuistic Learning," 406. See also Lawlis's introduction to Deloney, *Novels*, xxix.

16. This overt class allegiance is perhaps the reason so many scholars interested in labor in the period have focused almost exclusively on Deloney's prose fiction. See for example Hentschell, *Culture of Cloth in Early Modern England*, 51–71; Rollison, "Discourse and Class Struggle," 184–89;

Biester, "Shaming the Fool"; Suzuki, *Subordinate Subjects*, 34–50; and Ladd, "Thomas Deloney and the London Weavers' Company."

17. *Transcript of the Registers of the Company of Stationers*, vol. 2, fol. 326b.

18. Greenham, *Two Learned and Godly Sermons* (STC 12325); Cotton, *Direction to the Waters of Life* (STC 5867.3); Broughton, *Treatise of Melchisedek Proving Him to Be Sem* (STC 3890.5); Broughton, *Our Lord His Line of Fathers from Adam* (STC 3874.5). On Gabriel Simson, see Ames and Herbert, *Typographical Antiquities*, 1263–66; and Willoughby, "Cover Design."

19. Hutton, *Black Dogge of Newgate* (STC 14029); subsequent citations to this work appear parenthetically in the text. On Hutton's life, see Shrank, "Hutton, Luke (d. 1598)"; and *Transcript of the Registers of the Company of Stationers*, fols. 4b, 6b.

20. Downame, *Spiritual Physicke to Cure the Diseases of the Soule* (STC 7147); *Table Declaring What Planet Dooth Raigne Euery Day* (STC 23634.5).

21. Murray, "Measured Sentences." See also Lievsay, "Newgate Penitents."

22. The charter did not originally specify a livery, a practice developed somewhat later. On the term "livery," see Chakravarty, "Livery, Liberty, and Legal Fictions"; Consitt, *London Weavers' Company*, 1–113; and Plummer, *London Weavers' Company*, 15–16.

23. Plummer, *London Weavers' Company*, 107.

24. Kathman, "Rise of Commercial Playing," 18–20. See also Lancashire, *London Civic Theatre*, 69–117.

25. Ward, *Metropolitan Communities*, 5–6.

26. On the right of livery companies to search households to enforce ordinances, see Rappaport, *Worlds within Worlds*, 111–17; Gustafsson, "Rise of Medieval Craft Guilds"; Wallis and Wright, "Evidence, Artisan Experience and Authority in Early Modern England"; and Berlin, "'Broken All in Pieces.'" See also the following cluster of essays in *Guilds, Society and Economy in London*: Wallis, "Controlling Commodities"; Homer, "Pewterers'

Company's Country Searches"; and Forbes, "Search, Immigration and the Goldsmith's Company."

27. Stow, *Survey of London* (STC 23345.5), 69.

28. Grocers, ironmongers, mercers, and drapers dominated the neighborhood. See Keene, Crouch, and Stedman, *Social and Economic Study of Medieval London*, 88–99.

29. Stow, *Survey of London* (STC 23345.5), 278. On the prominence of silk at this market, see Sutton, *Mercery of London*, 16, 470–73, 478.

30. Worshipful Company of Drapers, Apprentice Book, June 8, 1602; see also Society of Genealogists, "Boyd's Inhabitants" and "Stevens 2."

31. *Calendar of Manuscripts of the Most Honourable the Marquess of Salisbury, Hatfield House*, vol. 5, 248–49; Power, "London and the Control of the 'Crisis' of the 1590s"; and Suzuki, *Subordinate Subjects*, 28–34.

32. Indeed, in the same report about the silk-weaver denouncing the mayor are descriptions of several other apprentice riots and near riots in June of 1595. On apprentice riots in the period, see Archer, *Pursuit of Stability*, 1–9.

33. Consitt, *London Weavers' Company*, 314, 316.

34. Archer, *Pursuit of Stability*, 9–14.

35. GL, "Remembrancia," vol. 2, fol. 52 (#102).

36. See Rappaport, *Worlds within Worlds*, 117–23, 136–37, 156–61; and Korda, *Labors Lost*, 41–45.

37. Luu, *Immigrants and the Industries of London*, 92. Roger Finlay estimates that by 1600 London was host to about two hundred thousand people; see *Population and Metropolis*, 51.

38. For an overview of Elizabethan policies regarding immigration and industry, see Goose, "Immigrants and English Economic Development in the Sixteenth and Early Seventeenth Centuries"; and Yungblut, *Strangers Settled Here amongst Us*, 69–82.

39. Consitt, *London Weavers' Company*, 32–61.

40. Ibid., 188–91.

41. LMA, Worshipful Company of Weavers, Constitutional Records: Account and Memorandum Book, Known as the "Old Leidger Book," fols. 313r-v; and Consitt, *London Weavers' Company*, 198–200, 223–26. See also Sharpe, *Calendar of Letter-Books of the City of London*, 253.

42. Luu, *Immigrants and the Industries of London*, 175–81.

43. Wendelken, "Wefts and Worms," 75.

44. Dale, "London Silkwomen of the Fifteenth Century," 324–25.

45. *Calendar of the Plea and Memoranda Rolls of the City of London*, 99–106. For an account of these events more focused on the merchant stranger, see Pearsall, "Strangers in Late Fourteenth-Century London," 54–55.

46. The act included an exception for "corses," or bands, of silk brought in from Genoa. By 1464 the act was renewed without the exception for Genoese silks. See *Rotuli Parliamentorum*, 325, 506.

47. LMA, Worshipful Company of Weavers, Ordinance, Oath and Memorandum Book, fol. 31v; Consitt, *London Weavers' Company*, 229.

48. LMA, Worshipful Company of Weavers, Ordinance, Oath and Memorandum Book, fol. 14–18. Consitt, *London Weavers' Company*, 191–95. Korda, *Labors Lost*, 41–42; Plummer, *London Weavers' Company*, 61–62.

49. LMA, Worshipful Company of Weavers, Ordinance, Oath and Memorandum Book, fol. 32v; Consitt, *London Weavers' Company*, 230.

50. LMA, Ratification, by Lord Keeper of the Great Seal, Chief Justice of the King's Bench and Chief Justice of the Common Pleas of the Ordinances for Regulating the Weavers' Guild, m. 1; Consitt, *London Weavers' Company*, 292. The 1555 regulations are described in the minutes of the Court of Assistants in LMA, Worshipful Company of Weavers, Ordinance, Oath and Memorandum Book, fol. 32v.

51. Consitt, *London Weavers' Company*, 320.

52. Lacey, "Production of 'Narrow Ware' by Silkwomen in Fourteenth and Fifteenth Century England."

53. Luu, *Immigrants and the Industries of London*, 196.

54. Consitt, *London Weavers' Company*, 150.

55. For a general understanding of the status of yeoman, see Rappaport, *Worlds within Worlds*, 219–32.

56. Plummer, *London Weavers' Company*, 43.

57. Ward, *Metropolitan Communities*, 125–43.

58. On the Yeomanry of the Weavers' Company, see Consitt, *London Weavers' Company*, 144–46, and Plummer, *London Weavers' Company*, 43–54. As an example of the effective use of power within various livery companies, one might consider control over civic pageantry described by Tracey Hill. See Hill, *Pageantry and Power*, 55–56. On the Yeomanry of various companies, see Unwin, *Gilds and Companies of London*, 223–31; Unwin, *Industrial Organization in the Sixteenth and Seventeenth Centuries*, 57–61, 198–99, 208–10; and more recently, Carlin, "Liberty and Fraternities in the English Revolution," 226–30.

59. In 1648 the anonymous, comprehensive, and radical pamphlet *The Case of the Commonality of the Corporation of Weavers in London* complained that the company's leadership had dismissed the Yeomanry. The pamphlet cites several orders "That the Yeomandry did consist of sixteen persons." See *Case of the Commonality of the Corporation of Weavers in London* (ESTC R233790), 7.

60. Consitt, *London Weavers' Company*, 146–47.

61. See Unwin, *Gilds and Companies of London*, 217–42; and Carlin, "Liberty and Fraternities in the English Revolution," 227. Ward argues that the notion of widespread oligarchical rule within the livery companies has been overstated. While his standard, "that company officers were not always unified," is perhaps too high a bar to set, the point is well taken. A comprehensive study of advancement to the livery might shed greater light on the issue. At any rate, it is clear that the Weavers' Company was undergoing something of a crisis in terms of its insular leadership, and that

issue extended well into the seventeenth century. Ward, *Metropolitan Communities*, 5, 73–98.

62. State Papers Domestic, Edward VI to Charles I, Edward VI–James I: Addenda, 1591–1593, fol. 137.

63. NA, State Papers Domestic, Edward VI to Charles I, Elizabeth I, 1593 Jan.–Apr., fols. 222–228, 253.

64. Carew, *Certaine Godly and Necessarie Sermons* (STC 4616), sig. A1r.

65. Ibid., sig. T4r. *Geneva Bible*, fol. 315v.

66. Plummer, *London Weavers' Company*, 10–11.

67. Carew, *Certaine Godly and Necessarie Sermons* (STC 4616), sig. V2r.

68. Ibid., sigs. V3r–V4r.

69. Ibid., sig. Y1v.

70. Ingram, "Laurence Dutton, Stage Player," 122–25; Kathman, "Grocers, Goldsmiths, and Drapers," 25–28. See also Plummer, *London Weavers' Company*, 451. Matthew Steggle has located another set of Dutton brothers in the company, thus casting some doubt on the identity of Laurence Dutton. The point regarding an entrenched leadership in the company still stands, however. See Steggle, "John and Laurence Dutton."

71. Sutton, *Mercery of London*, 452.

72. On Taylor's role in his company, see Capp, *World of John Taylor*, 146–50, but also 8–11, 15–16, 30–33. See also Taylor, *To the Right Honorable Assembly, the Lords, Knights, Esquires, and Burgesses of the Honorable House of Commons in Parliament* (Wing T518).

73. Phillips, *English Fictions of Communal Identity*, 11–16.

74. Chambers, *Elizabethan Stage*, 98–99.

75. LMA, Worshipful Company of Weavers, Constitutional Records: Ordinance, Oath and Memorandum Book, Known as the "Ancient Book," fol. 1v. For a transcription, see Consitt, *London Weavers' Company*, 202.

76. Worshipful Company of Weavers, Constitutional Records, Ratification, by Lord Keeper of the Great Seal, Chief Justice of the King's Bench and Chief Justice of the Common Pleas of the Ordinances for Regulating the Weavers' Guild, m. 4; Consitt, *London Weavers' Company*, 303.

77. On the discipline of the French Church's consistory, see Littleton, "Geneva on Threadneedle Street," 265–342; and Cottret, *Huguenots in England*, 241–62.

78. Littleton, "Geneva on Threadneedle Street," 246.

79. Freeman, "Marlowe, Kyd, and the Dutch Church Libel," 50–51.

80. Consitt, *London Weavers' Company*, 312.

81. Ibid., 315.

82. Ibid., 316.

83. Ibid., 312.

84. On hospitality in early modern England, see Heal, *Hospitality in Early Modern England*.

85. Consitt, *London Weavers' Company*, 313–14.

86. LMA, Worshipful Company of Weavers, Constitutional Records: Ordinance, Oath and Memorandum Book, Known as the "Ancient Book," fols. 41a–42a.

87. Consitt, *London Weavers' Company*, 72–75, 153–54.

88. NA, State Papers Domestic, Supplementary, Exchequer, fol. 379.

89. Plummer, *London Weavers' Company*, 147–48.

90. See Wallis, "Labor, Law, and Training in Early Modern London."

91. Plummer, *London Weavers' Company*, 63–64. On women, and widows specifically, involved in the livery companies, see Crowston, "Women, Gender, and Guilds in Early Modern Europe"; Clark, *Working Life of Women in Seventeenth Century*, esp. 304, 160–71; Wiesner, *Women and Gender in Early Modern Europe*, 104–5, 125–28; Ogilvie, "Economics of Guilds," 172–75, 184; Korda, *Labors Lost*, 114–15, 253–54; and Epstein, *Wage Labor and the Guilds*, 122–23, 144–45. The cases of York and Bristol are instructive here as well. See Willen, "Guildswomen in the City of York"; Collins, "Jane Holt"; and Ben-Amos, "Women Apprentices in the Trades and Crafts of Early Modern Bristol."

92. On the differences in wages between men and women, Carew asserts that "it cannot be granted that there should

be difference more then halfe in halfe betweene them." Carew, *Certaine Godly and Necessarie Sermons*, sigs. V1v–V2r.

93. Plummer, *London Weavers' Company*, 61–64; Korda, *Labors Lost*, 41–43; and Rappaport, *Worlds within Worlds*, 38–42.

94. Unwin, *Gilds and Companies of London*, 329–51, esp. 349–51.

95. Epstein, *Wage Labor and the Guilds*, 3.

96. Consitt, *London Weavers' Company*, 314.

97. Ibid., 314.

98. These details are related in the mayor's report of his own investigation into the petition. GL, "Remembrancia," vol. 2, fols. 50v–51r (#98). See also Consitt, *London Weavers' Company*, 316–17.

99. Hoyle, "Petitioning as Popular Politics in Early Sixteenth-Century England," 366–67.

100. GL, "Remembrancia," vol. 2, fols. 50v–51r (#98); Consitt, *London Weavers' Company*, 318.

101. The items from Muggins's household are listed in the inventory, NA, Records of the Chancery . . . Wm. Mouggings. The design of the falcon is curious, perhaps copied from Queen Elizabeth's own heraldry. See Le Rougetel, "Rose of England."

102. On these wall hangings, see Hamling, *Decorating the Godly Household*, 87, 208–11; James, "Domestic Painted Cloths in Sixteenth-Century England"; Mander, "Painted Cloths"; Richardson, *Domestic Life and Domestic Tragedy in Early Modern England*, 88–90; Olson, *Arras Hanging*; and Santos, "'The knots within.'"

103. James, "Domestic Painted Cloths," 145–46; Mander, "Painted Cloths," 140.

104. James, "Domestic Painted Cloths," 159; see also James, *Women's Voices in Tudor Wills*, 241–44.

105. Richardson, *Domestic Life and Domestic Tragedy in Early Modern England*, 66, 74–76, 80, 90, 97–98. See also the several entries in *Tudor Wills Proved in Bristol*, 16, 32, 50–51, 88.

106. O'Connell, "Elizabethan Bourgeois Hero-Tale"; Davies, "'Monuments of Honour'"; Robertson, "Adventures of Dick Whittington"; and Ward, *Culture, Faith,*

and Philanthropy in Early Modern England, 27–67.

107. Ward, *Metropolitan Communities*, 1–26; Fitzgerald, *Drama of Masculinity and Medieval English Guild Culture*; Davies, "'Writying, making, and engrocyng'"; De Munck, "Artisans, Products and Gifts."

108. Wallis, "Apprenticeship and Training in Premodern England"; Griffiths, *Youth and Authority*, 299–302.

109. Kilburn-Toppin, "'Discords Have Arisen and Brotherly Love Decreased'"; Ben-Amos, *Culture of Giving*, 169–93; Consitt, *London Weavers' Company*, 108–11.

110. Bishop, "Speech and Sociability"; Branch, *Faith and Fraternity*, 45–46, 170–71; Richardson, "Craft Guilds and Christianity in Late-Medieval England."

111. Ben-Amos, *Culture of Giving*, 95–106.

112. Kilburn-Toppin, "Material Memories of the Guildsmen"; Plummer, *London Weavers' Company*, 449–50.

113. Fry, *Historical Catalogue of the Pictures, Herse-Cloths and Tapestry at Merchant Taylor's Hall*, 68; Tittler, *Face of the City*, 154–55, 175.

114. I am here indebted to Raymond Williams's reflection on the word "community" in Williams, *Politics and Letters*, 118–19. See also Andrew Gordon's excellent discussion of the terms in *Writing Early Modern London*, 1–10.

115. GL, "Remembrancia," vol. 2, fols. 50v (#98).

116. Deloney, *Proper New Ballad, Breefley Declaring the Death and Execution of 14. Most Wicked Traitors* (STC 6563.5).

117. Consitt, *London Weavers' Company*, 312–13.

118. Babington, *English Bastille*, 41–44.

119. Consitt, *London Weavers' Company*, 317.

120. Ibid., 317.

121. GL, "Remembrancia," vol. 3, fols. 17–19 (#18).

122. Ward, *Metropolitan Communities*, 129.

123. Plummer, *London Weavers' Company*, 44; GL, Worshipful Company of Weavers, Ordinance and Memorandum Book, fols. 179–81, 188–92.

124. Luu, *Immigrants and Industries*, 205–6; Plummer, *London*

Weavers' Company, 150–52; GL, Worshipful Company of Weavers, Ordinance and Memorandum Book, fols. 215, 298.

125. Hutton, Black Dogge of Newgate (STC 14029), unspecified sig. corresponding to A2r.

126. BL, Lansdowne MS vol. 81.30, fol. 76.

127. Hentschell, Culture of Cloth in Early Modern England, 55.

128. BL, Lansdowne MS vol. 81.30, fol. 76.

129. Consitt, London Weavers' Company, 314.

130. Ibid., 314.

131. Lurking here is an early modern urban "moral economy," not unlike that explored in the rural communities of eighteenth-century England or twentieth-century Southeast Asia. See Thompson, "Moral Economy of the English Crowd in the Eighteenth Century"; and Scott, Moral Economy of the Peasant.

132. Consitt, London Weavers' Company, 314.

CHAPTER 2

The epigraph for this chapter is drawn from Crabbe, Poeticall Works of George Crabbe, 50.

1. See Consitt, London Weavers' Company, 123; and Plummer, London Weavers' Company, 125–26.

2. See Hill, Pageantry and Power, 34. On Michaelmas Day, see Cressy, "Protestant Calendar and the Vocabulary of Celebration," 33, 51–52.

3. LMA, Parish Registers, St. Mildred, Poultry, fol. 26v. Parish registers vary in the information provided. While virtually all record the date of christening, St. Mildred's typically includes a date of birth for each child.

4. On holy days and their relation to baptism in early modern England, see Kitson, "Religious Change and the Timing of Baptism in England."

5. Church of England, Booke of Common Prayer (STC 16326), sig. L8v.

6. On the seasonal pattern of burials, see Boulton, Neighbourhood and Society, 49–59. One should note that this pattern varies across England. See Dobson, Contours of Death and Disease in Early Modern England, 203–20.

7. Cressy, Birth, Marriage, and Death, 28–31. See also Schwartz, Milton and Maternal Mortality, 29–48; Schofield, "Did Mothers Really Die?"; and Dobbie, "Attempt to Estimate the True Rate of Maternal Mortality."

8. Sorocold, The Supplications of Saints (STC 22932), 298.

9. Ibid., 297–311.

10. LMA, Parish Registers, St. Mildred, Poultry, fol. 31v. Note that the register uses Old Style dating. Susan Sorocold's burial is listed on March 16, 1604.

11. On infant mortality in Elizabethan England, see Wrigley and Schofield, Population History of England, 249–50; Dobson, Contours of Death and Disease in Early Modern England, 160–83. See also Boulton, Neighbourhood and Society, 55–57; and Rappaport, Worlds within Worlds, 67–77.

12. Sorocold, Supplications of Saints (STC 22932), 310.

13. LMA, Parish Registers, St. Mildred, Poultry, fol. 31v.

14. See Cleugh, "Teaching in Praying Words?" 17–25.

15. LMA, Parish Registers, St. Mildred, Poultry, fols. 25v, 26v.

16. Sorocold, Supplications of Saints (STC 22932), sig. P2v.

17. On ambivalent attitudes regarding childbirth, see Paster, Body Embarrassed, 163–214.

18. See Howard, "Imagining the Pain and Peril of Seventeenth-Century Childbirth," 372–73; and Fissel, Vernacular Bodies, 43–47.

19. On the ways in which early modern birthing established a community of women, see Gowing, Common Bodies, 154–76; and Pollock, "Childbearing and Female Bonding in Early Modern England." On early modern childbirth and neonatal care, see Crawford, Blood, Bodies, and Families in Early Modern England, 79–112. Paige Martin Reynolds suggests that a number of early modern plays evince an anxiety about the way women dominated the birthing

process. See "Sin, Sacredness, and Childbirth in Early Modern Drama."

20. Gibbs, "New Duties for the Parish Community in Tudor London"; Kümin, *Shaping of a Community*; Kümin, *Communal Age in Western Europe*, 40–52; and Wrightson, "Politics of the Parish in Early Modern England." Although focused on rural areas, Steve Hindle's study of poor relief, *On the Parish?*, is indispensable to understanding the administrative functions of the parish.

21. Stow, *Survey of London* (STC 23345.5), 274–75.

22. Ibid.; Milbourn, *History of the Church of St. Mildred the Virgin*, 15. Iken is listed as churchwarden in 1584. See LMA, Parish Registers, St. Mildred, Poultry, fol. 21. For Iken's will, see NA, Prerogative Court of Canterbury . . . Will Registers, Thomas Iken, fols. 169r–v. See also Society of Genealogists, "Boyd's Inhabitants," 14124.

23. Just three months after his death, the parish register lists the baptism of "Sara the daughter Thomas Iken, deceased." LMA, Parish Registers, St. Mildred, Poultry, fol. 24v.

24. On Tusser's poetry, see McRae, *God Speed the Plough*, 146–51, 206–8; Skura, *Tudor Autobiography*, 126–48; and Rosenberg, "Point of the Couplet."

25. Tusser, *Fiue Hundredth Points of Good Husbandry* (STC 24380), fol. 7b. The importance of thrift to Tusser runs throughout his books, but see for example fols. 7b–8a and 57b–58a.

26. On the Poultry Compter, see Howard, *Theater of a City*, 69, 73–75, 79; and Shaw, "Position of Thomas Dekker in Jacobean Prison Literature," 370–71, 374–75, 384, 391.

27. On Tusser's popularity, see Stevenson, *Praise and Paradox*, 277; and Farmer and Lesser, "What Is Print Popularity?" 28–29.

28. Stow, *Survey of London* (STC 23345.5), 274. Part of the epitaph was written onto the final page of the 1580 printing held at the Folger Shakespeare Library. See Tusser, fol. 90a.

29. LMA, Parish Registers, St. Mildred, Poultry, fol. 19r.

30. On Tusser and mid-Tudor populism, see Oldenburg, "Thomas Tusser and the Poetics of the Plow."

31. An unfortunately not very detailed list of significant monuments in and around St. Mildred's may be found in Stow, *Survey of London* (STC 23345.5), 274–75.

32. Milbourn, *History of the Church of St. Mildred the Virgin*, 13, 15, 24, 26. On property holdings in the Poultry, see Keene, Crouch, and Stedman, *Social and Economic Study of Medieval London*, 58–102.

33. Hobson's notoriety was kept alive by these works. Johnson's jestbook was reprinted in 1610, and Heywood's play was reprinted numerous times throughout the seventeenth century.

34. Johnson dedicated the book to Sir William Stone, who, like Hobson, was a haberdasher. Johnson writes that the book contains "many quick flashes of the witty jests of old Hobson the merry Londoner, lately cittyzen of good estimation, and I thinke not alltogether forgotten of your worship." Several of the episodes take place in the Poultry. See Johnson, *Pleasant Conceites of Old Hobson the Merry Londoner* (STC 14688), sig. A1r.

35. On the significance of church monuments in early modern England, see Phillippy, *Shaping Remembrance from Shakespeare to Milton*; Owen, *Identity, Commemoration and the Art of Dying Well*; Llewellyn, *Funeral Monuments in Post-Reformation England*; and Sherlock, *Monuments and Memory in Early Modern England*.

36. Comments about Haseldon appear in Munday's additions to Stow's *Survey*. See Stow, *Survey of London* (STC 23345.5), 274. These events are summarized in part by Milbourn, *History of the Church of St. Mildred the Virgin*, 8–11.

37. On Tipper's reputation, see Stone, *Crisis of the Aristocracy*, 415–16. See also Kitching, "Quest for Concealed Lands," 72–75; and Cottret, *Huguenots in England, Immigration and Settlement*, 63–64.

38. In addition to Milbourn's summary, several primary documents inform this summary of the case of concealed lands in the Poultry. See NA, State Papers Domestic,

Supplementary, Exchequer, fol. 303; NA, Records of the Exchequer, Depositions Taken by Commission.

39. See Cressy, *Birth, Marriage, and Death*, 149–72; Coster, *Baptism and Spiritual Kinship in Early Modern England*, 45–74; and Wilson, *Ritual and Conflict*, 181–200. For a broad view of early modern baptism as ritual, see Muir, *Ritual in Early Modern Europe*, 24–27, 185–86.

40. LMA, Parish Registers, St. Mildred, Poultry, fol. 35v. On this entry, see Knutson, "Caliban in St. Mildred Poultry"; Habib, *Black Lives in the English Archives*, 141–42; and Dimmock, "Converting and Not Converting 'Strangers' in Early Modern London," 462, 474. See also Britton, *Becoming Christian*.

41. On fonts in early modern baptism, see Coster, *Baptism and Spiritual Kinship in Early Modern England*, 57–70; Cressy, *Birth, Marriage, and Death*, 140–48; Whiting, *Reformation of the English Parish Church*, 36–52.

42. Church of England, *Booke of Common Prayer* (STC 16326), sig. N6r.

43. Ibid., sig. N6r.

44. Ibid., sig. N6v.

45. Ibid., sigs. N6v–O1r.

46. Dimmock, "Converting and Not Converting 'Strangers' in Early Modern London," 474.

47. On the role of godparents in the period, see Coster, *Baptism and Spiritual Kinship in Early Modern England*, 195–221.

48. On the desire for an increase in public baptisms, see ibid., 52–53.

49. Despite the state's best efforts at uniformity, there was some divergence in baptismal practice in early modern England. Some disliked the sign of the cross; others debated the use of the ancient fonts. Deviations and compromises then signal the boundaries of particular parish communities.

50. On the parish as the basis for local community, see French, *People of the Parish*; and Kümin, *Communal Age in Western Europe*, 40–54. On the *Booke of Common Prayer*'s role in national identity, see Rosendale, *Liturgy and Literature in the Making of Protestant England*, 34–69.

51. See Cressy, *Birth, Marriage, and Death*, 197–229; Wilson, *Ritual and Conflict*, 201–10; Fissel, *Vernacular Bodies*, 43–46; Rushton, "Purification or Social Control"; and Lee, "Men's Recollections of a Women's Rite." One should also consult Keith Thomas's early discussion of churching, *Religion and the Decline of Magic*, 38, 59–61.

52. On the "churching seat" and other aspects of churching, see Coster, "Purity, Profanity, and Puritanism"; Coster, *Baptism and Spiritual Kinship in Early Modern England*, 54, 67, 71, 95; Newell, "Thanksgiving of Women after Childbirth"; and Muir, *Ritual in Early Modern Europe*, 28–33. For a contrast to these readings, see Knodel, "Reconsidering an Obsolete Rite"; and Ray, "View from the Childwife's Pew."

53. McPherson, "Dramatizing Deliverance and Devotion"; Cressy, *Birth, Marriage, and Death*, 201–2; Wilson, *Ritual and Conflict*, 43–44.

54. Sorocold, *Supplications of Saints* (STC 22932), 308–9.

55. Donne, *Sermons of John Donne*, 168–83.

56. Ibid., 171. Italics in original. For a reading of Donne in terms of the sexual revulsion these lines betray, see Back, "(Re)Placing Donne in the History of Sexuality." On Donne, churching, and gender, see Hodgson, *Gender and the Sacred Self in John Donne*, 36–50; and Johnson, "Recovering the Curse of Eve." See also Cressy, *Birth, Marriage, and Death*, 19.

57. See Wilson, *Ritual and Conflict*, 159, 195–99.

58. Totaro, "Mother London," 154. Similarly, Julia Combs, "Fountains of Love," finds in Dorothy Leigh's description of breastfeeding powerful symbols of love and authority.

59. Deloney, *Novels*, 328.

60. Wilson, *Ritual and Conflict*, 201–17; Wilson, *Making of Man-Midwifery*, 25–46. See also Schwartz, *Milton and Maternal Mortality*, 15–28; and Pollock, "Childbearing and Female Bonding in Early Modern England."

61. On these two midwives and the larger network of midwives in early modern London, see Harkness, *Jewel House*, 69, 271.

62. LMA, Parish Registers, St. Michael, Cornhill, fol. 91v; St. Mildred, Poultry, fols. 25r, 26r.

63. William Waterstone was buried in February 1592. By 1596, Dorothy Waterstone had married Edmond Townsend and subsequently left the parish. LMA, Parish Registers, St. Mildred, Poultry, fols. 24v, 27r.

64. Milbourn, *History of the Church of St. Mildred the Virgin*, 15.

65. Ibid., 15; Society of Genealogists, "Boyd's Inhabitants," 14126.

66. Milbourn, *History of the Church of St. Mildred the Virgin*, 15; Fisher, *Catalogue of Most of the Memorable Tombes, Grave-stones, Plates, Escutcheons, or Atchievement* (Wing F1014), 18.

67. LMA, Parish Registers, St. Mildred, Poultry, fols. 26r, 27r. See also Society of Genealogists, "Boyd's Inhabitants," 9239.

68. LMA, Parish Registers, St. Mildred, Poultry, fol. 27v.

69. Ibid. Several years earlier, Joos de Prill was sanctioned for "immorality" at the Dutch Church. See Hessels, *Register of the Attestations or Certificates of Membership, Confessions of Guilt*, 225; Kirk and Kirk, *Returns of Aliens in the City and Suburbs of London, 1598-1625*, 270; and Kirk and Kirk, *Returns of Aliens in the City and Suburbs of London from the Reign of Henry VIII to James I*, 463.

70. LMA, Parish Registers, St. Mildred, Poultry, fol. 27v.

71. Foster, *London Marriage Licenses*, 1260.

72. *Registers of the University of Oxford*, vol. 2, pt. 2, 94. On Sorocold's life, see Wright, "Sorocold, Thomas."

73. *Remains Historical and Literary Connected with the Palatine Counties of Lancaster and Chester*, 32, 142; *Spending of the Money of Robert Nowell*, 170.

74. Sorocold, *Supplications of Saints* (STC 22932), 326-27.

75. NA, Prerogative Court of Canterbury . . . Will Registers, Thomas Lane. Lane was churchwarden at St. Mildred's in 1587-88. LMA, Parish Registers, St. Mildred, Poultry, fols. 27v-28r. Archer discusses Lane's demands; see *Pursuit of Stability*, 71.

76. Sorocold, *Supplications of Saints* (STC 22932), 277-87, 319-22, 328-32.

77. Ibid., 288-91.

78. LMA, Worshipful Company of Haberdashers, Register of Apprenticeship Bindings, fol. 149v.

79. LMA, Parish Registers, St. Mildred, Poultry, fols. 22r-27v.

80. Muldrew, "'Hard Food for Midas,'" 88; Muldrew, *Economy of Obligation*, 98-102. See also Wordie, "Deflationary Factors in the Tudor Price Rise," 48-70; Wennerlind, *Casualties of Credit*, 17-43; and Spence, *Women, Credit, and Debt in Early Modern Scotland*, 4-6.

81. On such networks, see Muldrew, *Economy of Obligation*, 95-119; Kawana, "Trade, Sociability, and Governance in an English Incorporated Borough"; and Briggs, *Credit and Village Society in Fourteenth-Century England*.

82. Muldrew, *Economy of Obligation*, 108-9.

83. On these numbers and the rise in lawsuits over debt in the early modern period, see Stretton, "Written Obligations, Litigation and Neighbourliness," 193; and Brooks, *Pettifoggers and Vipers of the Commonwealth*, 67-71, 95, 105-6, 110.

84. On the various translations of the line, see Noll, *In the Beginning Was the Word*, 61; and Gottschall, "Pater Noster and the Laity in England," 4-7.

85. Sorocold, *Supplications of Saints* (STC 22932), sig. A12r.

86. See Kermode, *Three Renaissance Usury Plays*, 1-78.

87. Sandys, *Sermons Made by the Most Reuerende Father in God* (STC 21713), 176. This passage and others were cobbled together as "testimony" in Blaxton, *English Vsurer* (STC 3129), 9-44.

88. Muldrew, *Economy of Obligation*, 63-64, 106.

89. Ibid., 148-72.

90. The scholarship on church seating is considerable: Marsh, "Order and Place in England"; Wrightson, "Politics of the Parish," 32-35; Tittler, "Seats of Honour, Seats of Power"; Dymond, "Sitting Apart in Church"; Pittman, "Social Structure and Parish Community of St. Andrew's

Church." On gender segregation in early modern English churches, see Aston, "Segregation in Church"; Gowing, *Gender Relations in Early Modern England*, 51-53; and Flather, *Gender and Space in Early Modern England*, 135-73.

91. This order is theoretical, based on wealth recorded in the lay subsidy, 1598-1600. Wealth and craft were further established by cross-referencing with Society of Genealogists, "Boyd's Inhabitants." See Boyd's numbers 1625, 13925, 23833, 24145, 24630, 36916, 37490, 45758, 45759, and 45937. Boyd's is, of course, incomplete in its survey of London citizens. For Tudnam's profession, see LMA, Parish Resisters, St. Mildred, Poultry, fol. 24r; and Grantham, *List of the Wardens of the Grocers' Company from 1345-1907*, 22.

92. Throughout the period in question, the register at St. Mildred's listed churchwardens across the top of each page. LMA, Parish Registers, St. Mildred, Poultry, fols. 23v-29v.

93. Shepard, *Accounting for Oneself*, 82-113.

94. On these more formal instruments of credit, see Muldrew, *Economy of Obligation*, 96, 109-15.

95. Ibid., 111-14. See also Kerridge, *Trade and Banking in Early Modern England*, 34-39; and Jones, *God and the Moneylenders*, 130-31.

96. Muldrew, *Economy of Obligation*, 201-10, 274-82.

97. On the homoerotics of *The Merchant of Venice*, see Sinfield, "How to Read *The Merchant of Venice* without Being a Heterosexist." On the relation between sexuality and credit, see Kleinberg, "*Merchant of Venice*"; Shell, *Money, Language, and Thought*, 47-83; and Patterson, "Bankruptcy of Homoerotic Amity in Shakespeare's *Merchant of Venice*."

98. *Merchant of Venice*, 1.3.11. On the conflation of moral and economic well-being, see Muldrew, *Economy of Obligation*, 148-51. See also Shepard, *Accounting for Oneself*, 82-113; and Heal, "Food Gifts, the Household and the Politics of Exchange in Early Modern England," 46-47.

99. See David Hawkes's discussion of debtor's prison in *Culture of Usury in Renaissance England*, 150-55.

100. LMA, Parish Registers, St. Mildred, Poultry, fol. 27v. See also Society of Genealogists, "Boyd's Inhabitants," 36916.

101. LMA, Parish Registers, St. Mildred, Poultry, fol. 27r-v.

102. NA, Prerogative Court of Canterbury . . . Will Registers, Thomas Childe.

103. See NA, Prerogative Court of Canterbury . . . Wills Registers, Hugh Morrall, fols. 253r-v. See also LMA, Parish Registers, St. Mary Magdalen, Milk Street, fol. 5v.

104. On Robert Nicholson's bankruptcy, see Jones, *Foundations of Bankruptcy*, 42-43.

105. Milward's daughter, Susan, was christened at St. Christopher le Stocks on December 27, 1606. Humphrey Milward's wife, Judith, was buried on June 21, 1603. Humphrey Milward was buried at the church on June 7, 1608. LMA Parish Registers, St. Christopher le Stocks, fols. (unsigned) 10r, 51r, 52r.

106. The property is described in Milward's will: NA, Prerogative Court of Canterbury . . . Will Registers, Humfrey Milward. On the Red Lion, see Gurr, *Shakespearean Stage*, 42, 141-45, 158-59; Berry, "First Public Playhouses, Especially the Red Lion"; and Loengard, "Elizabethan Lawsuit."

107. NA, Prerogative Court of Canterbury . . . Will Registers, Humfrey Milward. See also Society of Genealogists, "Boyd's Inhabitants," 877. In a demonstration of Milward's wealth and influence, Milward's daughter, Mary, would go on to marry Sir Thomas Hayes, sheriff (1604-5) and mayor (1614-15). See Cokayne, *Some Account of the Lord Mayors and Sheriffs of the City of London*, 68-69.

108. LMA, Parish Registers, St. Magnus the Martyr, fols. 41r, 118v, 119r.

109. NA, Prerogative Court of Canterbury . . . Will Registers, George Maunsell; see also Society of Genealogists, "Boyd's Inhabitants," 19568.

110. The terms of the loan are described in NA, Records of the Chancery . . . Wm. Mouggings.

111. Muldrew, *Economy of Obligation*, 110.

112. On the legal process in such cases, see Conyers, *Wiltshire Extents for Debts*, 1–13.

113. The men's names, listed on the inquisition, all appear in the lay subsidy: NA, Records of the Exchequer, Three Subsidies, 1598 Oct. 1, rots. 1 and 2. I have further cross-referenced these with the parish registers of St. Stephen, Coleman St., and St. Margaret, Lothbury LMA, Parish Registers, St. Stephen Coleman St.; St. Margaret, Lothbury. From Coleman Street: Walrond (fol. 42r), Betts (fol. 146v), Floud or Floyd (fols. 63r, 65r, 66v, 75r), Horne (innholder and churchwarden: fols. 90v, 158r), Morris ("Brown baker": fol. 155r), Leather (fols. 94v, 128r, 146r), Allen (shoemaker and churchwarden: fols. 90v, 91v, 165v), Mercer (fol. 70v), and Butler (saddler: fol. 145v). From Lothbury: Symondes (fol. 13r) and Gassley (fols. 12v, 17r). On St. Stephen's, albeit from later decades, see Johns, "Coleman Street."

114. LMA, Parish Registers, St. Botolph, Bishopsgate, fols. 25v, 29v, 33v, 38v.

115. For example, Dunwell participated in the inquisition postmortem of Thomas Cookys and Elizabeth Roche. See *Abstracts of Inquisitions Post-Mortem*, 77–78, 88.

116. Stow, *Abridgement of the English Chronicles* (STC 23332), 402.

117. LMA, Parish Registers, St. Magnus the Martyr, fols. 39v, 40r–v, 43r. See also *Allegations for Marriage Licenses Issued by the Bishop of London*, 178. It is worth noting that Martha Maunsell and Elizabeth Houghton, daughters of George Maunsell and Simon Hougton respectively, were baptized on the same day. See fol. 41r.

118. On bedding in the period, see Richardson, *Domestic Life and Domestic Tragedy in Early Modern England*, 64–103.

119. Halliday was a founding member of the East India Company. Lowe was mayor of London in 1604, and Halliday followed him as mayor the next year. See Society of Genealogists, "Boyd's Inhabitants," 15487 and 8957.

120. On goods as savings, see Spufford, *Great Reclothing of Rural England*, 117–18; and Shepard, *Accounting for Oneself*, 42–43, 298.

121. I am here thinking of R. H. Tawney's remarkable description of poverty in rural China: "There are districts in which the position of the rural population is like that of a man standing permanently up to the neck in water, so that even a ripple is sufficient to drown him." See *Land and Labor in China*, 77.

122. Stow, *Survey of London* (STC 23345.5), 122.

123. Italics in the original. Taylor, *Water-Cormorant* (STC 23813), sig. E4v. A year earlier Taylor had neared this false etymology turned epithet in *The Cold Tearme*, where he describes "a Broker, a base Houndsditch hound." See *Cold Tearme* (STC 23910).

124. Rowley, *Match at Mid-Night* (STC 21421).

125. Lupton, *London and the Countrey Carbonadoed and Quartred into Seuerall Characters* (STC 16944), 57.

126. To draw attention to the pun, I have retained the spelling of "courtesy" as found in the quarto and folio. On epithets in *The Merchant of Venice* see Vienne-Guerrin, "'You Have Rated Me'"; and on this pun in particular, see Andrews, "Textual Deviancy in *The Merchant of Venice*."

127. Dekker, *Rod for Run-Awayes* (STC 6520), sigs. C1v–C2r; Jonson, *Workes of Benjamin Jonson* (STC 14752), sig. D2r.

128. See, for example, Robert Greene's use of the phrase "powling pence" in *A Quip for an Upstart Courtier* (STC 12301s.3), sig. B2v; or Thomas Nashe's similar use of the phrase "powling pence" along with his pun "Peter to pay Powle" in *Haue with You to Saffron-Walden* (STC 18369), sig. B2r–v.

129. Stow, *Survey of London* (STC 23345.5), 123.

130. On the moral economy, see Muldrew, "Interpreting the Market"; See also Shepard, *Accounting for Oneself*, 35, 313. One should also consult Thompson, "Moral Economy of the English Crowd in the Eighteenth Century."

131. Shepard, *Accounting for Oneself*, 120–22; Lemire, *Business of Everyday Life*, 58–60; Lemire, "Secondhand Clothing Trade in Europe and Beyond."

132. *Tudor Economic Documents*, 361.

133. Textiles and fabrics made up as much as 80 percent of all pawned goods

in England from 1600 through 1830. See Lemire, *Business of Everyday Life*, 92–96; and Jones and Stallybrass, *Renaissance Clothing*, 26–32. On women's involvement in taking out of loans, see Korda, *Labors Lost*, 45–46, 58–60, 67–71; and Lemire, "Secondhand Clothing Trade in Europe and Beyond," 152–53. On Henslowe as pawnbroker, see Korda, "Household Property/Stage Property"; and Carson, *Companion to Henslowe's Diary*, 22–34.

134. Stubbes, *Anatomie of Abuses* (STC 23376), sigs. K8r–v.

135. Ibid., sigs. K7v–K8r.

136. William Rider, Lord Mayor of London, to Sir Robert Cecil, in *Calendar of Manuscripts of the Most Honourable Marquess of Salisbury, Hatfield House*, vol. 11, 132.

137. I render the Latin thus: "Quod Will[elmu]s Movggings in p[re]d[icto] bre[vi]s no[m]i[n]atus laicus est & non est invent[us] in balli[v]a n[ost]ra."

138. LMA, Parish Registers, St. Mildred, Poultry, fol. 27v.

139. Boyd lists the given name as Joseph, but the records of the Drapers appear as "Prince Jacobo aurifabro," reasonably translated as "Prince, James goldsmith." There was, moreover, a James Prince among the goldsmiths at this time, whereas I can find no Joseph Prince in the lists of goldsmiths in London. See *London Goldsmiths*, 227.

140. Worshipful Company of Drapers, Freedom Admissions Book, 1567–1655, and Quarterage Book, 1617–27, fol. 244. See also Boyd, *Roll of the Drapers' Company*, entry for "Stevens."

141. On Stephenson's musical career, see the entry for "Beeland, Ambrose" in Ashbee et al., *Biographical Dictionary of English Court Musicians*, cxxxviii.

142. See Wallis, "Labor, Law, and Training," 800–802; and Leunig, Minns, and Wallis, "Networks in the Premodern Economy," 433.

CHAPTER 3

The epigraph for this chapter comes from *Poem on the History of Queen Hester* (Wing P2696), 6.

1. Boulton, *Neighbourhood and Society*, 19.

2. Ibid., 24. See also Rendle, *Old Southwark*, 272–75.

3. *Acts of the Privy Council of England, 1617–1619*, 172; *Acts of the Privy Council of England, 1597–1598*, 435.

4. Stow, *Survey of London* (STC 23345.5), 168.

5. Boulton, *Neighbourhood and Society*, 64.

6. See Nelson, "Shakespeare and Southwark."

7. Greg, *Henslowe's Diary*, 298.

8. See entries in Chambers, *Elizabethan Stage*, 237, 312, 314, 317–19, 329, 333–36, 338, 340, 345.

9. Ibid., 338; LMA, Parish Registers, St. Saviour, Southwark, Bermondsey, fol. 46or (December 31, 1607).

10. Chambers, *Elizabethan Stage*, 298, 299, 313, 314, 325, 339, 348.

11. Ibid., 331, 340. This is by no means an exhaustive list.

12. Habib and Salkeld, "Resonables of Boroughside, Southwark," 140–41.

13. Sutton, *Englands First and Second Summons* (STC 23502), 28.

14. Field, *Remonstrance of Nathan Field*, 8.

15. *Diary of Philip Henslowe*, 244, 245, 246, 249, 274.

16. Other plays likely based on Deloney's writing were being performed on the other side of the Thames. The *Lost Plays Database* lists *The Six Yeomen of the West*, *The Six Clothiers of the West*, and *Tom Dough, Part Two* as all likely based on Deloney's *Thomas of Reading*. On the relationship between Dekker and Deloney, see Christensen, "Being Mistress Eyre in Dekker's *The Shoemaker's Holiday* and Deloney's *The Gentle Craft*"; and Mortenson, "Economics of Joy in *The Shoemakers' Holiday*."

17. Kemp, *Kemps Nine Daies Wonder* (STC 14688), sigs. D3r–v.

18. See Boulton, *Neighbourhood and Society*, 65–68, 70–71.

19. See Fumerton, *Unsettled*.

20. Stow, *Survey of London* (STC 23345.5), 329, 340.

21. Groom, "John Siberch (d. 1554)." See also Boulton, *Neighbourhood and Society*, 63–64. On the medieval immigrant communities, see Carlin, *Medieval Southwark*, 149–68; and Rendle, *Old Southwark*, 262–66.

22. I am here assuming that clothing is part of the textile industry. Boulton, *Neighbourhood and Society*, 66.

23. Ibid., 62–63.

24. The subsidy was taken in 1598, 1599, and 1600. NA, Records of the Exchequer, Three Subsidies, 1598 Dec. 12, rot 7; 1598 Oct. 1, rot 15; 1600 Oct. 1, rot 1.

25. On the lay subsidy, see Boulton, *Neighbourhood and Society*, 104–19; Braddick, *Parliamentary Taxation in Seventeenth-Century England*, 64–125; and Jurkowski, Smith, and Crook, *Lay Taxes in England and Wales*, xli–xlv, 168–69.

26. On the status of subsidy payers, see Boulton, *Neighbourhood and Society*, 146. See also Braddick, *Parliamentary Taxation in Seventeenth-Century England*, 77.

27. Boulton, *Neighbourhood and Society*, 65. This may, moreover, reflect a downward economic turn in the suburbs. Based on the 1589 assessment, Archer estimates subsidy payers in the parish to have been around 27 percent. See *Pursuit of Stability*, 71.

28. This issue came to a head in 1642 when parishioners insisted on replacing some members of the vestry. *Fifth Report of the Royal Commission on Historical Manuscripts*, 17, 24.

29. Archer, *Pursuit of Stability*, 73.

30. Schofield and Wrigley, "Infant and Child Mortality in England in the Late Tudor and Early Stuart Period."

31. On the watching of bodies, see Cressy, *Birth, Marriage, and Death*, 425–32. See also Tarlow, *Ritual, Belief and the Dead in Early Modern Britain and Ireland*, 128–29; and Koslofsky, *Reformation of the Dead*, 95–96.

32. Church of England, *Booke of Common Prayer*, sigs. P7v–P8v.

33. Balmford, *Short Dialogve concerning the Plagves Infection* (STC 1338), 58–59.

34. Church of England, *Booke of Common Prayer*, sigs. Q1r–v.

35. See Duffy, *Stripping of the Altars*, 301–76; Gittings, "Urban Funerals in Late Medieval and Reformation England"; and Binski, *Medieval Death*, 29–69.

36. NA, Prerogative Court of Canterbury . . . Will Registers, John Crowle. See also Carlin, *Medieval Southwark*, 86–87.

37. On these guilds generally, see Duffy, *Stripping of the Altars*, 141–54, 455–56; and Rousseau, *Saving the Souls of Medieval London*. On Southwark's fraternities, see Rendle, *Old Southwark*, 88–99; and Carlin, *Medieval Southwark*, 87–89, 97–99. Clive Burgess offers a useful study of fraternities at the parish level; see "London Parishioners in Times of Change."

38. Such payments occur regularly in pre-Reformation wills by parishioners of St. Olave's. They also sometimes include payments to "the brotherhood of Jesus," another guild associated with St. Olave's. Occasionally payment was made to the altar rather than the guild maintaining the altar. Early on this may have reflected an understanding that prayers would follow, but by the 1540s the wording may also have reflected a Protestant attitude or a concern with the status of the fraternities themselves, granting payments not for the fraternities themselves but for the altars with which they were associated. NA, Prerogative Court of Canterbury . . . Will Registers, Cristofer Cravyn, Henry Fitzjohn, John Skylborne, and John Stephyns.

39. NA, Prerogative Court of Canterbury . . . Will Registers, Edward Vaughan.

40. On funerals in Reformation England, see Phillippy, *Women, Death and Literature*, 83–86; Gittings, *Death, Burial and the Individual in Early Modern England*, 39–59; Houlbrouke, *Death, Religion and the Family in England*, 255–94. For a broader view of the rituals around funeral in the early modern period, see Muir, *Ritual in Early Modern Europe*, 50–59.

41. On the use of bells, see Cressy, *Birth, Marriage, and Death*, 421–25; Gittings, *Death, Burial and the Individual in Early Modern England*, 32–35; and Marsh, "'At it ding don.'" The maintenance of the bells at St. Olave's is evident on most pages of the vestry account books; see Society of

Antiquaries of London, St. Olave, Southwark, Churchwardens, fols. 47a, 48b, 49a, 51a, 51b.

42. Adams, *Deuills Banket* (STC 110.5), 209–10. See also Cressy, *Birth, Marriage, and Death*, 422.

43. Hooker, *Works of Mr. Richard Hooker* (Wing H2631), 291.

44. Aubrey, *Natural History and Antiquities of the County of Surrey*, 60; Stow, *Survey of London* (STC 23345.5), 457.

45. Aubrey, *Natural History and Antiquities of the County of Surrey*, 62.

46. Stow includes descriptions of six such monuments. Stow, *Survey of London* (STC 23345.5), 457–58.

47. See Phillippy, *Women, Death and Literature*, 7–11; Brady, *English Funerary Elegy in the Seventeenth Century*, 32–61; and Houlbrooke, "Civility and Civil Observances in the Early Modern English Funeral."

48. Jay, *Sermon Preacht at the Funerall of the Lady Mary Villiers* (STC 14479), 32–33.

49. Pigman, *Grief and English Renaissance Elegy*, 20–22.

50. Doolittle, *Mourner Directory* (Wing D1888), 66.

51. Ibid., 120. See also Hibbert, *Waters of Marah Drawn Forth in Two Funeral Sermons* (Wing H1794), 10, 66.

52. On the prevalence of elegies for children in the early modern period, see Anselment, "'Teares of Nature.'" See also Phillippy, *Women, Death and Literature*, 148–56.

53. LMA, Parish Registers, St. Olave, Bermondsey, Southwark, fol. 106v.

54. Ibid., fol. 116v.

55. Ibid., fols. 124v, 133v.

56. A Robert Redman appeared before the governors of Bridewell as a vagrant in 1602 in the same week that a Suzan Muggins also appeared at Bridewell. Although no record survives of William Muggins appearing to bail out a kinswoman, the coincidence of the name of Muggins's apprentice appearing alongside a Muggins is curious. LMA, Royal Hospitals of Bridewell and Bethlem, Minutes of the Court of Governors, fols. 361r–v.

57. LMA, Parish Registers, St. Olave, Bermondsey, Southwark, fol. 103r.

58. James Muggins appears as a master haberdasher in 1594: LMA, Worshipful Company of Haberdashers, Register of Apprenticeship Bindings, fol. 157r.

59. LMA, Parish Registers, St. Mary Magdalen, Old Fish Street, fols. 108v, 109v, 110v.

60. Blower's shop was on Lambeth Hill near Old Fish Street. He appears in the parish register of St. Mary Magdalen, Old Fish Street, multiple times. Ibid., fols. 25v, 26r, 26v, 114r, 115r.

61. James Muggins married Mary Wrighte in 1588. Ibid., fol. 51r.

62. LMA, Parish Registers, St. Olave, Bermondsey, Southwark, fols. 106v, 116v, 124v.

63. Ibid., fols. 133v, 137r, 139r.

64. Boulton, *Neighbourhood and Society*, 71–73.

65. LMA, Parish Registers, St. Olave, Bermondsey, Southwark, fol. 116v.

66. Worshipful Company of Parish Clerks, *A Generall Bill for 8 Weeks Shewing All the Burials and Christninges* (STC 16743.1).

67. Dekker, *1603. The Wonderfull Yeare* (STC 6535), sig. D2r.

68. Herring, *Modest Defence of the Caveat Given to the Wearers of Impoisoned Amulets* (STC 13248), sig. B1r.

69. Balmford, *Short Dialogve concerning the Plagves Infection* (STC 1338), 57–58.

70. The numbers here are based on bills of mortality. As has already been mentioned, plague deaths were accompanied by a rise in non-plague deaths, and readers may want to factor in a broader sense of mortality in and around the parish. Worshipful Company of Parish Clerks, *Buried in London* (STC 16743.9); Worshipful Company of Parish Clerks, *True Bill of the Whole Number That Hath Died* (STC 1997:26). On the additional 124 burials, see LMA, Parish Registers, St. Olave, Bermondsey, Southwark, fols. 134r–135r.

71. Scholars have long linked Deloney to St. Giles because his son Richard was christened there on October 16, 1586. It is possible that Richard Deloney died within several weeks. The burial of "Richard sonne of John Delony (weav[er])" occurred on

December 21, 1586. To my knowledge, no one has noted the July 27 burial of "Thomas Deloney servant with George Avery, weaver." "Servant" here is the generalized term for apprentice, and the name and age along with the record of the balladeer's association with the church points to not irrefutable but still significant evidence for this Thomas Deloney to be the son of Muggins's fellow weaver-poet. George Avery had been buried a week and a half earlier, on July 12. His five-year-old daughter, Alice, was buried two days after Deloney. St. Giles, like St. Olave's in Southwark, was extremely hard hit by the plague. LMA, Parish Registers, St. Giles, Cripplegate, fols. 193v, 191v, 194r. On the christening of Richard Deloney and his possible burial, see fols. 92v and 93v.

72. LMA, Parish Registers, St. Olave, Bermondsey, Southwark, fol. 75r. The family of Thomas Black, a fisherman in the neighboring parish, had been hit by the plague in mid-July, so perhaps Mary had contracted the disease during a visit with her cousins. The relation between Mary Black and Thomas Black's household is necessarily speculative: migration in the period was such that it is now very difficult to attribute a special meaning to proximity, especially with a fairly common name that might be spelled variously as Blake, Black, or Bleake. Thomas Black was buried on July 30, 1603. LMA, Parish Registers, St. Saviour, Southwark, fol. 340v.

73. Totaro, *Suffering in Paradise*, 52–57; Slack, *Impact of the Plague*, 44–50, 199–226; Wilson, *Plague in Shakespeare's London*, 10–13.

74. In 1666, Thomas Clark described his own miserable experience of quarantine, where

> The Daughter dareth not approach the Mother;
> Nor dares one Brother to come at another.
> The Father may not his own Child come near,
> Nor may the Child the Parent see for fear.
> The Mother doth bewail her Child at distance;

The Child oft wants the Mother's kind assistance. (Totaro, *Plague Epic in Early Modern England*, 265).

Not much is known of Clark, but it is difficult to imagine that the humble Muggins household would have had space to keep the infected very far from the healthy.

75. I have included Anne Muggins in this list of members of the household because there is no solid evidence that she was not in the household in 1603. There is a remote possibility that she had gone to live with a relative, John Muggins, however. On September 17, 1603, St. Giles, Cripplegate records the burial of "Anne daughter of John Muggins mercer." There is no corresponding record of christening for a daughter of John Muggins named Anne. LMA, Parish Registers, St. Giles, Cripplegate, fol. 203v.

76. Balmford, *Short Dialogve concerning the Plagves Infection* (STC 1338), 6.

77. Clapham, *Epistle Discoursing vpon the Present Pestilence* (STC 5339), sig. B4v. See also the discussion of Clapham in Slack, *Impact of the Plague*, 233–35; Gilman, *Plague Writing in Early Modern England*, 146–52; Totaro, *Suffering in Paradise*, 45–46; and Wallis, "Plagues, Morality and the Place of Medicine in Early Modern England," 5–6, 9–10.

78. Balmford, *Short Dialogve concerning the Plagves Infection* (STC 1338), 59.

79. Ibid., 60–61.

80. Ibid., 67.

81. W. T., *Casting VP of Accounts of Certain Errors* (STC 1717:05), sigs. C3v–C4r.

82. Balmford, *Short Dialogve concerning the Plagves Infection* (STC 1338), 10.

83. Church of England, *Booke of Common Prayer*, sigs. B6r–B7v; Church of England, *Certaine Praiers Collected out of a Fourme of Godly Meditations* (STC 16524). See also Totaro, *Plague in Print*, 17–48.

84. Muggins's prayer, for instance, echoes one of the state's plague prayers: the phase "turne us, and wee shall be turned unto thee" from one of the authorized prayers of 1603 appears in Muggins's prayer as "Turne vs vnto thee, and we shall be turned" (sig. D4r). See Church of England, *Certaine*

Prayers Collected out of a Forme of Godly Meditation (STC 16523), sig. B4v.

85. Smith, "Personifications of Plague in Three Tudor Interludes." Smith similarly reads Muggins's personification of London as "subsum[ing] individual crimes under the aegis of society as a whole." See "Playhouse as Plaguehouse in Early Modern Revenge Tragedy," 80.

86. On the pun hear/here, particularly in epitaphs, see Newstok, *Quoting Death in Early Modern England*, 1–2, 36–45, 150–52.

87. Scott Wayland notes a proliferation of elegies in Reformation England and suggests that in some sense they fill the void left by Catholicism's more elaborate funeral practices. See "Religious Change and the Renaissance Elegy."

88. See Kay, *Melodious Tears*, 7–12.

89. Scodel, "Genre and Occasion in Jonson's 'On My First Sonne'"; Riggs, *Ben Jonson*, 93–97.

90. Greenfield, "Cultural Functions of Renaissance Elegy," 81–82.

91. Jonson, *Workes of Benjamin Jonson* (STC 14752), 780–81.

92. I am here, in part, indebted to Patrick J. Mahony's subtle psychological reading of the poem. See Mahony, "Ben Jonson's 'best piece of poetrie'"; and Martin, "Name of the Father in 'On My First Son.'"

93. See Meskill, *Ben Jonson and Envy*, 136.

94. Phillippy, *Women, Death and Literature*, 161; Pigman, *Grief and English Renaissance Elegy*, 88–90.

95. This corresponds loosely to Pigman's notion of rigorism in mourning. See *Grief and English Renaissance Elegy*, 88–90.

96. On the tension between public and private in Jonson, see Meyer, "Public Statements and Private Losses of Ben Jonson and Katherine Philips"; and Winner, "Public and Private Dimensions of Jonson's Epitaphs."

97. See Brady, *English Funerary Elegy in the Seventeenth Century*, 62–89.

98. Gilman, *Plague Writing in Early Modern England*, 165.

99. Phillippy, *Women, Death and Literature*, 121–22.

100. It might be reasonable to suppose that the "onely Phisicke women can bestow" is aimed at the object "greefe"; in other words, that the only cure for grief is tears, and that women, in the early modern construction of gender, are more apt to cry.

101. Puttenham, *Arte of English Poesie* (STC 20519.5), 37–38.

102. Ibid., 39.

103. Thorne, "'O lawful let it be / That I have room . . . to curse awhile,'" 121.

104. On early modern women and literacy, see Wiesner, *Women and Gender in Early Modern Europe*, 141–73; Eales, *Women in Early Modern England*, 34–45; Snook, *Women, Reading, and the Cultural Politics of Early Modern England*; and Willen, "Godly Women in Early Modern England."

105. Wrightson, *Earthly Necessities*, 49–50.

106. Jones and Stallybrass, *Renaissance Clothing*, 7–11, 21–22, 28.

107. See Frye, *Pens and Needles*, 116–59; Hamling and Richardson, *Day at Home in Early Modern England*, 212–15; Jones and Stallybrass, *Renaissance Clothing*, 148–59; Cabot, "Patter Sources of Scriptural Subjects in Tudor-Stuart Embroideries"; Mazzola, *Learning and Literacy in Female Hands*, 26–30; and Winner, *Cheerful and Comfortable Faith*, 64–72.

108. Frye, *Pens and Needles*, 116–59. See also, Jones and Stallybrass, *Renaissance Clothing*, 137, 156–59.

109. Jonson and Patterson, *Notes of Ben Jonson's Conversations with William Drummond of Hawthornden*, 25. See also Riggs, *Ben Jonson*, 95.

110. *Geneva Bible*, fols. 254v–255r.

111. Cawdry, *Treasurie or Store-House of Similes* (STC 4887), 349.

112. Herbert's poem, too, complicates theology's positive view of death, of course.

113. Brady, *English Funerary Elegy in the Seventeenth Century*, 37; Heller, *Mother's Legacy in Early Modern England*, 168–71.

114. Boethius, *Boke of Comfort Called in Laten Boetius de Consolatione Philosophie* (STC 3200), sig. B2r; Augustine, *Certain Select Prayers* (STC 924), sig. A8v; Foxe, *Sermon of Christ Crucified* (STC 11242.3), sig. T2r; Jewel, *Second Tome of Homilees* (STC 13669), 546.

115. Froide, "Marital Status as a Category of Difference," 240, 262–63.
116. LMA, Royal Hospitals of Bridewell and Bethlem, Minutes of the Court of Governors, fols. 337v, 361r. On prostitution, see Capp, *When Gossips Meet*, 179–80, 192–94; Karras, *Common Women*, 48–64; and Gowing, *Gender Relations in Early Modern England*, 14–15, 19.

CHAPTER 4

The epigraph for this chapter is drawn from Hull, *Exposition vpon a Part of the Lamentations of Jeremie* (STC 1312:06), sig. B1r.
1. Church of England, *Certaine Prayers Collected out of a Forme of Godly Meditation* (STC 16523), sig. A3r. *Certaine Prayers* was revised at each visitation of the plague from 1563 onward, but remained substantially similar over time. See Totaro, *Plague in Print*, 17–48. See also Raffe, "Nature's Scourges"; and Mears, "Public Worship and Political Participation in Elizabethan England." Finally, see Mears et al., *National Prayers*, xlvii–cv, 240–53.
2. Balmford, *Short Dialogve concerning the Plagves Infection* (STC 1338), sig. A4r.
3. Ibid., sigs. A2v–A3r.
4. Amid controversy surrounding Udall's *Diotrephes*, Huntington arranged for Udall to move from his ministry at Kingston-upon-Thames to Newcastle-upon-Tyne where, according Udall, he "joyned in the ministery of the word there with two godly men, Mr. *Houldesworth* the Pastor, and Mr. *Bamford* a [pr]eacher, through whose joynt labours God vouchsafed so to draw the people to the love of the word." The original says, "Mr. Bamford, a teacher." Given what is known about Balmford at the time as well as the context of the sentence, it seems clear that "teacher" is a printer's error for "preacher." See Udall, *New Discovery of Old Pontifical Practises* (Wing U14), 1.
5. Balmford's removal from the ministry at Newcastle is briefly touched on in Fenwicke, *Christ Ruling in Midst of His Enemies* (Wing F719), sig. A2r. The date of Balmford's transfer to Southwark can be estimated with some accuracy. In late August 1600, he is listed as godfather to Toby Barker, the son of Newcastle merchant John Barker. It cannot have been much after this that Balmford relocated. By January 1601 William Morton appears as Newcastle's vicar. Although it has been presumed that he replaced Holdesworth, who died in 1596, Morton's appearance in the records of Newcastle corresponds with Balmford's appearance in Southwark. See Barnes, *Memoirs*, 299.
6. See Balmford, *Position Maintained by J. B* (STC 13345). On Hastings as patron, see Cross, *Puritan Earl*, 99–135.
7. On the controversy around games of chance in early modern England, see Chovenak (sic., actual surname is Chovanec), "'What is there in three dice?'"; and Willen, "Case of Thomas Gataker."
8. Balmford, *Short and Plaine Dialogue concerning the Vnlawfulnes of Playing at Cards* (STC 1335), sig. B1r.
9. Tudor, *By the Queen, by the Grace of God Queene of England, Fraunce, and Ireland* (STC 8171); Stuart, *Basilikon Doron* (STC 14353), 123–24.
10. Gataker, *On the Nature and Vse of Lots* (STC 11670). Gataker expanded his attack on Balmford in the subsequent 1623 printing. On Gataker as polemicist, see Willen, "Thomas Gataker and the Use of Print in the English Godly Community."
11. Balmford, *Modest Reply to Certaine Answeres* (STC 1336).
12. Gataker, *Just Defence of Certaine Passages in a Former Treatise* (STC 11666a).
13. LMA, Parish Registers, St. Olave, Bermondsey, Southwark, fol. 274r. Like most of the other forty-eight burials in the parish that day, Balmford had probably died of the plague. On the plague of 1625, see Gilman, *Plague Writing in Early Modern England*, 191–213; and Wilson, *Plague in Shakespeare's London*, 129–76.
14. Balmford, *Short and Plaine Dialogue concerning the Vnlawfulnes of Playing at Cards* (STC 1335), sig. A2v.
15. Ibid., sig. B4r.
16. Without knowing that Muggins attended Balmford's church, Philippy rather remarkably reads these two texts in relation

to each other, no doubt picking up on some of their shared characteristics. See *Women, Death and Literature*, 122.

17. Balmford, *Short Dialogve concerning the Plagves Infection* (STC 1338), 6; Geneva Bible, fol. 300v.

18. Balmford, *Short Dialogve concerning the Plagves Infection* (STC 1338), 72–73.

19. Balmford, *Short and Plaine Dialogue concerning the Vnlawfulnes of Playing at Cards* (STC 1335), sig. A2r. A broadside printing of the same also included the dedication. See Balmford, *To the Maior, Aldermen, and Inhabitants of N.* (STC 13357).

20. Balmford received multiple payments in 1579 and 1580 designated as "towarde his exhibicon at Oxford." *Records of the Worshipful Company of Carpenters*, vol. 5, 103, 120, 136.

21. *Records of the Worshipful Company of Carpenters*, vol. 7, 411.

22. Ibid., 426, 453, 454, 485.

23. Ibid., 165.

24. Balmford, *Position Maintained by J. B. . . . Treason* (STC 13345). Balmford, *Carpenters Chippes* (STC 1334).

25. Balmford, *Short Catechisme* (STC 1337), sig. A2v. The pamphlet was reprinted in 1610. Balmford entered St. Mary Hall, Oxford, in 1570. He is listed as the recipient of a bachelor of arts in 1579. See *Registers of the University of Oxford*, vol. 2, pt. 2, 33, 43; *Registers of the University of Oxford*, vol. 2, pt. 3, 84, 89.

26. Balmford, *Short Catechisme* (STC 1337), sig. A2r.

27. Ibid., sigs. A2r, A4v. Italics in the original.

28. Seaver, *Wallington's Worlds*, 138–42.

29. Roberts, *Puritanism and the Pursuit of Happiness*, 54–55, 104–6.

30. Reynolds, *Godly Reformers and their Opponents in Early Modern England*, 91; Greaves, "Origins and Early Development of English Covenant Thought," 31.

31. See Carrington, *Two Schools*, 46–49.

32. Burrage, *True Story of Robert Browne*, 44–45.

33. Ibid., 38–39.

34. Bredwell, *Rasing of the Foundations of Brownisme* (STC 3599), 139.

35. Ibid., 138–39.

36. Burrage, *True Story of Robert Browne*, 146–80.

37. Ibid., 145. Rippon's trade and identity as a parishioner of St. Olave's is confirmed by an entry in St. Olave's parish register in August 1592. LMA, Parish Registers, St. Olave, Bermondsey, Southwark, fol. 59v.

38. Carlson, *Elizabethan Non-conformist Texts*, vol. 6, 219, 245–46.

39. BL, Harley MS 6948, fol. 61. See also Burrage, *True Story of Robert Browne*, 34–36; Culpepper, *Francis Johnson and the Separatist Influence*, 63–64, 155, 159.

40. Jacob, *Defence of the Churches and Ministery of Englande* (STC 14335), sigs. X2r–X3v; Johnson, *Answer to Maister H. Jacob* (STC 14658), sig. A4r.

41. NA, Prerogative Court of Canterbury . . . Will Registers, 1384–1858, Daniel Bucke.

42. Ibid.

43. On this episode, see Pederson, *Unity in Diversity*, 96–98; and Mortimer, *Reason and Religion in the English Revolution*, 50–53.

44. See Lake, *Boxmaker's Revenge*, 221–57; Pederson, *Unity in Diversity*, 96–98; and Willen, "Thomas Gataker and the Use of Print in the English Godly Community," 358.

45. See Brachlow, *Communion of Saints*, 56–64, 101–6, 136–41, 185–93, 220–25, 256–62; Paul, "Henry Jacob and Seventeenth-Century Puritanism"; Ha, *English Presbyterianism*, 50–55, 97–98, 115–19; and Morgan, "Henry Jacob, James I, and Religious Reform."

46. As far as I can tell, no record of Samuel Balmford's christening exists. Records suggest that he was born in 1601 (NA, Records of the Exchequer, Licenses to Pass beyond the Seas, fol. 43v); the will of Edmund Cordell of St. Olave's lists "Samuel Balmford son of Mr. James Balmford" (LMA, Original Wills, Diocese of Winchester . . . Edmund Cordell). See Nijenhuis, "Resolutions of Dutch Church Assemblies concerning English Ministers in the Hague," 82–94; and Sprunger, "Archbishop Laud's Campaign against Puritanism at the Hague."

47. Haigh, "Taming of Reformation."
48. Balmford was buried at St. Olave's on July 20, 1625: LMA, Parish Registers, St. Olave, Bermondsey, Southwark, fol. 274.
49. Bredwell systematically attributes "assembly" to the Church of England and "conventicle" to Brownists, but throughout the period the words were used interchangeably. Bredwell, *Rasing of the Foundations of Brownisme* (STC 3599), 125–43.
50. See Narveson, *Bible Readers and Lay Writers in Early Modern England*, 20–28, 200–215; and Bremer, *Lay Empowerment and the Development of Puritanism*, 17.
51. Barne, *Sermon Preached at Pauls Crosse* (STC 1464.8), sig. C2v.
52. Hyperius, *Course of Christianitie* (STC 11755), 213–15.
53. Parr, *Grounds of Diuintie Plainely Discouering the Mysteries of Christian Religion* (STC 19314), 36; Rogers, *Seuen Treatises* (STC 21215), 291; Downame, *Guide to Godlynesse* (STC 7143), 645. See also Narveson's in-depth discussion of these texts: Narveson, *Bible Readers and Lay Writers in Early Modern England*, 23–27.
54. 1 Samuel 7:8–10, *Geneva Bible*, fols. 123v–124r.
55. Consitt, *London Weavers' Company*, 312.
56. *Geneva Bible*, fols. 243r, 321v, 368r, 90r, 106r.
57. See Healy, *Fictions of Disease in Early Modern England*, 55–58; Totaro, *Suffering in Paradise*, 12.
58. Gilman, *Plague Writing in Early Modern England*, 45.
59. On the Psalms in Elizabethan England, see Prescott, "Evil Tongues at the Court of Saul"; and Hamlin, *Psalm Culture and Early Modern English Literature*.
60. Deuteronomy 32:15, *Geneva Bible*, fol. 95v.
61. Deuteronomy 32:23, *Geneva Bible*, fol. 95r.
62. There is some debate about how to read Deuteronomy 32. For an overview of dominant interpretations, see Weitzman, "Lessons from the Dying."
63. Muggins may have intuited the strong connection between Deuteronomy 32 and Jeremiah. Indeed, William L. Holladay has provides a meticulous argument for the influence of Deuteronomy 32 on the book of Jeremiah. See "Elusive Deuteronomists, Jeremiah and Proto-Deuteronomy."
64. Frontain, "'Man Which Have Affliction Seene,'" 135.
65. *Geneva Bible*, fol. 312v.
66. Trapp, *Commentary or Exposition upon the XII Minor Prophets* (Wing T2043), 82.
67. Christian, *Spenserian Allegory and Elizabethan Biblical Exegesis*, 37.
68. For the epithet "the weeping prophet," see (among others) Cannon, *Lachrimae* (STC 4577), 9; Reading, *Faire Warning Declaring the Comfortable Vse of Sicknesse and Health* (STC 20789), 34; and Watson, *Upright Mans Character and Crown* (Wing W1146), 29. For the less common title of "the mourning prophet," see Baker, *Wicked Mans Plot Defeated* (Wing B524), 145; and Taylor, *XXV Sermons* (Wing T408), 180.
69. Balmford, *Short Dialogve concerning the Plagves Infection* (STC 1338), 61; Totaro, *Suffering in Paradise*, 12.
70. Hooke, *Sermon Preached in Paules Church* (STC 13703), sigs. C2r–v.
71. *Geneva Bible*, fols. 308r, 309r, 210r, 313v, 315r.
72. Dod and Cleaver, *Two Sermons on the Third of the Lamentations of Jeremie* (STC 6951).
73. Ibid., 10.
74. On masculinity and weeping, see Vaught, *Masculinity and Emotion in Early Modern English Literature*, 1–24; and Capp, "'Jesus Wept' but Did the Englishman?'"
75. On a scriptural basis for an alternative masculinity developing in the period, see Capp, "'Jesus Wept' but Did the Englishman?'" 100–101.
76. Dod and Cleaver, *Two Sermons on the Third of the Lamentations of Jeremie* (STC 6951), 11–13.
77. Ibid., 38.
78. Ibid., 37–38.
79. The earliest instance of "jeremiad" in the *OED* is from 1780. While the term may have been in use sometime before that, it does not appear to have been current in the early seventeenth century (its close

cousin, the "hosead," was named in 1983 by Michael McGiffert). On jeremiads at Paul's Cross (and more generally) see Morrissey, "Paul's Cross Jeremiad and Other Exhortations." One should also see Walsham, *Providence in Early Modern England*, 281–325; Collinson, *This England*, 167–92; and McGiffert, "God's Controversy with Jacobean England." Scholarship on the jeremiad in America (though sometimes overstating a difference with English examples) should also be consulted: see Miller, *New England Mind*, 27–40; and Bercovitch, *American Jeremiad*. The Americanist exploration of the jeremiad is too extensive to cover in a footnote, but in addition to the two classics of Miller and Bercovitch, there have been several important studies of the jeremiad and race. See Howard-Pitney, *Afro-American Jeremiad*; Moses, *Black Messiahs and Uncle Toms*, 30–48; Harrell, *Origins of the African American Jeremiad*; and Bell, *Bearing Witness to African American Literature*, 26–40.

80. See this trio of essays by McGiffert: "Covenant, Crown, and Commons in Elizabethan Puritanism"; "Grace and Works"; and "God's Controversy." On the political import of jeremiads, see Killeen, *Political Bible in Early Modern England*, 34, 61–63.

81. Collinson, *This England*, 176. See also Neelakanta, *Retelling the Siege*.

82. Thus, Nicholas Lesse's *A Looking Glass for England* (STC 84.5) meditated on Deuteronomy, Isaiah, and Matthew; Thomas Lodge and Robert Greene's play depicting the biblical story of Jonah was titled *A Looking Glasse for London and England* (STC 16679); and several decades later Edward Calumy's fasting sermon before the House of Commons, a meditation on Jeremiah 18, was titled *Englands Looking-Glasse* (Wing C236).

83. Jeremiah 9:1, Lamentations 1:16. *Geneva Bible*, fols. 310r, 331v.

84. Threats of plague occur in Jeremiah 24:10, 29:18, 25: 29–31. Jeremiah frequently addresses social injustices. See, for example, 5:20, 21:11, 22:13; Jeremiah demands the freeing of servants in chapter 34. Jeremiah is imprisoned in chapters 20, 32, and 37–38. For an overview of the ethics in Jeremiah and Lamentations from a theological perspective, see Houston, *Contending for Justice*, 80–84; and on Jeremiah's notion of social justice alongside other Old Testament prophets, see Malchow, *Social Justice in the Hebrew Bible*, 31–49.

85. Lamentations 5:1. *Geneva Bible*, fol. 332r.

86. On the development of English prophetic poetry, see King, *English Reformation Literature*, 11–12, 242; Norbrook, *Poetry and Politics in the English Renaissance*, 28–52; and Doelman, *James I and the Religious Culture of England*, 39–56.

87. Crowley, *Voyce of the Laste Trumpet* (STC 6094), sigs. A7v, C4r, C6v, D1r. See also Jones, "'O London, London.'"

88. This tradition is best outlined by Norbrook, *Poetry and Politics in the English Renaissance*.

89. *Geneva Bible*, 331r.

90. See, for example, Udall, *Commentarie vpon the Lamentations of Jeremy* (STC 24494), 2–3; Hull, *Exposition vpon a Part of the Lamentations of Jeremie* (STC 1312:06), 20–21; and Tossanus, *Lamentations and Holy Mournings of the Prophet Jeremiah* (STC 2779.5), 3–4.

91. *Lachrymae Londinenses* (STC 16753), 6–7.

92. On the plague, isolation, and urban population growth, see Munro, *Figure of the Crowd in Early Modern London*, 184–91.

93. *Geneva Bible*, fols. 310r–v.

94. Tossanus, *Lamentations and Holy Mournings of the Prophet Jeremiah* (STC 2779.5), sig. B4v. See also the deeply misogynistic work of Bentley, *Sixt Lampe of Virginitie* (STC 1894), 106–7.

95. Trapp, *Commentary or Exposition upon These Following Books of Holy Scripture* (Wing T2044), 255.

96. Claassens, "Calling the Keeners," 66. See also O'Connor, *Jeremiah*, 66–68. On the idea of the weeping women as engaged in excessive mourning, see Phillippy, *Women, Death and Literature*, 121.

97. Withington, *Society in Early Modern England*, 138, 134–68.

98. This mode of prophesying is in marked contrast to a more personal, introspective prophesying that existed alongside it. See Smith, *Perfection Proclaimed*, 23–72.

99. Luke 16, *Geneva Bible*, fol. 32v.
100. Matthew 25:14–30, *Geneva Bible*, fol. 14v.
101. Fumerton, *Unsettled*, 12. See also Shepard, *Accounting for Oneself*, 118–27; Rappaport, *Worlds within Worlds*, 150–53, 157–65; and Merritt, *Social World of Early Modern Westminster*, 257–307.
102. Muggins's "deuouring drones" may owe something to Thomas Tusser's "A Sonet against a Slaunderous Tongue," which questions the need for any "sucking drones, in hiues where bees abide." See Tusser, *Fiue Hundred Pointes of Good Husbandrie* (STC 24380), fol. 61b. On the "commonwealth of bees" and insect fables more generally, see Patterson, *Fables of Power*, 78–79; Egan, *Green Shakespeare*, 70–72; and Holstun, "The Spider, the Fly, and the Commonwealth."
103. Stow, *Survey of London* (STC 23345.5), 448–49. See also Shugg, "Prostitution in Shakespeare's London."
104. Ungerer, "Prostitution in Late Elizabethan London," 161.
105. Adams, *Deuills Banket Described in Foure Sermons* (STC 110.5), 4.
106. *Returne of the Knight of the Poste from Hell* (STC 20905), sig. F2v; A. R., *True and Wonderfull a Discourse Relating to a Strange and Monstrous Serpent* (STC 20569), sig. C2r; Braithwaite, *Strappado for the Diuell* (STC 3588), 165; Dekker, *1603. The Wonderfull Yeare* (STC 6535), sig. D1r.
107. Given that the brothels here are disguised as alehouses, "lye" may also be a pun about deception.
108. On the visual and the auditory in prophetic verse, see Hyde, "Vision, Poetry, and Authority in Spenser."
109. Jeremiah 13:15, *Geneva Bible*, fol. 312r.
110. Jan Dumolyn and Jelle Haemers argue that the proverb primarily meant that the voice of the people needed to be heeded whether wise or not. I note, however, that Thomas Digges wrote in 1590 that "*vox populi* be manie times for truth termed *vox Dei*: especiallie when it is grounded vpon long trial and experience." This does not, of course, negate Dumolyn and Haemers, but there is at least in England a rhetorical attempt to equate *populi* and *Dei*. See

Dumolyn and Haemers, "'Bad Chicken Was Brooding,'" 54; and Digges, *A Breife and True Report of the Proceedings of the Earle of Leycester for the Reliefe of the Towne of Sluce* (STC 7284), 5.
111. See the discussion of Troynovant in Manley, "Fictions of Settlement," 209.
112. Dekker, *Magnificent Entertainment* (STC 6510), sig. B2r.
113. On the motif of imperial Rome in the Jacobean court, see Howarth, *Images of Rule*, 33–34; Goldberg, *James I and the Politics of Literature*, 46–54; and Kewes, "Julius Caesar in Jacobean England."
114. Spenser, *Shepheardes Calender* (STC 23089), fol. 41v.
115. Ibid., fol. 43v.
116. Pask, *Emergence of the English Author*, 32–33, 103–5. See also Norbrook, *Poetry and Politics in the English Renaissance*, 53–82.
117. LMA, Parish Registers, St. Bride, Fleet Street, fol. 175r.

EPILOGUE

The epigraph for this chapter comes from Muggins, *London's Mourning Garment*, sig. D4r.
1. Muggins, *London's Mourning Garment* (Bodleian Library, Gough, London, 153).
2. Digges, *Englands Defence* (Wing D1471), sig. A2r.
3. Pestana, "Rainborowe [Rainsborough], William."
4. See Moote, *Great Plague*; Wallis, "Plagues, Morality and the Place of Medicine"; Slack, *Impact of the Plague*, 223–24, 244–54; Gilman, *Plague Writing in Early Modern England*, 215–44; and Totaro, *Suffering in Paradise*, 169–83.
5. Defoe, *Journal of the Plague Year*, 20.
6. Phillips, "'At Home in His Repair,'" 229.
7. I am here translating/paraphrasing Grendi; see "Ripensare la Microstoria?," 544.
8. Centers for Disease Control and Prevention, "Pregnancy Mortality Surveillance System"; U.S. Department of Justice, Office

of Justice Programs, "Correctional Populations in the United States"; U.S. Department of Housing and Urban Development, Office of Community Planning and Development, *2018 Annual Homeless Assessment Report (AHAR) to Congress*, 1; Mishel and Schieder, "CEO Pay Remains High"; Semega, Fontenot, and Kollar, "Income and Poverty in the United States: 2016."

APPENDIX

1. Sir John Swinnerton, merchant-taylor (1564–1616). At the time Swinnerton was sheriff and alderman. He would go on to be mayor.
2. *the Vertuous minde, respecteth not so much . . .*: a paraphrase of Seneca.
3. King James VI of Scotland, made King James I of England following Queen Elizabeth I's death in 1603.
4. AGAMEMNONS *gallant trayne*: Agamemnon led the Greek forces against Troy.
5. *the Change*: the Royal Exchange, established in 1571, was London's commercial center, located just east of Muggins's household in the Poultry.
6. SOL, FA: shorthand for the musical scale.
7. VIVE LE ROYE: long live the king.
8. *skarlet rich*: scarlet robes were worn by London's aldermen.
9. *Free-men*: those who had gained the right to retail in the city either by patrimony or the completion of apprenticeship in one of London's livery companies.
10. *Marchant-strangers*: London was host to a number of merchants from the continent, especially those of the Hanseatic League.
11. CESAR: that is, King James, who sometimes styled himself as a Roman emperor.
12. PIGMALION . . . *Prospectious strange*: In Ovid's *Metamorphoses*, Pygmalion is a talented sculptor who carves the likeness of a beautiful woman out of ivory. Pygmalion's wish that the statue might come to life is granted by Aphrodite. Appeles was a celebrated ancient Greek artist described in Pliny the Elder's *Natural History*.
13. *times of Custome past*: a reference to "lying in," the period in which a new mother stays indoors with the infant.
14. Henry and Elizabeth (Bess) were the names of Muggins's children who died in Southwark.
15. *Sampler*: embroidery often featuring images or words.
16. ATROPOS: the eldest of the three Fates of Greek mythology.
17. The widow here worries about being forced into prostitution. The image of water in a sieve recalls the Elizabethan emblem for virginity.
18. BRVTE: the legendary descendent of Aeneas, Brutus, was said to have founded Britain.
19. ICARVS: Son of Daedalus, the craftsman who designed the Labyrinth, which held the Minotaur. To escape imprisonment Daedalus devises wings of feathers held together by wax. Daedalus warns his son not to fly to high nor too low. Icarus, excited by flight goes so high that the wax melts and he crashes to his death. Icarus, then, was an emblem of ambition or hubris, while safe flight (i.e., neither too high nor too low) appears as a symbol of moderation.
20. *King* DAVIDS *chance*: An allusion (and perhaps typographical error for) King David's choice: seven (or three) years of famine, three months of exile and flight from enemies, or three days of pestilence. David commits to God's mercy, and his people suffer three days of plague, which only ceases when David prays that he alone be punished. See 1 Chronicles 21:12–19 and 2 Samuel 24:13–15 as well as several seventeenth-century sermons, such as Larke, *Practice of Thankefulnesse* (STC 15252.5); and Struther, *True Happines* (STC 23371).
21. NABALS: a miserly figure from the Bible who refuses aid to David and his servants. See 1 Samuel 25.
22. *goe without A* LOATE: The sense seems to be "without delay." *Loate* is enigmatic. The word should rhyme with "take," and so might have been "lake," an archaic term for "fight" and for fine linen. Lait (a look or

glance) is another possibility. All of these seem to imply urgency.

23. HOWNDESDITCH: Houndsditch, a street north of London's walls, notorious for its pawnbroker population.

24. *a powling groat*: a fee for the drafting of a bill.

25. *poore Lazers woes ... fed glutton*: Reference to Luke 16 in which Lazarus begs at a rich man's gate. The rich man refuses Lazarus. Lazarus ascends to heaven while the rich man descends to hell.

26. *priuate oath*: oath of office for various city officials.

27. *nursing, fathers*: a phrase from Isaiah 49:23 indicating the responsibility of rulers to care for their subjects.

28. *tallents*: a reference to Matthew 25: 14–30, the parable of the five talents (a unit of money). A master leaves his three servants in charge of 8 talents. Two servants use the talents to profit while one buries the money for safekeeping. The two servants who put the money to use and profit are rewarded while the servant who kept the money from circulation is punished.

29. *The number, numberlesse ... LONDONS eye*: this stanza describes brothels disguised as alehouses.

30. *Your Wiues shall flourish ... Your Children prosper*: an allusion to Psalm 128.

31. *My crowned CESAR and his Peerlesse Queene ... with their princely sonne*: King James, Queen Anne of Denmark, and their son, Henry, Prince of Wales.

32. *(the Phisition of our soules) for Balme to cure our Sores*: proverbial, but also an allusion to Jeremiah 8:22, "Is there no balme at Gilead? Is there no Phisitio[n] there?" which the Geneva Bible glosses as the people's expectation that "priests shulde haue bene the phisitions of their soules."

33. *great is thy goodnesse*: Psalm 31:19.

34. *powred out thy blessings vpon vs*: Isaiah 44:3.

35. *the fatte of the earth, and fed vs with the dewe of heauen*: Genesis 27:28, 27:39.

36. *the sword hath not deuoured vs*: Deuteronomy 32:41.

37. *whereas other Nations sit in darkenesse*: an allusion to Matthew 4:16 or Luke 1:79; *and grope at Noone day*: Deuteronomy 28:29 and Job 5:14; *sunne of righteousnes*: Malachi 4:2.

38. *dropped as the deaw ... showres*: Deuteronomy 32:2.

39. *first fruites of the spirit ... latter raine*: Deuteronomy 26:2 and Joel 2:23.

40. *Wine is bitter as the Wine of Sodom, and our grapes as the grapes of Gomorrah*: Deuteronomy 32:32.

41. *seede of the wicked corrupt children*: a direct quote from Isaiah 1:4; *a rebellious people*: probable allusion to Isaiah 30:9; *waxen fat, we spurne with the heele*: Deuteronomy 32:15; *vnruly Heifar*: Hosea 4:16.

42. *fulnes of bread ... our iniquities*: Ezekiel 16:49 on Sodom.

43. *like a man of warre*: Exodus 15:3; *thou hast whet thy sword, thou hast bent thy bow*: Psalms 7:12–13; *like a Gyaunt refreshed with wine*: Psalm 78:66.

44. *voyce of lamentation and mourning is heard in our Cities*: Jeremiah and Lamentations; *as when thou slewest the first borne of Egypt*: Exodus 11:5.

45. *Our houses are left desolate*: Matthew 23:38, a passage linked to Jeremiah 22:5; *men abhorre their owne inheritance*: a reworking of Psalm 106:40.

46. *the Streates and high wayes mourne*: Amos 5:16, linked to Lamentations 1:4.

47. *like the swift Dromedorie*: Jeremiah 2:23.

48. *Or like the Asse in the mountaines, which draweth in the ayre at her pleasure*: Jeremiah 2:24; *comforted the weake and feeble knees*: a paraphrase of Isaiah 35:3; *we haue not wept with them that weepe*: Romans 12:15.

49. *pride and presumption of his heart*: Isaiah 9:9.

50. *thine hand is stretched out, to smite*: phrasing can be found in Exodus 3:20, Exodus 9:15, and Jeremiah 21:5–6.

51. *Turne vs ... we shall be turned*: Lamentations 5:21.

52. *Draw thou vs ... oyntments*: Song of Solomon 1:2–3.

53. *Touch our flinty hearts ... as the stonie Rocke which Moses smote*: Numbers 20:11 and Ezekiel 11:19 and 36:26.

54. *the calues of our lips*: Hosea 14:2; *a sacrifice of prayse and thankesgiuing . . . myrth and gladnesse*: Jeremiah 33:11.

55. *cup of indignation . . . dregs of thy furie*: Isaiah 51:17–22 and Jeremiah 25:15.

56. *ashamed and confounded at their presence*: Psalm 83:16–18.

57. *the spirit of wisedome, counsell and vnderstanding*: an important application of Isaiah 11:2–5.

58. *our downe sitting and our vprising . . . our going foorth, and our comming in*: Psalm 139:2 and 121:8, respectively.

59. *the hammer of thine indignation*: Jeremiah 51:20; *breakest in peices like a Potters vessell*: Jeremiah 19:11 and Psalm 2:9; *stubburnesse of our owne hearts*: Jeremiah 9:14 and 11:8.

60. *liue vnto righteousnesse*: Peter 2:24; *from vertue to vertue*: a reworking of Psalm 84:7.

61. *Albones*: Saint Alban on Woodstreet.

62. *Lumbarstr.*: Abbreviation for Lombard Street.

63. *Dennis Back-Church*: St. Dionis Backchurch.

64. *Ethelborow within Bishopsg*: St. Ethelburga's Bishopsgate.

65. *Fan-Church*: Fenchurch.

66. *Auntlins parish*: St. Antholin's Parish at Budge Row near Soper Lane.

67. *Buttols*: St. Botolph.

68. *Magnus parish*: the parish of George Maunsell, who pressed charges against Muggins for debt.

69. *Steuens in Colman-street*: several of the men who assessed the value of the goods in the Muggins's household hailed from this parish.

70. *Mary le Bloooe*: St. Mary le Bow.

71. *Mary Mountawe*: St. Mary Monthaw.

72. *Maudlins*: Magdalen's.

73. *Mighels Bassie shaw*: St. Michael Bassishaw.

74. *Olaues in Southwarke*: the parish of William Muggins during the plague of 1603.

75. *Mildreds Poultry*: the parish of William Muggins's household until 1598.

76. *Templeb.*: Temple Bar.

77. *Pest-house*: established in 1594, London's Pest House was designed as a place for those suffering from leprosy and the plague.

78. As the original owner of the Huntington Library copy learned, the numbers do not in fact add up to 377,717.

BIBLIOGRAPHY

PRIMARY SOURCES, MANUSCRIPTS

British Library (BL)
Harley MS 6948
Lansdowne MS vol. 81.30

Guildhall Library (GL)
"Remembrancia," vols. 2 and 3
Worshipful Company of Weavers, Ordinance and Memorandum Book, 1577–1645, CLC/L/WC/A/030/MS04647

London Metropolitan Archives (LMA)
Original Wills, Diocese of Winchester, Archdeaconry Court of Surrey, 1480–1858, Edmund Cordell, DW/PA/05/1627/22
Parish Registers
   All Saints, Edmonton, DRO/040/A/01/001
   St. Benet, Gracechurch, P69/BEN2/A/001/MS05671
   St. Botolph, Bishopsgate, P69/BOT4/A/001/MS04515/001
   St. Bride, Fleet Street, P69/BRI/A/004/MS06538
   St. Christopher le Stocks, P69/CRI/A/001/MS04421/001
   St. Dunstan's in the West, P69/DUN2/A/001/MS10342
   St. Giles, Cripplegate, P69/GIS/A/001/MS6418
   St. Magnus the Martyr, P69/MAG/A/001/MS11361
   St. Margaret, Lothbury, P69/MGT1/A/001/MS04346/001
   St. Mary le Bow, P69/MRY7/A/001/MS04996
   St. Mary Magdalen, Milk Street, P69/MRY9/A/002/MS6984
   St. Mary Magdalen, Old Fish Street, P69/MRY10/A/001/MS11529
   St. Michael, Cornhill, P69/MIC2/A/002/MS4062
   St. Mildred, Poultry, P69/MIL2/A/001/MS4429/001
   St. Olave, Bermondsey, Southwark, P71/OLA/009
   St. Saviour, Southwark, P92/SAV/3001
   St. Stephen, Coleman St., P69/STE1/A/002/MS04449/001
Royal Hospitals of Bridewell and Bethlem, Minutes of the Court of Governors, 1598–1604, CLC/275/MS33011/004
Worshipful Company of Haberdashers, Register of Apprenticeship Bindings, 1591–1596, CLC/L/HA/C/011/MS15860/002
Worshipful Company of Weavers, Constitutional Records
   Account and Memorandum Book, Known as the "Old Leidger Book," 1441–1741, CLC/L/WC/A/027/MS04646
   Ordinance, Oath and Memorandum Book, Known as the "Ancient Book," CLC/L/WC/A/025/MS04645
   Ratification, by Lord Keeper of the Great Seal, Chief Justice of the King's Bench and Chief Justice of the Common Pleas of the Ordinances

for Regulating the Weavers' Guild, CLC/L/WC/A/014/MS04630

National Archives, Kew, UK (NA)
Prerogative Court of Canterbury and Related Probate Jurisdictions, Will Registers, 1384–1858
Daniel Bucke (February 18, 1604), PROB 11/103/265
Thomas Childe (January 21, 1598), PROB 11/91/37
Cristofer Cravyn (November 15, 1535), PROB 11/25/412
John Crowle (June 22, 1528), PROB 11/22/529
Henry Fitzjohn (October 15, 1524), PROB 11/21/439
Thomas Iken (March 19, 1591), PROB 11/77/220
Thomas Lane (August 26, 1594), PROB 11/84/185
George Maunsell (March 14, 1597), PROB 11/89/220
Humfrey Milward (January 6, 1609), PROB 11/113/9
Hugh Morrall (April 11, 1618), PROB 11/131/372
John Skylborne (October 29, 1504), PROB 11/14/330
John Stephyns (17 October 1543), PROB 111/29/454
Edward Vaughan (10 June 1561), PROB 11/44/234
Records of the Chancery as Central Secretariat, Extents for Debts, Series II, 38 Elizabeth, Wm. Mouggings, C 239/62/3
Records of the Exchequer, and Its Related Bodies, with Those of the Office of First Fruits and Tenths, and the Court of Augmentations. Records of the King's Remembrancer
Depositions Taken by Commission, E 134/35&36 Eliz/Mich22
Licenses to Pass beyond the Seas, 1631 Dec.–1632 Dec., E 157/16
Particulars of Account and other records relating to Lay and Clerical Taxation,
Three Subsidies: December 12, 1598 E 179/146/369, rot 7; October 1, 1598 E179/146/371, rot 1 and 2; October 1, 1599 E179/146/394, rot 15; October 1, 1600 E179/146/407, rot 1
State Papers Domestic
Edward VI to Charles I, Secretaries of State, Letters and Papers
Edward VI–James I, Addenda, 1591–1593, SP 15/32
Elizabeth I, 1593 Jan.-Apr., SP 12/244
Elizabeth I, 1603 Jan.–Mar. and undated, SP 12/287
James I, 1607 Jan.–Mar., SP 14/26
Charles II to George III, Secretaries of State, Letters and Papers
Supplementary, Exchequer, SP 46/38

Society of Antiquaries of London
St. Olave, Southwark, Churchwardens, SAL/MS/236

Society of Genealogists
"Boyd's Inhabitants of London," compiled by Percival Boyd

Worshipful Company of Drapers
Apprentice Book
Freedom Admissions Book, 1567–1655
Quarterage Book, 1617–27

Worshipful Company of Goldsmiths
Apprentice Book 1

PRIMARY SOURCES: PRINT, INCLUDING CALENDARS AND PRINTED TRANSCRIPTIONS

Note: STC and Wing numbers refer to texts accessed through Early English Books Online.

Abstracts of Inquisitions Post-Mortem Relating to the City of London Returned into the Court of Chancery, Part III, 19–45 Elizabeth, 1577–1603. London: London and Middlesex Archaeological Society, 1908.
Acts of the Privy Council of England, 1597–1598. Vol. 28. London, 1929.
Acts of the Privy Council of England, 1617–1619. Vol. 36. London, 1929.

Adams, Thomas. *The Deuills Banket Described in Foure Sermons*. London: Thomas Snodham for Ralph Mab, 1614. STC 110.5.

Aelian, Claudius. *A Registre of Hystories Conteining Martiall Exploites of Worthy Warriours, Politique Practises of Ciuil Magistrates, Wise Sentences of Famous Philosophers, and Other Matters Manifolde and Memorable*. Trans. Abraham Fleming. London: Thomas Woodcocke, 1577. STC 164.

Allegations for Marriage Licenses Issued by the Bishop of London, 1520–1610. Vol. 1. Ed. Joseph Lemuel Chester. London, 1887.

A. R. *True and Wonderfull a Discourse Relating to a Strange and Monstrous Serpent*. London: John Trundle, 1614. STC 20569.

A. T. *A Rich Store-House or Treasury for the Diseased*. London: Ralph Blower, 1596. STC 23606.

Augustine, Saint. *Certain Select Prayers*. London: John Day, 1574. STC 924.

Averell, William. *A Dyall for Dainty Darlings*. London: Thomas Kackette, 1584. STC 978.

Baker, Thomas. *The Wicked Mans Plot Defeated, or, The Wicked Man Laughed out of Countenance*. London, 1656. Wing B524.

Balmford, James. *Carpenters Chippes: or Simple Tokens of Vnfeined Good Will, to the Christian Friends of James Balmford, the Unworthie Seruant of Jesus Christ, a Poore Carpenters Sonne*. London: Richard Boyle, 1607. STC 1334.

———. *A Modest Reply to Certaine Answeres, Which Mr. Gataker B. D. in His Treatise of the Nature, & Use of Lotts, Giveth to Arguments in a Dialogue concerning the Vnlawfulness of Games Consisting in Chance*. London: Richard Boyle, 1623. STC 1336.

———. *A Position Maintained by J. B. before the Late Earle of Huntingdon: viz. Priests Are Executed Not for Religion but for Treason*. London, 1600. STC 13345.

———. *A Short and Plaine Dialogue concerning the Vnlawfulnes of Playing at Cards or Tables, or Any Other Game Consisting in Chance*. London: Richard Boyle, 1593. STC 1335.

———. *A Short Catechisme, Svmmarily Comprizing the Principall Points of Christian Faith*. London: Felix Kyngston for Richard Boyle, 1607. STC 1337.

———. *A Short Dialogve concerning the Plagves Infection*. London: Richard Boyle, 1603. STC 1338.

———. *To the Maior, Aldermen, and Inhabitants of N*. London: Richard Boyle, 1600. STC 13357.

Barley, William. *The Deligtful History of Celestina the Faire*. Abel Jeffes for William Barley, 1596. STC 4910.

Barne, Thomas. *A Sermon Preached at Pauls Crosse the Thirteenth of June, the Second Sunday in Trinitie Tearme 1591*. Oxford, UK: Joseph Barnes, 1591. STC 1464.8.

Barnes, Ambrose. *Memoirs of the Life of Mr. Ambrose Barnes, Late Merchant and Sometime Alderman of Newcastle upon Tyne*. Durham: Andrews & Co., 1867.

Bayly, Lewis. *The Practise of Pietie Directing a Christian How to Walke That He May Please God*. London: John Hodgets, 1613. STC 1602.

Bentley, Thomas. *The Sixt Lampe of Virginitie Conteining a Mirrour for Maidens and Matrons*. London: Thomas Dawson for William Seres, 1582. STC 1894.

Blaxton, John. *The English Vsurer, or Vsury Condemned*. London: John Norton, 1634. STC 3129.

Boethius. *The Boke of Comfort Called in Laten Boetius de Consolatione Philosophie*. London: Robert Langdon, 1535. STC 3200.

Bownd, Nicholas. *Medicines for the Plague*. London: Adam Islip for Cuthbert Burbie, 1604. STC 3439.

Boyd, Percival. *Roll of the Drapers' Company*. Ann Arbor: University of Michigan, 1934.

Braithwaite, Richard. *A Strappado for the Diuell Epigrams and Satyres Alluding to the Time, with Diuers Measures of No Lessse Delight*. London: Richard Redmer, 1615. STC 3588.

Bredwell, Stephen. *The Rasing of the Foundations of Brownisme*. London: John Windet, 1588. STC 3599.

Broughton, Hugh. *Our Lord His Line of Fathers from Adam*. London: Gabriel Simson and William White, 1595. STC 3874.5.

———. *A Treatise of Melchisedek Proving Him to Be Sem*. London Gabriel Simson and William White, 1591. STC 3890.5.

Bullein, William. *A Dialogue Bothe Pleasaunte and Pietiful Wherein Is a Goodly Regimente against the Fever Pestilence with a Consolacion and Comfort against Death*. London: John Kingston, 1564. STC 4036.5.

Byron, Lord George Gordon. *The Works of Lord Byron*. Vol. 1. Ed. Ernest Hartley Coleridge. London: Scribner, 1903.

Calendar of the Cecil Papers in Hatfield House. Vol. 18, *1606*. Ed. M. S. Giuseppi. London, 1940.

Calendar of Manuscripts of the Most Honourable the Marquess of Salisbury, Hatfield House, Hertfordshire. Vol. 5. London: Eyre and Spottiswoode, 1894.

Calendar of the Manuscripts of the Most Honourable the Marquess of Salisbury, Preserved at Hatfield House, Hertfordshire. Vol. 9. London: Eyre and Spottiswoode, 1902.

Calendar of the Manuscripts of the Most Honourable the Marquess of Salisbury, Preserved at Hatfield House, Hertfordshire. Ed. R. A. Roberts. Vol. 11, *1601*. London: His Majesty's Stationery Office, 1906.

Calendar of the Manuscripts of the Most Honourable the Marquess of Salisbury. Vol. 18, *1606*. London: Eyre and Spottiswoode, 1940.

Calendar of the Plea and Memoranda Rolls of the City of London. Vol. 2, *1364–1381*. Ed. A. H. Thomas. London: His Majesty's Stationery Office, 1929.

Calumy, Edward. *Englands Looking-Glasse*. London: J. Raworth for Christopher Meredith, 1642. Wing C236.

Cannon, Nathanael. *Lachrimae: or Lamentations over the Dead*. London: Felix Knyghton for William Welby, 1616. STC 4577.

Carew, Thomas. *Certaine Godly and Necessarie Sermons*. London: George Potter, 1603. STC 4616.

Carlson, Leland H., ed. *Elizabethan Non-conformist Texts*. Vol. 6, *The Writings of John Greenwood and Henry Barrowe, 1591–1593*. London: Routledge, 1970.

The Case of the Commonality of the Corporation of Weavers in London. London, 1648. ESTC R233790.

Cawdry, Robert. *A Treasurie or Store-House of Similes Both Pleasaunt, Delightfull, and Profitable, for All Estates of Men in Generall*. London: Thomas Creede, 1600. STC 4887.

Chapman, George. *The Plays and Poems of George Chapman: The Comedies*. Ed. Thomas Marc Parrott. London: Routledge, 1914.

Chettle, Henry. *A True Bill of the Whole Number That Hath Died in the Cittie of London, the City of Westminster, the City of Norwich, and Divers Other Places, since the Time This Last Sicknes of the Plague Began in Either of Them*. London: J. R. for John Trundle, 1603. STC 16743.2.

Church of England. *Booke of Common Prayer*. London: Robert Barker, 1603. STC 16326.

———. *Certaine Praiers Collected out of a Fourme of Godly Meditations, Set Foorther by Her Majesties Authoritie in the Great Mortalitie*. London: Christopher Barker, 1593. STC 16524.

———. *Certaine Prayers Collected out of a Forme of Godly Meditation*. London: August 1603. STC 16523.

Clapham, Henoch. *A Description of New Jerushalem*. London: Valentine Simmes, 1601. STC 5336.5.
———. *An Epistle Discoursing vpon the Present Pestilence Teaching What It Is, and How the People of God Should Carrie Themselues towards God and Their Neighbour Therein*. London: T[homas] C[reede] for the Widow Newbery, 1603. STC 5339.
The Confession of a Paenitent Sinner. London: Henry Gosson, 1635. STC 5627.
Cotton, Roger. *A Direction to the Waters of Life*. London: Gabriel Simson and William White for William Barley, 1592. STC 5867.3.
Coverdale, Miles. *Certain Most Godly, Fruitful, and Comfortable Letters of Such True Saintes and Holy Martyrs*. London: John Day, 1564. STC 5886.
Crabbe, George. *The Poetical Works of George Crabbe*. Ed. R. M. Carlyle. Oxford, UK: Oxford University Press, 1914.
Crowley, Robert. *The Voyce of the Laste Trumpet*. London: Robert Crowley, 1549. STC 6094.
Defoe, Daniel. *A Journal of the Plague Year*. London: E. Nutt, J. Roberts, A. Dodd, and J. Graves, 1722.
———. *The Life and Action of Moll Flanders*. London: Thomas Read, 1723. ESTC T070316.
Dekker, Thomas. *The Magnificent Entertainment*. London: Thomas Creede, Humphrey Lownes, Edward Allde, and Others for Thomas Man, the Younger, 1604. STC 6510.
———. *A Rod for Run-Awayes, Gods Tokens, of His Feareful Judgments, Sundry Wayes Pronounced vpon This City, and on Severall Persons, Both Flying from It, and Staying in It*. London: John Trundle, 1625. STC 6520.
———. *1603. The Wonderfull Yeare. Wherein Is Shewed the Picture of London Lying Sicke of the Plague*. London: Thomas Creede, 1603. STC 6535.
———. *Troia Nova Triumphans*. London: Nocholas Okes for John Wright, 1612. STC 6530.

Deloney, Thomas. *The Garland of Good Will*. London: Printed for Edward Brewster and Robert Bird, 1628. STC 6553.5.
———. *The Novels of Thomas Deloney*. Bloomington: Indiana University Press, 1961.
———. *A Proper New Ballad, Breefley Declaring the Death and Execution of 14. Most Wicked Traitors*. London: Edward Allde, 1586. STC 6563.5.
———. *A Proper New Sonet Declaring the Lamentation [of Beckles in] Suffolke*. London: Robert Robinson for Richard Colma[n], 1586. STC 6564.
———. *The Queenes Visiting of the Campe at Tilsburie*. London: John Wolfe for Edward White, 1588. STC 6565.
———. *Strange Histories*. London: Printed for William Barley, 1602. STC 6566.
———. *Strange Histories*. London: Ralph Blower for William Barley, 1612. STC 6568.
———. *Thomas of Reading*. London: Ralph Blower for Thomas Pavier, 1612. STC 6569.
———. *The Works of Thomas Deloney*. Ed. Francis Oscar Mann. Oxford, UK: Clarendon Press, 1912.
de Mornay, Philippe. *The True Knowledge of a Mans Owne Selfe*. Trans. Anthony Munday. London: J. R. for William Leake, 1602. STC 18163.
The Diary of Philip Henslowe from 1591–1609. Ed. J. Payne Collier. London: Shakespeare Society, 1845.
Digges, Thomas. *A Breife and True Report of the Proceedings of the Earle of Leycester for the Reliefe of the Towne of Sluce*. London: Thomas Orwin, 1590. STC 7284.
———. *Englands Defence. A Treatise concerning INVASION*. London: Francis Haley, 1680. Wing D1471.
A Discourse on Mans Life. London: Henry Gosson, 1629. STC 6907.
Dod, John, and Robert Cleaver. *Two Sermons on the Third of the Lamentations of Jeremie*. London: Felix Knyghtson for Jonas Man, 1608. STC 6951.

Donne, John. *The Sermons of John Donne.* Vol. 5. Ed. George R. Potter and Evelyn M. Simpson. Berkeley: University of California Press, 1959.

Doolittle, Thomas. *The Mourner Directory, Guiding Him to the Middle Way betwixt the Two Extreams, Defect, Excess of Sorrow for His Dead to Which Is Added, the Mourners Soliloquy.* London: J.A. for Thomas Cockerill, 1693. Wing D1888.

Downame, John. *A Guide to Godlynesse, or a Treatise of a Christian Life.* London: Felix Kingston for Ed[mond] Weaver and W[illiam] Bladen, 1622. STC 7143.

———. *Spiritual Physicke to Cure the Diseases of the Soule.* London: Gabriel Simson for William Jones, 1600. STC 7147.

Drayton, Michael. *Poems.* London: Nicholas Ling, 1605. STC 7216.

Fenwicke, Sir John. *Christ Ruling in Midst of His Enemies, or, Some First Fruits of the Churches Deliverance Budding Forth out of the Crosse and Sufferings and Some Remarkable Deliverances of a Twentie Yeares Sufferer.* London: Benjamin Allen, 1643. Wing F719.

Fetherston, Christopher. *A Dialogve agaynst Light, Lewde, and Lasciuouus Dauncing.* London: Thomas Dawson, 1582. STC 10835.

Field, Nathan. *The Remonstrance of Nathan Field, One of Shakespeare's Company of Actors, Addressed to a Preacher in Southwark, Who Had Been Arraigning against the Players at the Globe Theatre in the Year 1616, Now First Edited from the Original Manuscript.* Ed. J. W. Halliwell-Phillipps. London, 1865.

Fifth Report of the Royal Commission on Historical Manuscripts. London: Eyre and Spottiswoode, 1876.

Fisher, Payne. *The Catalogue of Most of the Memorable Tombes, Grave-Stones, Plates, Escutcheons, or Atchievement in the Demolisht or Yet Extant Churches of London.* London, 1668. Wing F1014.

Foster, Joseph, ed. *London Marriage Licenses, 1521–1869.* London: Bernard Quaritch, 1887.

Foxe, John. *Actes and Monuments.* London: John Daye, 1583. STC 11225.

———. *A Sermon of Christ Crucified.* London: John Daye, 1570. STC 11242.3.

Gascoigne, George. *The Poesies of George Gascoigne, Esquire.* London: Henry Bynneman for Richard Smith, 1575. STC 11636.

Gataker, Thomas. *A Just Defence of Certaine Passages in a Former Treatise concerning the Nature and Vse of Lots against Such Exceptions and Oppositions as Have Beene Made Thereunto by Mr. J. B.* London: John Haviland for William Bladen, 1623. STC 11666a.

———. *On the Nature and Vse of Lots a Treatise Historicall and Theologicall.* London: Edward Griffin for William Bladen, 1619. STC 11670.

The Geneva Bible: A Facsimile of the 1560 Edition. Madison: University of Wisconsin Press, 1969.

Gilbart, Thomas. *A Declaration of the Death of John Lewes.* London: Richard Jones, 1583. ESTC S923693. Society of Antiquaries of London.

Godskall, James. *The Arke of Noah for the Londoners That Remaine in the Cittie to Enter in.* London: Thomas Creede, 1604. STC 11935.

Greene, Robert. *A Quip for an Upstart Courtier.* London: John Wolfe, 1592. STC 12301s.3.

Greenham, Richard. *Two Learned and Godly Sermons.* London Gabriel Simson and William White for William Jones, 1595. STC 12325.

Hall, Joseph. *An Holy Panegyrick.* London: John Pindley for Samuel Macham, 1613. STC 12673.

Hanson, John. *Time Is a Turne-Coate. Or Englands Three-Fold Metamorphosis Wherin Is Acted the Pensiue Mans Epilogomena, to Londons Late Lamentable Heroicall Comi-Tragedie.* London: J. H., 1604. STC 12750.

Hawkins, John. *A Salade for the Simple.* London: Abel Jeffes for William Barley, 1595. STC 12960.

Herbert, George. *The Complete English Poems.* London: Penguin Books, 1991.

Herring, Francis. *Modest Defence of the Caveat Given to the Wearers of Impoisoned Amulets, as Preservatives from the Plague.* London: Arnold Hatfield for William Jones, 1604. STC 13248.

Hessels, Jan Hendrick, ed. *Register of the Attestations or Certificates of Membership, Confessions of Guilt, Certificates of Marriage, Betrothals, Publications of Banns &c Preserved in the Dutch Reformed Church, Austin Friars, London, 1568–1872.* London: David Nutt, 1892.

Hewitt, John, ed. *Rhyming Weavers and Other Country Poets of Antrim and Down.* 1974. Reprint, Belfast, UK: Blackstaff, 2004.

Heywood, Thomas. *The Rape of Lucrece.* London: Edward Allde for Nathaniel Butter, 1608. STC 13360.

Hibbert, Henry. *Waters of Marah Drawn Forth in Two Funerall Sermons.* London: W. Hunt for Francis Coles, 1654. Wing H1794.

Holinshed, Raphael. *Third Volume of the Chronicle, Beginning at Duke William the Norman.* London: Henry Denham, 1586. STC 13569.

Holland, Henry. *Spirituall Preseruatiues against the Pestilence.* London: Thomas Creede for John Browne, 1603. STC 13589.

Homer. *Seaven Bookes of the Iliades of Homere, Prince of Poets.* Trans. George Chapman. London: John Windet, 1598. STC 13632.

———. *Ten Books of Homer's Iliades.* Trans. Arthur Hall. London: Ralph Newberie, 1581. STC 13630.

Hooke, Christopher. *A Sermon Preached in Paules Church in London and Published for the Instruction and Consolation of All That Are Heauie Harted, for the Wofull Time of God His Generall Visitation.* London: Edward Allde, 1603. STC 13703.

Hooker, Richard. *The Works of Mr. Richard Hooker (That Learned and Judicious Divine), in Eight Books of Ecclesiastical Polity.* London: Andrew Crooke, 1666. Wing H2631291.

Hull, John. *An Exposition vpon a Part of the Lamentations of Jeremie.* London: Bernard Alsop, 1618. STC 1312:06.

Hutton, Luke. *The Black Dogge of Newgate.* London: Gabriel Simson and William White, 1596. STC 14029.

Hyperius, Andreas. *The Course of Christianitie: or, As Touching the Dayly Reading and Meditation of the Holy Scriptures Very Requisite and Necessary for All Christians of What Estate or Condition Soeuer.* Trans. John Ludham. London: Henry Bynneman, 1579. STC 11755.

Jacob, Henry. *A Defence of the Churches and Ministery of Englande Written in Two Treatises, against the Reasons and Obiections of Maister Francis Iohnson, and Others of the Separation Commonly Called Brownists.* Middleburgh, UK: Richard Schilders, 1599. STC 14335.

Jay, George. *A Sermon Preacht at the Funerall of the Lady Mary Villiers, Eldest Daughter of the Right Honble Christopher Earle of Anglesey.* London: Thomas Harper, 1626. STC 14479.

Jewel, John. *The Second Tome of Homilees of Such Mattters as Were Promised and Intituled in the Former Part of Homilees.* London: Richard Jugge and John Cawood, 1571. STC 13669.

Johnson, Francis. *An Answer to Maister H. Jacob His Defence of the Churches and Minstery of England.* Place unknown, 1600. STC 14658.

Johnson, Richard. *The Pleasant Conceites of Old Hobson, the Merry Londoner.* London: George Eld for John Wright, 1607. STC 14688.

Jonson, Ben. *The Workes of Benjamin Jonson.* London: William Stansby, 1616. STC 14752.

Jonson, Ben, and Ronald F. Patterson, ed. *Notes of Ben Jonson's Conversations*

with William Drummond of Hawthornden. London: Blackie and Son, 1923.
Kempe, William. *Kemps Nine Daies Wonder, Performed in a Daunce from London to Norwich.* London: E. A. for Nicholas Ling, 1600. STC 14923.
Kirk, R. E. G., and Ernest F. Kirk. *The Returns of Aliens in the City and Suburbs of London from the Reign of Henry VIII to James I.* Aberdeen: Huguenot Society of London, 1902.
———. *The Returns of Aliens in the City and Suburbs of London, 1598–1625.* Aberdeen: Huguenot Society of London, 1907.
Lachrymae Londinenses: or, Londons Lamentations and Teares for Gods Heauie Visitation of the Plague of Pestilence. London: H. Holland and G. Gibbs, 1626. STC 16753.
Larke, Nicholas. *The Practice of Thankefulnesse; or Davids Choyse Direction How to Prayse God in an Exposition and Application vpon the Whole Sixtie Sixe Psalme.* London: G. P. for Roger Jackson, 1622. STC 15252.5.
Lesse, Nicholas. *A Looking Glasse for England.* London: John Charlewood for Henry Car and Thomas Butter, 1590. STC 84.5.
Lodge, Thomas, and Robert Greene. *A Looking Glasse for London and England.* London: Thomas Creede, 1594. STC 16679.
The London Goldsmiths, 1200–1800. Ed. Sir Ambrose Heal. Cambridge, UK: Cambridge University Press, 1935.
Lupton, Donald. *London and the Countrey Carbonadoed and Quartred into Seuerall Characters.* London: Nicholas Okes, 1632. STC 16944.
Marriage Licenses Issued by the Bishop of London, 1520–1610. Vol. 1. Ed. Joseph Lemuel Chester. London, 1887.
Middleton, Thomas. *Collected Works.* Ed. Gary Taylor and John Lavagnino. Oxford, UK: Oxford University Press, 2010.
Moffett, Thomas. *The Silkewormes and Their Flies: Liuely Described in Verse.* London: Valentine Simmes for Nicholas Ling, 1599. STC 17994.
More, Richard. *The Carpenters Rule.* London: Felix Kyngston, 1602. STC 18075.
Muggins, William. *Londons Mourning Garment, or Funerall Teares: Worne and Shed for the Death of Her Wealthy Cittizens, and Other Her Inhabitants.* London: Ralph Blower, 1603. Bodleian Library, Gough, London, 153.
———. *Londons Mourning Garment, or Funerall Teares: Worne and Shed for the Death of Her Wealthy Cittizens, and Other Her Inhabitants.* London: Ralph Blower, 1603. STC 18248.
Munday, Anthony. *Metropolis Coronata, the Triumphes of Ancient Drapery.* London: George Purslowe, 1615. STC 18275.
———. *The Third and Last Part of Palmerin.* London: J. R. for William Leake, 1602. STC 19165.
Nashe, Thomas. *The Anatomie of Absurditie.* London: John Charlewood for Thomas Hacket, 1589. STC 18364.
———. *Haue with You to Saffron-Walden.* London: John Danter, 1596. STC 18369.
Nicholas, Thomas. *A Pleasant Dialogue betweene a Lady Called Listra, and a Pilgrim concerning the Gouerment and Common Weale of Crangalor.* London: John Charlewood, 1579. STC 18335.5.
Ovid. *The .XV. Bookes of P. Ouidius Naso, Entytuled Metamorphosis.* London: Willyam Seres, 1567. STC 18956.
Parr, Elnathan. *The Grounds of Diuintie Plainely Discouering the Mysteries of Christian Religion.* London: Nicholas Okes for Samuel Man, 1614. STC 19314.
Peacham, Henry. *The Period of Mourning Disposed into Sixe Visions.* London: T. S. for John Helme, 1613. STC 19513.5.
Petowe, Henry. *Londoners Their Entertainment in the Countrie. Or the Whipping of Runaways Wherein Is Described London Miserie. The Covnties Crveltie. And Mans

Inhvmanitie. London: H. L. for C. B., 1604. STC 19807.
Phillips, John. *The Play of Patient Grissel*. Ed. Ronald B. McKerrow and W. W. Greg. London: Printed for the Malone Society by Charles Whittingham & Co. at the Chiswick Press, 1909.
Poem on the History of Queen Hester; an Eleygy on the Death of Lord Chief Justice Hales; and Other Occasional Poems. London: William Leech, 1680. Wing P2696.
Puttenham, George. *The Arte of English Poesie*. London: Richard Field, 1589. STC 20519.5.
Ravenscroft, Thomas. *A Briefe Discourse of the True (but Neglected) Vse of Charact'ring the Degrees, by Their Perfection, Imperfection, and Diminution in Measurable Musicke*. London: Edward Allde for Thomas Adams, 1614. STC 20756.
Reading, John. *A Faire Warning Declaring the Comfortable Vse of Sicknesse and Health*. London: Bernard Alsop for John Hodgets, 1621. STC 20789.
Records of the Worshipful Company of Carpenters. Vol. 5, *Wardens' Account Book, 1571–1591*. Ed. John Ainsworth. Oxford, UK: Oxford University Press, 1937.
Records of the Worshipful Company of Carpenters. Vol. 7, *Wardens' Account Book, 1592–1614*. Ed. A. M. Millard. Oxford, UK: Oxford University Press, 1968.
Registers of the University of Oxford. Vol. 2, part 2. Ed. Andrew Clarke. Oxford, UK: Clarendon Press, 1887.
Registers of the University of Oxford. Vol. 2, part 3. Ed. Andrew Clarke. Oxford, UK: Clarendon Press, 1888.
Remains Historical and Literary Connected with the Palatine Counties of Lancaster and Chester. Vol. 31, *Chetham Society. Stanley Papers*, part 2. Manchester, UK: Chetham Society, 1882.
The Returne of the Knight of the Poste from Hell with the Divels Aunswere to the Supplication of Pierce Penilesse, with Some Relation of the Last Treasons.

London: John Windet for Nathaniel Butter, 1606. STC 20905.
Rinaldi, Orazio. *The Royal Exchange*. London: John Charlewood for William Wright, 1590. STC 12307.
Robinson, Richard. *Certain Selected Histories for Christian Recreations*. London: Henry Kirkham, 1577. STC 21118.
Rogers, Richard. *Seuen Treatises Containing Such Direction as Is Gathered out of the Holie Scriptures*. London: Felix Kyngston for Thomas Man and Robert Dexter, 1603. STC 21215.
Rotuli Parliamentorum; ut et Petitiones, et Placita in Parliamento. Vol. 5. Ed. John Strachey. London: Chambre des Lords, 1832.
Rowley, William. *A Match at Mid-Night*. London: Augustine Matthews for William Sheares, 1633. STC 21421.
Sandys, Edwin. *Sermons Made by the Most Reuerende Father in God*. London: Henrie Midleton for Thomas Chard, 1585. STC 21713.
Seneca, Lucius Annaeus. *The Woorke of the Excellent Philosopher Lucius Annaeus Seneca concerning Benefyting That Is Too Say the Dooing, Receyuing, and Requyting of Good Turnes*. Trans. Arthur Golding. London: John Day, 1578. STC 22215.
Shakespeare, William. *The Historie of Henrie the Fourth*. London: P. S. for Andrew Wise, 1598. STC 22280.
———. *The Norton Shakespeare*. Ed. Stephen Greenblatt et al. New York: Norton, 2016.
Sharpe, Reginald Robinson. *Calendar of Letter-Books of the City of London: Letter-Book K, Temp. Henry VI*. London, 1911.
Smith, Sir Thomas. *De Republica Anglorum: The Maner of Gouernement or Policie of the Realme of England*. London: Henrie Midleton for Gregorie Seton, 1583. STC 22857.
Smith, Wentworth. *The Hector of Germanie*. London: Thomas Creede for Josias Harrison, 1615. STC 22871.
Sorocold, Thomas. *The Supplications of Saints: A Book of Prayers Divided*

into *Three Parts*. London: Nicholas Bourne, 1612. STC 22932.

The Spending of the Money of Robert Nowell. Ed. Alexander Grosart. Privately Printed, 1877.

Spenser, Edmund. *The Shepheardes Calender*. London: Hugh Singleton, 1579. STC 23089.

Stow, John. *The Abridgement of the English Chronicles*. London: Company of Stationers, 1618. STC 23332.

———. *Survey of London*. London: Nicholas Bourn, 1633. STC 23345.5.

Struther, William. *True Happines, or King Dauids Choice Begunne in Sermons, and Now Digested into a Treatise*. Edinburgh: R. Young for John Wood. STC 23371.

Stuart, James (James VI and I). *Basilikon Doron*. London: Richard Field for John Norton, 1603. STC 14353.

Stubbes, Philip. *The Anatomie of Abuses*. London: Richard Jones, 1583. STC 23376.

Sutton, Thomas. *Englands First and Second Summons, Two Sermons Preached at Paules Crosse, the One the Third of Januarie 1612; the Other the Fifth of Februarie, 1615*. London: Nicholas Okes for Matthew Law, 1616. STC 23502.

Swynnerton, John. *A Christian Loue-Letter*. London: William Jaggard, 1606. STC 23558.

A Table Declaring What Planet Dooth Raigne Euery Day and Houre Enduring for Euer. London: Gabriel Simson for William Kirkham, 1598. STC 23634.5.

Taylor, Jeremy. *XXV Sermons*. London: E. Cotes for Richard Royston, 1653. Wing T408.

Taylor, John. *The Cold Tearme, or The Frozen Age, or, The Metamorphosis of the River of Thames*. London, 1621. STC 23910.

———. *To the Right Honorable Assembly, the Lords, Knights, Esquires, and Burgesses of the Honorable House of Commons in Parliament*. London: John Hammond, 1642. Wing T518.

———. *The Water-Cormorant His Complaint against a Brood of Land-Cormorants*. London: George Eld, 1622. STC 23813.

Thayre, Thomas. *A Treatise of the Pestilence*. London: E. Short, 1603. STC 23929.

Thom, William. *Rhymes and Recollections of a Hand-Loom Weaver*. London: Smith, Elder, and Co., 1845.

Thomas, Roger. *Anglorum Lachrimae in a Sad Passion Complaining the Death of Our Late Soueraigne*. London: William White for Thomas Pavier, 1603. STC 14671.

Tossanus, Daniel. *The Lamentations and Holy Mournings of the Prophet Jeremiah with a Lamentable Paraphrase and Exhortation*. London: John Windet for Humfrey Bate, 1587. STC 2779.5.

A Transcript of the Registers of the Company of Stationers of London, 1554–1640 A.D. Vol. 2. Ed. Edward Arber. London: Privately Printed, 1875.

A Transcript of the Registers of the Company of Stationers of London, 1554–1640 A.D. Vol. 3. Ed. Edward Arber. London: Privately Printed, 1876.

Trapp, John. *A Commentary or Exposition upon These Following Books of Holy Scripture Proverbs of Solomon, Ecclesiastes, the Song of Songs, Isaiah, Jeremiah, Lamentations, Ezekiel & Daniel*. London: Robert White for Nevil Simmons and Thomas Basset, 1660. Wing T2044.

———. *A Commentary or Exposition upon the XII Minor Prophets*. London: Phlemon Stephens, 1654. Wing T2043.

Tudor, Elizabeth (Elizabeth I). *By the Queen, by the Grace of God Queene of England, Fraunce, and Ireland*. London: Thomas Purfoote, 1588. STC 8171.

Tudor Economic Documents. Vol. 1. Ed. Eileen Power and R. H. Tawney. London: Longman, 1924.

Tudor Wills Proved in Bristol, 1546–1603. Ed. Sheila Lang and Margaret McGregor. Bristol, UK: Bristol Record Society, 1993.

Tusser, Thomas. *Fiue Hundredth Points of Good Husbandry*. London: Richard Tottel, 1580. STC 24380.
Udall, John. *A Commentarie vpon the Lamentations of Jeremy*. London: Joan Orwin for Thomas Man, 1593. STC 24494.
———. *A New Discovery of Old Pontifical Practises for the Maintenance of the Prelates Authority and Hierarchy*. London: Stephen Bowtell, 1643. Wing U14.
Watson, Thomas. *The Upright Mans Character and Crown*. London: Ralph Smith, 1657. Wing W1146.
Webbe, Edward. *The Rare and Most Wonderfull Things Which Edward Webbe an Englishman Borne, Hath Seene in his Troublesome Travailes*. London: Abel Jeffes for William Barley, 1595. STC 25153.
Wild, Robert. *Alas Poore Scholler, Whither Wilt Thou Goe?* London: s. n., 1641. STC 25632.
Wilson, Thomas. *The Rule of Reason, Conteinying the Art of Logique, Set Forth in Englishe*. London: Richard Grafton, 1551. STC 25809.
Worshipful Company of Parish Clerks. *Buried in London and in the Places Neere Adjoyning*. London: John Windet, 1603. STC 16743.9.
———. *A Generall Bill for 8 Weeks Shewing All the Burials and Christninges within the City of London and the Liberties Thereof, and All the Burials in Other Parishes in the Skirts of the City and out of the Freedome and Other Places Neare vnto the Citty: That Is to Say, from the 14 of July 1603 to the 8 of September 1603*. London: John Windet, 1603. STC 16743.1.
———. *A True Bill of the Whole Number That Hath Died*. London: I. Roberts for John Trundle, 1603. STC 1997:26.
W. T. *A Casting VP of Accounts of Certain Errors, Being Answered in Items, to the Summa Totalis*. London: Thomas Creede, 1603. STC 1717:05.

SECONDARY SOURCES

Achinstein, Sharon. "Plagues and Publication: Ballads and the Representation of Disease in the English Renaissance." *Criticism* 34.1 (1992): 27–49.
Ackroyd, Peter. *London: A Biography*. New York: Vintage, 2001.
Addison, Catherine. "Little Boxes: The Effects of the Stanza on Poetic Narrative." *Style* 37.2 (2003): 124–43.
Ames, Joseph, and William Herbert. *Typographical Antiquities: Or an Historical Account of the Origin and Progress of Printing in Great Britain and Ireland*. Vol. 3. London, 1790.
Andrews, John F. "Textual Deviancy in *The Merchant of Venice*." In *The Merchant of Venice: New Critical Essays*, ed. John W. Mahon and Ellen Macleod Mahon, 169–70. New York: Routledge, 2006.
Anselment, Raymond A. "'The Teares of Nature': Seventeenth-Century Parental Bereavement." *Modern Philology* 91.1 (1993): 26–53.
Appleby, Andrew B. "Nutrition and Disease: The Case of London, 1550–1750." *Journal of Interdisciplinary History* 6 (1975): 1–22.
Archer, Ian. *The Pursuit of Stability: Social Relations in Elizabethan London*. Cambridge, UK: Cambridge University Press, 1991.
———. "Swinnerton, John." Rev. Alison Shell. In *Oxford Dictionary of National Biography*, ed. H. C. G. Matthew and Brian Harrison. Oxford, UK: Oxford University Press, 2004. Online ed., ed. David Cannadine, January 2008.
Ashbee, Andrew, with David Lasocki, Peter Holman, and Fiona Kisby. *A Biographical Dictionary of English Court Musicians, 1485–1714*. Vol. 1. New York: Routledge, 2018.
Aston, Margaret. "Segregation in Church." *Studies in Church History* 27 (1990): 237–94.
Aubrey, John. *The Natural History and Antiquities of the County of Surrey*. Vol. 5. London: E. Curll, 1719.

Babington, Anthony. *The English Bastille: A History of Newgate Gaol and Prison Conditions in Britain, 1188–1902.* London: Macconald, 1972.

Back, Rebecca Ann. "(Re)Placing Donne in the History of Sexuality." *English Literary History* 72.1 (2005): 259–89.

Bassett, Margery. "Newgate Prison in the Middle Ages." *Speculum* 18.2 (1943): 233–46.

Bell, Bernard W. *Bearing Witness to African American Literature: Validating and Valorizing Its Authority, Authenticity, and Agency.* Detroit: Wayne State University Press, 2012.

Bellhouse, D. R. "London Plague Statistics in 1665." *Journal of Official Statistics* 14.2 (1998): 207–34.

Ben-Amos, Ilana Krausman. *The Culture of Giving: Informal Support and Gift-Exchange in Early Modern England.* Cambridge, UK: Cambridge University Press, 2008.

———. "Women Apprentices in the Trades and Crafts of Early Modern Bristol." *Continuity and Change* 6.2 (1991): 227–52.

Bercovitch, Sacvan. *The American Jeremiad.* Madison: University of Wisconsin Press, 1978.

Bergeron, David M. *English Civic Pageantry, 1558–1642.* Rev. ed. Lawrence: University of Kansas Press, 2003.

———. *Textual Patronage in English Drama, 1570–1640.* Farnham, UK: Ashgate, 2006.

Berlin, Michael. "'Broken All in Pieces': Artisans and the Regulation of Workmanship in Early Modern London." In *The Artisan and the European Town, 1500–1900*, ed. Geoffrey Crossick, 75–91. Aldershot, UK: Scolar Press, 1997.

Berry, Herbert. "The First Public Playhouses, Especially the Red Lion." *Shakespeare Quarterly* 40.2 (1989): 133–48.

Betteridge, Tom. *Literature and Politics in the English Reformation.* Manchester, UK: Manchester University Press, 2004.

Biester, James. "Shaming the Fool: Jack and Anti-Jack." *English Literary Renaissance* 31.2 (2001): 230–39.

Binski, Paul. *Medieval Death: Ritual and Representation.* Ithaca, N.Y.: Cornell University Press, 1996.

Bishop, Jennifer. "Speech and Sociability: The Regulation of Language in the Livery Companies of Early Modern London." In *Cities and Solidarities: Urban Communities in Pre-modern Europe*, ed. Justin Colson and Arie van Steensel, 208–24. New York: Routledge, 2017.

———. "'Utopia' and Civic Politics in Mid-Sixteenth-Century London." *Historical Journal* 54.4 (2011): 933–53.

Blair, Kirstie, and Mina Gorji, eds. *Class and Canon: Constructing Labouring-Class Poetry and Poetics, 1750–1900.* New York: Palgrave, 2013.

Boulton, Jeremy. *Neighbourhood and Society: A London Suburb in the Seventeenth Century.* Cambridge, UK: Cambridge University Press, 1987.

Brachlow, Stephen. *The Communion of Saints: Radical Puritans and Separatist Ecclesiology, 1570–1625.* Oxford, UK: Oxford University Press, 1989.

Braddick, M. J. *Parliamentary Taxation in Seventeenth-Century England: Local Administration and Response.* Suffolk, UK: Boydell, 1994.

Brady, Andrea. *English Funerary Elegy in the Seventeenth Century: Laws in Mourning.* New York: Palgrave, 2006.

Branch, Laura. *Faith and Fraternity: London Livery Companies and the Reformation, 1510–1603.* Boston: Brill, 2017.

Branch, Lori. "The Rejection of Liturgy, the Rise of Free Prayer, and Modern Religious Subjectivity." *Restoration: Studies in English Literary Culture, 1660–1700* 29.1 (2005): 1–28.

Bremer, Francis. *Lay Empowerment and the Development of Puritanism.* New York: Palgrave, 2015.

Briggs, Chris. *Credit and Village Society in Fourteenth-Century England.* Oxford, UK: Oxford University Press, 2009.

Briggs, Julia. "Middleton's Forgotten Tragedy *Hengist, King of Kent*." *Review of English Studies* 41.164 (1990): 479–95.

Britton, Dennis Austin. *Becoming Christian: Race, Reformation, and Early Modern Romance*. Fordham: Fordham University Press, 2014.

Brooks, Chris W. *Pettifoggers and Vipers of the Commonwealth: The "Lower Branch" of the Legal Profession in Early Modern England*. Cambridge, UK: Cambridge University Press, 1986.

Burgess, Clive. "London Parishioners in Times of Change: St. Andrew Hubbard, Eastcheap, c. 1450–1570." *Journal of Ecclesiastical History* 53.1 (2002): 38–63.

Burke, Victoria E. "Ann Bowyer's Commonplace Book (Bodleian Library Ashmole MS 51): Reading and Writing among the 'Middling Sort.'" *Early Modern Literary Studies* 6.3 (2001): 1–128.

Burrage, Champlin. *The True Story of Robert Browne (1550?–1633), Father of Congregationalism*. Oxford, UK: Oxford University Press, 1906.

Cabot, Nancy Graves. "Patter Sources of Scriptural Subjects in Tudor-Stuart Embroideries." *Bulletin of the Needle and Bobbin Club* 30.1–2 (1946): 3–17.

Capp, Bernard. "'Jesus Wept' but Did the Englishman? Masculinity and Emotion in Early Modern England." *Past & Present* 224.1 (2014): 75–108.

———. *When Gossips Meet: Women, Family and Neighborhood in Early Modern England*. Oxford, UK: Oxford University Press, 2003.

———. *The World of John Taylor, the Water-Poet, 1578–1653*. Oxford, UK: Clarendon Press, 1994.

Carlin, Martha. *Medieval Southwark*. London: Hambledon Press, 1996.

Carlin, Norah. "Liberty and Fraternities in the English Revolution: The Politics of London Artisan's Protests, 1636–1659." *International Review of Social History* 39.2 (1994): 223–54.

Carrington, Richard. *Two Schools: A History of St. Olave's and St. Saviour's Grammar School Foundation*. London: Governors of the St. Olave's and St. Saviour's Grammar School Foundation, 1971.

Carson, Neil. *A Companion to Henslowe's Diary*. Cambridge, UK: Cambridge University Press, 1988.

Centers for Disease Control and Prevention, "Pregnancy Mortality Surveillance System." June 4, 2019. https://www.cdc.gov/reproductivehealth/maternal infanthealth/pregnancy-mortality -surveillance-system.htm.

Chakravarty, Urvashi. "Livery, Liberty, and Legal Fictions." *English Literary Renaissance* 42.3 (2012): 365–90.

Chambers, E. K. *The Elizabethan Stage*. Vol. 2. Oxford, UK: Clarendon Press, 1945.

Childs, Jessie. *God's Traitors: Terror and Faith in Elizabethan England*. Oxford, UK: Oxford University Press, 2014.

Chovenak (Chovanec), Kevin. "'What is there in three dice?': The Role of Demons in the History of Probability." In *Renaissance Papers, 2013*, ed. Jim Pearce and Joanna Kucinski, 17–30. Suffolk, UK: Boydell & Brewer, 2014.

Christensen, Ann C. "Being Mistress Eyre in Dekker's *The Shoemaker's Holiday* and Deloney's *The Gentle Craft*." *Comparative Drama* 42.4 (2008): 451–80.

Christian, Margaret. *Spenserian Allegory and Elizabethan Biblical Exegesis: A Context for "The Faerie Queene."* Manchester, UK: Manchester University Press 2016.

Christmas, William J. *Lab'ring Muses: Work, Writing, and the Social Order in English Plebian Poetry, 1730–1830*. Newark: University of Delaware Press, 2001.

Claassens, Juliana M. "Calling the Keeners: The Image of the Wailing Woman as Symbol of Survival in a Traumatized

World." *Journal of Feminist Studies in Religion* 26.1 (2010): 63–77.
Clark, Ann. *The Working Life of Women in the Seventeenth Century*. 1919. Reprint, London: Routledge, 1968.
Cleugh, Hannah. "Teaching in Praying Words? Worship and Theology in the Early Modern English Parish." In *Worship and the Parish Church in Early Modern Britain*, ed. Natalie Mears and Alec Ryrie, 11–30. Farnham, UK: Ashgate, 2013.
Clode, Charles Matthew. *Memorials of the Guild of Merchant Taylors of the Fraternity of St. John the Baptist*. London: Harrison and Sons, 1875.
Cohn, Samuel K. *Cultures of Plague: Medical Thinking at the End of the Renaissance*. Oxford, UK: Oxford University Press, 2010.
Cohn, Samuel K., and Guido Alfani. "Households and Plague in Early Modern Italy." *Journal of Interdisciplinary History* 38.2 (2007): 177–205.
Cokayne, George Edward. *Some Account of the Lord Mayors and Sheriffs of the City of London during the First Quarter of the Seventeenth Century, 1601–1625*. London: Phillimore and Co., 1897.
Collins, Jessica. "Jane Holt, Milliner, and Other Women in Business: Apprentices, Freewomen and Mistresses in the Clothworkers' Company, 1606–1800." *Textile History* 44.1 (2013): 72–94.
Collinson, Patrick. *Archbishop Grindal, 1519–1583: The Struggle for a Reformed Church*. Berkeley: University of California Press, 1979.
———. *This England: Essays on the English Nation and Commonwealth in the Sixteenth Century*. Manchester, UK: Manchester University Press, 2011.
Combs, Julia. "Fountains of Love: The Maternal Body as Rhetorical Symbol of Authority in Early Modern England." *Journal of Early Modern Studies* 7.2 (2018): 55–71.
Consitt, Frances. *The London Weavers' Company*. Vol. 1, *From the Twelfth Century to the Close of the Sixteenth Century*. Oxford, UK: Clarendon Press, 1932.
Conyers, Angela, ed. *Wiltshire Extents for Debts, Edward I–Elizabeth I*. Vol. 28. Wiltshire, UK: Wiltshire Record Society, 1973.
Coster, Will. *Baptism and Spiritual Kinship in Early Modern England*. 2002. Reprint, New York: Routledge, 2016.
———. "Purity, Profanity, and Puritanism: The Churching of Women, 1500–1700." In *Women in the Church*, ed. W. J. Sheils and Diana Wood, 377–87. Oxford, UK: Basil Blackwell, 1990.
Cottret, Bernard. *The Huguenots in England: Immigration and Settlement, c. 1550–1700*. Cambridge, UK: Cambridge University Press, 1991.
Crawford, Patricia. *Blood, Bodies, and Families in Early Modern England*. 2004. Reprint, New York: Routledge, 2014.
Cressy, David. *Birth, Marriage, and Death: Ritual, Religion, and the Life Cycle in Tudor and Stuart England*. Oxford, UK: Oxford University Press, 1997.
———. "Describing the Social Order of Elizabethan and Stuart England." *Literature & History* 3 (1976): 29–44.
———. *Literacy and the Social Order: Reading and Writing in Tudor and Stuart England*. Cambridge, UK: Cambridge University Press, 1980.
———. "The Protestant Calendar and the Vocabulary of Celebration in Early Modern England." *Journal of British Studies* 29.1 (1990): 31–52.
Cross, Claire. "Noble Patronage in the Elizabethan Church." *Historical Journal* 3.1 (1960): 1–16.
———. *The Puritan Earl: The Life of Henry Hastings, Third Earl of Huntingdon, 1536–1595*. New York: St. Martin's Press, 1966.
———. "Udall, John (c. 1560–1592/3)." In *Oxford Dictionary of National Biography*, ed. H. C. G. Matthew and Brian Harrison. Oxford, UK: Oxford University Press, 2004. Online ed., ed. David Cannadine, January 2008.
Crowston, Clare. "Women, Gender, and Guilds in Early Modern Europe: An

Overview of Recent Research." *International Review of Social History* 53, no. S16 (2008): 19–44.

Culpepper, Scott. *Francis Johnson and the Separatist Influence*. Macon, Ga.: Mercer University Press, 2011.

Cummings, Robert. "The Province of Verse: Sir Thomas More's Twelve Rules of John Picus of Mirandula." In *Elizabethan Translation and Literary Culture*, ed. Gabriela Schmidt, 201–27. Berlin: De Gruyter, 2013.

Cummins, Neil, Morgan Kelly, and Cormac Ó Gráda. "Living Standards and Plague in London, 1560–1665." *Economic History Review* 69.1 (2016): 3–34.

Dale, Marian K. "London Silkwomen of the Fifteenth Century." *Economic History Review* 4.3 (1933): 324–35.

Davies, Matthew. "'Monuments of Honour': Clerks, Histories and Heroes in the London Livery Companies." In *The Fifteenth Century X: Parliament, Personalities and Power. Papers Presented to Linda S. Clark*, ed. Hannes Kleineke, 143–65. Suffolk, UK: Boydell and Brewer, 2011.

———. "'Writyng, making, and engrocyng': Clerks, Guilds and Identity in Late Medieval London." In *Medieval Merchants and Money: Essays in Honour of James L. Bolton*, ed. Martin Allen and Matthew Davies, 21–41. London: School of Advanced Study, University of London, 2016.

De Munck, Bert. "Artisans, Products and Gifts: Rethinking the History of Material Culture in Early Modern Europe." *Past and Present* 224.1 (2014): 38–74.

Dimmock, Matthew. "Converting and Not Converting 'Strangers' in Early Modern London." *Journal of Early Modern History* 17 (2013): 457–78.

Dobb, Clifford. "London's Prisons." In *Shakespeare in His Own Age*, ed. Allardyce Nicoll, 87–100. Cambridge, UK: Cambridge University Press, 1976.

Dobbie, B. M. Willmott. "An Attempt to Estimate the True Rate of Maternal Mortality, Sixteenth to Eighteenth Centuries." *Medical History*, 26.1 (1982): 79–90.

Dobson, Mary J. *Contours of Death and Disease in Early Modern England*. Cambridge, UK: Cambridge University Press, 1997.

Doelman, James. *James I and the Religious Culture of England*. Suffolk, UK: Boydell and Brewer, 2000.

Dorsinville, Max. "Design in Deloney's *Jack of Newbury*." *PMLA* 88.2 (1973): 233–39.

Duffin, Ross W. "To Entertain a King: Music for James and Henry at the Merchant Taylors Feast of 1607." *Music and Letters* 83.4 (2002): 525–41.

Duffy, Eamon. *The Stripping of the Altars: Traditional Religion in England, 1400–1580*. New Haven, Conn.: Yale University Press, 1992.

Dumolyn, Jan, and Jelle Haemers. "'A Bad Chicken Was Brooding': Subversive Speech in Late Medieval Flanders." *Past & Present* 214 (2012): 45–86.

Dymond, David. "Sitting Apart in Church." In *Counties and Communities: Essays on East Anglian History*, ed. Carol Rawcliffe, Roger Virgoe, and Richard Wilson, 213–24. Norwich, UK: Centre of East Anglian Studies, 1996.

Eales, Jacqueline. *Women in Early Modern England, 1500–1700*. New York: Routledge, 2005.

Egan, Gabriel. *Green Shakespeare: From Ecopolitics to Ecocriticism*. New York: Routledge, 2006.

Eisenstein, Elizabeth L. *The Printing Press as an Agent of Change*. 1-vol. ed. Cambridge, UK: Cambridge University Press, 1979.

Ellinghausen, Laurie. *Labor and Writing in Early Modern England, 1567–1667*. Farnham, UK: Ashgate, 2008.

———. "'Their labour doth returne rich golden gaine': Fishmongers' Pageants and the Fisherman's Labor in Early Modern London." *Comparative Drama* 51.2 (2017): 134–56.

Epstein, Steven A. "Craft Guilds." In *The Oxford Encyclopedia of Economic*

History, 1:35–39. Oxford, UK: Oxford University Press, 2003.

———. *Wage Labor and the Guilds in Medieval Europe*. Chapel Hill: University of North Carolina Press, 1991.

Farmer, Alan B., and Zachary Lesser. "What Is Print Popularity? A Map of the Elizabethan Book Trade." In *The Elizabethan Top Ten: Defining Print Popularity in Early Modern England*, ed. Andy Kesson and Emma Smith, 19–54. Farnham, UK: Ashgate, 2013.

Farmer, Sharon. *The Silk Industries of Medieval Paris: Artisanal Migration, Technological Innovation, and Gendered Experience*. Philadelphia: University of Pennsylvania Press, 2017.

Finlay, Roger. *Population and Metropolis: The Demography of London, 1580–1650*. Cambridge, UK: Cambridge University Press, 1981.

Finlayson, J. Caitlin. "Jacobean Foreign Policy, London's Civic Polity, and John Squire's Lord Mayor's Show, *The Tryumphs of Peace* (1620)." *Studies in Philology* 110.3 (2013): 584–610.

Fissel, Mary E. *Vernacular Bodies: The Politics of Reproduction in Early Modern England*. Oxford, UK: Oxford University Press, 2004.

Fitter, Chris. *Radical Shakespeare: Politics and Stagecraft in the Early Career*. New York: Routledge, 2012.

Fitzgerald, Christina M. *The Drama of Masculinity and Medieval English Guild Culture*. New York: Palgrave, 2007.

Flather, Amanda. *Gender and Space in Early Modern England*. Suffolk, UK: Boydell Press, 2007.

Forbes, John. "Search, Immigration and the Goldsmith's Company: A Study in the Decline of Its Powers." In *Guilds, Society and Economy in London, 1450–1800*, ed. Ian Anders Gadd and Patrick Wallis, 115–26. London: Centre for Metropolitan History Institute of Historical Research, 2002.

Forey, Madeleine. "'Bless thee, Bottom, bless thee! Thou art translated!': Ovid, Golding, and *A Midsummer Night's Dream*." *Modern Language Notes* 93 (1998): 321–29.

Freeman, Arthur. "Marlowe, Kyd, and the Dutch Church Libel." *English Literary Renaissance* 3.1 (1972): 44–52.

Freeman, Thomas. "'The Good Ministrye of Godlye and Vertuouse Women': The Elizabethan Martyrologists and the Female Supporters of the Marian Martyrs." *Journal of British Studies* 39.1 (2000): 8–33.

———. "The Rise of Prison Literature." *Huntington Library Quarterly* 72.2 (2009): 133–46.

French, H. R. *The Middle Sort of People in Provincial England, 1600–1750*. Oxford, UK: Oxford University Press, 2007.

French, Katherine L. *The People of the Parish: Community Life in a Late Medieval Diocese*. Philadelphia: University of Pennsylvania Press, 2001.

Froide, Amy M. "Marital Status as a Category of Difference: Singlewomen and Widows in Early Modern England." In *Singlewomen in the European Past, 1250–1800*, eds. Judith M. Bennett and Amy M. Froide, 236–69. Philadelphia: University of Pennsylvania Press, 1999.

Frontain, Raymond-Jean. "'The Man Which Have Affliction Seene': Donne Jeremiah, and the Fashioning of Lamentation." In *Centered on the Word: Literature, Scripture, and the Tudor-Stuart Middle Way*, ed. Daniel W. Doerksen and Christopher Hodgkins, 127–47. Newark: University of Delaware Press, 2004.

Fry, Frederick M. *A Historical Catalogue of the Pictures, Herse-Cloths and Tapestry at Merchant Taylor's Hall*. London: Chapman Hall, Ltd., 1907.

Frye, Susan. *Pens and Needles: Women's Textualities in Early Modern England*. Philadelphia: University of Pennsylvania Press, 2010.

Fumerton, Patricia. *Unsettled: The Culture of Mobility and the Working Poor in Early Modern England*. Chicago: University of Chicago Press, 2006.

Gadd, Ian Anders, and Patrick Wallis, eds. *Guilds, Society and Economy in London, 1450–1800*. London: Centre for Metropolitan History Institute of Historical Research, 2002.
Gibbs, Gary. "New Duties for the Parish Community in Tudor London." In *The Parish in English Life, 1400–1600*, ed. Karen L. French, Gary Gibbs, and Beat Kümin, 163–77. Manchester, UK: Manchester University Press, 1997.
Gilman, Ernest B. *Plague Writing in Early Modern England*. Chicago: University of Chicago Press, 2009.
Ginzburg, Carlo. *The Cheese and the Worms: The Cosmos of a Sixteenth-Century Miller*. Baltimore: Johns Hopkins University Press, 1976.
Ginzburg, Carlo, and Carlo Poni. "The Name of the Game: Unequal Exchange and the Historiographic Marketplace." In *Microhistory and the Lost Peoples of Europe*, ed. Edward Muir and Guido Ruggiero, 1–10. Baltimore: Johns Hopkins University Press, 1991.
Gittings, Clare. *Death, Burial and the Individual in Early Modern England*. London: Croom Helm, 1984.
———. "Urban Funerals in Late Medieval and Reformation England." In *Death in Town: Urban Responses to the Dying and the Dead, 100–1600*, ed. S. Bassett, 170–78. London: Leicester University Press, 1992.
Gleed, Paul. "'I Lov'd Thee Best': London as Male Beloved in Isabella Whitney's 'The Manner of Her Wyll.'" *London Journal* 37 (2012): 1–12.
Goldberg, Jonathan. *James I and the Politics of Literature: Jonson, Shakespeare, Donne, and Their Contemporaries*. Baltimore: Johns Hopkins University Press, 1983.
Goose, Nigel. "Immigrants and English Economic Development in the Sixteenth and Early Seventeenth Centuries." In *Immigrants in Tudor and Early Stuart England*, ed. Nigel Goose and Lien Luu, 137–60. Brighton, UK: Sussex Academic Press, 2005.
Gordon, Andrew. *Writing Early Modern London: Memory, Text, and Community*. New York: Palgrave, 2013.
Gottschall, Anna Edith. "The Pater Noster and the Laity in England, c. 700–1560, with Special Focus on the Clergy's Use of the Prayer to Structure Basic Catechetical Teaching." Ph.D. diss., University of Birmingham, 2016.
Gowing, Laura. *Common Bodies: Women, Touch, and Power in Seventeenth-Century England*. New Haven, Conn.: Yale University Press, 2003,
———. *Gender Relations in Early Modern England*. London: Routledge, 2012.
———. "Girls on Forms: Apprenticing Young Women in Seventeenth-Century London." *Journal of British Studies* 55.3 (2016): 447–73.
Grantham, Wilson, ed. *List of the Wardens of the Grocers' Company from 1345–1907*. London, 1907.
Gray, Marion W. "Microhistory as Universal History." *Central European History* 34.3 (2001): 419–31.
Greaves, Robert L. "The Origins and Early Development of English Covenant Thought." *The Historian* 31.1 (1968): 21–35.
Green, Ian. *Print and Protestantism in Early Modern England*. Oxford, UK: Oxford University Press, 2000.
Greenberg, Stephen. "The Plague, the Printing Press, and Public Health in Seventeenth-Century England." *Huntington Library Quarterly* 67.4 (2004): 508–27.
Greenfield, Matthew. "The Cultural Functions of Renaissance Elegy." *English Literary Renaissance* 28.1 (1998): 75–94.
Greg, Walter W., ed. *Henslowe's Diary, Part II: Commentary*. London: A. H. Bullen, 1908.
Grendi, Edoardo. "Ripensare la Microstoria?" *Quaderni Storici* 86 (1994): 539–49.

Griffiths, Arthur. *The Chronicles of Newgate*. London: Chapman and Hall, 1884.

Griffiths, Paul. *Lost Londons: Change, Crime and Control in the Capital City, 1550–1660*. Cambridge, UK: Cambridge University Press, 2008.

———. *Youth and Authority: Formative Experience in England, 1560–1640*. Oxford, UK: Clarendon Press, 1996.

Groom, Matthew. "John Siberch (d. 1554), the First Cambridge Printer: New Finding from English Records." *Transaction of the Cambridge Bibliographical Society* 12.4 (2003): 403–13.

Gurr, Andrew. *The Shakespearean Stage, 1574–1642*. Cambridge, UK: Cambridge University Press, 2009.

Gustafsson, Bo. "The Rise of Medieval Craft Guilds: An Economic-Theoretical Interpretation." *Scandinavian Economic History* Review 35.1 (1987): 1–40.

Ha, Polly. *English Presbyterianism, 1590–1640*. Stanford, Calif.: Stanford University Press, 2011.

Habib, Imtiaz H. *Black Lives in the English Archives, 1500–1677: Imprints of the Invisible*. Aldershot, UK: Ashgate, 2008.

Habib, Imtiaz, and Duncan Salkeld. "The Resonables of Boroughside, Southwark: An Elizabethan Black Family Near the Rose Theatre." *Shakespeare* 11.2 (2015): 135–47.

Haigh, Christopher. "The Taming of Reformation: Preachers, Pastors and Parishioners in Elizabethan and Early Stuart England." *History* 85.280 (2000): 572–88.

Halliday, Stephen. *Newgate: London's Prototype of Hell*. Stroud, UK: Sutton, 2006.

Hamlin, Hannibal. *Psalm Culture and Early Modern English Literature*. Cambridge, UK: Cambridge University Press, 2004.

Hamling, Tara. *Decorating the Godly Household: Religious Art in Post-Reformation Britain*. London: Paul Mellon Centre for Studies in British Art, 2011.

Hamling, Tara, and Catherine Richardson. *A Day at Home in Early Modern England: Material Culture and Domestic Life, 1500–1700*. New Haven, Conn.: Yale University Press, 2017.

Harkness, Deborah E. *The Jewel House: Elizabethan London and the Scientific Revolution*. New Haven, Conn.: Yale University Press, 2007.

Harrell, Willie J., Jr. *Origins of the African American Jeremiad: The Rhetorical Strategies of Social Protest and Activism, 1760–1861*. Jefferson, N.C.: McFarland, 2011.

Hart, Charles J. "Old Chests." *Birmingham and Midland Institute: Archaeological Section: Transactions and Proceedings* 18 (1892): 60–94.

Hawkes, David. *The Culture of Usury in Renaissance England*. New York: Palgrave, 2010.

Heal, Felicity. "Food Gifts, the Household and the Politics of Exchange in Early Modern England." *Past and Present* 199 (2008): 41–70.

———. *Hospitality in Early Modern England*. Oxford, UK: Oxford University Press, 1990.

Heale, Elizabeth. "Misogyny and the Complete Gentleman in Early Elizabethan Printed Miscellanies." *Yearbook of English Studies* (2003): 233–47.

Healy, Margaret. *Fictions of Disease in Early Modern England: Bodies, Plagues and Politics*. New York: Palgrave, 2001.

Heaton, Gabriel, and James Knowles. "'Entertainment Perfect': Ben Jonson and Corporate Hospitality." *Review of English Studies* 54.217 (2003): 587–600.

Heinenmann, Margot. *Puritanism and the Theatre: Thomas Middleton and Opposition Drama under the Early Stuarts*. Cambridge, UK: Cambridge University Press, 1980.

Heller, Jennifer. *The Mother's Legacy in Early Modern England*. 2011. Reprint, New York: Routledge, 2016.

Hentschell, Roze. *The Culture of Cloth in Early Modern England: Textual Construction of National Identity*. Farnham, UK: Ashgate, 2008.

Hertz, Gerald B. "The English Silk Industry in the Eighteenth Century." *English Historical Review* 24.96 (1909): 710–27.

Hill, Christopher. *The Bible in Seventeenth-Century English Politics: The Tanner Lectures on Human Values*. London: Penguin, 1991.

Hill, Tracey. *Anthony Munday and Civic Culture: Theatre, History and Power in Early Modern London, 1580–1633*. Manchester, UK: Manchester University Press, 2004.

——. *Pageantry and Power: A Cultural History of the Early Modern Lord Mayor's Show, 1585–1639*. Manchester, UK: Manchester University Press, 2010.

Hindle, Steve. *On the Parish? The Micro-Politics of Poor Relief in Rural England*. Oxford, UK: Oxford University Press.

Hodgson, Elizabeth M. A. *Gender and the Sacred Self in John Donne*. Newark: University of Delaware Press, 1999.

Hogan, A. P. "Thematic Unity in Chapman's *Monsieur D'Olive*." *Studies in English Literature* 11.2 (1971): 295–306.

Holladay, William L. "Elusive Deuteronomists, Jeremiah and Proto-Deuteronomy." *Catholic Biblical Quarterly* 66.1 (2004): 55–77.

Holstun, James. "The Spider, the Fly, and the Commonwealth: Merrie John Heywood and Agrarian Class Struggle." *English Literary History* 71.1 (2004): 53–88.

Homer, Ronald F. "The Pewterers' Company's Country Searches and the Company's Regulation of Prices." In *Guilds, Society and Economy in London, 1450–1800*, ed. Ian Anders Gadd and Patrick Wallis, 101–14. London: Centre for Metropolitan History Institute of Historical Research, 2002.

Houlbrooke, Ralph. "Civility and Civil Observances in the Early Modern English Funeral." In *Civil Histories: Essays Presented to Sir Keith Thomas*, ed. Brian Harrison and Paul Slack, 67–86. Oxford, UK: Oxford University Press, 2000.

——. *Death, Religion and the Family in England, 1480–1750*. Oxford, UK: Oxford University Press, 1998.

Houston, Walter. *Contending for Justice: Ideologies and Theologies of Social Justice in the Old Testament*. New York: T & T Clark, 2006.

Howard, Jean. *Theater of a City: The Places of London Comedy, 1598–1642*. Philadelphia: University of Pennsylvania Press, 2007.

Howard, Sharon. "Imagining the Pain and Peril of Seventeenth-Century Childbirth: Travail and Deliverance in the Making of an Early Modern World." *Social History of Medicine* 16.3 (2003): 367–82.

Howard-Pitney, David. *The Afro-American Jeremiad: Appeals for Justice in America*. Philadelphia: Temple University Press, 1990.

Howarth, David. *Images of Rule: Art and Politics in the English Renaissance, 1485–1649*. Berkeley: University of California Press, 1997.

Hoyle, Richard W. "Petitioning as Popular Politics in Early Sixteenth-Century England." *Historical Research* 75 (2002): 365–89.

Hyde, Thomas. "Vision, Poetry, and Authority in Spenser." *English Literary Renaissance* 13.2 (1983): 127–45.

Imhof, Arthur E. *Lost Worlds: How Our European Ancestors Coped with Everyday Life and Why Life Is So Hard Today*. Charlottesville: University of Virginia Press, 1996.

Ingram, William. "Laurence Dutton, Stage Player: Missing and Presumed Lost." *Medieval and Renaissance Drama in England* 14 (2001): 122–43.

Ioppolo, Grace. "Revision, Manuscript Transmission and Scribal Practice in Middleton's *Hengist, King of Kent, or, The Mayor of Queensborough*." *Critical Survey* 7.3 (1995): 319–31.

James, Susan E. "Domestic Painted Cloths in Sixteenth-Century England: Imagery, Placement, and Ownership." *Medieval Clothing and Textiles* 9 (2013): 139–60.

———. *Women's Voices in Tudor Wills, 1485–1603: Authority, Influence, and Material Culture.* Farnham, UK: Ashgate, 2015.

Johns, Adrian. "Coleman Street." *Huntington Library Quarterly* 71.1 (2008): 33–54.

Johnson, Jeffrey. "Recovering the Curse of Eve: John Donne's Churching Sermons." *Renaissance and Reformation / Renaissance et Réforme* 23.2 (1999): 61–71.

Jones, Ann Rosalind, and Peter Stallybrass. *Renaissance Clothing and the Materials of Memory.* Cambridge, UK: Cambridge University Press, 2001.

Jones, Mike Rodman. "'O London, London': Mid-Tudor Literature and the City." *Review of English Studies* 68.287 (2017): 883–901.

Jones, Norman. *God and the Moneylenders: Usury and Law in Early Modern England.* Oxford, UK: Basil Blackwell, 1989.

Jones, W. J. *The Foundations of Bankruptcy: Status and Commissions in the Early Modern Period.* Philadelphia: American Philosophical Society, 1979.

Jurkowski, M., C. L. Smith, and D. Crook. *Lay Taxes in England and Wales, 1188–1688.* London: Public Records Office Publications, 1998.

Karras, Ruth Mazo. *Common Women: Prostitution and Sexuality in Medieval England.* Oxford, UK: Oxford University Press, 1996.

Kathman, David. "Grocers, Goldsmiths, and Drapers: Freemen and Apprentices in the Elizabethan Theater." *Shakespeare Quarterly* 55.1 (2004): 1–49.

———. "The Rise of Commercial Playing in 1540s London." *Early Theatre* 12.1 (2009): 15–38.

Kaufmann, Peter Iver. "'Much in Prayer': The Inward Researches of Elizabethan Protestants." *Journal of Religion* 73.2 (1993): 163–82.

Kawana, Yoh. "Trade, Sociability, and Governance in an English Incorporated Borough: 'Formal' and 'Informal' Worlds in Leicester, c. 1570–1640." *Urban History* 33.3 (2006): 324–49.

Kay, Dennis. *Melodious Tears: The English Funeral Elegy from Spenser to Milton.* Oxford, UK: Oxford University Press, 1990.

Keene, Derek, David Crouch, and John Stedman. *Social and Economic Study of Medieval London: The Walbrook Study: A Summary Report with Appendix (Containing Property Histories and Indexes).* London: Centre for Metropolitan History, 1987.

Kermode, Lloyd Edward, ed. *Three Renaissance Usury Plays.* Manchester, UK: Manchester University Press, 2014.

Kerridge, Eric. *Trade and Banking in Early Modern England.* Manchester, UK: Manchester University Press, 1988.

Kewes, Paulina. "Julius Caesar in Jacobean England." *Seventeenth Century* 17.2 (2002): 155–86.

Kilburn-Toppin, Jasmine. "'Discords Have Arisen and Brotherly Love Decreased': The Spatial and Material Contexts of the Guild Feast in Early Modern London." *Brewery History* 150 (2013): 28–38.

———. "Gifting Cultures and Artisanal Guilds in Sixteenth- and Early Seventeenth-Century London." *Historical Journal* 60.4 (2017): 865–87.

———. "Material Memories of the Guildsmen: Crafting Identities in Early Modern London." In *Memory before Modernity: Practices of Memory in Early Modern Europe,* ed. Judith Pollman, Johannes Müller, and Jasper van der Steen, 166–81. Boston: Brill, 2013.

Killeen, Kevin. *The Political Bible in Early Modern England.* Cambridge, UK: Cambridge University Press, 2017.

King, John N. *English Reformation Literature: The Tudor Origins of the Protestant Tradition.* Princeton, N.J.: Princeton University Press, 1982.

———. *Foxe's "Book of Martyrs" and Early Modern Print Culture*. Cambridge, UK: Cambridge University Press, 2011.

Kirsch, Arthur. "'Twixt Two Extremes of Passion, Joy and Grief': Shakespeare's *King Lear* and Last Plays." *Yale Review* 103.1 (2015): 26–47.

Kitching, C. J. "The Quest for Concealed Lands in the Reign of Elizabeth I: The Alexander Prize Essay." *Transactions of the Royal Historical Society* 24 (1974): 63–78.

Kitson, P. M. "Religious Change and the Timing of Baptism in England, 1538–1750." *Historical Journal*, 5.2 (2009): 269–94.

Kleinberg, Seymour. "*The Merchant of Venice*: The Homosexual as Anti-Semite in Nascent Capitalism." In *Literary Visions of Homosexuality*, ed. Stuart Kellogg, 113–26. New York: Haworth, 1983.

Knodel, Natalie. "Reconsidering an Obsolete Rite: The Churching of Women and Feminist Liturgical Theology." *Feminist Theology* 5.14 (1997): 106–25.

Knutson, Roslyn. "A Caliban in St. Mildred Poultry." In *Shakespeare and Cultural Traditions: The Selected Proceedings of the International Shakespeare Association World Conference, Tokyo, 1991*, ed. Tetsuo Kishi, Roger Pringle, and Stanley Wells, 110–26. Newark: University of Delaware Press, 1994.

Korda, Natasha. "Household Property/Stage Property: Henslowe as Pawnbroker." *Theatre Journal* 48.2 (1996): 185–95.

———. *Labors Lost: Women's Work and the Early Modern English Stage*. Philadelphia: University of Pennsylvania Press, 2011.

Koslofsky, Craig. *The Reformation of the Dead: Death and Ritual in Early Modern Germany, 1450–1700*. New York: St. Martin's Press, 1999.

Kowaleski, Maryanne, and Judith M. Bennett. "Crafts, Gilds, and Women in the Middle Ages: Fifty Years after Marian K. Dale." *Signs: Journal of Women in Culture and Society* 14.2 (1989): 474–501.

Kümin, Beat. *The Communal Age in Western Europe, c. 1100–1800*. New York: Palgrave, 2013.

———. *The Shaping of a Community: The Rise and Reformation of the English Parish, 1400–1560*. Aldershot, UK: Scolar Press, 1996.

Lacey, Kay. "The Production of 'Narrow Ware' by Silkwomen in Fourteenth and Fifteenth Century England." *Textile History* 18.2 (1987): 187–204.

Ladd, Roger A. "Thomas Deloney and the London Weavers' Company." *Sixteenth Century Journal* 32.3 (2001): 981–1001.

Lake, Peter. *The Boxmaker's Revenge: "Orthodoxy," "Heterodoxy" and the Politics of the Parish in Early Stuart London*. Stanford, Calif.: Stanford University Press, 2001.

Lamb, Mary Ellen. "*A Midsummer Night's Dream*: The Myth of Theseus and the Minotaur." *Texas Studies in Literature and Language* 21.4 (1979): 478–91.

Lancashire, Anne. *London Civic Theatre: City Drama and Pageantry from Roman Times to 1558*. Cambridge, UK: Cambridge University Press, 2002.

Landry, Donna. *The Muses of Resistance: Laboring-Class Women's Poetry in Britain, 1739–1796*. Cambridge, UK: Cambridge University Press, 1990.

Lavin, J. A. "William Barley, Draper and Stationer." *Studies in Bibliography* 22 (1969): 214–23.

Lee, Becky R. "Men's Recollections of a Women's Rite: Medieval English Men's Recollections regarding the Rite of Purification of Women after Childbirth." *Gender and History* 14.2 (2002): 224–41.

Lemire, Beverly. *The Business of Everyday Life: Gender, Practice and Social Politics in England, c. 1600–1900*. Manchester, UK: Manchester University Press, 2005.

———. "The Secondhand Clothing Trade in Europe and Beyond: Stages of Development in a Changing Material World, c. 1600–1850." *Textile: Cloth and Culture* 10.2 (2012): 144–63.

Le Rougetel, Hazel. "The Rose of England." *RSA Journal* 136 (1988): 742–44.

Leunig, Tim, with Chris Minns and Patrick Wallis. "Networks in the Premodern Economy: The Market for London Apprenticeships, 1600–1749." *The Journal of Economic History* 71.2 (2011): 413–43.

Levi, Giovanni. "On Microhistory." In *New Perspectives on Historical Writing*, 2nd ed., ed. Peter Burke, 97–119. University Park: Pennsylvania State University Press, 2001.

Lievsay, John Leon. "Newgate Penitents: Further Aspects of Elizabethan Pamphlet Sensationalism." *Huntington Library Quarterly* 7.1 (1943): 47–69.

———. "William Barley, Elizabethan Printer and Bookseller." *Studies in Bibliography* 8 (1956): 218–25.

Linebaugh, Peter. *The London Hanged: Crime and Civil Society in the Eighteenth Century*. New York: Penguin, 1993.

Linton, Joan Pong. "Jack of Newbery and Drake in California: Domestic and Colonial Narratives of English Cloth and Manhood." *English Literary History* 59.1 (1992): 23–51.

Littleton, Charles Galton. "Geneva on Threadneedle Street: The French Church of London and Its Congregation, 1560–1625." Ph.D. diss., University of Michigan, 1996.

Llewellyn, Nigel. *Funeral Monuments in Post-Reformation England*. Cambridge, UK: Cambridge University Press, 2000.

Lobanov-Rostovsky, Sergei. "The Triumphes of Golde: Economic Authority in the Jacobean Lord Mayor's Show." *English Literary History* 60.4 (1993): 879–98.

Loengard, Janet S. "An Elizabethan Lawsuit: John Brayne, His Carpenter, and the Building of the Red Lion." *Shakespeare Quarterly* 34.3 (1983): 298–310.

Loomis, Catherine. *The Death of Queen Elizabeth I: Remembering and Reconstructing the Virgin Queen*. New York: Palgrave, 2010.

Loose, Margaret A. *The Chartist Imaginary: Literary Form in Working-Class Political Theory and Practice*. Columbus: Ohio State University Press, 2015.

Lost Plays Database. Ed. Roslyn L. Knutson and Matthew Steggle. Washington, D.C.: Folger Shakespeare Library. https://lostplays.folger.edu/.

Lucking, David. "Translation and Metamorphosis in *A Midsummer Night's Dream*." *Essays in Criticism* 61.2 (2011): 137–54.

Luu, Lien Bich. *Immigrants and the Industries of London, 1500–1700*. Farnham, UK: Ashgate, 2005.

Mackerness, E. D. "Thomas Nashe and William Cotton." *Review of English Studies* 25.100 (1949): 342–46.

Mahony, Patrick J. "Ben Jonson's 'best piece of poetrie.'" *American Imago* 37.1 (1980): 68–82.

Malchow, Bruce V. *Social Justice in the Hebrew Bible: What Is New and What Is Old*. Collegeville, Minn.: Liturgical Press, 1996.

Mander, Nicholas. "Painted Cloths: History, Craftsmen and Techniques." *Textile History* 28.2 (1997): 119–48.

Manley, Lawrence. "Fictions of Settlement: London 1590." *Studies in Philology* 88.2 (1991): 201–24.

Marchant, E. C. "Rivers, Antony (*fl.* 1601–1606)." Rev. Alison Shell. In *Oxford Dictionary of National Biography*, ed. H. C. G. Matthew and Brian Harrison. Oxford, UK: Oxford University Press, 2004. Online ed., ed. David Cannadine, January 2008.

Marsh, Christopher. "'At it ding don': Recreation and Religion in the English Belfry, 1580–1640." In *Worship in the Parish Church in Early Modern England*, ed. Natalie Mears and Alec

Ryrie, 173–96. Farnham, UK: Ashgate, 2013.

———. "Order and Place in England, 1580–1640: The View from the Pew." *Journal of British Studies* 44.1 (2005): 3–26.

Martin, J. W. "English Protestant Separatism at Its Beginnings: Henry Hart and the Free-Will Men." *Sixteenth Century Journal* 7.2 (1976): 55–74.

Martin, Matthew. "The Name of the Father in 'On My First Son.'" *Ben Jonson Journal* 15.2 (2008): 159–74.

Martin, Patrick, and John Finnis. "The Secret Sharers: 'Anthony Rivers' and the Appellant Controversy, 1601–2." *Huntington Library Quarterly* 69.2 (2006): 195–238.

Maslen, R. W. "The Healing Dialogues of William Bullein." *Yearbook of English Studies* 38.1–2 (2008): 119–35.

Mathur, Maya. "An Attack of the Clowns." *Journal for Early Modern Cultural Studies* 7.1 (2007): 33–55.

Mazzola, Elizabeth. *Learning and Literacy in Female Hands, 1520–1698*. New York: Routledge, 2013.

McDermott, Ryan. *Tropologies: Ethics and Invention in Early Modern England, c. 1350–1600*. Notre Dame, Ind.: University of Notre Dame Press, 2016.

McGiffert, Michael. "Covenant, Crown, and Commons in Elizabethan Puritanism." *Journal of British Studies* 20.1 (1980): 35–52.

———. "God's Controversy with Jacobean England." *American Historical Review* 88.5 (1983): 1151–74.

———. "Grace and Works: The Rise and Division of Covenant Divinity in Elizabethan Puritanism." *Harvard Theological Review* 75.4 (1982): 463–502.

McIntosh, Marjorie Keniston. *Working Women in English Society, 1300–1620*. Cambridge, UK: Cambridge University Press, 2005.

McPherson, Kathryn R. "Dramatizing Deliverance and Devotion: Churching in Early Modern England." In *Performing Maternity in Early Modern England*, ed. Kathryn M. Moncrief and Kathryn R. McPherson, 131–42. Farnham, UK: Ashgate, 2007.

McRae, Andrew. *God Speed the Plough: The Representation of Agrarian England, 1500–1660*. Cambridge, UK: Cambridge University Press, 1996.

Mears, Natalie. "Public Worship and Political Participation in Elizabethan England." *Journal of British Studies* 51.1 (2012): 4–25.

Mears, Natalie, with Alasdair Raffe, Stephen Taylor, Philip Williamson, and Lucy Bates. *National Prayers: Special Worship since the Reformation*. Vol. 1, *Special Prayers, Fasts and Thanksgivings in the British Isles, 1533–1688*. London: Boydell Press, 2013.

Merritt, J. F. *The Social World of Early Modern Westminster: Abbey, Court and Community, 1525–1640*. Manchester, UK: Manchester University Press, 2005.

Meskill, Lynn S. *Ben Jonson and Envy*. Cambridge, UK: Cambridge University Press, 2009.

Meyer, Sheree L. "The Public Statements and Private Losses of Ben Jonson and Katherine Philips: The Poet as Bereaved Parent." *Explorations in Renaissance Culture* 19 (1993): 173–82.

Milbourn, Thomas. *The History of the Church of St. Mildred the Virgin, Poultry, in the City of London*. London: John Russell Smith, 1872.

Miller, Perry. *The New England Mind: From Colony to Province*. Cambridge, Mass.: Harvard University Press, 1953.

Mishel, Lawrence, and Jessica Schieder. "CEO Pay Remains High Relative to the Pay of Typical Workers and High-Wage Earners." *Economic Policy Institute*, July 20, 2017.

Moote, Alanson Lloyd. *The Great Plague: The Story of London's Most Deadly Year*. Baltimore: Johns Hopkins University Press, 2004.

Morgan, John. "Henry Jacob, James I, and Religious Reform, 1603–1609: From

Hampton Court to Reason-of-State." *Church History* 86.3 (2017): 695–727.

Morrissey, Mary. "The Paul's Cross Jeremiad and Other Exhortations." In *Paul's Cross and the Culture of Persuasion in England, 1520–1640*, ed. Torrance Kirby and P. G. Stanwood, 421–38. Boston: Brill, 2014.

Mortenson, Peter. "The Economics of Joy in *The Shoemakers' Holiday*." *Studies in English Literature* 16.2 (1976): 241–52.

Mortimer, Sarah. *Reason and Religion in the English Revolution: The Challenge of Socinianism*. Cambridge, UK: Cambridge University Press, 2010.

Moses, Wilson Jeremiah. *Black Messiahs and Uncle Toms: Social and Literary Manipulations of a Religious Myth*. University Park: Pennsylvania State University Press, 1993.

Muir, Edward. *Ritual in Early Modern Europe*. Cambridge, UK: Cambridge University Press, 2005.

Muldrew, Craig. "'Th'ancient Distaff' and 'Whirling Spindle': Measuring the Contribution of Spinning to Household Earnings and the National Economy in England, 1550–1770." *Economic History Review* 65.2 (2012): 498–526.

———. *The Economy of Obligation: The Culture of Credit and Social Relations in Early Modern England*. New York: St. Martin's Press, 1998.

———. "'Hard Food for Midas': Cash and Its Social Value in Early Modern England." *Past and Present* 170 (2001): 78–120.

———. "Interpreting the Market: The Ethics of Credit and Community Relations in Early Modern England." *Social History* 18.2 (1993): 163–83.

Munkhoff, Richelle. "Reckoning with Death: Women Searchers and the Bills of Mortality in Early Modern London." In *Rhetorics of Bodily Disease and Health in Medieval and Early Modern England*, ed. Jennifer C. Vaught, 119–34. Farnham, UK: Ashgate, 2010.

———. "Searchers of the Dead: Authority, Marginality, and the Interpretation of Plague in England, 1574–1665." *Gender and History* 11.1 (1999): 1–29.

Munro, Ian. *The Figure of the Crowd in Early Modern London*. New York: Palgrave, 2005.

Murphy, Paul Thomas. *Toward a Working-Class Canon: Literary Criticism in British Working-Class Periodicals, 1816–1858*. Columbus: Ohio State University Press, 1994.

Murray, Molly. "Measured Sentences: Forming Literature in the Early Modern Prison." *Huntington Library Quarterly* 72.2 (2009): 147–67.

Murray, Tessa. *Thomas Morley: Elizabethan Music Publisher*. Martlesham, UK: Boydell, 2014.

Narveson, Kate. *Bible Readers and Lay Writers in Early Modern England: Gender and Self-Definition in an Emergent Writing Culture*. Farnham, UK: Ashgate, 2012.

Neelakanta, Vanita. *Retelling the Siege of Jerusalem in Early Modern England*. Newark: University of Delaware Press, 2019.

Nelson, Alan H. "Shakespeare and Southwark." *Drama and Pedagogy in Medieval and Early Modern England*, ed. Elisabeth Dutton and James McBain. *Swiss Papers in English Language and Literature* (2015): 159–72.

Netzloff, Mark. "Public Diplomacy and the Comedy of State: Chapman's *Monsieur D'Olive*." In *Authority and Diplomacy from Dante to Shakespeare*, ed. Jason Powell and Will Rossiter, 185–97. London: Ashgate, 2013.

Newell, Rachel C. "The Thanksgiving of Women after Childbirth: A Blessing in Disguise?" In *Exploring the Dirty Side of Women's Health*, ed. Mavis Kirkham, 38–52. New York: Routledge, 2007.

Newman, Kira L. S. "Shutt Up: Bubonic Plague and Quarantine in Early Modern England." *Journal of Social History* 45.3 (2012): 809–34.

Newstok, Scott. *Quoting Death in Early Modern England*. New York: Palgrave, 2009.
Nicholl, Charles. *A Cup of News: The Life of Thomas Nashe*. London: Routledge, 1984.
Nijenhuis, W. "Resolutions of Dutch Church Assemblies concerning English Ministers in the Hague, 1633–1651." *Nederlands archief voor kerkgeschiedenis / Dutch Review of Church History* 62.1 (1982): 77–101.
Noll, Mark A. *In the Beginning Was the Word: The Bible in American Public Life, 1492–1783*. Oxford, UK: Oxford University Press, 2016.
Norbrook, David. *Poetry and Politics in the English Renaissance*. 2002. Reprint, Oxford, UK: Oxford University Press, 1984.
Northway, Kara. "'To kindle an industrious desire': The Poetry of Work in Lord Mayors' Shows." *Comparative Drama* 41.2 (2007): 167–92.
O'Connell, Laura Stevenson. "The Elizabethan Bourgeois Hero-Tale: Aspects of an Adolescent Consciousness." In *After the Reformation: Essays in Honor of J. H. Hexter*, ed. Barbara C. Malament, 267–90. Manchester, UK: Manchester University Press, 1980.
O'Connor, Kathleen M. *Jeremiah: Pain and Promise*. Minneapolis: Augsburg Fortress Publishers, 2011.
Ogilvie, Sheila. "The Economics of Guilds." *Journal of Economic Perspectives* 28.4 (2014): 169–92.
Oldenburg, Scott. "Thomas Tusser and the Poetics of the Plow." *English Literary Renaissance* 49.3 (2019): 273–303.
Olson, Rebecca. *Arras Hanging: The Textile That Determined Early Modern Literature*. Newark: University of Delaware Press, 2013.
Owen, Kirsty. *Identity, Commemoration and the Art of Dying Well*. Oxford, UK: British Archaeological Reports, 2010.
Pask, Kevin. *Emergence of the English Author: Scripting the Life of the Poet in Early Modern England*. Cambridge, UK: Cambridge University Press, 1996.
Paster, Gail Kern. *The Body Embarrassed: Drama and the Disciplines of Shame in Early Modern England*. Ithaca, N.Y.: Cornell University Press, 1993.
Patterson, Annabel. *Fables of Power: Aesopian Writing and Political History*. Durham, N.C.: Duke University Press, 1991.
Patterson, Steve. "The Bankruptcy of Homoerotic Amity in Shakespeare's *Merchant of Venice*." *Shakespeare Quarterly* 50 (1999): 9–32.
Paul, Robert S. "Henry Jacob and Seventeenth-Century Puritanism." *Hartford Quarterly* 7 (1967): 92–113.
Pearl, Valerie. "Change and Stability in Seventeenth-Century London." *London Journal* 5 (1979): 3–34.
Pearsall, Derek. "Strangers in Late Fourteenth-Century London." In *The Stranger in Medieval Society*, ed. F. R. P. Akehurst and Stephanie Cain Van D'Elden. St. Paul: University of Minnesota Press, 1997.
Peck, Linda Levy. "Problems in Jacobean Administration: Was Henry Howard, the Earl of Northampton, a Reformer?" *Historical Journal* 19.4 (1976): 831–58.
Pederson, Randall J. *Unity in Diversity: English Puritans and the Puritan Reformation, 1603–1689*. Boston: Brill, 2014.
Pender, Patricia. *Early Modern Women's Writing and the Rhetoric of Modesty*. New York: Palgrave, 2012.
Pestana, Carla Gardina. "Rainborowe [Rainsborough], William." In *Oxford Dictionary of National Biography*, ed. H. C. G. Matthew and Brian Harrison. Oxford, UK: Oxford University Press, 2004. Online ed., ed. David Cannadine, January 2008.
Phillippy, Patricia. "London's Mourning Garment: Maternity, Mourning and Royal Succession." In *Maternal Measures: Figuring Caregiving in the Early Modern Period*, 319–32. Aldershot, UK: Ashgate, 2000.

———. *Shaping Remembrance from Shakespeare to Milton*. Cambridge, UK: Cambridge University Press, 2018.
———. *Women, Death and Literature in Post-Reformation England*. Cambridge, UK: Cambridge University Press, 2002.
Phillips, Joshua. *English Fictions of Communal Identity, 1485–1603*. Farnham, UK: Ashgate, 2010.
Phillips, Patrick. "'At Home in His Repair': The Reformation of Plague in Jonson's Epitaphs for John Roe." *Ben Jonson Journal* 17.2 (2010): 222–41.
Pigman, G. W. *Grief and English Renaissance Elegy*. Cambridge, UK: Cambridge University Press, 1985.
Pittman, Susan. "The Social Structure and Parish Community of St. Andrew's Church, Clastock, as Reconstituted from Its Seating Plan, c. 1587–8." *South History* 20–21 (1998–99): 44–67.
Plummer, Alfred. *The London Weavers' Company, 1600–1970*. London: Routledge, 1972.
Pollock, Linda. "Childbearing and Female Bonding in Early Modern England." *Social History* 22.3 (1997): 286–306.
Potter, Ursula. "Tales of Patient Griselda and Henry VIII." *Early Theatre* 5.2 (2002): 11–28.
Power, M. J. "London and the Control of the 'Crisis' of the 1590s." *History* 70.230 (1985): 371–85.
Prescott, Anne Lake. "Evil Tongues at the Court of Saul: The Renaissance David as a Slandered Courtier." *Journal of Medieval and Renaissance Studies* 21 (1993): 163–86.
Prior, Mary. "Women and the Urban Economy: Oxford, 1500–1800." In *Women in English Society, 1500–1800*, ed. Mary Prior, 102–13. 1985. Reprint, London: Routledge, 1991.
Prothero, Iorwerth. *Radical Artisans in England and France, 1830–1870*. Cambridge, UK: Cambridge University Press, 1997.
Quitslund, Beth. *The Reformation in Rhyme: Sternhold, Hopkins and the English Metrical Psalter, 1547–1603*. Aldershot, UK: Ashgate, 2008.
Raffe, Alasdair. "Nature's Scourges: The Natural World and Special Prayers, Fasts and Thanksgivings, 1541–1866." In *God's Bounty? The Churches and the Natural World*, ed. Peter Clarke and Tony Claydon, 237–47. Studies in Church History 46. Cambridge, UK: Cambridge University Press, 2010.
Rappaport, Steve. *Worlds within Worlds: Structures of Life in Sixteenth-Century London*. Cambridge, UK: Cambridge University Press, 1989.
Ray, Donna K. "A View from the Childwife's Pew: The Development of Rites around Childbirth in the Anglican Communion." *Anglican and Episcopal History* 69.4 (2000): 443–73.
Renders, Hans. "The Limits of Representativeness: Biography, Life Writing, and Microhistory." In *Theoretical Discussion of Biography: Approaches from History, Microhistory, and Life Writing*, ed. Hans Renders and Binne de Haan, 195–209. Lewiston, N.Y.: Edwin Mellen Press, 2012.
Rendle, William. *Old Southwark and Its People*. London: Drewett, 1878.
Reuter, O. R. "Some Notes on Thomas Deloney's Indebtedness to Shakespeare." *Neuphilologische Mitteilungen* 87.2 (1986): 255–61.
Reynolds, Matthew. *Godly Reformers and Their Opponents in Early Modern England: Religion in Norwich, c. 1560–1643*. London: Boydell and Brewer, 2005.
Reynolds, Paige Martin. "Sin, Sacredness, and Childbirth in Early Modern Drama." *Medieval and Renaissance Drama in England* 28 (2015): 30–48.
Richardson, Catherine. *Domestic Life and Domestic Tragedy in Early Modern England: The Material Life of the Household*. Manchester, UK: Manchester University Press, 2006.
Richardson, Gary. "Craft Guilds and Christianity in Late-Medieval England: A Rational-Choice Analysis."

Rationality and Society 17.2 (2005): 139–89.
Riggs, David. *Ben Jonson: A Life.* Cambridge, Mass.: Harvard University Press, 1989.
Roberts, S. Bryn. *Puritanism and the Pursuit of Happiness: The Ministry and Theology of Ralph Venning, c. 1621–1674.* Woodbridge, UK: Boydell Press, 2015.
Robertson, Emma, with Michael Pickering, and Marek Korczynski. "'And Spinning with Voices Meet, Like Nightingales They Sung Full Sweet': Unravelling Representations of Singing in Pre-industrial Textile Production." *Cultural and Social History* 5.1 (2008): 11–31.
Robertson, James. "The Adventures of Dick Whittington and the Social Construction of Elizabethan London." In *Guilds, Society and Economy in London, 1450–1800*, ed. Ian Anders Gadd and Patrick Wallis, 51–66. London: Centre for Metropolitan History Institute of Historical Research, 2002.
Robertson, James C. "Reckoning with London: Interpreting the 'Bills of Mortality' before John Graunt." *Urban History* 23.3 (1996): 325–50.
Robisheaux, Thomas, ed. "Microhistory Today: A Roundtable Discussion." *Microhistory and the Historical Imagination: New Frontiers*, ed. Thomas Robisheaux, Thomas V. Cohen, and István M. Sijártó, special issue, *Journal of Medieval and Early Modern Studies* 47.1 (2017): 7–52.
Robisheaux, Thomas, Thomas V. Cohen, and István M. Sijártó, eds. *Microhistory and the Historical Imagination: New Frontiers*, special issue, *Journal of Medieval and Early Modern Studies* 47.1 (2017).
Rollins, Hyder E. "Deloney's Sources for Euphuistic Learning." *PMLA* 51.2 (1936): 399–406.
———. "'King Lear' and the Ballad of 'John Careless.'" *Modern Language Review* 15.1 (1920): 87–89.

Rollison, David. *Commonwealth of the People: Popular Politics in England's Long Social Revolution, 1066–1649.* Cambridge, UK: Cambridge University Press, 2010.
———. "Discourse and Class Struggle: The Politics of Industry in Early Modern England." *Social History* 26.2 (2001): 166–89.
Rosenberg, Jessica. "The Point of the Couplet: Shakespeare's *Sonnets* and Tusser's *One Hundreth Pointes of Good Husbandrie*." *English Literary History* 83.1 (2016): 1–41.
Rosendale, Timothy. *Liturgy and Literature in the Making of Protestant England.* Cambridge, UK: Cambridge University Press, 2007.
Rousseau, Marie-Hélène. *Saving the Souls of Medieval London: Perpetual Chantries at St. Paul's Cathedral, c. 1200–1548.* New York: Routledge, 2011.
Rudd, Niall. "Pyramus and Thisbe in Shakespeare and Ovid." In *Shakespeare's Ovid: "The Metamorphosis" in the Plays and Poems*, ed. A. B. Taylor, 113–25. Cambridge, UK: Cambridge University Press, 2000.
Rushton, Peter. "Purification or Social Control: Ideologies of Reproduction and the Churching of Women after Childbirth." In *The Public and the Private*, ed. Eva Gamarnikow, 118–31. London: Heinemann, 1983.
Ryrie, Alec. *Being Protestant in Reformation Britain.* Oxford, UK: Oxford University Press, 2013.
Santos, Kathryn Vomero. "'The knots within': Translations, Tapestries, and the Art of Reading Backwards." *Philological Quarterly* 95.3-4 (2016): 343–57.
Schmidt, Albert J. "Thomas Wilson and the Tudor Commonwealth: An Essay in Civic Humanism." *Huntington Library Quarterly* 23.1 (1959): 49–60.
Schofield, Roger. "Did Mothers Really Die? Three Centuries of Maternal Mortality in 'The World We Have Lost.'" In *The World We Have Gained: Histories of Population and Social*

Structure, ed. Richard M. Smith and Keith Wrightson, 231–60. Oxford, UK: Oxford University Press, 1986.

Schofield, Roger, and E. A. Wrigley. "Infant and Child Mortality in England in the Late Tudor and Early Stuart Period." In *Health, Medicine, and Mortality in the Sixteenth Century*, ed. Charles Webster, 61–95. Cambridge, UK: Cambridge University Press, 1979.

Schwartz, Louis. *Milton and Maternal Mortality*. Cambridge, UK: Cambridge University Press, 2009.

Scodel, Joshua. "Genre and Occasion in Jonson's 'On My First Sonne.'" *Studies in Philology* 86.2 (1989): 235–59.

Scott, James C. *The Moral Economy of the Peasant: Rebellion and Subsistence in Southeast Asia*. New Haven, Conn.: Yale University Press, 1976.

Seaver, Paul. "Puritan Preachers and Their Patrons." In *Religious Politics in Post-Reformation England*, ed. Kenneth Fincham and Peter Lake, 128–42. Suffolk, UK: Boydell and Brewer, 2006.

———. *Wallington's World: A Puritan Artisan in Seventeenth-Century London*. Stanford, Calif.: Stanford University Press, 1985.

Semega, Jessica L., with Kaylar R. Fontenot and Melissa A. Kollar. "Income and Poverty in the United States: 2016." September 12, 2017. https://www.census.gov/library/publications/2017/demo/p60-259.html.

Sensback, Jon F. *Rebecca's Revival: Creating Black Christianity in the Atlantic World*. Cambridge, Mass.: Harvard University Press, 2005.

Shaw, Phillip. "The Position of Thomas Dekker in Jacobean Prison Literature." *PMLA* 62.2 (1947): 366–91.

Shell, Marc. *Money, Language, and Thought: Literary and Philosophical Economics from the Medieval to the Modern Era*. Berkeley: University of California Press, 1982.

Shepard, Alexandra. *Accounting for Oneself: Worth, Status, and the Social Order in Early Modern England*. Oxford, UK: Oxford University Press, 2015.

Sherlock, Peter. *Monuments and Memory in Early Modern England*. Aldershot, UK: Ashgate, 2008.

Shrank, Cathy. "Hutton, Luke (d. 1598), Highwayman and Writer." In *Oxford Dictionary of National Biography*, ed. H. C. G. Matthew and Brian Harrison. Oxford, UK: Oxford University Press, 2004. Online ed., ed. David Cannadine, January 2008.

———. *Writing the Nation in Reformation England, 1530–1580*. Oxford, UK: Oxford University Press, 2004.

Shugg, Wallace. "Prostitution in Shakespeare's London." *Shakespeare Studies* 10 (1977): 291–303.

Sinfield, Alan. "How to Read *The Merchant of Venice* without Being a Heterosexist." In *Alternative Shakespeares*, vol. 2, ed. Terence Hawkes, 123–40. London: Routledge, 1996.

Skura, Meredith Ann. *Tudor Autobiography: Listening for Inwardness*. Chicago: University of Chicago Press, 2008.

Slack, Paul. *The Impact of Plague in Tudor and Stuart England*. London: Routledge, 1985.

Smith, Melissa. "Personifications of Plague in Three Tudor Interludes: *Triall of Treasure*, *The longer thour liuest, the more foole thou art*, and *Inough is as good as a feast*." *Literature and Medicine* 26.2 (2007): 364–85.

———. "The Playhouse as Plaguehouse in Early Modern Revenge Tragedy." *Journal of the Washington Academy of Sciences* 89 1–2 (2003): 77–86.

Smith, Nigel. *Perfection Proclaimed: Language and Literature in English Radical Religion, 1640–1660*. Oxford, UK: Clarendon Press, 1989.

Snook, Edith. *Women, Reading, and the Cultural Politics of Early Modern England*. New York: Routledge, 2005.

Snyder, Jane McIntosh. "The Web of Song: Weaving Imagery in Homer and the Lyric Poets." *Classical Journal* 76.3 (1981): 193–96.

Spence, Cathryn. *Women, Credit, and Debt in Early Modern Scotland*. Manchester, UK: Manchester University Press, 2016.

Sprunger, Keith L. "Archbishop Laud's Campaign against Puritanism at the Hague." *Church History* 44.3 (1975): 308–20.

Spufford, Margaret. *The Great Reclothing of Rural England: Petty Chapmen and Their Wares in the Seventeenth Century*. Winchester, UK: Hambledon Press, 1984.

Staton, Walter F., Jr. "Ovidian Elements in *A Midsummer Night's Dream*." *Huntington Library Quarterly* 26 (1962): 165–78.

Steggle, Matthew. "John and Laurence Dutton, Leaders of the Queen's Men." *Shakespeare Quarterly* 70.1 (2019): 32–51.

Stevens, Martin. "The Royal Stanza in Early English Poetry." *PMLA* 94.1 (1979): 62–76.

Stevenson, Laura Caroline. *Praise and Paradox: Merchants and Craftsmen in Elizabethan Popular Literature*. Cambridge, UK: Cambridge University Press, 1984.

Stone, Lawrence. *The Crisis of the Aristocracy, 1558–1641*. Oxford, UK: Oxford University Press, 1965.

Stretton, Thomas. "Written Obligations, Litigation and Neighbourliness, 1580–1680." In *Remaking English Society: Social Relations and Social Change in Early Modern England*, ed. Steve Hindle, Alexandra Shepard, and John Walter, 189–209. Aberdeen, UK: Boydell, 2013.

Sullivan, Ceri. "Early Modern Creative Industrialists." *Studies in Philology* 103.3 (2006): 313–28.

Sutton, Anne F. *The Mercery of London: Trade, Goods, and People*. Farnham, UK: Ashgate, 2005.

Suzuki, Mihoko. *Subordinate Subjects: Gender, the Political Nation, and Literary Form in England, 1588–1699*. 2003. Reprint, London: Routledge, 2018.

Syme, Holger Schott. "Thomas Creede, William Barley, and the Venture of Printing Plays." In *Shakespeare's Stationers: Studies in Cultural Bibliography*, ed. Marta Straznicky, 28–46. Philadelphia: University of Pennsylvania Press, 2013.

Tarlow, Sarah. *Ritual, Belief and the Dead in Early Modern Britain and Ireland*. Cambridge, UK: Cambridge University Press, 2011.

Tawney, R. H. *Land and Labor in China*. London: George Allen and Unwin, 1932.

Taylor, Gary. "The Embassy, the City, the Text: *Cardenio* Performed in 1613." In *The Quest for Cardenio: Shakespeare, Fletcher, and the Lost Play*, ed. David Carnegie and Gary Taylor, 286–308. Oxford, UK: Oxford University Press, 2012.

Taylor, Hillary. "The Price of the Poor's Words: Social Relations and the Economics of Deposing of One's 'Betters' in Early Modern England." *Economic History Review* 72 (2019): 828–47.

Taylor, Lou. *Mourning Dress: A Costume and Social History*. London: George Allen and Unwin, 1983.

Theilmann, John, and Frances Cate. "A Plague of Plagues: The Problem of Plague Diagnosis in Medieval England." *Journal of Interdisciplinary History* 37.3 (2007): 371–93.

Thomas, Keith. *Religion and the Decline of Magic*. New York: Weidenfeld and Nicholson, 1971.

Thompson, E. P. "The Moral Economy of the English Crowd in the Eighteenth Century." In *Customs in Common*, by E. P. Thompson, 185–258. New York: Penguin, 1991.

Thorne, Alison. "'O lawful let it be / That I have room . . . to curse awhile': Voicing the Nation's Conscience in Female Complaint in *Richard III*, *King John*, and *Henry VIII*." In *This England, That Shakespeare*, ed. Willy Maley and Margaret Trudeau-Clayton, 105–26. Farnham, UK: Ashgate, 2010.

Thornton, Peter. "Two Problems." *Furniture History* 7 (1971): 61–71.
Thrupp, Sylvia. "The Gilds." In *The Cambridge Economic History of Europe from the Decline of the Roman Empire*, vol. 3, ed. M. M. Postan, E. E. Rich, and E. Miller, 230–80. Cambridge, UK: Cambridge University Press, 1963.
Tittler, Robert. *Face of the City: Civic Portraiture and Civic Identity in Early Modern England*. Manchester, UK: Manchester University Press, 2007.
———. "Seats of Honour, Seats of Power: The Symbolism of Public Seating in the English Urban Community, c. 1560–1620." *Albion* 2 (1992): 205–23.
———. *Townspeople and Nation: English Urban Experiences, 1540–1640*. Stanford, Calif.: Stanford University Press, 2001.
Totaro, Rebecca. "Mother London and the Madonna Lactans in England's Plague Epic." *Medieval and Renaissance Lactations: Images, Rhetorics, Practices*, ed. Jutta Gisela Sperling, 163–80. Farnham, UK: Ashgate, 2013.
———, ed. *The Plague Epic in Early Modern England: Heroic Measures, 1603–1720*. Farnham, UK: Ashgate, 2012.
———. *The Plague in Print: Essential Elizabethan Sources, 1558–1603*. Pittsburgh: Duquesne University Press, 2010.
———. *Suffering in Paradise: The Bubonic Plague in English Literature from More to Milton*. Pittsburgh: Duquesne University Press, 2005.
Tricomi, Albert. "The Focus of Satire and the Date of *Monsieur D'Olive*." *Studies in English Literature* 17.2 (1977): 281–94.
Tuck, Anthony. "Stories at the Loom: Patterned Textiles and the Recitation of Myth in Euripides." *Arethusa* 42.2 (2009): 151–59.
Twigg, Graham. "Plague in London: Spatial and Temporal Aspects of Mortality." *Epidemic Disease in London*, ed. J. A. J. Champion. *Centre for Metropolitan History, Working Papers Series* 1 (1993): 1–17.
Tyacke, Nicholas. "The Puritan Paradigm of English Politics, 1558–1642." *Historical Journal* 53.3 (2010): 527–50.
Ungerer, Gustav. "Prostitution in Late Elizabethan London: The Case of Mary Newborough." *Medieval and Renaissance Drama in England* 15 (2003): 138–203.
Unwin, George. *The Gilds and Companies of London*. London: Methuen, 1908.
———. *Industrial Organization in the Sixteenth and Seventeenth Centuries*. London: Cass and Company, 1957.
U.S. Department of Housing and Urban Development, Office of Community Planning and Development. *The 2018 Annual Homeless Assessment Report (AHAR) to Congress*, December 2018.
U.S. Department of Justice, Office of Justice Programs. "Correctional Populations in the United States, 2016." *Bureau of Justice Statistics*, April 2018, NCJS 251211.
Vaught, Jennifer C. *Masculinity and Emotion in Early Modern English Literature*. London: Routledge, 2008.
Vienne-Guerrin, Nathalie. "'You Have Rated Me': Insults in *The Merchant of Venice*." *Litteraria Pragensia* 23 (2013): 82–96.
Waddington, John. *Surrey Congregational History*. London: Jackson, Walford, and Hodder, 1866.
Wallis, Patrick. "Apprenticeship and Training in Premodern England." *Journal of Economic History* 68.3 (2008): 832–61.
———. "Controlling Commodities: Search and Reconciliation in the Early Modern Livery Companies." In *Guilds, Society and Economy in London, 1450–1800*, ed. Ian Anders Gadd and Patrick Wallis, 85–100. London: Centre for Metropolitan History Institute of Historical Research, 2002.
———. "Labor, Law, and Training in Early Modern London: Apprenticeship

and the City's Institutions." *Journal of British Studies* 51.4 (2012): 791–819.
———. "Plagues, Morality and the Place of Medicine in Early Modern England." *English Historical Review* 121.490 (2006): 1–24.
Wallis, Patrick, and Catherine Wright. "Evidence, Artisan Experience and Authority in Early Modern England." In *Ways of Making and Knowing: The Material Culture of Empirical Knowledge*, ed. Pamela H. Smith, Harold J. Cook, and Amy R. W. Meyers, 134–58. Ann Arbor: University of Michigan Press, 2014.
Walsham, Alexandra. *Providence in Early Modern England*. Oxford, UK: Oxford University Press, 2001.
Ward, Joseph P. *Culture, Faith, and Philanthropy in Early Modern England: Londoners and Provincial Reform in Early Modern England*. New York: Palgrave, 2013.
———. *Metropolitan Communities: Trade Guilds, Identity, and Change in Early Modern London*. Stanford, Calif.: Stanford University Press, 1997.
Watt, Tessa. *Cheap Print and Popular Piety, 1550–1640*. Cambridge, UK: Cambridge University Press, 1991.
Wayland, Scott. "Religious Change and the Renaissance Elegy." *English Literary Renaissance* 29.3 (2009): 429–59.
Weitzman, Steven. "Lessons from the Dying: The Role of Deuteronomy 32 in Its Narrative Setting." *Harvard Theological Review* 87.4 (1994): 377–93.
Wendelken, Rebecca Woodward. "Wefts and Worms: The Spread of Sericulture and Silk Weaving in the West before 1300." In *Medieval Clothing and Textiles*, vol. 10, ed. Robin Netherton and Gale R. Owen-Crocker, 59–77. Suffolk, UK: Boydell, 2014.
Wennerlind, Carl. *Casualties of Credit: The English Financial Revolution, 1620–1720*. Cambridge, Mass.: Harvard University Press, 2011.
Whatley, Christopher A. "'It Is Said That Burns Was a Radical': Contest, Concession, and the Political Legacy of Robert Burns, ca. 1796–1859." *Journal of British Studies* 50.3 (2011): 639–66.
White, Micheline. "A Biographical Sketch of Dorcas Martin: Elizabethan Translator, Stationer, and Godly Matron." *Sixteenth Century Journal* 30.3 (1999): 775–92.
White, Paul Whitfield. "Reforming Mysteries' End: A Look at Protestant Intervention in English Provincial Drama." *Journal of Medieval and Early Modern Studies* 29.1 (1999): 121–47.
Whiting, Robert. *The Reformation of the English Parish Church*. Cambridge, UK: Cambridge University Press, 2010.
Whittle, Jane. "A Critique of Approaches to 'Domestic Work': Women, Work and the Pre-industrial Economy." *Past and Present* 243 (2019): 35–70.
Wiesner, Merry E. *Women and Gender in Early Modern Europe*. Cambridge, UK: Cambridge University Press, 2000.
Wiles, David. *Shakespeare's Clown: Actor and Text in the Elizabethan Playhouse*. Cambridge, UK: Cambridge University Press, 1987.
Willen, Diane. "The Case of Thomas Gataker: Confronting Superstition in Seventeenth-Century England." *Sixteenth Century Journal* 43.4 (2012): 727–49.
———. "Godly Women in Early Modern England: Puritanism and Gender." *Journal of Ecclesiastical History* 43.4 (1992): 561–80.
———. "Guildswomen in the City of York, 1560–1700." *The Historian* 46.2 (1984): 204–18.
———. "Thomas Gataker and the Use of Print in the English Godly Community." *Huntington Library Quarterly* 70.3 (2007): 343–64.
Williams, Raymond. *Politics and Letters*. London: Verso, 1979.
Willoughby, Edwin Eliott. "The Cover Design." *Library Quarterly:*

Information, Community, Policy 8.1 (1938): 118–19.

Wilson, Adrian. *The Making of Man-Midwifery: Childbirth in England, 1660–1770.* Cambridge, Mass.: Harvard University Press, 1995.

———. *Ritual and Conflict: The Social Relations of Childbirth in Early Modern England.* New York: Routledge, 2016.

Wilson, Frank P. *The Plague in Shakespeare's London.* Oxford, UK: Oxford University Press, 1927.

Winner, Jack D. "The Public and Private Dimensions of Jonson's Epitaphs." In *Classic and Cavalier: Essays on Jonson and the Sons of Ben*, ed. Claude J. Summer and Ted-Larry Pebworth, 107–19. Pittsburgh: University of Pittsburgh Press, 1982.

Winner, Lauren F. *A Cheerful and Comfortable Faith: Anglican Religious Practice in the Elite Households of Eighteenth-Century Virginia.* New Haven, Conn.: Yale University Press, 2010.

Withington, Phil. *Society in Early Modern England. The Vernacular Origins of Some Powerful Ideas.* Cambridge, UK: Polity Press, 2010.

Witte, Ann E. "Bottom's Tangled Web: Texts and Textiles in *A Midsummer Night's Dream*." *Cahiers Élisabéthains: A Journal of English Renaissance Studies* 56.1 (1999): 25–39.

Wood, Andy. "Fear, Hatred, and the Hidden Injuries of Class in Early Modern England." *Journal of Social History* 39.3 (2006): 803–26.

Wordie, J. R. "Deflationary Factors in the Tudor Price Rise." *Past and Present* 154 (1997): 32–70.

Wright, Stephen. "Sorocold, Thomas." In *Oxford Dictionary of National Biography*, ed. H. C. G. Matthew and Brian Harrison. Oxford, UK: Oxford University Press, 2004. Online ed., ed. David Cannadine, January 2008.

Wrightson, Keith. *Earthly Necessities: Economic Lives in Early Modern Britain.* New Haven, Conn.: Yale University Press, 2002.

———. "Estates, Degrees, and Sorts: Changing Perceptions of Society in Tudor and Stuart England." In *Language, History and Class*, ed. Penelope J. Cornfield, 31–52. London: Basil Blackwell, 1991.

———. "The Politics of the Parish in Early Modern England." In *The Experience of Authority in Early Modern England*, ed. Adam Fox, Paul Griffiths, and Steve Hindle, 10–46. New York: Palgrave, 1996.

———. *Ralph Tailor's Summer: A Scrivener, His City and the Plague.* New Haven, Conn.: Yale University Press, 2011.

———. "'Sorts of People' in Tudor and Stuart England." In *The Middling Sort of People: Culture, Society, and Politics in England, 1550–1800*, ed. Jonathan Barry and Christopher Brooks, 28–51. New York: St. Martin's Press, 1994.

Wrigley, E. A., and Roger S. Schofield. *The Population History of England, 1541–1871: A Reconstruction.* Cambridge, UK: Cambridge University Press, 1989.

Wunderli, Richard. *The Peasant Fires: The Drummer of Niklashausen.* Bloomington: Indiana University Press, 1992.

Yungblut, Laura Hunt. *Strangers Settled Here amongst Us: Policies, Perceptions, and the Presence of Aliens in Elizabethan England.* London: Routledge, 1996.

INDEX

Adams, Thomas, 116, 162
Adamson, Thomas, 169–70
aliens, 50, 52, 70
   churches of, 60–61, 65, 68, 69, 89
   merchant strangers, 29, 165, 178, 216n45
   in Southwark,113
   and weavers, 52–5˙5, 60–65, 68–70, 72, 149
   See also xenophobia
Allde, Edward, 33, 67
Alleyn, Edward, 111
Anderson, Edmund, 10, 97–99, 106
apprentices, 12, 37–38, 47, 50, 52–54, 56, 66–67, 90, 103, 121, 158, 207n4
   and riot, 51–52, 65, 70, 215n32
   rules regarding, 50, 52–54, 56, 62–63, 68–69
   See also individual apprentices under Muggins, William

ballads and balladry, 15, 17, 19–20, 23, 24, 25, 28, 30, 46–47, 67, 70, 112, 152
Balmford, James, 41, 115, 120–21, 123–24, 140–47, 151, 160
   and carpenters 142–44
   games of chance 141–42
   in Newcastle 142–43
   in Oxford 143
   and the plague 120–21, 123–24, 140, 142
   John Udall, relationship with, 141, 147
   theology of 144, 146–47, 151
   See also Balmford, Samuel
Balmford, Samuel, 143, 147
Barley, William, 2–3, 15
Bible, The, 7, 17, 24, 26, 140, 141, 171
   Deuteronomy, 26, 62, 150–51
   Ephesians, 150
   Hebrews, 150

Hosea, 26, 150, 153
Isaiah, 26, 27, 115, 123, 142, 155, 160
Jeremiah, 26–27, 43, 56, 57, 150, 151–54, 155, 157, 163
Lamentations, 27, 57, 139, 151–53, 155–56, 163
lay readers of, 19, 145, 147–48
Leviticus, 61, 62
Matthew, 160
Muggins's Bible, 10, 27, 28, 33, 147, 150
Numbers, 150
as relating to the present, 150, 151, 153, 158, 160, 172
Samuel, 148–49, 150, 151
Billingsley, Sir Henry (Lord Mayor of London), 33–34
bills of mortality, 4, 5, 30–31, 10, 133, 136
Blower, Ralph, 15, 33, 119, 167, 175
Booke of Common Prayer, 78, 146
   christenings in, 83–84, 146
   churching in,85
   funeral service in, 115
   and the plague, 124, 140
Boyle, Richard, 141
Bredwell, Stephen, 145
Browne, Robert, 144–45, 146, 147
Bucke, Daniel, 146–47
Bullein, William, 31
Burby, Cuthbert, 33

Careless, John, 17–20, 22, 23–24
Carew, Thomas, 56–57, 64
carpenters, 9, 16, 33–34, 111, 143–44
   dedications to, 33–34, 143–44
   payments for university studies, 143
Cawdry, Robert, 133
Chettle, Henry, 30

Childe, Thomas, 95–96
churching, 85–88, 96, 97
Clapham, Henoch 34, 123
class, 3, 8–14, 22, 44, 58, 59, 72, 113, 143, 164
　See also middling sort
Cleaver, Robert, 25, 152–53
Condell, Henry, 34
conventicles, 144, 145, 147
Conyhope Lane, 51, 81, 89, 98, 107
Coverdale, Miles, 19
credit. See debt and credit
Crowley, Robert, 155

Day, John, 111
debt and credit, 3, 7, 10, 13, 22, 27, 37, 38, 41, 42, 49, 60, 75, 76, 80–81, 91–106, 107, 110, 114, 130, 137, 149, 155, 163, 167, 171
Defoe, Daniel, 45, 170
Dekker, Thomas, 4, 34, 101
　and debt, 80
　and the plague, 4, 101–2, 120
　Shoemaker's Holiday, The, 112
Deloney, Thomas, 17, 19–20, 22, 24, 28, 46–47, 50, 112–13, 142
　children of, 121
　on churching, 87–88
　death of, 120
　Garland of Goodwill, 20
　Gentle Craft, The, 15, 47, 112
　Jack of Newbury, 21–23, 47, 112
　Muggins, relationship with, 15–17, 28, 33, 41, 46, 50, 51, 171
　and Thomas Nashe, 15, 20, 47
　petition, involvement in, 23, 41, 49–73, 167, 171
　and printers, 15, 103
　Strange Histories, 15
　Thomas of Reading, 15, 47, 87–88
Diggins, Christopher, 145–46
Dod, John, 25, 152–53
Donne, John, 85–86, 115, 151
Downame, John, 49, 148
drapers, 37, 78, 107
Drayton, Michael, 34
Dutton, John, 57–60
Dyer, Sir Edward, 82

elegy, 43, 125–37, 111, 156–57, 163, 170
Elizabeth I (queen), 46, 56, 67, 82, 90, 154, 166
　funeral of, 4, 30
　opinion of games of chance, 141

epitaph, 79–82, 84, 110, 112, 117–18, 126–27

Field, Nathan, 112
freedom of the city, 12, 47, 57, 66, 143
funeral monuments, 79–82, 88, 110, 117–18
funerals, 30, 42–43, 67, 96–97, 110, 114–20, 125, 129, 156, 157

Gataker, Thomas, 141
Globe Theatre, 38, 111, 160
Greene, Robert, 30, 34
grocers, 8, 14, 51, 81, 90, 113
guilds (craft). See livery companies; *and individual crafts*
guilds (religious), 113, 115–16,

haberdashers, 51, 81, 90, 93, 99, 119
Hall, Joseph, 34
Halliday, Leonard, 99, 105, 106
Hart, Sir John (Lord Mayor of London), 34
Harvey, Gabriel, 20
Haselden, John, 82
Hastings, Henry, Earl of Huntingdon, 141
Heminges, John, 34–35
Henslowe, Philip, 104, 111
Herbert, George, 26, 134
Herring, Francis, 120
Heywood, Thomas, 20, 81
Hobson, William, 81–82
homelessness, 7, 13, 43, 134, 136, 137, 172
Hooke, Christopher, 151–52
Houndsditch, 100–104, 164
Hutton, Luke 47–9, 68
　Black Dogge of Newgate, The, 48–50, 69–70, 101, 112

immigrants. See aliens

Johnson, Francis, 146–47
Johnson, Richard, 81
Jonson, Ben, 3, 35, 38, 80, 131,
　Everyman in His Humor, 102, 111
　"On My First Sonne," 42, 110–11, 125–28, 171
Jugge, Joan, 47

Kemp, William, 17, 112–13
King James, 3, 4, 7, 17, 25, 29, 30, 70, 141, 156, 164–66

lace and lacemaking, 1, 10, 50, 51, 53, 56, 64, 71, 98

Langland, William, 154
lay subsidy, 10, 36–37, 38, 42, 98, 114, 119, 140
Lee, Sir Robert (Lord Mayor of London), 35
Leke, Henry, 144
livery companies, 3, 12, 33, 42, 50, 55, 62–64, 66–67, 69, 76, 82
  oligarchy in, 50, 54–58
  as regulatory, 62
  Twelve Great, 9, 50
  See also individual crafts
London
  infant mortality in, 76–77
  as a new Jerusalem, 27, 40, 152, 155–56
  personification of, 3, 7–8, 9, 13, 40, 60, 70–72, 155
  as a new Troy, 165
  See also individual parishes and streets
Lord Mayors of London, 9, 25, 37, 50, 53, 69
  See also Swinnerton, Sir John; *and other individual mayors*
Lord Mayor's Show, 8–9, 34
London's Mourning Garment
  biblical allusions in, 26–27, 142, 147–51, 156–57, 159–60, 163
  classical allusions in, 29–30, 156, 165–66
  copies of, 31, 169, 212n132
  dedication in, 2, 13, 14, 29–30, 32–35, 142
  elegies in, 27, 43, 125–37, 140, 156–57, 163, 170
  as epic, 7, 8, 14, 27, 110, 125, 128, 154, 156
  family in debt in, 7, 13, 41, 100–105, 130, 155, 163
  Londoners, indifference of, in, 3, 7, 43, 49, 71–72, 77, 91, 103, 128, 129, 134, 136, 138, 149, 156, 158, 163, 164, 170
  meter in, 28–29, 155
  and the "mourning garment" genre, 30
  mourning women in, 7, 43, 91, 111, 119, 128–37, 149, 155, 155–58, 162, 163
  organization of, 2, 7, 40, 150
  as plague pamphlet, 31, 87, 150, 162
  prayer in, 2, 7, 26–27, 28, 40, 62, 84, 124–25, 140, 147, 149–51, 154–55, 156, 158
  petition, relation to, 13, 61–62, 69–73, 124, 136, 171,
  printer's device in, 2–3, 15, 159
  prophetic elements of, 27, 43, 140, 154–67, 170–71, 172
  rhyme in, 28–29, 71, 135
  royal entry in, 3, 7, 29, 70, 164–65
  table of the dead in, 2, 14, 30–31, 40–41, 110

Lowe, Thomas, 99, 105, 106
Lupton, Donald, 101

Maddison, Lionel, 142
Marston, John, 38
Martin, Thomas, 18–19
mercers, 10, 34, 51, 57, 58, 98
microhistory, 38–41, 171–72
Middleton, Thomas (dramatist), 8, 22, 25
Middleton, Sir Thomas (Lord Mayor of London), 8
middling sort, 10–13, 14, 15–16, 22, 27, 35–37, 41, 43–44, 46–47, 51, 58, 66, 75, 76, 81, 90–93, 95, 100, 110, 121, 130, 142–44, 164, 171
  See also class
midwives. 42, 76, 82–83, 88
Milward, Humphrey, 41, 96–99, 106
mourning, 17, 27, 132–34, 136, 155–58, 170
  and Christian outlook, 30, 151–54
  as communal, 4, 7, 42–43, 91, 110–11, 129, 165
  and the education of women, 1, 3, 27–28, 130
  gowns or garments, 3, 32, 96, 170
  and masculinity, 152–53
  moderation in, 42, 118–19, 125–28
  and women, 8, 43, 91, 111, 128–37, 149, 155–58, 163
Muggins, William
  and Henry Beste (apprentice), 2, 6, 41, 119, 122, 124
  and Mary Black (apprentice), 1–2, 5, 41, 51, 53, 64, 119, 121–22, 124
  books read by, 7, 10, 19, 25–35, 66, 150–51
  possible death of, 167
  debt of 10, 13, 37, 38, 42, 96–100, 105–6, 114, 171
  extended family of, 119–20, 136
  information about, lack of, 35, 38
  inventory of household of, 10, 33, 13, 28, 50, 65
  Jeremiah, identification with, 26–27, 43, 151, 153–57, 163
  and Anne Muggins (daughter), 75–76, 82–84, 88, 89, 90, 96, 98–99, 107, 122
  and Elizabeth Muggins (daughter), 2, 27, 37, 38, 51, 84, 88, 89, 99, 122, 124, 129–30, 148–49, 151
  and Henrie Muggins (son), 89, 90, 106–7, 109, 114–15, 118–19, 120, 130, 129–32

Muggins, William (*continued*)
   and James Muggins (son), 108, 119–20, 122, 134
   and Mary Muggins (daughter), 108, 119–20, 122, 134
   and Robert Muggins (son), 108, 119, 122, 134
   and William Muggins (son), 119, 120
   petition, involvement in, 9, 10, 11, 12–13, 23, 37–38, 41, 51–73, 167, 171
   and religion, 26, 139–47, 148, 171–72
   and Robert Redman (apprentice), 2, 119, 124
   and Thomas Stephenson (apprentice), 38, 51, 107
   See also *London's Mourning Garment*
mulberry tree, 17, 209n63
Munday, Anthony, 9, 34, 82, 102–3

Nashe, Thomas, 15, 20, 22, 47
Nycolls, Crystian, 117–18

pawnbrokers, 13, 94, 99, 101–4, 161, 164
parish, the
   as site of community, 42, 76, 78–79, 82, 84, 88, 92, 110
   church, 42, 78–79, 116
   effects of plague on, 5–6, 77
   laity, role of, in, 78–79, 84–85
   poor relief within, 6, 78
   registers of, 35–36, 37, 81, 113, 119–20
   seating in church of, 93–94
   vestry, of 89–90, 114
   See also *individual parishes*
patronage, 14
   civic, 33–35, 47, 142–44
   theatre, 58–59
Peacham, Henry, 34
Philpot, John, 18–19
plague, the, 1–7, 26–27, 28–29, 30–32, 40–41, 43–44, 77, 84, 91, 99–100, 110–11, 119, 120–37, 139–42, 148–67, 170–72
   causes of, 8, 72, 137, 158
   economic impact, of 7, 13, 71–72, 99–105
   pamphlets about, 20, 31, 35, 87, 101–2, 140–42, 147, 162
   plague orders/state response, to 6, 26, 42, 110, 120, 122, 123–24, 125, 139–40, 147
   quarantine during, 2, 6, 42, 120, 122–25, 126, 131, 139, 151, 153, 166, 170
   sermons during, 4, 31, 151–54
   of 1625, 118, 141, 155
   of 1665, 170
   symptoms of, 1, 132
playing cards, 10, 141–42
Pliny the Elder, 30
Popham, John, 68–70
prayer, 26, 83, 116, 149, 158, 163, 165
   during the plague 124, 140, 151–53
   for the souls of the dead 115–16
   in Sorocold's *Supplications of Saints* 76–78, 85, 89, 90, 92
   See also *The Booke of Common Prayer*; *London's Mourning Garment*: prayer in
prison, 16, 42, 94–96, 97, 145–46, 171, 172
   King's Bench, 18, 23, 92
   Newgate, 15, 17–18, 41, 45–51, 96, 105, 145
   Poultry Compter, 80–81, 101, 105
   See also Hutton, Luke
prostitution, 13, 29, 136, 161–64
Puttenham, George, 129
Psalms, 26, 132, 150, 164

quarantining, 2, 6, 42, 120, 122–25, 126, 131, 139, 151, 153, 166, 170
Quarles, Francis, 151

Ravenscroft, Thomas, 34
Resonable, John, 111
rhyme royal, 28–29
Rippon, Roger, 145–46, 147
Rogers, Richard, 148
Rowley, William, 101
Ryder, Sir William (Lord Mayor of London), 34

samplers, 130
Sandys, Edwin, 93
Shakespeare, Edmund, 111
Shakespeare, William, 23, 38, 111, 129
   Cardenio, 34
   Coriolanus, 160
   Hamlet, 38, 111
   Henry IV, part one, 22, 24
   Henry V, 111
   Julius Caesar, 111
   King Lear, 20
   Merchant of Venice, 42, 76, 93, 94, 101
   Midsummer Night's Dream, A, 16–17, 23, 38, 70

Rape of Lucrece, 29
Romeo and Juliet, 38
Twelfth Night, 22, 38
Venus and Adonis, 23
Sidney, Sir Philip, 14, 38
silk, 10, 64–65, 70–71, 98–99, 130
  production of, 1, 17, 50, 52–54, 89
  sale of 11–12, 56–57, 67, 69, 107, 111
silkworms, 17
Simson, Gabriel, 33, 41, 46, 47–48, 49–50, 67–68, 69–70, 71, 73
Skinner, Sir Thomas (Lord Mayor of London), 34
Slaney, Sir Stephen (Lord Mayor of London), 70, 75
Smith, Thomas, 13, 39, 43, 44
Smith, Wentworth, 34
Sorocold, Thomas, 42, 76–77, 78, 81, 82–84, 85–86, 87, 89–91, 92, 141
Spenser, Edmund, 38, 140, 154, 166–67
Spencer, Sir John (Lord Mayor of London), 51–52, 65, 67–68, 97
spinning and spinsters, 21–22, 54, 56, 63–64, 69, 89
St. Giles' parish in Cripplegate, 5–6, 33, 40, 46, 103, 121
St. Mildred's parish in the Poultry, 35–37, 41, 42, 51, 75–108, 109, 110, 117, 204
  St. Olave's parish, Southwark, 1–2, 5–6, 36–37, 38, 42–43, 107–8, 109–17, 120–24, 139–42, 144–47, 154, 160, 161, 163, 204
Stow, John, 78, 81, 101, 102, 109, 112, 113, 161–62
Street, Peter, 111
St. Saviour's parish, Southwark, 109, 111–12, 113, 114, 145, 154, 161, 163
Sutton, Thomas, 111–12
Swinnerton, Sir John, 2, 14, 32, 33–35, 67, 142, 171, 176

Taylor, John, 16, 58, 101
theaters and theater companies, 14, 38, 57, 96, 111–13, 160
Thom, William, 22–23
Tipper, William, 82

Totaro, Rebecca 3, 8, 35, 87, 173
Towne, Thomas, 111
Trapp, John, 151
Tusser, Thomas, 79–81

Udall, John, 141, 147, 230n4

Venning, Ralph, 144

weavers
  and petitions, 9, 10, 11, 12–13, 23, 37–38, 41, 51–73, 167, 171
  and poetry, 15–23
  and religion, 24–25
  representations of, 16–17, 21–25
  and women in, 1, 21–22, 53–54, 56, 62, 63–64, 69, 89, 119
  Worshipful Company of, 9–10, 14, 16, 23–24, 37–38, 41–42, 49–69, 70, 75–76
  Yeomanry of, 12, 37, 55, 59–69, 171
  See also lace and lacemaking; silk; spinning and spinsters
Webster, John, 38
Weintraub, Scott Adam, 11
White, William, 47
Wild, Robert, 25
wills, 36, 66, 79, 90, 95–97, 115–16, 146, 226n38
Wilson, Thomas, 32–33
Wither, George, 155, 171
women
  and the cloth trade, 1, 21–22, 53–54, 56, 62, 63–64, 69, 89, 119
  community of, 43, 76, 85, 88–91, 111, 137
  education, 1, 3, 27–28, 130
  and life in the parish, 42
  and motherhood, 2, 7–8, 13, 27, 41, 42, 76–78, 85–89, 90–91, 106–7, 122–23, 128–37, 149, 155–58, 172
  and mourning, 8, 43, 91, 111, 128–37, 149, 155–58, 163
Wotton, Anthony, 146

xenophobia, 60–61

www.ingramcontent.com/pod-product-compliance
Lightning Source LLC
Chambersburg PA
CBHW022042290426
44109CB00014B/947